To Richard —
with best wishes,
Robert W. Kill
8-21-12

Pitcairn Island,
the *Bounty* Mutineers
and Their Descendants

Pitcairn Island, the *Bounty* Mutineers and Their Descendants

A History

Robert W. Kirk

Foreword by Herbert Ford

McFarland & Company, Inc., Publishers

Jefferson, North Carolina, and London

LIBRARY OF CONGRESS CATALOGUING-IN-PUBLICATION DATA

Kirk, Robert W., 1937–
Pitcairn Island, the Bounty mutineers and their descendants :
a history / Robert W. Kirk ; foreword by Herbert Ford.
p. cm.
Includes bibliographical references and index.

ISBN 978-0-7864-3471-8
illustrated case binding : 50# alkaline paper ∞

1. Pitcairn Island — History. 2. Bounty Mutiny, 1789.
3. Pitcairn Island — Biography. 4. Pitcairn Island — Genealogy.
5. Christian, Fletcher, 1764–1793 — Family. I. Title.

DU800.K57 2008   996.1'8 — dc22   2008010254

British Library cataloguing data are available

On the cover: *Bounty Searches for a Home* by John Hagan
(Pitcairn Islands Study Center);
Thursday October Christian (1790–1831),
first of the second generation born on Pitcairn Island

Manufactured in the United States of America

McFarland & Company, Inc., Publishers
Box 611, Jefferson, North Carolina 28640
www.mcfarlandpub.com

For my friends since we were fourteen,
Ronald A. Cooper and George H. Smith —
the brothers I never had.

Acknowledgments

The writing of this book was made easier by having access to some superb sources. I found my friend the late Sven Wahlroos's *Mutiny and Romance in the South Seas: A Companion to the Bounty Adventure*, Robert B. Nicolson's *The Pitcairners*, David Silverman's *Pitcairn* and Herbert Ford's *Pitcairn—Port of Call* valuable in this work. Herbert Ford, director of the Pitcairn Study Center at Pacific Union College in Angwin, California, has been most helpful to me in my research; he has my deepest gratitude. I have used the resources of numerous libraries and Web sites. Friends Squire and Ailsa Speedy of Auckland have sent me articles from the *New Zealand Herald*, for which I am most grateful. I am also grateful to cruise companions Bob and Donnalee Cook of Ontario, Canada, for permission to use superb photos taken at Pitcairn. My wife Barbara's encouragement, critical appraisal and technical support in reproducing illustrations have been invaluable. Conversations and email communications with Pitcairners have proven essential to the evolution of this work, and my sincere thanks goes out to all who helped along the way.

Contents

What a little spot it appears on the vast Pacific! a mere rock apparently incapable to resist the mighty waves of so vast an ocean.

— M. Fortescue Moresby, 1853

South Pacific Ocean

Places Mentioned in the Text

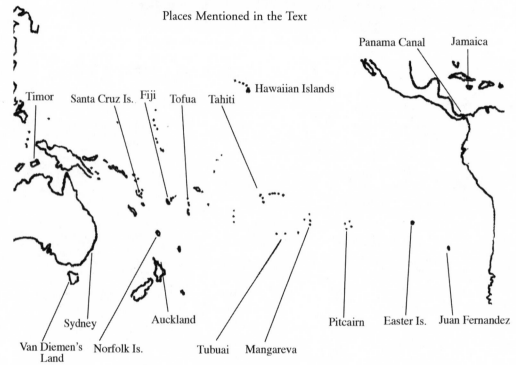

Map by Robert Kirk.

Foreword

by Herbert Ford

In author Robert Kirk's use of Fortescue Moresby's description of Pitcairn Island there is implied far more for study than a mere rock's stubborn resistance against the ever-pounding surf of the mighty Pacific Ocean; there is the far greater battle of the lives of the Pitcairn people. Not only have they endlessly battled against the Pacific's tides, tidal waves and fierce storms, they have also had to do battle with the consequences of their utter remoteness from the rest of the world, and all that has meant in both material and psychological terms. To the commuter zipping daily along the rails from Long Island into New York City, or the gold miner dredging for treasure outside Johannesburg, or the television producer fretting over a story line in Tokyo, the isolation of today's handful of people on Pitcairn Island and its consequences is simply incomprehensible. This book suggests, but can in no way replicate, the cut-off-from-the-world–ness of the Pitcairners; one must live on that tiny, remote, volcanic isle, lost as it is in the far reaches of the South Pacific Ocean, to know its life struggle.

It is in digging into the less often touched on aspects of Pitcairn life that this book finds some of its greatest value. There will be found in the pages that follow a considerable number of previously unexplored yet interesting crannies of Pitcairn life that have been either passed over or are glossed over in earlier volumes about Pitcairn Island. Most especially is this true of Pitcairn life in the more recent decades.

The sweep of Pitcairn's unusual history is found here in a measure of engrossing detail that is sure to fire the mind of anyone with a spark of adventure in his or her blood. The lives of the principals of the *Bounty*-Pitcairn saga — Bligh, Christian, Adams, Hill, Nobbs and others — come alive through the author's skillful writing in a way that is at once both gripping and captivating.

Pitcairn Island, the Bounty Mutineers, and Their Descendants will rightly command the attention of all adventure lovers, as well as that of the worldwide body of *Bounty*-Pitcairn students and scholars whose numbers continue to grow. It has certainly captured mine.

Dr. Herbert Ford is Director of the Pitcairn Islands Study Center, Pacific Union College, Angwin, California.

Introduction: The Island as Icon

Village in the Spotlight

An editor of *The Pitcairn Miscellany*, the monthly island newsletter, observed that "Pitcairners are a unique group of people whose day-to-day lives are frequently exposed to the public through books, television, magazines, newspapers and other publications, including *Miscellany*.... The names of many ordinary Pitcairn folk are known the world over. Some don't mind at all, while others accept that this has to be."[1]

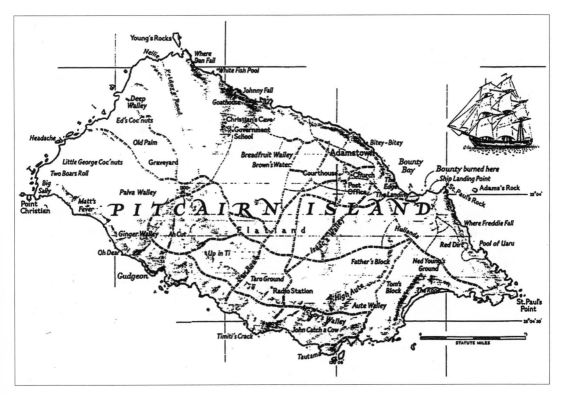

Map of Pitcairn Island. Courtesy of the Pitcairn Island Study Center.

Pitcairners are famous. Except for royalty, there is no other extended family of three or four dozen individuals, people without remarkable talent, stunning appearance, or notable accomplishment — quite ordinary individuals — who have been so studiously inspected, so celebrated, so invasively reported by the world's media. Pitcairn Island is a public icon and its inhabitants are like a royal family in that their celebrity has been determined by heredity and, like kings and queens, their existence subsidized by taxpayers' largess. If the name Windsor reflects splendor in Britain, the names Christian and Young reflect romance and daring in the South Seas. These Pitcairn "royals" live not in palaces but in a haphazardly arranged hamlet on a minuscule rock about half way between Chile and New Zealand. They inhabit one of the most isolated spots on earth. They are descendants of the perpetrators of the most notorious mutiny in all of history — that of His Majesty's Armed Vessel *Bounty*. The blood of mutineers and of sultry Polynesian women surges in their veins.

The Christian, Young, Brown and Warren families have their community's origin, history, and pedigrees documented in and by a library/study center, internet discussion groups, Web sites, a philatelic research organization, tons of newsprint, detailed genealogical charts, documentary films, and Hollywood extravaganzas. By the end of the twentieth century, an estimated twelve hundred books, thirty-two hundred magazine articles and uncounted newspaper articles had been published about the mutiny and the mutineers' descendants.[2] Readers of these articles express concern that if the population of Pitcairn Island becomes too small, the island will have to be abandoned. The visible embodiment of a romantic legend will no longer inhabit the refuge of their ancestors.

Pitcairn Island is maintained by the British government as one of a few remaining small possessions, fragments of a once vast empire upon which, prior to about 1960, the sun shone brilliantly. The other remnants — Anguilla, Ascension, Bermuda, British Indian Ocean Territory, British Virgin Islands, Cayman Islands, Falkland Islands, Gibraltar, Montserrat, St. Helena, Turks and Caicos Islands, and Tristan da Cunha — all have larger populations than Pitcairn. All of these minuscule leftovers have compelling stories, but none as compelling as that of Pitcairn.

The purpose of colonies has always been to enhance the well-being of the mother country strategically or financially, but Pitcairn has always been an exception. It was, from its incorporation into empire, totally useless to Britain's strategic and financial well-being — and so it remains. It has no valuable resources. It has no harbor. It has no airport. It has no missile defenses. It has no beach worthy of the name and even if it did it cannot host any appreciable number of tourists at one time. The Pitcairn economy is based on the production and sale of curios for a world truly awash in curios. There is scant profit in curios, as lovingly produced as each is, so the islanders' purchasing power is minimal; they have never kept the factories of the English Midlands humming.

Financially, maintaining Pitcairn as a possession is costly to Britain, though she has spent relatively little on the island until the last quarter century. If the Pitcairners declared independence tomorrow, Whitehall would be momentarily stunned but ultimately a few million pounds ahead. The British government helps maintain and police Pitcairn because the British feel an obligation to the Pitcairners; these people of mixed English-Polynesian descent are as much British subjects as those in Bristol or Bath. The British feel an obligation because the population is too small to become a sovereign nation. If Pitcairners were pure Polynesians they would long ago have been granted independence as the world's tiniest republic or added to French Polynesia. But London can hardly cast adrift descendants of the participants in a spectacularly romantic event that ranks among the best historic tales of the British people — the *Bounty* mutiny.

Birth of an Icon

Though the uninhabited Pitcairn Island was discovered in 1767, it remained unvisited. In 1790 nine *Bounty* mutineers settled Pitcairn after ridding themselves of their intolerable master and commander, William Bligh. They brought Polynesian men and women to work for them and bear their children. For the next eighteen years nobody knew what had become of these criminals and their companions. In 1808, Captain Mayhew Folger of the American sealing vessel *Topaz* found one surviving mutineer, John Adams, Polynesian women, and mixed-race children. The settlement's existence was little publicized. Nobody came to arrest and hang the last of the mutineers. Adams was found again in 1814 by the ships *Briton* and *Tagus* of the Royal Navy. News of that discovery reached Europe and America, and from time to time, a few more ships put in at Pitcairn. As they did, the *Bounty* story unfolded bit by bit. Word reached other nations that an idyllic community of God-fearing young people lived on the remote rock, motivated by the Bible to live in peace, piety and harmony. If the description could be believed, the people had formed a true Christian utopia. Public interest heightened in 1831 when British Admiralty official Sir John Barrow published *The Eventful History of the Mutiny and the Piratical Seizure of H.M.S. Bounty*, the first comprehensive story of events leading to and including Pitcairn's settlement.

Since the publication of Barrow's history, Pitcairn has never entirely left the public's imagination, though when crowded out by more momentous events, it retreated into the recesses of arcane historical occurrences. In the mid-nineteenth century, whaling vessels stopped at this utopia for fresh produce and water; their reports helped keep interest about the community alive. About twenty years after Barrow's book came out, the Rev. Thomas Boyes Murray issued *Pitcairn: The Island, The People, and the Pastor*; by 1860, 30,000 copies had been sold. In the mid-nineteenth century, American and British Sunday school pupils read tracts in which the lives of pious Pitcairners were portrayed in the hope they would be emulated. The most popular American writers of their time, Mark Twain and Jack London, each wrote a short story about Pitcairn. Twain wrote "The Great Revolution on Pitcairn" about a dictator very much like Joshua Hill, and London wrote "The Seed of McCoy," whose protagonist is modeled after the much-praised magistrate James Russell McCoy. That the public read and appreciated these stories indicates that readers at the turn of the twentieth century were very much aware of Pitcairn Island and its inhabitants.

The first *Bounty* motion picture came out in 1916, a silent Australian production that drew minimal attention. The second, in 1933, was also an Australian production, *In the Wake of the Bounty*. Producer Charles Chauvel mixed a fictional narrative with footage from Chauvel's own visit to Pitcairn. This film is memorable because a hitherto unknown actor named Errol Flynn played mutineer Fletcher Christian. Flynn was quoted later as confessing, "I was without the least idea of what I was doing."[3]

It was not until the mid–1930s with the publication of Nordhoff and Hall's novels, the tremendously popular —*Mutiny on the Bounty*, *Men against the Sea*, and *Pitcairn's Island*— that interest in the colony was truly awakened. The "*Bounty* Trilogy" presented the drama of the mutiny, of Bligh's epic voyage across the South Pacific in an open boat, as well as interracial passion and brutal murders on Pitcairn. In the first few years after publication, an estimated twenty-five million people read one or more of these books.

Popular interest in the *Bounty* and Pitcairn truly exploded in 1935, when the film *Mutiny on the Bounty* was released. Charles Laughton played a cruel Bligh, dispensing harsh expletives and severe lashings. Clark Gable played Bligh's victim, a handsome, long-suffering

Fletcher Christian. Producers sent a teacher's manual to American high school classes to encourage students to discuss the events portrayed in the film. Within six weeks during the deep Depression year that it came to theaters, an estimated six hundred thousand people lined up to see Laughton having Gable flogged. Loew's theaters showed *Mutiny* exclusively.[4]

In 1962, Trevor Howard was Bligh, and Marlon Brando was Christian in the next cinematic production. Brando was paid six million dollars to take Howard's verbal abuse; he used some of the money to buy the Society island of Tetiroa. He was aware that three *Bounty* crewmen — Millward, Burkitt and Churchill — had tried to desert to Tetiroa before the mutiny. Brando agreed it was a good place to get away.

Hollywood continued to remake the story. In 1984, in a satisfying version which famously portrayed bare-breasted Tahitian maidens, Anthony Hopkins played the captain and Mel Gibson the petulant midshipman. These films have helped to keep the *Bounty* legend alive in the public imagination.

In 1940, further interest was added when the British Crown Agents brought out a spectacular regular postal issue, Pitcairn's first. Pictured on the eight stamps were HMAV *Bounty*; Bligh; artist Robert Dodd's 1808 engraving of Bligh being put off in the ship's launch; King George VI facing away from arch-mutineer Fletcher Christian; Bounty Bay; the *Bounty* itself with full sails unfurled; John Adams and his house; a map showing the island's location; breadfruit; and Pitcairn's major product at the time, oranges. It is arguably the most compelling set of stamps issued by the hundred-odd British Empire and Commonwealth postal entities. Hundreds of thousands of stamp collectors became acquainted with Pitcairn and its founding through adding this issue to their albums.

In 2002, a descendant of Captain Bligh auctioned off items Bligh had carried with him in his open boat voyage after the mutiny. Interest was astonishing. The coconut shell Bligh had used as a cup and on which he inscribed, "The cup I eat my miserable allowance out of," went for $111,135; and the bullet he used to ration out food to his starving mates sold for $58,900.[5] In June 2005 approximately a hundred people, many of whom had actually been to Pitcairn, convened at the Pier in St. Petersburg, Florida, to meet and exchange information about their favorite island. The Pitcairn Conference was sponsored by Friends of Pitcairn, an ad hoc internet group. Nearby sails fluttered in the breeze aboard a replica of the *Bounty*, built in the 1960s for the film starring Marlon Brando; it was used more recently in a *Pirates of the Caribbean* sequel. Fletcher Christian's descendants Tom and his wife Betty traveled from their remote home to attend the conference, as did Pitcairners Nola and Reynold Warren.[6]

Take away Christians and Youngs and Pitcairn becomes a remote rock where an occasional tourist looks down at the patch of water where the *Bounty* was burned, stares up at the triangular cave opening where Fletcher Christian brooded and stared out to sea, visits the grave of patriarch John Adams, goes to the Seventh-day Adventist church to see the *Bounty* Bible, and perhaps wanders through the historic cemetery. Without the descendants of mutineers, Pitcairn would be an empty shell, just as London would lose its scarlet and gold luster if the guard stopped changing and the royal standard above Buckingham Palace were instead pinned up inside the Victoria and Albert Museum. The presence of the mutineers' pedigreed descendants perpetuates the island's status as an icon.

This book is a new history of Pitcairn Island and its people, taking the reader from prehistory to the aftermath of the sexual abuse convictions that threaten the very existence of the colony in the first decade of the twenty-first century. Many books, some superb like Caroline Alexander's *The Bounty,* cover the mutiny and its aftermath. Of all of the dramatic episodes of history, the mutiny on the *Bounty* certainly doesn't need still another retelling. However, this work includes the mutiny's causes and the mutiny itself and its consequences because that background is essential for an understanding of what has taken place in the last two centuries on Pitcairn. Events of the mutiny are included not only because of their compelling interest, but because a retelling offers an opportunity to explain what I modestly — but confidently — assert to be the *true* reason that Fletcher Christian mutinied against William Bligh. A number of books chronicle Pitcairn nineteenth-century history; most of these stop around 1914 with the opening of the Panama Canal. No other book offers extensive coverage of twentieth- and early twenty-first-century events.

My interest in Pitcairn began at a junior high stamp club meeting when I was offered in trade a short set of the 1940 first Pitcairn Islands stamp issue. I immediately went to the library to find out about Adams and Christian and the *Bounty*. I read the Nordhoff and Hall trilogy. This information was new to me and as the story unfolded it came as an exciting surprise. From age thirteen my interest never waned.

On an Adventist Sabbath morning, February 1, 1986, I achieved a decades-long dream by going ashore at Pitcairn. A few months earlier Jim Snyder, the cruise director for the *Lindblad Discoverer*, an eighty-five-passenger luxury expedition ship, phoned and offered my wife Barbara and me a six-week cruise from Chile to Papua New Guinea, in return for which I was to deliver a series of lectures about the Pacific islands we were to visit. Jim told me that I had been recommended by Professor Robin W. Winks of the Yale University history department. Why had Robin recommended me? I wondered. I soon recalled what I had said that led to my appointment as lecturer.

I had spent a recent summer at Yale University enrolled in a seminar which focused on the history of the British Empire. A National Endowment for the Humanities scholarship enabled me to study under Dr. Winks, recognized as one of the world's greatest authorities on British imperialism. At a cocktail party this superb teacher told Barbara and me that he would lecture about South Pacific history on a six-week cruise from Punta Arenas, Chile, to Port Moresby, Papua New Guinea.

"Are you going to Pitcairn Island?" I asked.

"Yes," he replied.

"You are so lucky," I said with considerable enthusiasm. I drew out the word "so" for emphasis. "I would give my right arm to go to Pitcairn Island."

Jim Snyder later told me that Robin had suffered a recurrence of malaria, contracted on a previous expedition to the Solomon Islands, and was unable to deliver lectures for Lindblad. Robin had selected me, he said, because "I've never seen anyone who was more enthusiastic about going anywhere." Going to Pitcairn as a lecturer aboard the *Lindblad Discoverer* in 1986, and again as lecturer aboard *Discovery World* in 2004, was a dream twice realized. I also realized that a real need exists for a comprehensive history of the island. This book is the result.

CHAPTER 1

Pitcairn Discovered

An Island Named for a Young Gentleman

On Thursday July 2, 1767, Captain Philip Carteret recorded the European discovery of Pitcairn Island. Carteret wrote in the log of His Majesty's Ship *Swallow* that in the evening, from a distance of fifteen leagues [forty-five miles], "we discovered land to the northward of us. Upon approaching it the next day, it appeared like a great rock rising out of the sea. It was no more than five miles in circumference, and seemed to be uninhabited; it was, however, covered with trees, and we saw a small stream of fresh water running down one side of it." Carteret named the dark mass looming from the sea foam Pitcairn's Island, "it having been discovered by a young gentleman, son to Major Pitcairn of the marines...."[1]

The "young gentleman" was Midshipman Robert Pitcairn, born in Edinburgh in 1752. The fifteen-year-old won the bottle of brandy Captain Carteret had promised to the first man to sight land. Robert's father, Major John Pitcairn of the marines, was the officer who, on April 19, 1774, would shout, "Disperse ye Rebels," at Minutemen assembled outside Boston on Lexington Green. His unheeded command came moments before someone fired the "shot heard 'round the world," which was the first shot in the American Revolutionary War. Major Pitcairn did not live to enjoy his place in history for long; nearly two months later, he was mortally wounded at the Battle of Bunker Hill. At the conclusion of the voyage of the *Swallow*, Robert Pitcairn signed on to H.M.S. *Aurora*, whose mission was to convey officials from England to India. The *Aurora* was lost in 1770 somewhere between the Cape of Good Hope and the Asian mainland. Robert was dead at seventeen.

Carteret had begun his voyage the previous year, 1766, his slow, leaky ship sailing in tandem with Captain Samuel Wallis's *Dolphin*. The two captains had orders from the Admiralty to search in the Southern Hemisphere between Cape Horn and New Zealand for a great southern land mass thought to balance the northern Eurasian continent. The *Swallow* and *Dolphin* became separated on April 11, 1767, after fighting heavy storms in the Strait of Magellan. Carteret sailed westward on the twenty-fifth parallel, where he found Pitcairn Island. Carteret was unable to report discovering the continent — Terra Australis Incognita — because it did not exist. On his way home, he continued westward in his decrepit scurvy-ridden ship, rediscovering the Santa Cruz group of the Solomon Islands, which the Spaniard Mendaña had visited two hundred years earlier. Then he explored the coasts of New Britain and the

Bismarck Archipelago. That he was able to bring some of his crew home alive in a ship that should never have set sail from England was to his credit as master and commander. Carteret died in 1796, a rear admiral.

There is no barrier reef at Pitcairn Island to intercept the surf. In July — the Southern Hemisphere's winter — the sea, according to Carteret, was "extremely tempestuous, with long rolling billows from the southward, larger and higher than any I had seen before." As a result, Carteret did not land to explore, because "the surf, which at this season broke upon it with great violence, rendered it impossible." The "great rock" that Midshipman Pitcairn saw was the top of an extinct volcano, the base of which rose up at its greatest height at Pawala Ridge, 1,138 feet above the pounding sea. The midshipman saw sea cliffs nearly two hundred feet in height, composed of reddish brown and black volcanic rock. Midshipman Pitcairn could not have known that the island named for him measured almost two square miles (4.5 square kilometers). All that Captain Carteret could add about the isolated rock was that "It lies in latitude 20 degrees two minutes S longitude and 133 degrees 21 minutes W. and about a thousand leagues to the westward of the continent of America."[2] Carteret was wrong. Anyone attempting to find the island at the location Carteret recorded would fail. Carteret's error helped make the island a perfect mutineers' lair, a hideaway for those who did not want ever to be found. Pitcairn actually lies at 25° 04' S, and 130° 05' W. It is on approximately the same latitude as Asuncion, Paraguay, and Gabarone, Botswana, and about half way between latitudes of Brisbane and Rockhampton, Australia. Thus, it has a pleasant climate: a mean monthly temperature of seventy-five (24 degrees Celsius) in January, to sixty-six (19 degrees Celsius) in July. Rainfall is quite high; it averages eighty inches (2,000 mm) a year.

Henderson, Ducie and Oeno Islands

Carteret did not find Pitcairn Island's three uninhabited "dependencies," Henderson, Ducie and Oeno islands. In 1902, Britain confirmed possession of these specks of land and annexed them.

The largest is Henderson Island, approximately twelve square miles (31 square kilometers) and is about seven times larger than Pitcairn. It lies 101 miles from Pitcairn. Coral cliffs jut up on three sides and a sandy beach is found on the northern shore. The island is about a hundred feet in height. Henderson was the top of a volcano; it became a low-lying coral atoll and is now a raised coral island. A fringing reef allows boats through two passages, one at the east beach, but only at high tide. The island has a thick profusion of vines and sharp coral rock; the coral makes walking a challenge. Sighted in 1606, by the Spaniard Pedro Fernandez de Quiros, it was rediscovered in 1819 by Captain Henderson of H.M.S. *Hercules*. Henderson Island is located at 24° 22' S, and 128° 16' W. Approaching Henderson in a longboat in the 1990s, Dea Birkett wrote that, "the island sat like an iced cake on a sea of silver foil."[3]

If Pitcairners go to Oeno very occasionally, it is to get pandanus leaves, coconuts and fish, and for a holiday. From these leaves they weave baskets, fans and other curios to sell to visitors. Oeno is located at 23° 56' S and 130° 44' W. Oeno measures about two square miles and is a low atoll, covered by brush. The distance is 77 miles from Pitcairn. The captain of an American whaling ship, the *Oeno*, first reported the island in 1842.

Ducie is actually a large island and three smaller islands; the four surround a lagoon. The large island is Acadia, named for a ship that was wrecked there in 1881. Ducie is found

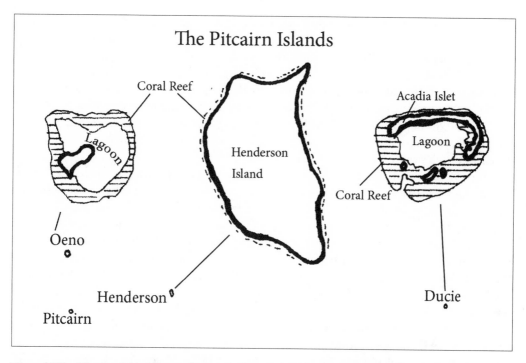

The Pitcairn Islands

Coral Reef

Acadia Islet

Lagoon

Lagoon

Henderson
Island

Coral Reef

Oeno

Henderson

Ducie

Pitcairn

Map of "The Pitcairn Island Dependencies." Oeno: 2 square mile atoll with one island, a lagoon, and reef. Henderson: 12.1 square mile raised limestone platform surrounded by reef. Ducie: 1.5 square miles. The main island is Acadia: A reef surrounds the lagoon. Map by Robert Kirk.

at 24º 40' S and 124º 48' W. Ducie was discovered on March 16, 1790, by Captain Edward Edwards of H.M.S. *Pandora*, the same officer who had been sent to apprehend the *Bounty* mutineers. Edwards named the mile-and-a-half square atoll for a naval captain, Francis Ducie. Two of the small islands are named Edwards Island and *Pandora* Island. (The fourth is Westward Island.) When he discovered Ducie, Edwards was only 283 miles from his quarry on Pitcairn but he did not know that, so he kept sailing on to Tahiti. It is difficult to land on Ducie due to the reef which rings it, and as a result, it is visited only rarely.

The Vanished Mangarevan Empire

Pitcairn Island was probably uninhabited when Carteret sighted it, and certainly without population in 1790, when the mutineers arrived to carve out a settlement amid its thick forests. Yet, Polynesian people had lived on its slopes and in its valleys in the past, and they left ample records to prove past residence. When he arrived, Fletcher Christian found stone tools and four maraes (temples), with stone statues that the mutineers destroyed as pagan relics. Archeologists have identified twenty-two petroglyphs at Down Rope on the western coast; they remain the most graphic evidence of Polynesian occupation. A crude stone figure saved from Pitcairn is in the Otago Museum in Dunedin, New Zealand. The mutineers ate fruit from trees that previous inhabitants had cultivated.

As Polynesians, the ancient Pitcairn Island inhabitants were related to Tahitians, Cook Islanders, Tongans, Samoans and others. All of these pre-literate people lived on islands within the so-called Polynesian Triangle—a hypothetical line linking, and including, all of New

Zealand, Easter Island, and the Hawaiian Islands. Polynesians made their way by canoe to Fiji and, by 1000 B.C.E., to Tonga and Samoa. Recent DNA studies of pigs which migrated with them suggest that Polynesians came initially from the coast of what is now Viet Nam about 3600 years ago.[4] They came most likely in large double-hulled canoes, navigating by stars, currents, clouds and the flights of birds. By the dawn of the Christian era, the Tongans and Samoans were separated by race and language from Melanesians in Fiji, New Caledonia, Vanuatu and the Solomons. Accomplishing astonishing long sea voyages, Polynesian mariners discovered and settled the islands within the Polynesian Triangle. About 900 c.e. they populated Pitcairn's nearest inhabited neighbor, Mangareva.

In 1991, a team known as the Pitcairn Islands Scientific Expedition performed extensive excavations on Pitcairn and Henderson. The team investigated a site at Water Valley on Pitcairn, which had been the residence of an ancient Polynesian family numbering eight to ten. The family had built terraces on three levels — for a house, for making tools, and for cooking. A landing place for fishing canoes was situated immediately below at a cove now called West Harbour. The archaeologists found hundreds of stone tools at the site, including adzes and awls. The middle terrace contained an earth oven that was similar, archaeologist Marshall Weisler pointed out, to that being used during the 1990s in the home of Pitcairn residents Reynold and Nola Warren. Weisler estimated the site to be about a thousand years old.[5]

The team noted the discarded remains of millions of fish and birds; they had been eaten by humans. Jared Diamond, author of *Guns, Germs and Steel* and *Collapse*, asked, "What happened to those original Pitcairn Islanders and to their vanished cousins on Henderson?" To answer that question, Diamond promoted a thesis formed by Dr. Weisler and his colleagues. The scientific team hypothesized that Polynesian colonists probably settled Pitcairn and Henderson from Mangareva.[6] Mangareva is the largest of the Gambier Islands, a little more than three hundred miles distant. Mangareva has a total land area of seven square miles. Its name means "Floating Mountain," an apt description of its two peaks which contrast it with its four lower and smaller neighboring islands.

Diamond explained Weisler's thesis as follows: On the hillsides of Mangareva, Polynesians cultivated sweet potatoes, yams, and taro. They also cultivated breadfruit and bananas. All of these are Polynesian staples. Between agriculture and fishing, Mangareva could support a population of several thousand. Mangareva also had pearl shells which could be carved into fish hooks. However, Mangareva lacked a vital article necessary for Polynesian culture: stone for tools such as adzes, used to chip and carve wood and stone.

Ancient Mangarevans called Pitcairn *Heragi*. At Down Rope on Pitcairn, below the petroglyphs, exists a major quarry of volcanic glass, suitable for making the sharp tools Mangarevans needed. Also on Pitcairn was a quarry of basalt, a stone which the Mangarevans and Henderson inhabitants needed for adzes. Pitcairn was incapable of supporting a large Polynesian population; Diamond estimates no more than a hundred. But not many people were required to quarry stone to be exported for tools.[7]

Centuries before Henderson was declared a piece of the British Empire it was, according to Weisler's thesis, along with Pitcairn part of a Mangarevan maritime empire. Sailing time in Polynesian outriggers was about four or five days between Mangareva and Henderson, and about a day between Pitcairn and Henderson. Using radiocarbon dating, Weisler established that this triangular trade flourished from about 1000 c.e. to 1450 c.e. Polynesian outriggers brought food from Mangareva to Pitcairn and Henderson. Pitcairn stone tools went to Mangareva and Henderson. Pearl shells and sea turtles were exported from Henderson to the other two islands.

Mangareva remained populated but Pitcairn and Henderson, by the time of European discovery, were not. Weisler linked the disappearance of the Pitcairn and Henderson populations to "a slowly unfolding environmental catastrophe" on Mangareva. Weisler concluded that the Pitcairn and Henderson populations were removed or died out because Mangarevans could no longer sustain their triangular trade. Due to soil erosion on Mangareva, ferns replaced trees. Ferns overran crop land and the food supply diminished. Without trees, islanders could no longer make canoes to fish or to sail to Pitcairn. In any event, they had no surplus food to bring to Pitcairn and Henderson. Mangarevans turned to cannibalism to satisfy protein deficiency; war became habitual. Diamond writes, "Chronic fighting broke out over the precious remaining cultivable land; the winning side redistributed the land of the losers...." Diamond thus concluded that "The disappearance of Pitcairn's and Henderson's populations must have resulted somehow from the severing of the Mangarevan umbilical cord."[8]

Weisler and Diamond posit that Henderson Islanders were trapped, there being no trees suitable for building canoes. Diamond thinks they may have been able to survive for several generations, adapting themselves to self-sufficiency, before their last member died. On Pitcairn, Diamond suggests that the stress of being trapped on the tiny island led to tensions which "may have exploded in mass murder, which later nearly did destroy the colony of *Bounty* mutineers on Pitcairn itself."[9] The Weisler expedition thesis is a logical explanation of a mystery that has long been waiting for a logical solution.

CHAPTER 2

Bread That Grows on Trees!

Sugar and Hunger in the West Indies

Pitcairn Island's story begins not only in the South Pacific but in the West Indies as well. The British had acquired West Indies colonies between 1624 and 1763, a period of 139 years of empire building at the expense of the original Caribs and Arawaks, of Africans bound into slavery, and of the Spanish and French from whom islands were taken. Britain's West Indies colonies at the time of the *Bounty* mutiny included sugar-producing colonies such as St. Christopher (St. Kitts), Nevis, Antigua, Montserrat, Barbados, and — the most important of all — Jamaica. All were totally dependent on slavery for the arduous process of sugar production.

The "plantocracy" — Caribbean sugar estate owners — were among the wealthiest families in the eighteenth century British Empire. Often absentees, the so-called West India Interest or their representatives sat in Parliament and constituted what Trinidad and Tobago's Prime Minister Eric Williams called "the most powerful lobby of the century."[1] They could rely on fifty or more members in Parliament to defend their profits. Profits allowed them to build fine plantation houses in the Caribbean, Georgian homes on London's elegant squares, and stately mansions in the English countryside.

Sugar was the most prized commodity of the century. But all British planters were faced with challenges that threatened sugar's profitability. A persistent challenge was competition from French sugar islands. French St. Domingue (today's Haiti) was larger than all the British islands combined and the French paid a smaller export tax on sugar than did British planters. Because the French could sell sugar for less, they had the benefit of European continental markets. To counter French competition, British planters increased production by cultivating new lands in Grenada, Tobago and elsewhere, but ironically throwing more sugar on a saturated market decreased the price they received. Moreover, after decades of producing sugar, soils became exhausted and planters were forced to cultivate less desirable lands.

For large or small planters, in good years as well as in bad, expenses remained the same. Chief among expenses was food for plantation slaves. These costs were sustainable so long as merchants from New York, Boston and Charleston exchanged corn, peas, beans, flour, rice, fish, beef, pork, and poultry for Caribbean molasses. When the London government declared an embargo on goods from the rebellious thirteen North American colonies, Caribbean planters lost a cheap and dependable source of food for their slaves.

In the war for American independence, Britain's continental enemies retaliated when the British Navy interrupted their shipments to the revolting colonies; French ships blockaded British sugar islands, preventing food from arriving. Moreover, privateers from the thirteen colonies intercepted shipments of sugar bound for Britain. When planters tried to make up for shortages by growing more food, severe hurricanes in 1780 and 1781 destroyed much of their work. To deprive the United States of capital, the British government forbade their West Indian subjects to buy food from the infant nation. One result was that by 1788, famine and disease took the lives of an estimated fifteen thousand slaves in Jamaica, a hundred in Antigua and four hundred on Nevis.[2] Whites feared that starving slaves would rise up in bloody revolt. What was really needed was a miracle food. If only slaves could pick their bread from trees...

Loaves for the Picking

Europeans had known about the existence of breadfruit for nearly a century. Writing in 1688, pirate-explorer William Dampier explained: "The bread-fruit (as we call it) grows on a large tree, as big and high as our largest apple trees: It hath a spreading head, full of branches and dark leaves. The fruit grows on boughs like apples; it is as big as a penny-loaf when wheat is at 5s. [shillings] the bushel; it is of a round shape and hath a thick tough rind. When the fruit is ripe, it is yellow and soft, and the taste is sweet and pleasant."[3]

Captain James Cook, who was considered in the 1770s the supreme authority on the South Seas, wrote, "The fruit is about the size of a child's head and the surface is reticulated not much unlike a truffle: it is covered with thin skin, and has a core about as big as the handle of a small knife." What Cook wrote next undoubtedly appealed to West Indies planters: "If a man plants ten of them in his life-time, which he may do in about an hour, he will as completely fulfill his duty to his own and future generations as the native of our less temperate climate can do by ploughing in the cold winter, and reaping in the summer's heat...."[4] Equally as enticing, if the fruit is pounded into paste, it can be preserved. Moreover, growers need not replant every year. As Cook explained, "...they spring from the roots of the old ones which run along near the surface of the ground." It gets better: According to Cook, in the Sandwich (Hawaiian) Islands, breadfruit trees "flourish with great luxuriance, on rising grounds. Where the hills rise almost perpendicularly in a great variety of peaked forms, their steep sides and deep chasms between them are covered with trees, among which those of the bread-fruit are observed particularly to abound."[5]

Sir Joseph Banks, Breadfruit Publicist

The Englishman who publicized breadfruit as a food for West Indies slaves was Sir Joseph Banks (1743–1820). At twenty-one, Joseph inherited his father's estates and became suddenly independently wealthy with an income of six thousand pounds a year. To put his fortune in perspective, a farm laborer might make twenty-five pounds a year and Bligh seventy pounds to serve as master of the *Bounty*. Like other heirs of his generation, Banks might have spent his patrimony gambling, womanizing, and drinking, but instead he became a botanical dilettante, a collector and classifier.

In 1766, the Royal Society decided to send observers to Tahiti to chart the transit of Venus. Orders of the Royal Society stated that accurate observation of the transit would "contribute greatly to the improvement of Astronomy on which Navigation so much depends...."[6] On May 5, 1768, the Admiralty chose Cook to command the expedition. The Royal Society petitioned the Admiralty, asking that "Joseph Banks esq., Fellow of the Society, a Gentleman of large fortune, who is well versed in natural history ... be received on board of the ship, under command of Captain Cook."[7] Banks's two dogs, a cat, and a renowned goat who had already circumnavigated the globe with Samuel Wallis without being consumed were brought aboard.

On April 13, 1769, Banks recorded his first personal discovery of breadfruit: "This morn early came to anchor in Port Royal bay King George the third's Island (Tahiti). Before the anchor was down we were surrounded by a large number of Canoes who traded very quietly and civilly, for beads chiefly, in exchange for which they gave Cocoa nuts Bread fruit both roasted and raw some small fish and apples."[8] So plentiful were breadfruit that the English traded one bead for four to six breadfruit. Banks wrote, "...while we Inhabitants of a changeable climate are obliged to Plow, Sow, Harrow, reap, Thrash, Grid, Knead and bake our daily bread and Each revolving year again to Plough, sow &c &c" the Tahitian gets breadfruit merely by picking it from a tree. The Tahitians' ease in obtaining food, Banks advised, allowed the islanders more time for making love.[9]

During the summer of 1771, the *Endeavour* returned Banks and Cook to England. King George III welcomed Banks at Windsor; king and botanist formed a friendship based on enjoyment of similar interests in improving agriculture. In 1778, Banks was elected president of the Royal Society and served in that prestigious office until his death in 1820. Corpulent, flashing mammoth bushy eyebrows, genuinely enamored of botany and natural history, Banks commanded attention; when he spoke, people listened. In 1779, he recommended Botany Bay as a future home for British convicts, recently denied admittance to the rebellious North American colonies. Banks was listened to also when he recommended that breadfruit be transplanted in the West Indies.

King George III's *Bounty* to the Planters

In July 1784, Hinton East, a Jamaica planter, told Banks that breadfruit would be "of infinite importance to the West Indian islands, in affording a wholesome and pleasant food to our negroes, which would have the great advantage of being raised with infinitely less labour than the plantain...."[10] A group of West Indies planters offered to pay for a ship owner to go to the South Seas and bring back breadfruit. No owner or captain applied for the risky venture.

On March 30, 1787, Banks wrote to the president of the Board of Trade: "It is full my opinion that the plan of sending out a vessel from England for the sole purpose of bringing the bread-fruit to the West Indies is much more likely to be successful...."[11] In early 1787, when Banks proposed the plan to George III, the king readily agreed and ordered the Lords of the Admiralty to begin preliminary preparations for an expedition. The proposal marked the first time a publically funded expedition was to sail to the South Pacific on a mission designed to sustain the profits of powerful private interests. The expedition would fail in its mission but its failure would lead to the establishment of the first British colony in Polynesia.

CHAPTER 3

Destination Tahiti

HMAV *Bounty*

The measures taken by the Lords of the Admiralty to bring South Seas breadfruit to the West Indies began with the purchase of a merchant vessel, the *Bethia*, and with the selection of Lieutenant William Bligh, at Banks's recommendation, as *Bethia*'s commander. Bligh came to Banks's attention through one of the richest West India planters, Duncan Campbell. Campbell was the uncle of William Bligh's wife, Elizabeth. Campbell had, in fact, sold the *Bethia* to the Admiralty. Lieutenant Bligh was in some respects a logical choice to direct the transport of breadfruit from Tahiti to Jamaica. He had served as ship's master on a voyage to Tahiti under Cook and had commanded ships to the West Indies sugar islands for Campbell.

"I was appointed to command her on the 16th of August, 1787," Bligh wrote of the *Bethia*. "Her burthen was nearly 215 tons, her extreme length on deck, 90 feet 10 inches; extreme breadth, 24 feet 3 inches, and height in the hold under the beams, at the main hatchway, 10 feet 3 inches." After Dino de Laurentiis made his film *Mutiny on the Bounty* in 1983, the replica that he built became a tourist attraction. Boarding it in Papeete harbor, one was struck by how tiny the ship was; two or three dozen tourists aboard seemed to crowd it. The vessel of which Bligh took command was only three years old. The navy spent £4,456 to refit and stock it. *Bethia* was renamed *Bounty* to call attention to the fact that the voyage constituted the king's bounty to the planters.

For reasons of economy, Banks had originally proposed that whatever ship was chosen to collect breadfruit should deliver convicts to Botany Bay, New South Wales, on the outward voyage. He soon realized that a convict ship and a floating nursery had to be configured entirely differently and he prudently retracted his proposal. The *Bounty*'s modifications were made at the expense of the ship's company's living space. Bligh wrote that "the great cabin was appropriated for the preservation of the plants, and extended as far forward as the after hatchway. It had two large sky-lights, and on each side three scuttles for air, and was fitted with a false floor cut full of holes to contain the garden pots, in which the plants were to be brought home."[1] The main cabin was enlarged to thirty feet. Gutters were installed to catch dripping water that needed to be used again. A large stove and stacks of firewood were intended to keep the plants warm in high latitudes. Three bulky ships' boats were carried on the deck.

William Bligh, 1754–1817. The notorious Captain Bligh, a superb navigator, was master of the *Bounty* until the mutiny, April 28, 1789. His harsh words led to his overthrow by Fletcher Christian. He later suffered more mutinies. Engraved from a painting by John Russell. Reproduced from William Bligh, *A Voyage to the South Seas*, London, 1792.

The ship's hold had been packed with gifts and trade goods for friendly Tahitians: 100 pounds of glass beads, 168 mirrors, 72 shirts, 1,000 pounds of nails, 576 knives, and over 2800 adzes, saws, drills and files. Little room was left. Crew, sheep, pigs, and goats ate and slept — and in the case of the animals, defecated — in an inadequate area, inadequately ventilated and inadequately lit. On deck, four four-pound cannon and ten swivel guns were mounted to deter aggression from hostile islanders.

Food was a compelling reason that men went to sea. The poor in eighteenth century Britain often had to skip meals. Mariners were promised three meals a day. Served on square wooden planks, they were characterized as three "square" meals. Food was an important component of Bligh's planning. In general and under the best of circumstances an eighteenth-century ship's provisions were not only unappetizing but would today be considered manifestly unhealthy: salt pork, dried beef, ship's biscuits, and dried peas. Custom aboard ships demanded that the oldest meat be served first, so even if the kitchen staff took on fresh meat in port, it was aged until it became unwholesome before it reached the table. If a sailor was unwilling to consume his meat, he could — and sometimes did — carve a curio from it. It polished well. Ship's biscuits were the staple of seagoing mess tables. These brown five-inch-diameter puck-hard wafers contained wheat, and sometimes pea flour, alum, chalk, lime, bone powder and maybe other mysterious ingredients. The standard eighteenth-century ship's diet led to scurvy, but Bligh was a knowledgeable commander who took precautions to protect his men from the debilitating disease. He stocked his ship with sauerkraut and a concoction known as portable soup. Author Richard Hough pointed out that a "piece" of portable soup, the ingredients of which had been boiled until "it lasted for ever," can be found in the National Maritime Museum at Greenwich.[2] Sauerkraut and portable soup served as anti-scorbutics and, with fresh fruit and vegetables taken on enroute when possible, accomplished their goal. Bligh lost no men to scurvy.

To wash down the unpalatable food, seamen could drink a gallon of beer a day, a pint of wine, and grog twice a day. Grog was rum diluted with water. Some sailors drank less on some days, saving up their ration for binge drinking on holidays.

The *Bounty*'s Company

In an age when sailors were impressed into involuntary naval service, Bligh had the luxury of admitting enthusiastic men who were eager to sail with him. The ship's destination was not announced, but waterfront banter made it to be Tahiti. Returning sailors told and retold stories about Tahiti's ready women, superb climate and seemingly limitless food. Aboard were nineteen able-bodied seamen. To be called "able-bodied" meant that a man could tie all necessary knots, could climb a hundred feet up a rope ladder to work on the rigging, and could steer the ship when assigned. An able-bodied seaman knew the arcane nomenclature of all parts of the ship. Such men were sought after and invaluable. An "ordinary" seaman was a man with previous experience at sea, but not yet as skillful or as knowledgeable as an able-bodied seaman. Many seamen preferred service in His Majesty's navy to that of merchant vessels. Royal Navy men-of-war had more hands than private ships, and that meant fewer watches to stand and less work per man. The pay of twenty-two shillings and six pence a month was similar to that of merchantmen and was more likely to be paid aboard naval vessels, on time and in full.

Among positions aboard the *Bounty* that were not found on other naval vessels were that of David Nelson, a botanist; William Brown, a gardener from Kew Gardens in London; and Michael Byrne, a blind fiddler employed by Bligh to ensure that the crew danced for exercise. The youngest of the crew was seventeen, the oldest forty. Bligh had personally selected every man except the gardeners. Richard Hough wrote that Bligh had signed aboard "a weak master, a drunken surgeon, an awkward carpenter, mainly second-rate petty and warrant officers, and a bunch of well-born 'young gentlemen' of negligible experience, together with the usual collection of roughs...."[3]

The Irascible Captain Bligh

William Bligh was born September 9, 1754, at Plymouth; his father was a customs officer. His parents enrolled him on the Royal Navy's books when he was seven; the boy did not sail before he was sixteen, but early enrollment gave him advantage later when seniority was a consideration for promotion. He had become a midshipman at seventeen and had sailed on three ships by twenty-one. William met his wife Elizabeth Betham at Douglas, on the Isle of Man, while he served aboard a naval ship searching the Irish Sea for smugglers.

A slightly corpulent man with remarkable energy, Bligh had sailed with Cook on his third voyage, aboard the *Resolution*, in 1777–79. Cook had appointed Bligh sailing master at age twenty-one, a singular honor and evidence of Bligh's navigation skills. However, as Arthur Herman points out, Bligh may have precipitated Cook's being clubbed to death in Hawaii when he ordered firing on a canoe full of islanders. Later, Bligh fought against the Dutch at Dogger Bank and at Gibraltar in the wars of the American Revolution. When Britain was finally at peace, having lost the thirteen colonies, Bligh returned to the Isle of Man and Elizabeth. Without a berth on a ship, he was put on half pay. It was then that Duncan Campbell gave him a job as commander of one of his merchant vessels, and the Blighs moved to London. William transported sugar and rum from the West Indies to London for Elizabeth's uncle.

Bligh had risen in rank the hard way — from the lower decks to command of the *Bounty* at age thirty-three. Most officers had been promoted through patronage. Boys of prominent families started as cabin boy and advanced to midshipman; some upper-class adolescents went off to Portsmouth for two years to study at the Naval Academy. These paths led most directly to officer's rank. Bligh had reason to be proud of his technical grasp of eighteenth-century navigation that had earned him his commission. Patrick O'Brian stated that Bligh was chosen because "most other officers with experience of the South Seas were either dead or too high in the rank for the *Bounty*...."[4] However, coming to the captain's cabin by way of the lower decks may have deprived him of the polish and social self-confidence of gentleman officers.

Almost certainly, the lower-deck route to the top supplied William Bligh with a venomous vocabulary. He was to display it often; as the only commissioned officer aboard, Bligh had numerous duties and was under stress. He planned a perfect voyage, an accomplishment that would lead to his promotion. He was determined not only to accomplish his mission but to do so without loss of life; he was determined to prevent scurvy and to keep his men healthy through cleanliness and exercise. The awful food was standard aboard all ships; nothing really could be done about that, but the *Bounty* was a sanitary vessel in that his men scrubbed down living areas every day. They were ordered to wash themselves and their clothing and to exercise for two hours in the evening by dancing to the sounds of Michael Byrne's fiddle.

The chief instrument of compulsion for unruly crew members was the whip, or cat-o'-nine-tails. When a captain wished to enforce the Articles of War, he ordered the bosun to take the whip out of a red bag in which it was kept. With the cat out of the bag (the origin of the term) and the miscreant lashed to the mast, the bosun was ordered to lay it on. Twenty or even a hundred lashes were not rare in His Majesty's navy. Men were lashed until their skin was frayed, then allowed time to partially heal, and brought back for more. Salt was rubbed into the wounds — to prevent infection. Bligh was not noted for physical abuse of his crew. He knew that flogging would endanger their health so they could not contribute to the completion of the perfectly-executed mission he envisioned. In comparison with commanders of fifteen voyages in the Pacific from 1766 to 1793, Bligh did not punish his men inordinately. Cliometricians who have counted strokes entered in ships' logs tell us that Bligh flogged fewer men than other commanders in the Pacific. Cook, and particularly George Vancouver, were far harsher with the lash than Bligh.

Rather, Bligh is infamous for tongue lashings. Bad tempered with no sense of humor, he was a verbal bully. Richard Hough wrote that Bligh's "aggressiveness is so poorly concealed that it is almost as if Bligh wants you to know there is going to be trouble."[5] No evidence exists to suggest that he complimented or praised underlings for performance. Bligh berated men for offenses real and imaginary. The crew was intimate with foul language, but not laid on in consistent torrents by the man who controlled their careers and very lives. Bligh, it would seem, was a man to avoid. On the other hand, no sooner had Bligh relieved his temper than he would change completely and speak in normal tones to the very person whose dignity he had a few minutes before taken away.

One reason for his bad language was that Bligh was bitter, even as he took command. He had complaints against his superiors. The chief— and entirely legitimate — complaint was that his sailing date had been delayed waiting for orders to arrive. Instead of addressing them to the Admiralty — which may have led to dismissal — or inscribing them in the *Bounty* log, on December 10, 1787, he wrote to his wife's uncle, his former employer Duncan Campbell. In this letter written to elicit sympathy, he blamed the *Bounty*'s disastrously late departure on unnecessarily delayed orders: "If there is any punishment that ought to be inflicted on a set of men for neglect, I am sure it ought on the Admiralty for my three weeks' detention at this place during a fine fair wind which carried all outward bound ships clear of the Channel but me, who wanted it most. This has made my task a very arduous one indeed for to get around Cape Horn at the time I shall be there.... I must do it if the ship will stand it at all or I suppose my character will be at stake." Bligh also felt his mission deserved higher rank: "Had Lord Howe sweetened this difficult task by giving me promotion I should have been satisfied...."

Moreover, Bligh was deeply dissatisfied with his pay: "The hardship I make known I lay under is, that they took me from a state of affluence from your employ with an income five hundred a year to that of a Lieut's pay 4/- [shillings] pr day...."[6] Crew members were to accuse Bligh of making up for his shortfall in pay by short-changing them in the galley; Bligh acted as his own purser, buying food and rationing it out to the ship's cook, so their accusations were far from baseless.

Bligh complained that he had to make do with too few able-bodied seamen. Nineteen were classified on the ship's muster as able-bodied, but of those Michael Byrne was the blind fiddler, Thomas Ellison was listed as a boy, Thomas Hall was the ship's cook, Henry Hillbrant the cooper, Robert Lamb the butcher, William Muspratt the tailor and assistant cook, and Richard Skinner served as barber. The remaining twelve had to stand most watches and sail the ship. Most captains preferred to sail with no fewer than one-third the ship's company as able-bodied seamen, which on the *Bounty* would be at least fifteen. Bligh had a master-at-arms — Charles Churchill — but no marines to keep order among his crew and to protect the ship from assault. With these unrepressed grievances Bligh set forth on his breadfruit mission.

Mr. Fletcher Christian

Fletcher Christian, whose aristocratic family was originally from the Isle of Man, was born at Moorland Close in Cumberland. Fletcher was the tenth son of an attorney and the brother of a professor of law. One uncle had served as high sheriff of Cumberland, and another as bishop of Carlisle. Three members of Parliament were among his first cousins. Christian might have studied law had his family not suffered financial reverses; under straitened circumstances, he opted to go to sea. Bligh described him after the mutiny in a "wanted" circular as, "Age 24, 5 feet, 9 inches in height, blackish or very dark brown complexion, dark brown hair, strongly made, a star tattooed on his left breast, tattooed on his backside; his knees stand a little out, and he may be called rather bow-legged."[7] Bligh did not describe the man's mood swings, which left Christian at times in a deep funk. Richard Hough stated that Christian was a "weak, moody, temperamental and sentimental young man," promoted above his ability to lead.[8]

Christian's family and that of Elizabeth Bligh enjoyed social links, which is how the young man had met William Bligh. In 1785, Bligh agreed to employ Fletcher Christian aboard Campbell's ship *Britannia* on the West Indies run. Christian had already served aboard H.M.S. *Eurydice* from India to England. Christian gladly subordinated himself to Bligh, a thoroughly knowledgeable mariner, though of a lower social class than his own. Christian showed his eagerness by offering to serve as an ordinary seaman until a midshipman's position became available. On March 2, 1788, Bligh named Christian as acting lieutenant aboard the *Bounty*. Bligh had it in his power to rescind this order at will. Nevertheless, Christian considered that he had made a favorable career move by linking himself to Bligh. At age twenty-two, Christian had found his patron, a skilled officer who would be promoted after bringing breadfruit to the West Indies, and who would recommend promotion for his protégé as well.

An Island That Once Was Paradise

A volcanic island surrounded by a barrier reef, Tahiti had become the favored watering and victualing stop for early voyagers from Europe. Divided among tribal chiefs, the island's lush 388 square miles contained enough breadfruit that plants could be removed without causing starvation among the Polynesian inhabitants.

Tahiti was not discovered by Magellan, Drake, Mendaña, Tasman, Schouten and Le Maire, Dampier, Roggeveen, Anson, Byron, or any other Spanish, Dutch, French or British explorers who ventured into the Pacific between 1521 and 1767. Tahiti was discovered on June 18, 1767, by Captain Samuel Wallis of H.M.S. *Dolphin*. James Cook later estimated the population at 240,000; more recent estimates put it at 30,000. Wallis named his discovery King George III Island. Wallis found there an extremely well developed Stone Age culture with a hierarchy of chiefs, aristocrats, priests, artisans, commoners, and slaves — all living in extended families. The preliterate people were polytheistic, worshipping a variety of gods and spirits at maraes. Unlike their ancestors in Polynesia's golden age of settlement, when mariners spread far beyond Samoa and Tonga to populate much of Oceania, the islanders voyaged within a more limited range. They were unaware of the existence of their fellow Polynesians in New Zealand, Easter Island and Hawaii.

From a European point of view, Tahitians lived idyllic lives. Their day was spent in a warm climate sleeping, singing, talking, playing sports, swimming, surfing and working just enough to supply their limited needs. They had time to dance, sing and make love and relate tales and memorize their lineages. They painfully submitted to their bodies' being decorated with elaborate tattoos; *Bounty* crew members would have themselves decorated as well. Tahitian bodies were at least partially covered with tapa, a cloth made from the bark of the mulberry tree. Sailors marveled at how fastidious Tahitians were in their habits, bathing frequently. Tahitians must have marveled at the unpleasant odor of the unwashed Europeans.

Hundreds of canoes surrounded Wallis's *Dolphin* when he arrived in 1767, menacing the visitors. After Wallis shot two men, the Tahitians decided that the voyagers had too much *mana*—super-natural power—to be confronted. Thereafter the islanders appeared to be friendly. As they became acquainted, language and custom confounded both English and Tahitians. When sailors made noises like chickens and pigs to request meat, Tahitians thought that was their language and replied with barnyard sounds. When the ship's surgeon removed his wig, a frightened Tahitian jumped overboard. When a large ram on board ran headlong into a Tahitian — they had never seen a ram — all the Tahitians leaped into Matavai Bay.

Having made friends with their visitors, Tahitians climbed aboard the *Dolphin* bringing fruit and offering their women. As worshipers of Te Atua, who was the Tahitians' concept of the supreme god, and of lesser gods and numerous spirits, they did not equate sex with sin. Sex to males and females alike was a natural function. The *Dolphin*'s crew expressed enthusiastic agreement.

For the Price of a Nail

When women offered themselves to the *Dolphin*'s sex-starved young crew, sailors gave them gifts of nails. Tahitians had never seen iron but they soon saw its utility. With nails, they could make superior fish hooks. With knives and axes they could work faster and more efficiently. Soon, girls and women expected a nail for sexual favors. Men pulled so many nails from their hammocks and later from bulkheads that the *Dolphin* was put in some danger of coming apart. A crew member bought a two-hundred-pound pig for a ten-penny nail. Then with inflation, the cost of a hog jumped to a large spike.

When the *Dolphin*'s crew returned to England with details of life among the Tahitians, Europeans learned about the lascivious entertainment offered by a troop of entertainers known as *arioi*. Their performances were called *heivas*, consisting of dancing, acting, singing and wrestling. All mundane activity stopped when villagers heard the flutes, drums and singing that signaled the arrival of these star-quality personalities. The village supported the male and female performers during their stay, which was often for several days. Cook noted as many as seven hundred arriving in seventy mammoth canoes; their arrival could present an economic strain for the host community. The *ariori* seemingly lived in a perpetual world of total sexual freedom, without permanent partners, all women in the group being available to all of the males. Any babies that resulted were aborted or killed. Abortion, the crew learned, was common among Tahitians, some women having aborted several babies. Abortion as a form of birth control was important in preventing the island from becoming hopelessly overpopulated.

The following year the French navigator Louis de Bougainville visited and named the island La Nouvelle Cythère. Spaniards with dreams of converting the islanders to Roman Catholicism arrived under Domingo de Boenechea and named the island Amat. James Cook visited three times—in 1769, 1774, and 1777. The British called it Otaheite, having failed to understand that "O" meant in the Tahitian Polynesian dialect, "It is"—"It is Tahiti." Tahiti was in 1788, by most accounts, as happy a society as existed on the planet. Any prolonged outside intrusion could transform it from perfect balance to catastrophe. That was the situation as the *Bounty*'s crew approached Matavai Bay for what was to be a prolonged visit.

At Sea with Captain Bligh

Bligh prepared for a voyage that would have assured him promotion, but events worked against him from the beginning. Bligh was ready to sail in early October. If he had been permitted to leave on time the *Bounty* would have reached Cape Horn and the Strait of Magellan in the southern summer—December—when conditions were optimum for passing from the South Atlantic to the South Pacific, as he had been ordered to do. The *Bounty*'s sailing date was delayed because Bligh had to wait for the Admiralty's orders. He was finally authorized to sail from Portsmouth on November 28, 1787, but the winds would not cooperate until, "On Sunday morning, the 23rd of December 1787, we sailed from Spithead, and passing through the Needles, directed our course down channel, with a fresh gale of wind at the East."[9] On the 23rd of December the *Bounty* should have been at or approaching Cape Horn if they were to get through to the South Seas.

When the *Bounty* put in at the Spanish port of Tenerife in the Canary Islands, Bligh became notably unreasonable. Referring to the journal kept during the voyage by Midshipman James Morrison, Sir John Barrow wrote, "It would appear from this important document that the seeds of discord, in the unfortunate ship *Bounty*, were sown at a very early period of the voyage." At Tenerife, Bligh demanded to inspect a cask of cheese brought from England. The captain declared that a portion had been stolen. James Morrison recalled, "The cooper declared that the cask had been opened before, while the ship was in the river [at Portsmouth] by Mr. Samuel's [ship's clerk] order and cheeses sent to Mr. Bligh's house—Mr. Bligh without making any further inquiry into the matter, ordered the allowance of cheese to be stopped from officers and men until the deficiency should be made good and told the cooper he would give him a damned good flogging if he said more about it."[10]

Sailing away from the Canaries, the crew were hopelessly late for smooth sailing around the tip of South America. Bligh might have made for the Cape of Good Hope, a much easier passage; he had the Admiralty's permission to do so. But with great obstinacy, from March 29 to April 22, Bligh used all of the considerable seamanship at his command to buck winds to get the *Bounty* around the Horn. The crew experienced "hard gales of westerly wind" and ultimately realized that "the season was now too far advanced for us to expect more favourable winds or weather."[11] "The weather continued to grow worse every day," James Morrison wrote, "hail, rain, sleet and snow or rather large flakes of half-formed ice alternately following each other in heavy squalls...."[12] Sails had become rigid, having been frozen by ice and snow. The crew had become too weak to continue to hoist ice-heavy sails and to work the slippery rigging.

At this point one might expect the foul-mouthed commander to unleash a volley of vituperation at procrastinating authorities who had put him in the position of attempting to bring his ship from one ocean to another in the wrong season. Instead he wrote, "Having maturely considered all circumstances, I determined to bear away for the Cape of Good Hope."[13] At Capetown, a Dutch port for over a century, the crew regained its health during thirty-eight days ashore. Some uncertain tension occurred at the Cape between Bligh and Christian; apparently Christian owed Bligh some money from a loan. We can never be certain to what extent that tension poisoned relations between the two men.

Six thousand miles eastward, the *Bounty* stopped in Van Diemen's Land and fought off attacks by hostile Tasmanians as shore parties searched for food, water and wood. Bligh, a hurried amateur ethnologist, described these Tasmanians, who were to die out entirely in less than a century: "Their colour ... is dull black: their skin is scarified about their shoulders and breast. They were of a middle stature, or rather below it. One of them was distinguished by his body being coloured with red oker, but all of the others were painted black, with a kind of soot, which they laid on so thick over their faces and shoulders, that it is difficult to say what they were like." Their voices sounded to Bligh "like the cackling of geese."[14]

Morrison wrote, "During this passage Mr. Bligh and his messmates the master and the surgeon fell out, and separated, each taking his part of the stock and retiring to live in their own cabins, after which they had several disputes and seldom spoke on duty, and even then with much apparent reserve."[15] The surgeon, described as being drunk all the time, could not have been a scintillating messmate for the captain.

Despite the captain's precautions to preserve his men's health, James Valentine, a seaman, contracted an illness while in Tasmania and when the alcoholic surgeon Huggan treated him, Valentine died. Not long after, Huggan literally drank himself to death. With the expiration of Valentine and Huggan went the captain's hope of bringing all of his men home alive.

CHAPTER 4

Captain Bligh v. Mr. Christian

Potting Plants in Paradise

On October 26, 1788, after nearly a year of sailing over 27,000 miles, Bligh wrote, "We saw Point Venus bearing S W by W, distant about 4 leagues. As we drew near, a great number of canoes came off to us. Their first inquiries were, if we were Tyo, which signified friends; and whether we came from Pretanie (their pronunciation of Britain), or from Lima." Tahitians climbed aboard in great numbers so that "in less than ten minutes, the deck was so full that I could scarce find my own people."[1]

Potting commenced on November 7. Breadfruit plants send out shoots or suckers from their roots and the shoots are clipped and replanted to produce new trees. Within a week most of the shoots had been potted. During the next twenty-four weeks the gardener and botanist and their workers continued potting and took care that each shoot took root properly. While they did their careful work, New South Wales was founded as a prison colony; George Washington was inaugurated first president of the United States; and in France, ominously, delegates brought *lettres de cachet* to the Estates General, an event which would lead King Louis XVI and Queen Marie Antoinette to the guillotine.

Bligh has been criticized for staying twenty-four weeks in Tahiti, long enough for his men to acclimate themselves to an indolent and erotic lifestyle. However, if the Admiralty had not delayed his orders two months, he could have arrived at Tahiti in August and left in September, making his way through the treacherous Endeavour (or Torres) Straits before typhoon season. Because November to April was the typhoon season in the seaway between Australia and New Guinea, Bligh was justified in waiting to leave in April.

On December 25, Bligh moved his ship from Matavai Bay six miles up the coast for better anchorage at a bay called Pare. Camp was set up ashore for the breadfruit tenders and their guards. Both Matavai Bay and Pare were in the larger loop of Tahiti's lop-sided figure-eight land mass. This larger loop was divided among three paramount chiefs, each of whom claimed superiority over three or four lesser chiefs within their territories. Pare was in the territory ruled by Chief Tinah. Tinah was born about 1751 and died in 1803. Bligh considered Tinah the most important chief on Tahiti because he controlled Matavai Bay and Pare. Tinah would later be called called Tu, and later yet, King Pomare I.

Chiefs like Tihah — the *ari'i* — had so much *mana* that everything they touched was affected; if a chief walked into a subject's house, the house became the chief's property because it became permeated with his *mana*. Therefore, chiefs had to be carried from place to place. Because chiefs were able to eat their fill of the best foods that their subjects could provide, they often became corpulent, so carrying them about was impractical. According to custom, when the chief sired a son, the baby was declared chief. The baby was more easily carried. The father, and even his father — the chief's grandfather and former chief— could now walk anywhere without affecting the area with their *mana*. Chief Tinah was married to Iddea. Both were over six feet tall and each was guessed to weigh three hundred pounds. Fortunately, Tinah and Iddea had a son, Prince Tu (later Pomare II, 1783–1821), who, at the time of the *Bounty*'s stay, was five years old and was carried everywhere. Nevertheless, Bligh treated Tinah, the boy's father, as chief.

According to his memoir, the *Bounty*'s master spent most days entertaining and being entertained by Tinah and Iddea. Bligh became Tinah's *tyo*, an adopted brother; in Tahitian custom, the two best friends for life exchanged names and could sleep with each other's wives, though there is no report that Bligh had sexual relations with Iddea. Each day, no matter how warm the temperature, to impress Tinah and Iddea, Bligh wore his full dress uniform. Bligh gave presents to Tinah and his family and served them lavish meals on board. By doing so, Bligh helped to enhance the power of this local ruler. Because of their geographical advantage in ruling bays that were essential to Europeans, Tinah's descendants would use European patronage and weapons to wrest control of the entire island for what was to become the Pomare dynasty, paramount lords of all of Tahiti.

Bligh's purpose in cementing friendship with Tinah was to continue to cultivate on shore an inordinate number of breadfruit plants, which would amount to 1,015, without causing animosity among the islanders. Bligh took a diplomatic approach, explaining to Tinah that, "on account of their good will, and from a desire to serve him [Tinah] and his country, King George had sent out those valuable presents to him; and will not you, Tinah, send something to King George in return?" "Yes," Tinah agreed, "I will send him any thing I have." Tinah now listed various items that he could send, including breadfruit. It was the moment Bligh had prepared for: "I told him the bread-fruit trees were what King George would like; upon which he promised me a great many should be put onboard, and seemed much delighted to find it so easily in his power to send anything that would be well received by King George."[2]

Like Bligh and Tinah, many of the ship's crew formed friendships with their own *tyos* among the tribesmen. Most of the crew, with time on their hands and having found willing female partners, also formed sexual liaisons ashore. James Morrison of the *Bounty* would describe women as "finely shaped," and "in general handsome and engaging, their eyes full and sparkling and black almost without exception, their noses of different descriptions, their mouths small, lips thin and red, and their teeth white and even and their breath sweet and perfectly free from taint." Morrison continued, "Their limbs in general are neat and delicate and ... many with the help of a fashionable dress would pass for handsome women even in England."[3]

Lighter skin in Tahiti was an indication of higher class. Many Tahitian females were more than willing to bear babies by European sailors, viewing babies with whiter skin as prestigious. Author Glynn Christian marveled that women coupled with sailors, "in spite of the horrors of the *Bounty* crew's foreskins, pubic hair, rotten teeth, execrable manners and a mantling of body odour and halitosis...."[4] Glynn Christian's distant ancestor Fletcher found a willing partner in Mi'Mitti, an aristocratic woman. Fletcher Christian, who had often been with Bligh during the voyage, now spent his time onshore, separating himself from his captain. Perhaps Bligh was envious or hurt or both. Bligh failed to realize how his crew, whose average age was twenty-four, preferred the comforts of Tahitian females to transporting breadfruit on an overcrowded ship with bad food and a foul-mouthed commander.

A Captain's Complaints

Bligh's problems with his crew worsened while anchored at Tahiti. Bligh recorded that during the night of January 5, 1789, a small cutter was reported missing. The captain mustered all hands and soon realized that Charles Churchill, the ship's corporal, and two seamen, William Muspratt and John Millward, had taken not only the cutter but arms and ammunition. Bligh recalled, "I went on shore to the chiefs, and soon received information, that the boat was at Matavai; and that the deserters had departed in a sailing canoe for the island Tehuroa [Tetiroa]." Bligh sent a party to apprehend them, but, "before they got half way, they met the boat with five of the natives, who were bringing her back to the ship." Bligh rewarded the Tahitian bounty hunters. He then summoned all hands, read the Articles of War, ordered twelve lashes administered to Churchill, and two dozen each to Muspratt and Millard. Thomas Hayward, the officer of the watch who should have thwarted the desertion, was placed in irons for eleven weeks for sleeping on duty. Since the *Bounty* left England, Bligh had ordered eight crew members flogged: Matthew Quintal, John Williams, Alexander Smith (a.k.a. John Adams), Isaac Martin, Charles Churchill, William Muspratt, John Millward and John Sumner; of these, all would be mutineers and the first four would be founding fathers of the Pitcairn settlement.

The following day, Bligh "discovered that the ship's cable had been cut near the water's edge, in such a manner that only one strand remained whole." As the crew attempted to secure the ship, chief Tinah and members of his family came on board. Bligh did not suspect the Tahitians of cutting the cable, but rather one or more of his own crew members. In a rare allusion in his own writing to his famous temper, he confessed how he frightened members of the royal family: "The anger which I expressed, however, created so much alarm, that [Tinah's father and mother] immediately quitted Oparre, and retired to the mountains in the midst of heavy rain...."[5]

Glossing over his own consistent rants and occasional orders for floggings, Bligh summed up events to the time of departing for home port: "Thus far, the voyage had advanced in a course of uninterrupted prosperity, and had been attended with many circumstances equally pleasing and satisfactory."[6] "Towards the later end of March," Morrison wrote, "we put the rigging in order and bent the sails and Mr. Nelson having collected upwards of a thousand fine bread fruit plants, with many others of value, we got ready for sea."[7]

An Impromptu Mutiny

Loaded with vegetables, fruit and fresh and salted chicken and pork, the *Bounty* sailed from Matavai Bay on April 4, 1789. Having been given a double allowance of grog, "everybody seemed in high spirits," according to Midshipman James Morrison, "and began already to talk of home, affixing the length of the passage and count up their wages and one would readily have imagined we had just left Jamaica instead of Tahiti so far onward did their flattering fancies waft them."[8] What should have been a routine voyage was to be aborted after only three and a half weeks.

On April 23, crew members went ashore at Nomuka in the Ha'apai Group of the Tonga Islands for wood, water, and any available food. Bligh placed Christian in an untenable position as head of the shore party; he ordered Christian and his men to go ashore but not to use arms in their own defense. When hostile Nomukans chased Christian and his companions back into their boats, Bligh "damned him for a cowardly rascal, asking him if he was afraid of a set of naked savages while he had arms, to which Mr. Christian answered, 'The arms are of no use when your orders prevent them from being used.'"[9]

Bligh failed to understand that his men were confused when he berated them constantly but ordered only mild punishments. Bligh failed to understand how far he could push Christian. Bligh's acid tongue and accusations compelled the sensitive midshipman to prefer any situation other than being a subordinate of the *Bounty*'s foul-mouthed master.

As April 28th dawned, the *Bounty* was sailing near Tofua, also in the Ha'apai Group. Christian commanded the early morning watch. Bligh recalled, "Just before sun-rising, while I was yet asleep, Mr. Christian with the master at arms, gunner's mate and Thomas Burkitt, seaman, came into my cabin and seizing me, tied my hands with a cord behind my back, threatening me with instant death if I spoke or made the least noise."[10] When Morrison saw Bligh, the captain was "in his shirt with his hands tied behind him and Mr. Christian standing by him with a drawn bayonet in his hand and his eyes flaming with revenge."[11] Master's mate John Fryer saw Bligh "standing by the mizen mast with his hands tied behind him and Christian holding the cord with one hand and a bayonet in the other." When Fryer tried to reason with Christian, Christian replied, "Hold your tongue Sir, I have been in hell for weeks past — Captain Bligh has brought all this on himself."[12]

In a desperate attempt to retain command, Bligh told Christian, "I'll pawn my honor, I'll give my bond, Mr. Christian, never to think of this if you desist." Christian replied, according to Morrison, "No Captain Bligh. If you had any honor things would never have come to this.... Tis too late. I have been in hell for this fortnight passed and am determined to bear it no longer."[13] Bligh also quoted Christian as having replied, "That — Captain Bligh — that is the thing; — I am in hell — I am in hell."[14] Witnesses said Christian emphasized the preposition *in*.

What was the mutiny's cause? Bligh asserted that the mutiny took place because, "The women of Otaheite are handsome, mild and cheerful in their manners and conversations, possessed of great sensibility, and have sufficient delicacy to make them admired and beloved." It was no wonder that, "a set of sailors, most of them devoid of connections, should be led away; especially when, in addition to such powerful inducements, they imagined it in their power to fix themselves in the midst of plenty, on one of the finest islands in the world, where they need not labour, and where the allurements of dissipation are beyond anything that be conceived."[15] Bligh did not explain why Wallis's or Bougainville's or Cook's men had not mutinied or deserted when they were in Tahiti.

What caused Christian to be "in hell," was that Bligh's daily rants were constant and culminated in Bligh's accusation the day before that Christian was a thief. Bligh had taken on coconuts at Nomuka, later ordered them brought on deck to be counted, and then claimed some had been stolen from him. When no officer would name a crew member as the thief, Bligh asserted that one of the officers had to be the culprit. Christian defended himself by replying, "...I hope you don't think me so mean as to be Guilty of Stealing yours." Bligh blasted Christian in front of the ship's company: "Yes you dam'd Hound I do — You must have stolen

them from me or you could give a
better account of them — God damn
you you Scoundrels you are all
thieves alike, and combine with the
Men to rob me — I suppose you'll steal
my Yams next, but I'll sweat you for
it you rascals I'll make half of you
jump overboard before you get
through Endeavour Streights."[16] Bligh
told Mr. Samuel to "Stop these villains grog, and give them but half a
pound of yams tomorrow and if they
steal then, I'll reduce them to a quarter."[17] Sven Wahlroos commented,
"Christian came from an unbroken
line of twenty-five generations of aris-
tocracy and none of his forefathers
would have let themselves be called
cowards or thieves without exacting
retribution."[18]

*The Mutineers Turning Lieut. Bligh and Part of the Officers
and Crew Adrift from His Majesty's Ship the Bounty.*
**Aquatint by Robert Dodd (1748–1816), painted in 1790.
Fletcher Christian forced Bligh and 18 others into the**
Bounty's **launch, April 28, 1789. After being repulsed at
Tofua in the Tonga Islands, Bligh commenced his epic
3,618-mile open boat voyage to Timor.**

Instead of plotting retribution, Christian immediately set about fabricating a raft to
extricate himself from his accuser. At some point in preparing to leave, he was convinced by
a shipmate that enough men, bullied too often and recalling the sweet rewards of life on
Tahiti, would side with him to depose Bligh. It was then he decided to disempower Bligh
and take his ship.

A number of historians have taken Bligh's excuse that the allure of Tahitian maidens was
the cause of the mutiny. R. B. Nicolson states in his *The Pitcairners*, "That the 'easy life' and
women of Tahiti were at the core of the mutiny cannot be doubted. The spur-of-the-moment
act of mutiny triggered off by Bligh's actions had its origins in the liaison between a British
sailor, too long at sea, and a Tahitian beauty hidden from sight on the island."[19]

Mr. Christian's Reason

It is probably correct to state that some — or perhaps most — mutineers participated in
order to return to Tahiti's women. However, Christian was the catalyst of the mutiny and it
is improbable there would have been any mutiny on that cruise had Christian not been aboard.
It is absurd to suggest that Christian gave up his career, committed a crime against his king
and country, embarrassed his family, stained his reputation, and put dozens of lives in danger to return to Mi'Mitti, his Tahitian lady. There was no apparent way he could have been
reunited with Mi'Mitti by building a single-man raft to get to the nearest Tongan islet. If he
had wanted to stay with her on Tahiti, he would have deserted and hid on Tahiti when his
ship sailed.

Christian mutinied because he thought his career was ended. In the eighteenth century,
officers depended for advancement on patronage. A man did not actually join His Majesty's
navy, but "in constitutional theory and in everyday practice, he was primarily a member of a
ship's company and not of the Navy as a whole."[20] It might be said that a man joined an

officer rather than the navy itself. When the crew was paid off at the end of an operation, the mariner would sign on the same ship again or look for another ship. Ideally, the next voyage would be under the same commanding officer. Commanders, for their part, attempted to staff their ships with men who had been loyal to them. As the senior officer advanced, the young officer would advance in rank under him. Christian might even have looked forward to command of a vessel after successful completion of the breadfruit mission. As Bligh's biographer Gavin Kennedy pointed out, "We do know that Bligh favoured Christian with promotion to Acting Lieutenant and that this almost guaranteed Christian an Admiralty promotion to this rank on his return to England."[21]

Christian did not cause a mutiny because he was called a scoundrel and rascal or because his yam allowance was halved. Christian deposed his commander because he had been accused of theft. Bligh's rant effectively ended Christian's career. As N. A. M. Rodger explained, the worst crimes aboard ship were murder, sodomy, "and after that theft, by far the most serious crime which was at all common. ... A thief among the ship's company destroyed its mutual bonds of trust and loyalty more swiftly than anything else." Roger concluded that "courts martial habitually treated theft much more severely than, say, mutiny or desertion."[22] As a result of the accusation, everything Christian had worked for was destroyed, and he knew it was within Bligh's power to have him court-martialed. If that were the case, Christian had lost his patron and could look forward to imprisonment and dismissal under the most dishonorable conditions, and — conceivably, though improbably — hanging.

What is surprising is that nobody attempted to thwart the mutiny. Morrison wrote, "The behaviour of the officers on this occasion was dastardly beyond description, none of them even making the least attempt to rescue the ship ... their passive obedience to Mr. Christian's orders even surprised himself."[23] What prevented loyalists from taking action may have been to some extent the same repugnance toward Bligh that motivated the mutineers.

There were several reasons for other crew members to join Christian's mutiny: their attraction to Christian as a natural leader, dislike of their captain, dread of the long voyage home, the allure of a sensual life on Tahiti with their Polynesian mates, and for those without family, as Sven Wahlroos suggests, the desire to return to a Tahitian *tyo*—"and thereby a loving family"— may all have been motivational forces.[24] In addition the *Bounty*'s company could not depend on Bligh as a high-ranking patron to advance their careers, and even if he were willing to do so, few wanted to sail with him again; thus, some felt their naval careers had become dispensable. And there was the matter of food. Though plentiful fresh meat, fruits and vegetables had been obtained on Tahiti before sailing, Bligh limited the men each day to six plantains and a ration of pork. Each man received a pound of yams when the plantains were exhausted. The men, whose work could be exhausting and who needed nourishment, had left an island with no shortages of food for a ship whose commander caused unnecessary hunger. Finally, any large group includes the rebellious, those who jump at the chance to defy authority and to seek illicit adventure. Everyone aboard the *Bounty* on mutiny morning were destined to have more adventure than any one of them had ever dreamed of.

CHAPTER 5

The Famous Captain Bligh

With Bligh in the *Bounty*'s Launch

The mutiny was bloodless. Fletcher Christian's anger and hurt made him determined to separate himself permanently from his captain, not to harm an erstwhile friend and patron. He might have had Bligh killed, but instead he gave Bligh a chance to live by rowing away in a ship's boat. First, Christian ordered the ship's jolly boat—a light craft carried at the stern—to be lowered, but it was found to be eaten with worms and unusable; then they lowered the cutter, which also leaked. The sailing master, John Fryer, had obviously been neglectful in not maintaining these boats, and Bligh himself could be criticized for not having inspected them and ordered repairs while anchored in Tahiti. Reluctantly, Christian gave Bligh and his companions the twenty-three-foot, two-masted ship's launch, which was sound. When Fryer saw Bligh entering the launch, he asked what the mutineers intended to do with him. "Damn his eyes," Fryer quoted seaman John Sumner as saying, "put him into the boat and let the bugger see if he can live upon three fourths of a pound of yams a day."[1] Eighteen men professed loyalty to Bligh and climbed into the boat. Seven more would have gone, but the launch's capacity was supposed to be fifteen and they were told there was no room for them.

Christian allowed the loyalists a tool chest, hammocks, clothing, rope, canvas, oars, sails, twine, lines, towline, a grapnel, and personal items. The mutineers threw into the launch 140 pounds of biscuits, 20 pounds of pork, some coconuts and moldy breadfruit, 28 gallons of water, 5 quarts of rum and 3 bottles of wine. Of great importance to master mariner Bligh were a compass, sextant, quadrant and book of tables, but he was given no pocket watch. "After having undergone a great deal of ridicule, and been kept some time to make sport for these unfeeling wretches," Bligh stated, "we were at length cast adrift in the open ocean."[2]

"A few hours before," Bligh wrote, "my situation had been peculiarly flattering. I had a ship in the most perfect order, and well stored with every necessary both for service and health: ... add to this, the plants had been successfully preserved in the most flourishing state: so that, upon the whole, the voyage was two-thirds completed." Moreover, Bligh continued, everyone on board was in perfect health. Making his way day by day in the launch Bligh had sufficient time to ponder how the act might have been thwarted: "Perhaps, if there had been marines on board, a sentinel at my cabin-door might have prevented it." Bligh attempted to

In this cave at Tofua, Tonga, Bligh and his companions in the *Bounty*'s launch sought shelter immediately after the mutiny. Hostile Tofuans killed quartermaster John Norton and menaced the others.
The crew threw precious clothing overboard, retarding the progress of the islanders, who stopped to
retrieve it, allowing Bligh's men to get away.

influence Admiralty opinion in his favor: "Had their mutiny been occasioned by any grievances, wither real or imaginary, I must have discovered symptoms of their discontent which
would have put me on my guard."[3]

More immediately, Bligh sought water and food on Tofua, the nearest island to the scene
of the mutiny. Tofua measures four by five miles. The launch crew landed on the north-west
coast at a beach approximately 150 yards long and here found a large cave for shelter. Using
Bligh's description, in March 1985, Bengt Danielsson, a veteran of the celebrated voyage of
the *Kon Tiki* with Thor Heyerdahl, was positive he had identified the cave.[4] Behind the cave
Bligh's men climbed a cliff to look for food and water. Bligh had hoped to befriend the
islanders so his men could wait at Tofua for rescue, but the crew were driven off by hostile
Tofuans. Islanders killed John Norton, the *Bounty*'s quartermaster, as they chased the launch
from shore. Bligh and his men saved themselves only by throwing clothing from the launch,
which Tofuans stopped to pick up from their canoes, thus retarding their pursuit.

With only cutlasses to defend themselves, Bligh and his men were unwilling to stop at
other Polynesian or Melanesian islands either for supplies or to wait for a ship to take them
home. Bligh realized then he would have to make for the nearest European settlement without stopping again for food or water. Bligh knew that a British prison colony was to be
established at Botany Bay in New South Wales, but he was reluctant to go there, as he had
no way to be certain that British ships had already arrived. The colony had actually been established in January 1788, but not where Bligh would have looked; it was founded near Botany

Bay in Sydney Harbor. There, the famous First Fleet disembarked 717 convicts with 200 copies of *Dissuasions from Stealing* and 200 copies of *Exercises against Lying,* with the expectation that the exiled felons would reform themselves through reading while pioneering a new continent.

Bligh headed instead for Dutch Timor; it was a distant 3,618 miles, a journey which was to be completed in forty-one days due to Bligh's superb seamanship. No more deaths resulted enroute. Bligh worked out rations: He told his crew that "no hope of relief for us remained ... till I came to Timor, ... where there was a Dutch settlement, but in what part of the island I knew not; they all agreed to live on 1 ounce of bread, and a quarter of a pint of water, per day." They took this minimal sustenance at 8 A.M., noon, and sunset.

Bligh noted that "every one seemed better satisfied with our situation than myself." In his book, *The Mutiny on* H.M.S. *Bounty,* the crew are depicted as perpetually satisfied with his leadership. Along the way, Bligh made notes and charted islands, recording twenty-three of the Fijis. Bligh's boatload of men were the first Europeans to have sailed through these palm-fringed islands. Cannibalistic Fijians jumped into their own boats and, looking for tasty human meat, chased the launch for miles. Every day, the boat's crew was plagued by rainstorms, blazing sun, and bitter cold. Bligh remembered being "so covered with rain and salt water, that we could scarcely see. We suffered extreme cold, and every one dreaded the approach of night. Sleep, though we longed for it, afforded no comfort."[5] Bligh knew that clouds and rain were essential for survival, because "Hot weather would have caused us to have died of thirst."[6] The boat was so overcrowded that "Our limbs were dreadfully cramped, for we could not stretch them out; and the nights were so cold and we [were] so constantly wet that, after a few hours sleep, we could scarce move."[7] Bligh drew maps for his men, encouraged them, made them sing and ordered them to get along with one another. The open voyage brought out the best in the irritable officer.

Planning to sail through the Endeavour Straits, Bligh sighted the Australian coast on May 28. The following day, he found an opening which allowed the boat to sail inside the Great Barrier Reef to what he named Restoration Island. There the crew rested for several days, "in the course of which we found oysters, a few clams, some birds, and water."[8] The men began to revive from their ordeal. Two days later, on nearby Sunday Island, Bligh became moody and chastised his men without real cause. A few men who were most unhappy planned a second mutiny against him. Bligh brandished his cutlass, determined to enforce his command with blood if necessary. Back in the launch, the men worked well together under their captain's leadership. Pitting his navigational skills against the challenging sea seemed to restore his calm.

In early June the men were suffering from body sores. Lethargic and famished, they slept much of the time; Bligh awakened each for his thrice daily bread and water allowance. On June 10, the surgeon's mate reported that the men were more dead than alive. Bligh knew he was close to Timor but he was obsessed with strict rationing. He denied his men extra bread and water. When they arrived, eleven days' rations would be left over, unconsumed.

On June 14, Bligh saw two square-riggers and a cutter against the backdrop of a jetty, a fort, and European colonial structures. They had reached Coupang, Timor, the closest European outpost. "It is not possible for me," Bligh wrote, "to describe the pleasure which the blessing of the sight of this land diffused among us." Either irrationally or vindictively, Bligh ordered the emaciated John Fryer to stay in the boat to guard its contents, as if there had been any contents worth guarding. Bligh summed up his own remarkable achievement in stating, "It appeared scarce credible to ourselves, that in an open boat and poorly provided, we should have been able to reach the coast of Timor in forty-one days, ... and not withstanding our extreme distress, no one should have perished in the voyage."[9] Naval official Sir John Barrow, a historian critical of Bligh in many respects, wrote, "To his discreet management of the men, and their scant resources, and to his ability as a thorough seaman, eighteen souls were saved from imminent and otherwise inevitable destruction."[10]

At Coupang, Bligh bought on credit, using his commission as a Royal naval officer as collateral, a small schooner, which he named H.M.S. *Resource*. Its purpose was to tow the launch to Batavia, Java, the chief port of the Dutch United East India Company. Reaching Batavia, the boat crew found it a notoriously unhealthy city. Having survived the launch voyage, four of the men died there of tropical diseases. On October 2, 1789, Bligh was bedridden with malaria. Two weeks later, when he was able to travel, Bligh sold H.M.S. *Resource* and the *Bounty*'s launch and used the proceeds to purchase passage home on a Dutch ship, *Vlydte*. Bligh took only his clerk and servant, leaving the survivors from his crew waiting for passage home on other ships. Two men — Lamb and Ledward — died on the trip home to England. In all, twelve of the nineteen men who climbed into Bligh's launch near Tofua survived to return to England.

Explaining the Loss of a Ship

On March 14, 1790, Bligh arrived in England. He told his superiors about how the *Bounty* had been lost through no conceivable fault of his own. The authorities could not allow mutineers to steal the king's ships with impunity. Ten days later the Admiralty decided to send H.M.S. *Pandora* to capture the mutineers.

The Admiralty then held a court martial aboard H.M.S. *Royal William* at Spithead in October; Bligh was made to answer for returning without his ship. Bligh had had sufficient time to rehearse his defense; he portrayed himself as a model commander and the mutineers as scoundrels whose cause was to return to illicit sex with primitive females. As expected, the Admiralty exonerated Bligh.

Though exonerated, Bligh was intensely bitter. He lashed out against Midshipman Peter Heywood, who had not, despite being a loyalist, been allotted space on the launch but had remained on the *Bounty* with Christian. Bligh told Heywood's anxious mother in a letter dated April 2nd, 1790, that "His baseness is beyond all description, but I hope you will endeavour to prevent the loss of him, heavy as this misfortune is, from afflicting you too severely. I imagine he is, with the rest of the mutineers, returned to Otaheite." To Peter's uncle, he wrote on March 26, 1790, that "I very much regret that so much baseness formed the character of a young man I had a real regard for, and it will give me much pleasure to hear that his friends can bear the loss of him without much concern." Admiralty official Sir John Barrow commented four decades later, "Some excuse may therefore be found for Bligh's hasty expressions uttered in moments of irritation. But no excuse can be found for his deeply and unfeelingly, without revocation, and in cold blood, inflicting a wound on the heart of a widowed mother, already torn with anguish and tortured with suspense for a beloved son, whose life was in imminent jeopardy."[11]

The *Bounty* mutiny did not harm Bligh's career. He became famous because of it, and the story of his brilliant voyage in the open boat aroused much public sympathy and admiration. The public was eager to know details of the mutiny and of the crew's sojourn among Tahiti's maidens. Seven weeks after Bligh's return the dramatic events of mutiny were transformed into public entertainment. On May 3, an advertisement for London's Royalty Theater promised an elaborate reenactment:

> Fact told in Action, called THE PIRATES, Or, the Calamities of Capt. Bligh Exhibiting a Full account of his Voyage, from his taking leave at the Admiralty, and shewing the *Bounty* falling down the River Thames — the Captain's reception at Otaheite, and exchanging the British manufactures for the bread Fruit — with an Otaheitian Dance, — an exact representation of the Seisure of Capt. Bligh, in the cabin of the *Bounty* by the Pirates, with the affecting scene of forcing the captain and his faithful followers into the Boat — their Distress at Sea, and Repulse by the natives of Timur [actually Tofua] — their miraculous arrival at the Cape of Good Hope, and their friendly reception by the governor.

The bill promised a grand finale featuring Hottentot dances and "their happy arrival in England."[12]

An entertaining writer, Bligh published *A Narrative of the Mutiny Onboard* H.M.S. *Bounty* in June 1790. The book was widely read. Even today, in reading Bligh, one journeys with a seemingly rational, interesting and humane companion. Only rarely, according to his own words, though faced with the desertion of three men, a nearly severed cable, and a quarrelsome launch complement, did he lose his temper. His book showed its author as a superb leader victimized by incompetent and immature sailors. At the height of his popularity, Bligh was introduced to King George III, promoted to commander and promoted a month later to post captain.

Bligh's Second Breadfruit Expedition

As post captain, Bligh had a promise to fulfill. His Majesty's government had promised breadfruit plants to the West Indian planters; therefore, Captain Bligh had to do it all over again — sail to Tahiti, pot breadfruit, and this time he had to deliver the miracle plants. Bligh sailed from Portsmouth Harbor on August 3, 1791, aboard H.M.S. *Providence* with a crew of 134. Just in case he lost his ship again, H.M.S. *Assistant*, with a crew of twenty-seven, accompanied *Providence*. This time he had onboard nineteen marines.

Bligh rounded the Cape of Good Hope and arrived in Tahiti on April 9, 1792. The ships left Tahiti July 19, 1792, after a stay of a little over three months. On December 17, 1792, Bligh arrived at St. Helena in the South Atlantic; there, as ordered, he gave the governor ten breadfruit pots and an assortment of other plants he had ordered potted. This time, in spite of the fact that Bligh continued to spew wounding insults to those on board, he completed his mission. The mission was completed because the Admiralty had done what it should have done for the *Bounty*'s mission: It supplied a contingent of marines to keep order, including a guard at the captain's cabin door at night. H.M.S. *Providence* was twice as large as the *Bounty*, providing sufficient room for men as well as plants. Bligh was promoted to captain, with a decent salary, and he had commissioned lieutenants serving under him.

Bligh left 544 breadfruit plants on St. Vincent and the rest at Port Royal, Jamaica. The Jamaican government gave Bligh a prize of a thousand guineas. Bligh was now modestly rich. The *Providence* and *Assistant* returned to England August 7. The West Indies sugar planters were less happy when their slaves found breadfruit insipid and refused to eat it. But nobody blamed Bligh for that.

There being no mutiny aboard H.M.S. *Providence*, one might assume that Bligh had been a paternal and humane commander. Bligh's second in command aboard was his nephew,

First Lieutenant Francis Godolphin Bond. In a letter to his brother, Bond wrote: "Yes, Tom, our relation had the credit of being a tyrant in his last expedition, where his misfortunes and good fortune have elevated him to a situation he is incapable of supporting with decent modesty. The very high opinion he has of himself makes him hold every one of our profession with contempt, perhaps envy. Nay, the navy is but a sphere for fops and lubbers to swarm in, without one gem to vie in brilliancy with himself. I don't mean to depreciate his extensive knowledge as a seaman and nautical astronome, but condemn that want of modesty, in self-estimation." There is no reason not to believe Bond when he stated, "Soon after leaving England I wished to receive instruction from this imperious master, until I found he publicly exposed any deficiency on my part in the Nautical Arts, &c." Bond then complained about the impossible work load that Bligh had assigned him, and that no decision could be made — not even a carpenter's nail driven — without his uncle's permission. Although Bligh had said nothing positive about his nephew during the voyage, Bond still held out hope for promotion.[13] Bond went on to command his own ship, the schooner *Netley*. He never sailed with Uncle William again.

While Bligh was making his epic voyage in the launch, furthering his career, and redeeming his promise to bring breadfruit to hungry slaves, the men who remained aboard the *Bounty* faced challenges of their own.

CHAPTER 6

With the Mutineers

Tensions at Tubuai

When Bligh and his companions were put off in the launch, twenty-five men remained on the *Bounty*. Of these, seven professed loyalty to Bligh but the launch was too crowded to accommodate them. To gain more space on the *Bounty*, the shrunken crew threw most of the now unwanted breadfruit trees into the Pacific.

Christian and his companions decided to settle on Tubuai, 350 miles south of Tahiti; Tubuai is one of the Austral Islands, now part of French Polynesia. Cook had charted the location of Tubuai in 1777 but did not land. Christian had found the island described in a book in Bligh's onboard library. Cook noted that Tubuai has no real harbor and is surrounded by a reef with a single passage. It measures three by five miles and is crowned by a peak that reaches 1,385 feet.

The men aboard the *Bounty* sailed for nearly a month before reaching the volcanic island. On May 24, 1789, the day after arriving at Tubuai, the crew clashed immediately with fifty or so boatloads of some of the island's estimated three thousand Polynesians. After shooting some twelve Tubuians, the crew became the first Europeans to land on the island, naming their landing place Bloody Bay.

Not long after the battle at Bloody Bay, they set sail once again for Tahiti. Mutineer John Adams recalled decades later, "We lacked women; and remembering Tahiti, where all of us had made intimate friendships, we decided to return there, so we could each obtain one."[1] The crew found that the only source of meat on Tubuai was rats. So, on Tahiti they collected pigs, goats, chickens, dogs, and a bull and cow, which Cook had left. They also brought with them eighteen Tahitian males and eleven females.

The *Bounty* arrived back at Tubuai on June 26. Those aboard were a disparate group — true rebels, loyalists hoping to go home, and Polynesians. They were a company who could follow the leader, Mr. Christian, or not, as they wished. They were a group which had no real cohesion at a time when unity was of vital importance to their safety. Fortunately this time the islanders were more hospitable, possibly because they equated the illness which broke out among them following the *Bounty*'s first visit as retribution of angry gods for their attack on the newcomers. Communication was relatively easy, as the Tubuians spoke a dialect related to Tahitian. Christian secured land from a friendly chief, Tummotoa, and all may have gone well, but Christian coveted land belonging to another chief, Taroatehoa. Taroatehoa gave the visitors a friendly welcome, and the land they wanted, accompanied by a feast.

The crew then made a series of mistakes. Their original host, Tummotoa, felt rebuffed when the British settled elsewhere, depriving him of the service of their superior weapons, so he joined forces with the third, and least friendly, chief, Tinnarow; the two chiefs warned the foreigners not to enter their tribal areas. Two-thirds of the island were now off-limits. Christian then let loose the three hundred pigs he had brought from Tahiti, and the pigs set about uprooting gardens which the islanders were counting on for food. Then Christian and his men began building a fort. It was to be enormous: 120 by 125 feet. The walls were to be eighteen feet thick and twenty feet high. Christian called it Fort George, after the sovereign whose ship he had commandeered. The purpose of the structure was to protect his men from the islanders and from the inevitable British war ship that would arrive some day. The mutineers hoisted the Union Jack over the construction area, and mounted the *Bounty*'s guns on the incomplete walls. The fort frightened the Tubuians, who saw it as a threat to themselves. The outline can yet be seen, but the area is overgrown.

Tubuai was a terrible choice as a secure settlement for the mutineers. They were unaware that while they were sleeping, the brig *Mercury* came close to shore. The crew of the *Mercury*, under command of Captain John Henry Cox, did not see the *Bounty* at anchor only because darkness had fallen. Interestingly, the *Mercury* was a privateer sailing under orders of King Gustaf III of Sweden (r. 1771–92), and had been sent to raid Russian settlements in Alaska; from 1788 to 1790, the two nations were at war over control of Finland. Cox's crew was British and no Swedes were onboard. Cox had promised Gustaf III a share of any profits to be wrested from the Russians. But when the *Mercury* crew reached Russian America they found the posts to be so pitifully poor that they did not waste time attacking. When the *Mercury* sailed away, it was only a matter of time that another ship would chance on the mutineers' settlement.

If Christian had been attuned to native politics and as good a diplomat as Bligh had been on Tahiti, the colony might have flourished. However, relations never improved between interlopers and Tubuians. Believing a rumor that the crew planned to kill them all and were digging a ditch — the fort's moat — to bury them, the islanders rose up and fought a vicious battle against the *Bounty*'s company. An estimated hundred Tubuians lost their lives in the battle. Sir John Barrow judged that "The mutineers' record of slaughter, wounding, theft, kidnapping, rape and wanton destruction of islander property ought by now to have removed them from the respectable company of history's victims. Whatever Bligh's personal manner, the mutineers had no justification for the crimes they committed once out of his jurisdiction."[2] Because the *Bounty*'s crew and later visiting crews brought venereal and other diseases, Tubuai's population was decimated; by 1823, it was estimated to be three hundred.[3]

Separating

Mr. Christian, as he was called, had obviously become first among his equals, but was not in full command. Vital decisions were made democratically. It had become obvious they had come to an island where they would never find peace and happiness. After three months on Tubuai, the *Bounty*'s crew voted sixteen to nine to return to Tahiti. Leaving Tubuai on September 15, they returned to Tahiti by the twentieth. Christian had no intention of remaining there to be caught and tried. Christian promised that those who wanted to remain on

Tahiti would be given a proportion of articles aboard the ship. The men who remained on Tahiti consisted of six who insisted they had not mutinied but for whom there was no room in the launch: Midshipman George Steward, Midshipman Peter Heywood, Charles Norman, blind fiddler Michael Byrne, armorer Joseph Coleman, boatswain's mate James Morrison, and carpenter's mate Thomas McIntosh; they patiently waited for a vessel to come from England to return them home. Nine others hoped that they could somehow hide out in the Society Islands when a ship did come from England to apprehend them. They were able-bodied seamen Thomas Ellison, Richard Skinner, Matthew Thompson, Thomas Burkett, John Sumner, John Millward, Henry Hillbrant, William Muspratt, and master-at-arms Charles Churchill.

The men who elected to stay aboard the *Bounty*, in addition to Christian, consisted of Midshipman Edward Young, gunner's mate John Mills, gardener William Brown, and able-bodied seamen John Williams, Matthew Quintal, John Adams (who had signed aboard as Alexander Smith), William McCoy, and Isaac Martin.[4] Christian, Quintal, McCoy, Mills, Adams and Young were to be the fathers of second-generation Pitcairners. The descendants of all but John Mills populate Pitcairn and Norfolk islands today; others are scattered in New Zealand, Australia and beyond. Williams, Brown and Martin were to die on Pitcairn Island without leaving progeny.

The nine who remained on the *Bounty* took three Polynesian men from Tahiti, one from Raiatea, and two from Tubuai; three of these six were stowaways. They took eighteen women, mostly from Tahiti. The mutineers kidnapped all but a few of these women by inviting them aboard for a party before sailing and preventing them from disembarking. Six were soon put ashore in Moorea, only nine miles from Matavai Bay, because they were judged to be too old. Isabella or Mi'Mitti, affectionately called Mainmast because she was tall, was Christian's companion; she had apparently remained aboard with Christian of her free will. McCoy's woman, Teio, called Mary, was the mother of the only child aboard, an infant daughter probably sired by a Polynesian.

Six Polynesian men were allocated three females to share: Nancy, Mareva, and Tinafanaea. The ratio of fifteen men to twelve women was to cause deadly complications in this tiny society. Christian should have put the three stowaways ashore. This singular mistake of Christian's matched Bligh's worst errors of judgment.

A quarter of a century later, the *Times* was able to piece together for its readers what had been known thus far of the mutineers. On December 16, 1815, the *Times* summarized the *Bounty*'s departure: "Christian, along with the remaining eight of the mutineers, having taken on board several of the natives of Otaheite, the greater part women, put to sea on the night between the 21st and 22nd of September, 1789; in the morning the ship was discovered from Point Venus, steering in a northwesterly direction; and here terminate the accounts given by the mutineers who were either taken or surrendered themselves at Matavai bay. They stated, however, that Christian on the night of his departure was heard to declare, that he should seek for some uninhabited island, and having established his party, break up the ship. From this period, no information respecting Christian and his party reached England for 20 years."[5]

The Extraordinarily Long Arm of the Law

On March 23, 1791, eighteen months after the men returned to Tahiti from Tubuai, H.M.S. *Pandora* anchored at Matavai Bay to bring the mutineers to justice. *Pandora* was a three-masted frigate carrying 24 guns and a crew of 120 under the command of Captain

Edward Edwards. The Admiralty's seriousness in apprehending the "pirates," as the mutineers were called, is indicated by the fact that the *Pandora* crew numbered two and a half times that of the *Bounty* when it was sent off to obtain breadfruit. Upholding authority appeared to be significantly more important to officialdom than saving the economy of the British West Indies. Sailing from England on November 7, 1790, Edwards was charged with capturing all the mutineers and bringing them back for trial as soon as possible. Approaching the Pacific from the tip of South America, Edwards discovered Ducie Island, one of four in the Pitcairn group. He was unaware that nine mutineers were hiding from him 357 miles away.

Fourteen of the *Bounty*'s men were living in Tahiti. Peter Heywood, like others of the refugees, had been invited to stay with his *tyo* and the *tyo*'s family. After he was apprehended, Heywood wrote to his mother, "Whilst we remained there we were used by our Friends (the Natives) with a Friendship, Generosity, & Humanity almost unparalleled, being such as never was equaled by the People of any civilised Nations, to the Disgrace of all Christians."[6]

The presence of the *Bounty*'s men altered Tahitian society. Some of the crew became mercenaries for local tribal chiefs. Churchill served as a mercenary in Tyarrabboo in the southeast. It was the territory of Churchill's *tyo*, the chief Vehiatua. Vehiatua ruled a few thousand people clustered in a pie-shape wedge of land. From time to time Vehiatua and his tribesmen fought with neighboring tribes, but appreciable territory did not change owners. This balance of power among Tahitian chiefs had existed as long as anyone could recall. Charles Churchill's friend Matt Thompson joined him because Thompson one day had encountered a Tahitian man walking with his family. When Thompson told the man to stop, the islander was unable to understand the order and kept walking. Thompson shot him to death, ostensibly to improve the Polynesians' English skills. To escape the wrath of the man's tribesmen, Thompson found it expedient to join Churchill. Shortly after, Vehiatua died and, as the chief's *tyo*, Churchill claimed the rank of chief, or *arii rahe* of Tyarrabboo. Thompson became madly envious at Churchill's hasty elevation in rank, so he shot Churchill and named himself chief of the tribe. Outraged at regicide, the good citizens of Tyarrabboo murdered the tyrant Thompson.

Following a complex series of internecine battles among local chiefs, in a mere year and a half gun-bearing mutineers helped the man who ruled Matavai and Pare, Tu (Bligh's *tyo* Tinah), beat his enemies at the neighboring island of Eimeo (Moorea). After that they conquered most of Tahiti. "It was a walkover," wrote historian David Howarth. "The fear of muskets made victory easy and immediate."[7] Tu held a ceremony in which chiefs swore fealty to their new paramount chief, and to emphasize their sincerity and positive intentions, the subdued chiefs slaughtered thirty of their fellow islanders in a ceremonial sacrifice.

Mutineers Apprehended and Boxed

Midshipman James Morrison, who had professed loyalty to Bligh, had directed the construction of a boat he named *Resolution*, a thirty-one-foot schooner, built entirely in Tahiti. The boat was a remarkable achievement that required the skills of the ship's carpenter, cooper, and armorer. Morrison was to discover that tapa cloth made flimsy sails, and without European canvas, the *Resolution* could not be sailed long distances. Thinking better of trying to get to another island when the *Pandora* arrived, and because he had taken no part in the crime, Morrison and Charles Norman, the armorer, disembarked and walked to Matavai Bay to surrender.

Morrison, Norman and other loyalists, glad for transportation home and expecting to be greeted warmly, were astonished when Edwards had them shackled along with those he identified as mutineers. Captain Edwards had brought *Bounty* midshipman Thomas Hayward from England, as third lieutenant, to identify the mutineers. Hayward remained bitter after the arduous voyage in the launch with Bligh to Coupang and failed to defend any of the men for their professed loyalty to Bligh. Peter Heywood, who also surrendered, explained to his mother that when the *Pandora* anchored, "my messmate and I went on board and made ourselves known"; and having learned that his good friend Thomas Hayward was on board and could vouch for his innocence of mutiny, found Hayward, who "received us very coolly, and pretended ignorance of our affairs.... Appearances being so much against us, we were ordered to be put irons" and treated as "piratical villains."[8] Sumner, Millward, Burkett, Muspratt, McIntosh and Hillbrant took to the mountains but were exposed by Tahitians and subsequently surrendered. Bligh wrote in his journal, "It may readily be believed that I found great satisfaction to hear of these men being taken by Captain Edwards except two who were killed by the Indians."[9]

Edwards had all fourteen confined to a special box he ordered built on deck. "*Pandora's* Box" measured eleven by fourteen feet. In this box fourteen men were transported across the South Pacific, suffering at times from intense heat, heavy rain and bitter cold. Two nine-inch air vents in the bulkhead allowed them to breathe. Each was shackled to the walls and floor of the box. Their toilet consisted of two buckets emptied twice a week. The fourteen — loyalists and mutineers alike — were guarded at all times by three men, one on top of the box. To prevent them from forming a plot to escape, they were forbidden to speak Tahitian among themselves. Prisoner Morrison later wrote to his mother that "we were all put in close confinement with both legs and both hands in irons, and were treated with great rigour, not being allowed even to get out of this den; and being obliged to eat, drink, sleep, and obey the calls of nature here.... My sufferings I have not power to describe...." Edwards described the box to the Admiralty as "airy and healthful."[10]

Edwards's cruelty may have been motivated in part by the fact that, as commanding officer in 1782, he had been the victim of a mutiny aboard H.M.S. *Narcissus.* When the mutiny was quelled, six were hanged and two others were lashed mercilessly. Edwards was an officer who hated mutineers.

Edwards commandeered the *Resolution,* which was put to use as the *Pandora's* tender; he placed nine of his men on board with orders to follow the *Pandora* home. Edwards took an additional four months getting his prisoners home because he attempted to search for the missing nine regardless of the fact that they might have been on any of 7,500 islands in the 63,855,093-square-mile Pacific. The *Pandora* crew searched most carefully in the Cook and Samoa groups.

At Palmerston Atoll in the Cook Islands, Edwards's crew found a mast and some stout poles which had been masts, yards or booms (spars) marked "*Bounty.*" Discovered in 1774, and named by Cook on his second voyage, Palmerston is protected by a barrier reef. Unlike Pitcairn, Palmerston is low and flat, very hot, sandy, and studded with palms. As at Pitcairn, one anchors far offshore at Palmerston and enters through a narrow channel. As at Pitcairn, getting to shore is a risky business, not so much due to crashing surf, but because it would be easy to miss the opening and wreck on the hard reef. Edwards ordered the atoll explored, hoping to find mutineers, but he was to be disappointed. The pieces of the *Bounty* had apparently floated from Tubuai.[11]

On May 24, 1791, Edwards sent the *Pandora's* jolly boat ashore at Palmerston, manned by a midshipman and four seamen. It then disappeared, probably wrecked on the vicious reef. Edwards was unable to find his five men so he sailed away. A month later, at Upolu in Samoa, the *Pandora* and *Resolution* became separated in a storm. They were scheduled to meet at Nomuka, a Tongan island. The *Resolution*, with its crew of nine, quickly ran out of drinking water, so it was imperative they land and obtain water. Under command of master's mate William Oliver, the *Resolution* crew sailed for Tofua, forty-five miles from the rendezvous point. There they traded nails for water but failed to meet the *Pandora*. Now Captain Edwards was missing fourteen men, one boat and one ship.

Sailing on near Vanikolo in the Santa Cruz group, now part of the Solomon Islands nation, the *Pandora* crew saw smoke signals. Impatient to find Christian and his cohorts, Edwards refused to stop to see if castaways needed rescue. Had Edwards investigated he may well have found survivors of the lost La Perouse expedition. Compte La Perouse, exploring for France, had set out in 1785, and in January 1788 sailed into Port Jackson in Sydney Harbour at the time of the arrival of the first convict fleet. After exchanging friendly greetings with the British officers, the French sailed away on March 10. Then they disappeared completely. It was not until 1826 that Captain Peter Dillon (1788–1847) found a sword hilt at Tikopia, a Polynesian outlier in the Solomons; it was inscribed J.F.G.P. (Jean François Galaup de la Perouse). Tikopians told Dillon that it been brought there from Vanikoro. Dillon found the wreckage of one of La Perouse's ships off Vanikoro, where *L'Astrolabe* and *La Boussole* had foundered in a storm. Islanders told Dillon that two survivors remained and had sought rescue at the time Edwards ordered *Pandora* to continue onward toward Endeavour Straits.

If the prisoners found life intolerable in *Pandora*'s box, their situation was about to worsen considerably. On August 28, 1791, the *Pandora* wrecked on the Great Barrier Reef. It broke up slowly over eleven hours. Three prisoners were unmanacled and let out of the box to help with the frantic work of trying to save the *Pandora*. Edwards ordered that the others remain shackled inside the box on the submerging deck. Writing in 1831, Sir John Barrow summed up Edwards for his readers: "It is true men are sometimes found to act the part of inhuman monsters, but then they are generally actuated by some motive of extraordinary excitement; here, however, there was neither; but on the contrary, the condition of the poor prisoners appealed most forcibly to the mercy and humanity of their jailor."[12]

Aboard the sinking *Pandora*, prisoner Peter Heywood recalled that the master-at-arms had dropped keys to the box so the prisoners could attempt to get out. By the time the drama concluded, thirty-one crew were dead and four prisoners had been drowned because they could not get out of the box in time. Eighty-nine of the *Pandora*'s company and ten prisoners were saved. In 1977, what remained of the *Pandora* was found under seventeen fathoms of water on the outer edge of a reef near Cape York. In 1997, the Queensland Museum sent an expedition to excavate what was left of Captain Edwards's ship.

The ninety-nine survivors rowed in four boats to an island in the Great Barrier Reef. The prisoners, bleached white from the box, were now left naked in the scorching sun. Peter Heywood told the Admiralty that the sun scorched skin off their bodies and their only recourse was to cover themselves with burning sand. Edwards and his company sheltered from the blistering sun under tents made of sails.

On September 15, 1791, the survivors navigated the four ship's boats to Coupang; for the last two weeks they had little food or water. Prisoners were bound hand and foot in the bottom of the boats. When the *Pandora*'s survivors reached Timor, they had completed a voyage of eleven hundred miles, about one-third of Bligh's launch journey. Mr. Timotheus Wanjon, governor of Timor, gave these refugees the same hospitality he had given Bligh and his men — except for Edwards's prisoners, who were jailed. It was the second time that Lieutenant Hayward, who had been aboard the *Bounty* launch, had limped ashore, half-dead, at the same place. At Coupang the *Pandora* survivors met eleven escapees from Australia; in a stolen longboat, the escapees had made their 3,254-mile voyage without formal navigation training. Sven Wahlroos wrote, "In maritime history the open-boat voyage of the escapees from Port Jackson to Timor deserves equal standing with the voyages of Bligh and Edwards."[13]

It was the profound misfortune of the Port Jackson eleven to run into Captain Edwards. After three weeks at Coupang, Edwards took his crew, *Bounty* prisoners and Port Jackson escapees aboard the Dutch ship *Rembang* to Semarang, Java, enroute to Batavia. At Semarang Edwards was astonished to find, after a separation of four months, the schooner *Resolution* riding in the harbor. The *Pandora* and *Resolution* sailed together once more and reached Batavia on November 7, 1791.

Edwards chartered transportation from the Dutch, dividing his own men, *Bounty* prisoners, and Port Jackson escapees among several ships. He did not have to provide transportation for sixteen of the *Pandora* crew; they died of tropical diseases in the pestilential Dutch East Indies. Edwards sailed aboard the Dutch East Indiaman *Vreedenberg* with the *Bounty* prisoners. They reached England on June 19, 1792. Captain Edwards had to report to his superiors that he had lost thirty-five men on the Great Barrier Reef, he had wrecked his ship, he was missing five men and the ship's jolly boat at Palmerston Island, and sixteen succumbed to disease in the East Indies. Edwards was promoted to the rank of rear admiral.

Court-Martials and Hangings

Article XIX of the Articles of War, promulgated Christmas Day 1749, stated clearly: "If any person in or belonging to the fleet shall make, or endeavour to make, any mutinous assembly, upon any pretense whatsoever, every person offending herein, and being convicted thereof by the sentence of the court martial, shall suffer death."[14] On September 12, 1792, aboard H.M.S. *Duke* in Portsmouth Harbor, the Admiralty opened a six-day court-martial of the ten *Bounty* crew members who had been accused of mutiny. Vice Admiral Lord Hood presided. Captain Bligh should have been the chief witness, but he had left to obtain breadfruit in August 1791.

On September 18, Lord Hood read the sentences. Peter Heywood, James Morrison, Thomas Ellison, Thomas Burkett, John Millward, and William Muspratt were sentenced to be hanged. Jo Coleman, Charles Norman, Tom McIntosh, and Michael Byrne were freed; before he had left England Bligh had vouched that these four men were innocent; unfortunately for them, Bligh had not informed Edwards of the fact. Heywood and Morrison received the king's pardon. While he was waiting for trial and then a pardon, Morrison wrote a detailed journal about Tahitian culture, and about his experiences aboard the *Bounty* and aboard the *Pandora*. Heywood busied himself with a Tahitian dictionary which would be used by the first English missionaries on that island. Now a free man, Heywood was soon promoted to midshipman with a berth aboard Lord Hood's flagship *Victory*. When Heywood died in 1831, he had attained the rank of admiral. Because William Muspratt's attorney Stephen Barney appealed on a technicality, the seaman received a stay, which ultimately prevented his execution.

On October 29, 1793, almost exactly four and half years after the event, three men paid the ultimate price for mutiny aboard HMAV *Bounty*. They were Tom Ellison, John Millward and Tom Burkett. The public hanging on the deck of H.M.S. *Brunswick* in Plymouth Harbor drew thousands of rapt spectators. Every seaman on every naval vessel was ordered to witness the execution. Men, women, and children rowed out to watch justice done. Slowly, gasping for air, each of the condemned was hoisted up by his neck. It was as good free entertainment as George III's government could provide.

Bligh: More Mutinies and Further Promotions

In 1794, Fletcher's brother Edward Christian published an account of the court martial proceedings, and an appendix. Although he was denied an official transcript of the proceedings, Stephen Barney, the lawyer for seaman Muspratt, gave Edward Christian his copious notes. Fletcher's brother then interviewed eleven surviving members of the *Bounty* crew; these interviews were done in the company of eminent witnesses such as the canon of Windsor and chaplain to the bishop of London. In the *Appendix* was testimony by survivors of the open launch voyage with Bligh and of the *Pandora*. Edward Christian was able to include quotes of Bligh's threats and expletives in the days and months preceding the mutiny. The sum total of the testimony showed that Bligh had verbally attacked his officers and crew, gratuitously and without moderation. Edward Christian wrote of the mutiny: " ... the crime itself in this instance may afford an awful lesson to the navy, and to Mankind, that there is a pressure, beyond which the best formed and principled mind must either break or recoil."[15] Public opinion gave Fletcher Christian the benefit of the doubt and many now blamed Bligh for giving the mutineers just cause. Professor Edward Christian's intention was to portray his brother as a well educated, well meaning officer from a good family, who had been pushed beyond the bounds of human endurance by his commander.

For his part, as Sven Wahlroos points out, Bligh considered himself "the most righteous, the most dutiful, the most efficient, the most caring of naval commanders" and was amazed that everyone else failed to realize his good intentions and actions.[16] Bligh wrote a reply to *The Appendix—An Answer to Certain Assertions Contained in the Appendix to a Pamphlet.* Edward Christian struck back with *Short Reply to Capt. William Bligh's Answer.*

On August 7, 1793, Bligh returned from Tahiti and Jamaica. Six months earlier, on February 1, 1793, the French Republic had declared war on Britain. This war continued to the Peace of Amiens, March 27, 1802, and then recommenced on May 16, 1803 and was ended only following Napoleon's final defeat on June 18, 1815, at Waterloo. Logic suggests that in this time of national emergency the Admiralty would enlist the services immediately of a brilliant navigator such as William Bligh. But his superiors caused him to languish at home for a year and a half in Lambeth on half pay and without command. Lord Chatham, First Lord of the Admiralty, refused him an audience, but welcomed Bligh's subordinate on the second breadfruit expedition, Lieutenant Portlock. Bligh was baffled because when he had returned after losing his ship, the king summoned him to Windsor and he had honors bestowed on him; now that he had completed his mission successfully, not even his fellow captains would receive him.

At last, in spring 1795, Captain Bligh was given command of *Warley*, a cruiser, and then H.M.S. *Calcutta* in August. Bligh acquitted himself well during the Napoleonic Wars. Nevertheless, on May 19, 1797, with captains of over a hundred other vessels at the Nore in the Thames Estuary, Bligh was once again the target of mutineers. This time fifty thousand seamen throughout the fleet struck over poor provisions and low pay. Bligh was expelled from his own vessel by the crew. To end the large-scale rebellion, the Admiralty met some demands and hanged the instigators.

At Copenhagen with Lord Horatio Nelson in 1801, Bligh helped achieve a brilliant if morally questionable victory. In 1805, Bligh was named a fellow of the Royal Society. In the same year he demanded the court martial of his subordinate Lieutenant John Frazier. At the hearing, Frazier accused Bligh of "outbursts of wrath, profanity, and violent nature." To prove Frazier wrong, Bligh called his boatswain "an audacious rascal, a vagrant and dastardly villain," and the master-at-arms "a Jesuit and an old rogue." The Admiralty admonished Bligh for "tyrannical and oppressive behaviour" and "abusive language," and told him to watch his tongue.17 Then they promoted Bligh to full captain.

In 1806, at the recommendation of his patron Joseph Banks, Bligh was named governor of New South Wales, the Australian prison colony. Although William and Elizabeth by now had six daughters, Bligh gladly accepted the appointment. This job, which paid the handsome sum of two thousand pounds per annum, would have challenged the most diplomatic of administrators. Bligh followed two governors who had been unable to end the debilitating trade in rum under control of the corrupt New South Wales Corps. To his credit, he attempted to control sheep-baron John MacArthur and to staunch the flow of rum. On January 26, 1808, hundreds of members of the Rum Corps marched on Government House, and acting under MacArthur's orders, staged a mutiny. They placed Governor Bligh under house arrest; Bligh was unable to return to England until April 1810, when London sent a new governor and more troops.

In 1811, Bligh was promoted to rear admiral. Three years before he died of the effects of cancer on December 7, 1817, he achieved the exalted rank of vice admiral. His outbursts finally silenced, Admiral William Bligh is buried in St. Mary Lambeth churchyard, across the Thames from Parliament.

A writer in *The United Service Journal* of April 1831 attempted to sum up Bligh's career: "Not only was the narrative which he published proved to be false in many material hearings, by evidence before a court-martial, but every act of his public life after this event, from his successive command of the *Director*, the *Glatton*, and the *Warrior*, to his disgraceful expulsion from New South Wales,—was stamped with an insolence, an inhumanity, and coarseness, which fully developed his character."18

CHAPTER 7

An Almost Perfect Hideaway

Mr. Christian Finds Pitcairn Island

Fletcher Christian knew that he needed an uninhabited refuge; he was aware that even if he had found an island with a friendly indigenous population, other Polynesians would visit by boat and word would leak out and His Majesty's vessels would be sent out from London to arrest him and his eight companions. Moreover, Christian understood that, "with the ignorant and racially prejudiced seamen" who were to settle with him, there would be no peace with Polynesian neighbors.[1]

Christian navigated the *Bounty* searching for a suitable home through the Cook Islands to Rarotonga, and through the Tongan Islands to Tongatapu. When the missionary John Williams arrived at Rarotonga in 1823, islanders told him that two generations earlier a floating garden with two waterfalls had come by sea to Rarotonga; the description, obviously, was of the *Bounty* with its water pumps operating; though most of the breadfruit may by that have time have been thrown off, enough plants remained to make the ship look like a nursery.

Perusing Bligh's library in the captain's quarters, Christian found enticing information in *Hawkesworth's Voyages*, published in 1773. Hawkesworth compiled a record of early English navigators in the South Pacific and quoted a passage about Pitcairn Island from Captain Philip Carteret's log, dated July 2, 1767. On about January 15, 1790, nine months after the mutiny, the *Bounty* crew and its Polynesian passengers saw a great rock rising from the sea at a distance. It was the only truly isolated uninhabited high island in the whole of the Pacific other than those near frozen Antarctica. Christian came to realize that Carteret had recorded its location as two hundred miles east of where the island was actually situated. As the latitude was correct, Christian merely kept sailing until he came to it. What could be more perfect for his purpose, he must have thought, than an island that did not exist on any chart?

Christian, with three mutineers and three Tahitians, rowed ashore on the west side to investigate. If the *Bounty* had arrived in the Southern Hemisphere's winter, it is unlikely they would have been able to land due to raging seas. Would they have waited a few months elsewhere, determined to have Pitcairn?

After an arduous climb where no path existed, they found the island to be thickly wooded with parau, banyan, palms and miro; the foliage was sufficient to hide a small community from the searching eyes aboard any ship that might someday pass. Because of its rich volcanic soil, the Polynesians who accompanied them called it *Fenua Maitai*, or *Good Land*. When Christian climbed back on the *Bounty* two days later, John Adams recalled it was with a happy and satisfied countenance. What could be better: An uninhabited island with fresh water, accessible only with difficulty and only in good weather, mischarted and unvisited by Europeans for twenty-three years.

No indentation on the island warrants even remotely the name harbor. The crew brought the *Bounty* around as near as they could to a small cove on the north shore. Ships are unable to anchor there and must be continually manned while passengers or crew go ashore. They guided the ship's boat over crashing waves in through the intricate narrow opening between rocks. They shot in to a tiny beach — the Landing. When they had explored the island earlier and stood on a cliff above the cove, they must have noted the treacherous path between the rocks and the swift left sweep they would have to make coming in; otherwise, it is unlikely they would have known where and how to bring the boat through. This hazardous opening serves well as a security door to which only the islanders to this day have a key; Pitcairn boatmen know the way in and deliver those visitors they wish to welcome.

A quarter century later Adams told about the first days on the island: "They soon erected tents with the sails &c. living chiefly on the ship's provisions with sea birds and fish which were very abundant. The place of encampment was near the landing place and was called by them 'Ship Landing,' now called 'Bounty Bay.'"[2]

The mutineers and the Polynesian men and women climbed a muddy incline that came to be called the *Hill of Difficulty*, up to the Edge, where the terrain flattened out somewhat. Exploring further, they eventually came to the summit of the western ridge of the mountain, with steep inclines and ravines to the west. Christian and his companions saw infinitely more trees than are present today. From the summit, facing west, one looks directly down into the ocean, but to the east is a fertile valley that slopes downward and is cut by ravines; this valley is the island's plateau, never flat but not as perpendicular as most of the island. Christian and his companions explored further and found "many caves and narrow defiles where a few determined men could make a stand against considerable numbers."[3]

Fletcher Christian was fortunate to have found Pitcairn. The island is indeed remote: 2,590 miles from Santiago, Chile; 4,695 from Sydney; and 1,312 from Tahiti. It is capable of supporting a community of substantial size; agriculture could be supplemented by fishing off shore for rock cod, mullet, mackerel, red snapper, and lobster. If the mutineers had gone to any other Pacific island they may have been apprehended or become protein for the inhabitants. Even on Pitcairn, not being apprehended was a matter of luck. If a British man-of-war had stopped in the 1790s, and its crew come ashore, the history of Pitcairn might have been cut short.

Pitcairn could be a nearly perfect hideout, but it could be little more. Only its relatively flat 88 acres, out of 1,118, are capable of sustainable agriculture. The rest of the land consists of angular slopes, cliffs, ravines, and deep narrow valleys. Eighty inches of rain a year makes mud a fact of Pitcairn life. It can never be a commercial entity because it lacks a harbor. It is too small for plantation agriculture. It lacks important natural resources. It is an island whose population without outside aid could barely exist, nothing more. Yet, for Christian and his cohorts, there was no finer place. For a generation nobody knew what had become of them.

The Mystery of the Missing Mutineers Solved

In 1808, Captain Mayhew Folger of the vessel *Topaz*, 140 days out of Boston, stumbled on the *Bounty* mutineers' hideout. Folger, named for his grandmother Elizabeth Mayhew's family which had owned Nantucket Island, was a pioneer in the lucrative South Pacific fur seal trade. In 1799, as captain of the *Minerva* out of Salem, Massachusetts, Folger headed for Mas a Fuera in the Juan Fernandez Islands, where his crew killed thousands of fur seals and carried the skins to Canton where they were purchased for as much as a dollar each. When the *Minerva* returned in May 1802, the first ship from Salem to have circumnavigated the globe, Folger turned over a profit of forty thousand dollars to the ship's owners. Having been well paid for his efforts, Folger married.

In 1807, Folger was given command of the *Topaz* with orders from its owners, Messrs. Boardman and Pope, to kill fur seals in the South Pacific, sell them in Canton, and return with a large profit. He stocked the *Topaz* with what he hoped was a sufficient supply of beef, pork, meal, peas, molasses, fish, flour. And he had put aboard copious amounts of rum and gin. His real troubles began in the South Atlantic where he ran into storms when he reached the Falklands in August. Folger recorded "Tremendous bad seas" and "very heavy gales" that menaced his ship on its voyage to Kerguelen Island, 2,200 miles south east of Cape Town. His route took him then to Van Diemen's Land, where he took on fuel and water. The *Topaz* anchored at the village of Hobart. On June 3, 1808, the governor of New South Wales, William Bligh, complained to Viscount Castlereagh "That the officers of the *Porpoise* when at the Derwent, commanded by Lieutenant Symons, received from the American ship *Topaz* ... upwards of Eight hundred gallons of Rum, and one hundred and fifty of Gin" and that most "was purchased by the Officers on their own private account, and afterwards Sold by them at two and three pounds per gallon."[4] This purchase helped precipitate the Rum Rebellion which deposed Governor Bligh.

Folger correctly anticipated that over-sealing had depleted the fur seal population of the Juan Fernandez Islands, and decided to look for richer populations of seals in southern waters. From Hobart the *Topaz* sailed to the Chatham Islands some 500 miles east of New Zealand looking for seals, but found only 600. At this point Mayhew Folger had been gone for nine months and had little to show for his labors. Folger and his crew needed fresh drinking water in order to continue their voyage and decided to sail for Pitcairn, which Captain Carteret had placed, if incorrectly, on the charts.

Tell-Tale Smoke on the Land

On February 6, 1808, Folger wrote in his log, "On approaching the shore saw a smoke on the land, at which I was very much surprised, it being represented by Captain Carteret as destitute of inhabitants."[5] Folger then saw three men rowing toward him in a "Tahitian-style canoe." Folger identified himself, his nationality, and his ship. One of the men replied from the canoe, "Where is America? Is it in Ireland?" Rather than "Ireland," the islander may more logically have asked, "Is it an island?" Folger was astonished that these Polynesian-appearing islanders spoke good English.

One of the men explained, "We are Englishmen because our father is an Englishman."

"Who is your father?" asked Folger.

"Aleck." The man referred to John Adams, who had signed aboard the *Bounty* for unknown reasons under the alias Alexander Smith.

"Who is Aleck?" asked Folger.

"Don't you know Aleck? Well, then, do you know Captain Bligh of the *Bounty*?"[6] In an instant Folger had solved a mystery that had intrigued the world for nineteen years.

The eldest of the three in the canoe was Thursday October Christian, eighteen-year-old son of Fletcher and Mi'Mitti. When told about the date change that takes place when one crosses from the west, an obviously flustered Thursday October Christian quickly changed his name to *Friday*. Later, on further reflection, Friday changed his name back to Thursday, and in fact named his son Thursday October Christian II. Bligh, so scrupulous in everything else navigational, had somehow failed to account for gaining a day by sailing east; therefore Fletcher's firstborn should have been named Wednesday October Christian. In any event, a man who renames his wife "Mainmast" and his son for the day and month of his birth either had a sense of humor or was particularly bitter at how his life had turned out and sought to ridicule those closest to him.

Folger and his crew learned that in January 1790, Fletcher Christian had settled eight mutineers, six Polynesian males, twelve Polynesian women and one baby on this forested and well watered island. The baby was Sully, daughter of Teio; her mother rolled Sully ashore in a barrel. Folger learned that five years after the landing, a ship had been sighted, so the island's inhabitants hid from sight. When the ship left, they found a jack-knife on a rock at the Landing. Between 1795 and 1808, they had sighted two other ships; the crews of neither landed. Folger and his companions were the first outsiders to meet the islanders.

Folger found Adams, eight Polynesian women and twenty-three children and teenagers on the island. Folger asked what had happened to the rest of the seamen and the Polynesian

men. John Adams told Folger a version of their death. Folger recorded in the log of the *Topaz* that Smith and seven others "took wives at Otaheite and Six men as Servants and proceeded to Pitcairn's Island ... which took place as near as he could recollect in 1790 — soon after which one of their party ran mad and drowned himself another died with a fever, and after they had remained about four years on the Island their Men Servants rose upon and killed Six of them, Leaving only Smith and he desperately wounded with a pistol Ball in the neck, however he and the widows of the deceased men arose and put all the Servants to death which left him the only Surviving man on the Island with eight or nine women and Several Small Children...."[7] Adams's story would change with the telling to successive visitors.

Adams, for his part, learned for the first

Friday [sic] Fletcher October Christian, Son of Fletcher Christian Mutineer of the Bounty. Drawing by John Shilibeer, 1814. From Shilibeer, *A Narrative of the Briton's Voyage to Pitcairn Island,* 1814. The son of Fletcher and Mi'Mitti, Thursday October Christian (1790–1831) was first of the second generation born on Pitcairn Island and first to die during the migration to Tahiti. He married Edward Young's widow, Teraura, who bore him three sons and three daughters.

time that a cataclysmic revolution had occurred in France and that the wars resulting from the revolution were sweeping over the continent and that Britain had been locked in war with Napoleon for six years. When Adams learned of Nelson's great victory in 1805 over the Spanish and French fleets at Trafalgar, he expressed patriotic pleasure. Folger told Adams that Bligh had reached England to report the mutiny and to name and describe the accused. Adams learned that those of the mutineers who had remained on Tahiti were taken to Plymouth, tried and some hanged.

Folger learned that Thursday October was the eldest of the second generation of Pitcairners. Fletcher Christian had sired three children; John Mills, two; Will McCoy, three; Matt Quintal, five; Edward Young, six and Alexander Smith (a.k.a. John Adams), four. Folger noted that, "All the children of the deceased mutineers speak tolerable English; some of them are grown to the size of men and women; and to do them justice, I think them a very humane and hospitable people; and whatever may have been the errors or crimes of Smith, the mutineer, in times back, he is at present a worthy man, and may be useful to navigators who traverse this immense ocean."[8] Folger stayed only five hours because he was unable to anchor in the deep sea near Bounty Bay and he worried that his ship might drift far from shore or, worse than that, onto the coastal rocks.

Out to sea the following day, Folger wrote a letter to friends, Philadelphia merchant Samuel Coates and his wife. Folger told the Coateses, "During all this time, Alec kept a regular Journal which had become very voluminous, from which he offered to let me have any Extracts I pleased, but as I staid only five hours with him, I declined it, not having time." The fact that Adams' writing ability was negligible makes it likely that the journal may have been kept by Edward Young. Folger wrote that Adams told him that after setting Bligh and his eighteen loyalists in the launch, the remaining twenty-four "steered for a Group of Islands, which were marked in the Chart, and said to be discovered by the Spaniards; after cruising a long time, they found no such islands existed, then they steered for Pitcairn's Island...." Either because Adams had left out the months of trying to settle Tubuai and returning most of the crew to Tahiti and then looking for a permanent home, or because Folger misunderstood, Folger's account omitted much detail. Folger summarized Adams's story for the Coateses: "In one or two Years after this Company arrived in the Island one of them died of sickness, and one jumped off the rocks in a fit of insanity, leaving only 7 of the Mutineers — four or five Years after this, the six Otaheit Servants rose in the Night, & killed 6 of the 7, leaving Alec only of the 9."

Folger described the island's lush agricultural products, mentioning that the islanders were handicapped by the lack of iron tools such as spades and saws. Although none of the children spoke "the Otaheit Tongue," they borrowed from Polynesian culture by going "almost naked; in general they are healthy and cleanly, being in the constant practice of bathing twice every day." Adams spoke both Tahitian and English, "but only one of [the women] cou'd talk English." Folger asked Adams's permission to publish an account of their meeting and "he said he did not care for all the Navy of England cou'd never find him, in the rocks he cou'd retire to in the Island...."[9] As parting gifts, Adams gave Folger the *Bounty*'s compass and the large silver Kendall's chronometer that both Bligh and Cook had used on two voyages to the South Seas.

Mayhew Folger's Most Unpleasant Year

Folger sailed for Mas a Tierra in the Juan Fernandez group, garrisoned at the time by Spain. It had been discovered in 1574 by a mariner named Juan Fernandez, probably sailing from Valparaiso.[10] Because his crew was suffering from scurvy, Folger had no choice but to land and ask aid of the authorities. After his men came ashore, the Spanish governor of the island ordered the shore battery to use the *Topaz* for target practice. Shells shredded the ship's rigging and broke her foremast. The governor summarily relieved Folger of the *Bounty*'s chronometer and forty thousand dollars. The chronometer was later purchased in Chile by a British citizen and found its way back to London by 1844. Today, one may watch it keeping accurate time in the National Maritime Museum at Greenwich. Folger and his crew were imprisoned by the governor and then taken aboard the hastily restored *Topaz* and shipped to Valparaiso. On March 29, 1809, Folger wrote to his wife from Valparaiso that twenty-one of his forty-nine men had deserted and that the last twelve months had been "the most unpleasant year of my Life."[11]

A Distracted Admiralty

The British had a major naval presence in Brazil in 1808. The previous year Napoleon's army had taken Lisbon, and with the help of the British fleet, the royal family fled to Rio de Janeiro. Officer Sir Sidney Smith was given command of the British navy's Brazil station at Rio. Smith then sent a Lieutenant William Fitzmaurice to Valparaiso to ask for the release by Spanish authorities of captured British sailors who had been aiding Chilean revolutionaries. Folger, who was free to roam the city, secured an appointment with Fitzmaurice and informed him of having found the last of the mutineers. Fitzmaurice wrote a report based on what Folger told him, dated October 10, 1808, addressed to the secretary of the Naval Office in London. Fitzmaurice sent this report to Rio de Janeiro and on March 14, 1809, Sir Sidney forwarded the report, together with an extract from the log of the *Topaz*, to the Admiralty.

The secretary of the Admiralty passed the letter on to the *Times*, the *Naval Review*, and the *Quarterly Review*; as a result, the discovery became public knowledge. Yet, naval authorities did nothing to apprehend Adams. It is easy enough to account for what Caroline Alexander characterized as "the apparent total lack of interest on the part of the Admiralty."[12] Britain was engaged in a titanic struggle, defending the home islands against Napoleon's formidable continental war machine. The British navy was active in Spain, Latin America, home waters, the Mediterranean, Caribbean, and the Indian Ocean. The Admiralty was unwilling to devote sufficient resources to apprehend one man half a world away who had committed a crime twenty years previously. And there was an element of disbelief. the *Quarterly Review* for February 1810 warned: "if this interesting relation rested solely on the faith which is due to Americans, with whom, we say with regret, truth is not always considered as a moral obligation, we should hesitate in giving it this publicity."[13]

By the end of 1809, the Spaniards returned the *Topaz* to Folger, and on May 27, 1810, after an absence of three years and fifty-one days, he returned to Boston. Even though their nations were now at war, on March 1, 1813, Captain Mayhew Folger wrote again to the Right Honorable Lords of the Admiralty, forwarding the *Bounty*'s compass, which the Spaniards had returned to him with his ship. In this letter, he outlined what he had learned from Adams. He concluded: "Should you wish any further information respecting Pitcairns Island or its inhabitants — a letter directed to me at Nantucket ... will be carefully attended to."[14] The Admiralty received the letter February 25, 1814. Folger received no reply. It was not until 1817 that Folger's discovery was announced in the United States, with the publication of *Narrative of Voyages and Travel* by Folger's friend Amasa Delano.

CHAPTER 8

Early Visitors: 1814–1825

1814: *Briton* and *Tagus*

After the *Topaz*, no vessel arrived at Bounty Bay for six years. On September 17, 1814, two British warships, H.M.S. *Briton* and H.M.S. *Tagus*, approached Pitcairn. According to island historian Rosalind Amelia Young, "The woman who first saw them ran to make it known to the rest by saying that 'two paafata [a wooden flooring erected on four posts, on which the feed for their goats was laid] were floating in toward the shore, with their posts turned wrong end up.'"[1] The officers aboard these vessels were unaware of Folger's report and, like Folger, thought Pitcairn to be uninhabited.

The *Briton* and *Tagus* were searching for the American sea raider Captain David Porter of the *Essex*; Porter had brought the War of 1812 from North America to the South Seas. The *Essex* was the first American warship to sail in the Pacific. In 1813 alone the *Essex* captured twenty-four British ships, "virtually destroying the British whaling fleet in the Pacific."[2] Some captured vessels had cargoes worth a hundred thousand pounds. Porter was able to write to the secretary of the U.S. Navy that "the actual injury we have done them may be estimated at two and a half millions of dollars."[3] On March 14, 1814, the Admiralty ordered one-armed Sir Thomas Staines of the *Briton*, who had fought alongside Bligh at Copenhagen, and Captain Philip Pipon of the *Tagus* to proceed to the South Pacific to protect the British whale fisheries. They were to sail to Valparaiso and from there to confront Porter's *Essex*, with its formidable thirty-two-pound carronades and six long guns. When they arrived at Valparaiso, they learned that British warships already had blocked the *Essex* for two months in the Chilean harbor and that Porter had been forced to surrender his ship. Staines and Pipon then sailed to Nuku Hiva to make certain American forces had departed from their hastily erected Fort Madison. Because the fort was abandoned, Staines and Pipon set sail once again for Valparaiso.

Enroute, on September 17, 1814, they "fell in with an island where none is laid down in the Admiralty or other charts...." At dawn they saw through their telescopes a community on the hillside. Then four canoes approached the *Briton*. "To my great astonishment," wrote Staines, "... every individual on the island (forty in number) spoke very good English, as well as Otaheitian."[4] On the day of the visit, *The Pitcairn Register*, a chronicle of major events on the island, reported, "John Mills killed by falling from the rocks."[5] About twenty-one years

52

old, he was the only son of *Bounty* gunner's mate John Mills. The youth had never married, and as a result, the name Mills never again appeared in the island *Register*.

Coming ashore for only a day, the crews were greeted by a flock of women and children. "They proved to be the descendants of the deluded crew of the *Bounty*, who from Otaheite, proceeded to the above mentioned island, where the ship was burnt," wrote Staines.[6] Staines stated, as reported in The *Times*, "A venerable old man named John Adams is the only surviving Englishman of those who last quitted Otaheite in her; and whose exemplary conduct and fatherly care of the whole of the little colony cannot but command admiration...."[7] The "venerable old man" was approximately forty-eight years old. Adams had signed on to the *Bounty* when he was twenty-two under the name Alexander Smith, but changed it to John Adams on Pitcairn when he felt he no longer needed an alias. Adams had been orphaned and raised in a poorhouse in Hackney, London. He was barely literate. Bligh described him being five feet five inches with brown complexion, brown hair, muscular and being distinguished by smallpox scars and plentiful tattoos.

John Adams, a.k.a. Alexander Smith (1757–1829). Regarded as their "father," Adams formed the second generation of Pitcairners into a pious, puritanical community. He was the last surviving mutineer. He sired three daughters and a son. Drawing by Captain Frederick William Beechey, 1825. Engraved by H. Adlard. Published in Beechey, *Narrative of a Voyage to the Pacific and Beering's Strait*, 1831.

Adams expected to be arrested immediately, stowed below in chains, and returned to England for hanging. He was not arrested because Adams' daughter Hannah pleaded, "Oh, do not, sir, take from me my father!"[8] and because Pipon was greatly touched by the piety and civility of the small Pitcairn community and confessed that, "In deed it would have been an act of great cruelty and inhumanity to have taken him from his family, who would be left in the greatest misery, and the settlement in all probability annihilated...." Pipon added a further — practical — reason for leaving Adams: "had we been inclined even to seize on old Adams, it would have been impossible to have conveyed him on board; again, to get onto the boats, we had to climb such precipices as were scarcely accessible to any but goats, and the natives and we had enough to do in holding on by the different boughs and roots of trees, to keep to our feet."[9]

Staines was impressed by "The pious manner in which all those born on the island have been reared, the correct sense of the religion which has been instilled in their young minds by this old man...."[10] Adams had been so intent on following what he recalled to be church strictures that he enforced fasting two days a week — Wednesday and Friday; he probably remembered not eating at the orphanage on Ash Wednesday and Good Friday. Eventually, he was persuaded by visitors to allow the islanders food on Wednesdays, but Fridays remained a fast day in Adams's lifetime. When they arose and when they went to bed, islanders sang hymns as a family and prayed together. On Sundays Adams held five religious observances for the community. Adams had created a gentle Christian utopia. Instead of being hanged, he would have a town — the administrative center of Britain's last Pacific colony — named for him. Ironically, a community founded by desperate criminals "out–Puritaned the Puritans and out–Victoriad the Victorians."[11]

Staines and Pipon found a mixed Polynesian-British community led by Adams, with a second generation speaking English, encouraging compulsory education, enjoying private property, living in plank-sided houses, and practicing Christianity according to the Church of England's *Book of Common Prayer*. Islanders let it be known emphatically that they considered themselves to be English, not Polynesian. It is interesting to note that no purely Polynesian children had been born on Pitcairn, although three Polynesian women had slept with six Polynesian men. It is possible that if a woman had conceived a purely Tahitian child she may have used a deep massage method of abortion that was widely practiced in Tahiti. The visitors found a mixed economy of barter and sharing. The *Times* on December 16, 1815, reported: "There was, it seems, besides private property, a sort of general stock, out of which articles were issued on account to the several members of the community; and for mutual accommodation, exchanges of one kind of provision for another were very frequent, as salt for fresh provisions, vegetables and fruit for poultry, fish, etc.; also when the stores of one family were low, or wholly expended, a fresh supply was raised from another, or out of the general stock to be repaid when circumstances were more favourable."[12]

Polynesian influence predominated in a number of areas. When a child fell down, any woman nearby would console it; children were raised in the Polynesian manner by the village women as a whole as much as by their birth mothers. Unlike in England, where privacy was a right, Pitcairners wandered into any home and when they sat down while a meal was in progress, they were served without question. On Pitcairn, one could pick and eat immediately a piece of fruit from a tree, no matter who owned the property; but, it was forbidden to pick fruit on another's land to carry away for future use or trade. The Polynesian influence was evidenced in thatch roofs made of pandanus leaves, by in-ground cooking methods, tapa cloth production, and weaving of baskets and hats. The Tahitian custom of women serving men before eating separately was firmly established in the early days of the settlement. The Tahitian method of spearing fish in preference to dropping a line with bait was retained.

Staines pictured for the Lords of the Admiralty what he saw on Pitcairn. The *Times* summarized:

> Their habitations are extremely neat. The little village of Pitcairn forms a pretty square, the houses at the upper end of which are occupied by the patriarch John Adams and his family, consisting of his old blind wife and three daughters from fifteen to eighteen years of age, and a boy of eleven; a daughter of his wife by a former husband, and a son-in-law. On the opposite side is the dwelling of Thursday October Christian, and in the centre is a smooth verdant lawn, on which the poultry are let loose, fenced in so as to prevent the intrusion of the domestic quadrupeds.

The visitors were impressed that "In their houses too they had a good deal of decent furniture, consisting of beds laid upon bedsteads, with neat coverings; they had also tables, and large chests to contain their valuables and clothing, which is made from the bark of a certain tree, prepared chiefly by the elder Otaheitian females." At least one of these rough unpainted houses had a second story. None had, or needed, fireplaces for keeping warm. An outbuilding or attached room was used for cooking.

Islanders ate two meals a day, one at approximately ten in the morning and the other at around four in the afternoon. Fruit, fish, vegetables, and occasionally meat composed the menu. A favorite dish was, and is, *pillihai*, which is a sort of cake consisting of yam and coconut meat. Each resident ate an estimated thousand yams a year.

The dress of the females beguiled the visitors. The women wore a sort of skirt — "a piece of linen reaching from the waist to the knees," and a "mantle thrown loosely over the shoulders, and hanging as low as the ankles," but the mantle "was frequently laid aside — and then the upper part of the body was entirely exposed." Men, when their European clothing deteriorated, wore a *maro*, which is a piece of tapa cloth passed through the legs and wound around the waist and cinched. Everyone wore a hat, woven from pandanus leaves. Females' topless attire notwithstanding, "Adams assured Staines and Pipon that since Christian's death there had not been a single instance of any young woman proving unchaste; nor any attempt at seduction on the part of the men."

Each person cultivated an assigned piece of land, using iron tools made laboriously from iron rescued from the *Bounty*. When a young man had sufficient productive property, he was ready to marry, and with Adams's blessing, chose a girl whom he had known his entire life. John Adams performed the ceremonies, using the same ring over and over again.[13]

When *Briton* and *Tagus* departed, Adams undoubtedly breathed a sigh of relief that he had not been hauled home in shackles. Sir John Barrow marveled that "The interesting account of Captains Sir Thomas Staines and Pipon, in 1814, produced as little effect on the government as that of Folger; and nothing more was heard of Adams and his family for twelve years nearly...."[14]

As news arrived of Pitcairn's rediscovery, London theatrical entrepreneurs manufactured fantasy out of the unfolding drama. In 1816, an impresario in London staged at the Royal Theater *A New Romantick Operatick Ballet Spectacle*. It was "founded on the recent Discovery of a numerous Colony, formed by and descended from, the Mutineers of the *Bounty* Frigate called Pitcairn's Island.... No money to be returned."[15] Then in 1823, at Sadler's Wells, appeared an aqua drama entitled *The Island or Christian and His Comrades*. This dramatization presented "the principal events of the Mutiny on Board the *Bounty* Armed Ship on her passage from Otaheite in 1787, the incidents of which have become interesting for being the origin of the singular and romantic population of Pitcairn's Island, lately discovered."[16]

1817: *Sultan*

On October 17, 1817, the ship *Sultan* arrived from Boston enroute to Mas a Fuera. Captain Caleb Reynolds recorded that he saw a small village on the north side of Pitcairn. Reynolds was rowed ashore when the sea had calmed "and soon had the boat loaded deep with yams, hogs, etc...." Reynolds traded one of the *Sultan*'s jolly boats for the food and for some copper bolts which had been salvaged from the *Bounty*. John Adams gave Reynolds two note books, in one of which he had written, "The Life Of John Adams, Born November the 4 or 5 in the Year Sixty Six at Sanford Hill in the parrish of St John Hackney My father was sarvent to Danel Bell Cole Merchant My father was drowned in the River Theames."[17] Through Captain Reynolds, the news of Adams's whereabouts reached his brother Jonathan at Wapping in London, and thus began a brief correspondence between the two men.

At her request, Captain Reynolds took away Teehuteatuaonoa, or Jenny, the wife of Isaac Martin. Reynolds returned her to her native Tahiti.

Jenny's Story

Jenny, born Teehuteatuaonoa on Tahiti, was the only member of the first generation Pitcairn women to have her story of the brutal first decade published. Jenny's account added some details to what had been learned from Adams. Her version of events added little to Adams's account to Captain Beechey in 1825 but rather corroborated his story. Jenny was the first person and the only one of the original settlers from the *Bounty* to leave Pitcairn. For 137 years historians had been unaware of the existence of her published interviews. In 1956, historian Henry E. Maude found her story, printed in the *Sydney Gazette* for July 17, 1819, and again on October 2, 1826, in the *Bengal Hurkaru*. The second article, from which the following information is taken, was republished in 1829 in the *United Service Journal and Naval and Military Magazine*. On Tahiti, Jenny told her story to Captain Peter Dillon and to Reverend Henry Nott, both of whom were fluent in Tahitian.

Tattooed on Jenny's arm was "AS 1789," signifying her relationship with Alexander Smith, actually John Adams. After serving as Adams's companion, she had become the companion of Isaac Martin. Jenny recalled that when the mutineers left Tubuai and returned to Tahiti, nine decided to stay aboard the *Bounty*, because they were "attracted by the native females who were in the ship, about nineteen in number...." Several women swam ashore off Tahiti when the opportunity presented itself, and six "who were rather ancient" were put ashore by the mutineers at Moorea. "Two months elapsed before land was seen, during which time all on board were much discouraged," but at last Fletcher Christian brought them to Pitcairn.

Because of foul weather, nobody went ashore until the third day after arrival, and then Christian, Brown, Williams, McCoy and three Tahitian men explored the island. After bringing what goods they wanted from the *Bounty* on rafts made of ship's hatches, three men set fire to the ship. "During the night all were in tears at seeing her in flames. Some regretted exceedingly they had not confined Capt. Bligh and returned to their native country...." Their temporary encampment was at the Landing, but "After a few weeks they ventured upon the high land, and began to erect more substantial buildings...."

After about a year, Williams's wife died of "a disease in her neck," and Williams demanded one of two women being shared by the Tahitian men. "Much afflicted," the wronged Tahitian men conspired to kill all of the mutineers. "One of the natives who remained with the English, was sent by Christian to the mountains, for the purpose of shooting the principal conspirator, whose name was Oopee, promising to reward him handsomely if he succeeded, but if he did not, to kill him. The man killed Oopee. [Oha?] The English men also had Tararo killed for taking back the woman Williams had taken from him. With four Tahitian men remaining, "the mutineers lived in a peaceable manner for some years."

On an unspecified date Manarii, a Tahitian male, stole a pig from McCoy and was beaten by McCoy severely. Teimua stole some yams and was chastised. These events helped the Tahitian men decide to kill the mutineers, and they "went about from day to day with their muskets, on a pretense of shooting wild-fowl." On Massacre Day, the Tahitian men shot Williams first, then Christian in his garden, then Mills, but McCoy ran to the higher elevations and saved himself. The killers then finished off Martin and Brown. Adams was shot in the neck and had two fingers broken, but "The women threw themselves on his body and at their entreaties his life was spared." Next Manarii shot Teimua, one of his compatriots. McCoy and Quintal hid in the mountains and killed Manarii. The next day about noon, when "one of the Otaheitian men was sitting outside of the house, and the other was lying on his back on the floor, one of the women took a hatchet and cleft the skull of the latter;

while at the same instant calling out to Young to fire, which he did, and shot the other native dead."

As Jenny continued, she enumerated the survivors: eleven Tahitian women and four Englishmen: Adams, Young, McCoy and Quintal. "In a drunken affray, Mathew Quintil was killed by three countrymen. M'Koy came by his death through drinking spirits, which brought on derangement, and caused him to leap into the sea, after having tied his own hands and feet." Young, she affirmed, died on Christmas Day, 1800, of natural causes.

Jenny said nothing of the Tahitian women's plots to kill the mutineers or to build a ship to leave the island. Jenny failed to specify her own role in the murders.[18] The value of Jenny's contribution is that it gives another version to compare with Adams's various accounts.

1819: *Hercules*

On January 18, 1819, Captain Henderson arrived as commander of the East India merchantman *Hercules*. The day before, he had sighted an island which he named for himself; it is the largest of Pitcairn's three uninhabited dependencies. British residents in India, readers of the *Calcutta Journal*, which had published a report on the Pitcairners, donated 3500 rupees. With this generous support, Captain Henderson was able to deliver a twenty-two-foot cutter, carpentry and agricultural tools, utensils, cutlery, dishes, cloth, guns, fishing gear, writing materials and other essential items to the grateful community.

At Bounty Bay, Henderson reported, "I then ascended the rocks, and was led through groves of bread-fruit, cocoanut, plantain and what they call the tea tree, till we reached their village, formed on an oblong square. Their dwellings are all of wood, and very ingeniously contrived so as to be shifted at pleasure, and were uncommonly clean."

Captain Henderson wrote, "I delivered to Adams the box of Books from the Missionary Society of London, and a Letter from Adams' brother at Wapping in London. I read this letter to him, giving him a description of his family, mentioning the death of one sister; and the prosperity of another. This affected him much, and he often repeated that he never expected to see this day, or indeed one of his countrymen more."[19]

1819: *Elizabeth*

On March 2, 1819, Captain Henry King of the American ship *Elizabeth* stopped. The previous day, King had sighted what had only a month and a half before been named Henderson Island. Not knowing that the *Hercules* had been there, he landed and carved the ship's name in a tree and named the island Elizabeth. For years afterward, it bore two names.

King was greeted at Bounty Bay when nine men climbed aboard, "came aft to the quarterdeck where I was, and taking me by the hand, gave it a hearty shake, and said, 'How do you do Captain.'" The captain and ship's surgeon went ashore. As Captain King described the experience, "When I got near the shore, I found the surf so violent, that I durst not attempt with my boat to go through it. I went in theirs, when one of them taking hold of me, bid me not fear, for should the boat upset, he would take me safe on shore We now entered the surf, when, to my surprise, a number of young women and children came half way into the surf to assist in landing the boat. These women ventured far beyond their depth, and assisted in bearing the boat up, by swimming and sustaining it with their hands. We landed safely, and were immediately met by John Adams, a hearty corpulent old man, who, like the rest, was naked, with the exception of a piece of cloth round his middle."

An indication that Adams had taken his Biblical reading too seriously was revealed in answer to King's question about Adams's unmarried daughter, Diana, whom Captain King was told had conceived a child. King wrote: "Adams having told me, prior to this, that his daughters were not married, I expressed my surprise to the wife of Christian. Old Adams hearing this, took me aside and gave me the following account: Notwithstanding his parental care of his daughters, Edward Quintral [sic] and Diana [Dinah] had committed an offence against the laws of God, for which he supposed them worthy of death, and accordingly gave orders that they should be shot; but as no person seeming willing to execute his orders, he made the necessary preparations for executing them himself, when he was strongly opposed by Auther Quintral [sic], who said that though the offence was certainly a great one, and the more so as a similar one had not been committed since the death of Christian, yet he did not conceive it to be a crime worthy of death. The rest being of the same opinion, Adams changed his mind also, but forbade them to marry." King felt that Adams had forbidden the marriage because he would have lost Diana as a field worker on his plot.[20] In return for provisions, King gave the islanders a whaleboat.

1820–22: The *Essex* and the *Surry*

On December 20, 1820, the island with two names — Henderson and Elizabeth — served as a haven for shipwreck survivors. The whaler *Essex*, from Nantucket, was destroyed by a forty-foot sperm whale. The crew reached Henderson. From there, all but three men left in two ship's boats for South America. After the boats became separated, three men were rescued by the brig *Indian* from London; the other boat was sighted 4,500 miles later, the men in a serious state of starvation. To stay alive, Captain Pollard and another survivor ate three crew members and the cabin boy.

Meanwhile Captain Thomas Raine of the *Surry* had sailed from Sydney on December 19, 1820, for Valparaiso to pick up a load of wheat for the hungry Australian colony. In Sydney, he had been given books and seeds donated for the Pitcairn colony. While in Valparaiso, he met Captain Pollard of the wrecked *Essex*. Pollard told Raine the whale that destroyed his ship was eighty or ninety feet long. Pollard also thought he had left three men on an island he identified as Ducie. Raine sailed to Ducie but found it uninhabited. On April 8, Raine and his crew rescued the three *Essex* survivors on Henderson. Three days later Raine, his crew and the three rescued men arrived at Pitcairn.

The *Surry*'s surgeon, Dr. David Ramsay, was fascinated by the anomaly of young islanders whose actions expressed fervent piety but whose appearances suggested — at least to Europeans — lascivious temptation. Ramsay described them as going "naked excepting that the men have a piece of cloth put round their middle and coming up between their legs," and the "women have a kind of petticoat which is very short and also a piece of cloth hanging over their breasts...."

Dr. Ramsay described their sport of sliding: "The islanders amused themselves by taking a flat board about 3 feet long, on the upper side smooth and on the under a ridge like a keel, and went out on a rock and waited till a large breaker came and when the top of it was close to them, away they went with the piece of wood under their belly on the top of this breaker and directed themselves by their feet into the little chanel formed by the rocks, so that when the surf left them they were up to their knees in water."[21] A later observer described how "older children, amusing themselves with their surf-boards, would dive out beneath the lofty breakers, and availing themselves of a succeeding series, approach the coast, borne onto the crest of a wave, with a velocity which threatened their instant destruction against the rocks; but, skillfully evading any contact with the shore, they again dived forth to meet and mount another of their foaming steeds."[22] Sliding was called *horue* in Tahiti and ceased to be practiced there when the missionaries took control in the early nineteenth century.

When islanders escorted Ramsay half way up the Hill of Difficulty, "they stopped and said prayers — they first sing a psalm then pray (on their knees) then sing a psalm again which concludes their services." Ramsay wrote, "We were welcomed on our arrival at the village, if I may call it so, by all the people as if we were their brothers or children. In fact they did not know what to do for us. The first house we went into was where they were making a kind of rum from the root of a particular tree and sugar cane mixed — there we sat down and had a glass of grog." In summary, wrote Dr Ramsay, "I have never at any time seen a more serious manner in devotion than at this time."[23]

Interested in languages, Dr. Ramsay noted that the second generation spoke their mothers' Tahitian and their fathers' English, or at least a comprehensible adaptation of English. Dr. Ramsay wrote as they spoke, attempting to capture speech patterns: "I like very much hear you talk — that very good — Captain Raine very funny man — we like to do well but we know not how — no good in doing wrong — when I do wrong something in my head tell me so." Raine found the residents "a well-made race, copper in colours, and having European features; both men and women quite stout, and their hair black and generally hanging down in ringlets...." Like some other visiting commanders, Captain Raine of the *Surry* left the islanders seeds for a variety of useful fruits, grains, and vegetables, plus tools, books, clothing, and manufactured articles.

Russell, 1822

Soon the piety of Pitcairners had become well known among South Seas mariners. When the whaler *Russell* arrived from New Bedford, Massachusetts, on March 8, 1822, Captain Frederick Arthur recorded in his diary the text of a bulletin he ordered posted aboard for the crew:

> As the island has been hitherto but little frequented, they will be less susceptible of fraud than a more general intercourse with the world would justify. It is desired that every officer and man will abstain from all licentiousness in word and deed, but will treat them kindly, courteously, and with the strictest good faith. As profane swearing has become an unfashionable thing even on board a man-of-war, it is quite time that it was laid aside by whalemen, particularly at this time. As these islanders have been taught to adore their Maker, and are not accustomed to hear His name blasphemed, they were shocked horror, when they heard some of the crew of an American ship swear, and said it was against the laws of God, their country, and their conscience.

When Arthur said goodbye to the Pitcairners, he felt it "a more affectionate leave than I ever did anywhere except my home."[24]

Commercial Agriculture

From 1813 to 1824, fifteen ships had arrived. As the islanders' reputations for honest dealing, piety and hospitality became known, the number increased to thirty-six between 1819 and 1830. Without using money, the islanders traded. They shared the items traded, as they had shared the labor that went into growing crops and conveying them through frenetic surf to the ships. They traded water, wood, and food for manufactured goods and foods that were not available on the island. With increased trade, islanders became more dependent on the products of the outside world, and as a result, they often shorted themselves on their own agricultural products. In order to grow more food, and to barter firewood, they cleared trees and brush from slopes and planted crops in expanded areas. Deforestation led to runoff and soil erosion, thus compromising their ability to sustain themselves without outside trade.

CHAPTER 9

Captain Beechey
Learns the Bloody Details

1825: Beechey of the *Blossom*

On December 5, 1825, Captain Frederick W. Beechey, commander of H.M.S. *Blossom*, hove to at Pitcairn Island. *Blossom* was the twentieth ship to call since 1808 when the refuge of the mutineers was first revealed. By this time Britain had been at peace for a decade and relied on eight Royal Navy squadrons in all seas, consisting of not much more than a hundred ships, to protect its possessions and, as Britain was at peace except for the occasional colonial uprising, to carry out explorations. These nine battle ships, thirty-three frigates and others made Britain the world's foremost naval power.[1] Sir John Barrow, Second Secretary to the Admiralty from the time of the Battle of Trafalgar in 1805 until his death in 1848, ordered Beechey to survey Arctic regions in the diminishing hope that a northwest passage between the Pacific and Atlantic could be found. Beechey was to visit Pacific islands as well, determining their correct position. One of these was Pitcairn. What made this visit historically memorable was Captain Beechey's curiosity and willingness to delay his departure for sixteen days while he spoke with Adams.

At nineteen, Beechey had fought for King George III against Andrew Jackson at the Battle of New Orleans; and at twenty-two, he had sailed to the Arctic as ship's artist. At age twenty-nine he was master of a British warship in the South Pacific. He would retire as a rear admiral, and in 1855 be elected president of the Royal Geographic Society the year before his death.

Having stopped at Pitcairn for food and water, he sought to learn "the particulars of every transaction connected with the fate of the *Bounty*...."[2] The *Blossom*'s crew remained the longest of all early visitors to Pitcairn. What Beechey learned from Adams he related in *A Narrative of a Voyage to the Pacific and Beerings Straits*, published in 1831. From this narrative, the reading public learned in some detail Adams's version of the full story of what happened to the desperate *Bounty* fugitives on Pitcairn.

Interview with a Mutineer

Adams's story changed with each telling. It is possible he was covering up his own guilt during the mutiny or in the deaths of one or more of his companions. It is probable he was

Interior of Pitcairn Island. Drawing by Captain Frederick William Beechey, 1825. Engraved by Edward Finden, 1830. Published in Beechey, *Narrative of a Voyage to the Pacific and Beering's Strait*, 1831. A competent artist, Beechey drew Adams in sailor's whites, and women and children in front of Thursday October Christian's house. Fletcher Christian's Cave looms above.

traumatized by the wound he received when others were massacred. Moreover, during the time of the massacre, Adams could not have seen all the events as they unfolded, even though he attempted to relate them. As William Goldhurst explains, "we can only say that the man was understandably confused," and that "the passage of years, might easily have led him to confuse the identities of the dead men and the incidents that had taken place."[3]

Young men, trailed by sixty-two-year-old Adams, scrambled up the *Blossom*'s side to greet the vessel's officers and men. The islanders were dressed in cast-off clothing from passing crews. Beechey noted that each man presented "a perfect caricature" of the English sailor. Some "had on long black coats without any other article of dress except trousers, some shirts without coats, and others waistcoats without either; none had shoes or stockings, and only two possessed hats...."[4]

Lieutenant George Peard, who served under Beechey, noted that "the quantity of Cocoanut oil they put in their hair does not afford the most agreeable odor."[5] Beechey, a competent artist, drew a picture of Adams, a tanned aging man with diminishing white hair, attired in seaman's whites.

The innocence of the thirty-six male and thirty female islanders struck Beechey and his crew. "Having no latches on their doors, they were ignorant of the manner of opening ours; and we were constantly attacked on all sides with, "Please may I sit down or get up, or go out of the cabin?" or, "Please to open or shut the door.""[6] Beechey found a small village of five houses, and across the island in a higher elevation, yam fields and temporary shelters for residents' use while cultivating the soil.

Beechey interviewed Adams, who bore "the inconvenience of considerable corpulence...."[7] Beechey stated that he used the diary of one of the dead mutineers, Midshipman Edward Young, to corroborate Adams's account of mutiny, murders, births, and survival. The diary has since been lost and we have only Beechey's word for its contents — indeed for its existence. Adams explained what were, in his opinion, the causes for the mutiny of April 28, 1789. Bligh had accused Christian of stealing coconuts. Adams told Lieutenant Peard that Bligh had also shorted his crew's rations: "He had given Pumpkins out to them in lieu of bread, and threatened to flog the first man who complained, and at Otaheite they were dissatisfied at having the bones, from which the pork had been cut for salting, given them instead of meat." Resentful of Bligh's accusation of theft and of the captain's parsimony, Christian refused Bligh's invitation to dinner the night before the mutiny. Instead, Christian determined to reach the nearest island and be done with Bligh. Another man suggested that Christian take the ship instead. "The whole affair was planned and executed in the short space of an hour."[8] Christian planned to leap overboard to kill himself if his hastily conceived mutiny failed and, "that there might be no chance of being saved, he tied a deep sea lead about his neck and concealed it within his clothes."[9] Other crew members contrasted visions of the affectionate welcome of their ladies in Tahiti to a half-year's voyage with inadequate rations grudgingly doled out by a captain whose pronouncements were venomous.

Fletcher Christian and his mates sailed for Tahiti, then Tubuai, and back to Tahiti. While sixteen remained on Tahiti, Christian and eight followers set out in the *Bounty* and, after searching much of the Pacific for a hiding place, Christian, "on reading Captain Carteret's account of Pitcairn Island, thought it better adapted to the purpose and accordingly shaped a course thither." Christian's next challenge was to actually find Pitcairn's Island. In January 1790, "Christian, with one of the seamen ... soon traversed the island sufficiently to be satisfied that it was exactly suited to their wishes." Christian noted that in addition to the precarious landing, "the mountains were so difficult of access, and the passes so narrow, that they might be maintained by a few persons against an army; and there were several caves, to which, in case of necessity, they might retreat, and where, as long as their provisions lasted, they might bid defiance to their pursuers."[10] A great gaping chasm looms on the mountain above Adamstown; it is known as Christian's Cave. Adams told Beechey that Christian sat in the cave from time to time, brooding over the fact that he may have sent Bligh and eighteen others to their deaths in the launch. He must also have scanned the horizon in a mixture of dread and hope that a ship would come and take him away.

After the settlers unloaded supplies and stripped the *Bounty* of sails and some planks, mutineer Mathew Quintal set the vessel on fire so they would not be easily discovered. Quintal watched it burn to its water line. Its remains are still in Bounty Bay, stripped over two centuries by islanders, treasure hunters, journalists, and scientists. Adams told Beechey that mutineers and Polynesians hauled the *Bounty*'s stores and supplies up to the Edge. The upward track had been scarcely improved, as William Beechey complained of being "obliged at times to have recourse to tufts of shrubs of grass for assistance...."[11]

Once their houses were erected, they made clothing from the sail cloth, their clothes now being in tatters. The nine seamen then divided the island among themselves, each taking arable land and sections of the shore from which to fish. The fifteen Polynesians received no land. The mutineers each took a Polynesian woman, leaving three for six Polynesian men to share. Fletcher Christian took Mi'Miti; Edward Young was with Teraura, called Susannah; John Adams had Puarai; Will Brown's mate was Teatuahitea or Sarah; Will McCoy's mate was Teio, called Mary; John Mills took Vahineatua; Matt Quintal lived with Tevara or Big Sullee; John Williams's companion was Faahotu or Fasto; and Isaac Martin was paired with Teehutea-tuaona, whom he called Jenny.

A Tale of Bloody Murder

The six Polynesian men never formed a single cultural group; Tararo was a chief from Raiatea and he had the woman Toofaiti, from Huahine, to himself. The woman Tinafanaea was shared by the men Titahiti and Oha; all were probably from Tubuai. Three Tahitian men — Manarii, Teimua, and Niau — shared Mareva as bed mate. As Lieutenant Peard explained, "The Otaheitans from friends were soon treated as servants, and being naturally adverse to work, were harshly used and beaten, particularly by McCoy and Quintal." McCoy was a troublesome individual with a knife scar on his belly. Matt Quintal, in his early twenties, was equally troublesome and was, according to Bligh, "very much tattooed." In spite of the feudal social order, Adams reported, island life went on peaceably for about six to eight months.

The peace was broken, Adams explained, when ship's armorer John Williams lost his mate Fasto and demanded Toofaiti, the wife of the Raiatean aristocrat, Tararo. This was the last insult for the Polynesian men; they decided to kill the Caucasians. But the women sang a song as warning: "Why does black man sharpen axe? to kill white man."[12] To placate the Caucasians, Manarii (a.k.a. Menalee) and Tararo's mate, Toofaiti, killed Tararo, one of the two instigators of the plot. After that the island was peaceful for two years.

After two years of involuntary labor and varying degrees of abuse, the Polynesian men reasoned that if they could rid the island of whites, they would have the land and women to themselves. On September 20, 1793 — during the week that the French Convention in Paris passed a law to arrest "enemies of the revolution," and President George Washington laid the cornerstone of the national capitol — Massacre Day took place on Pitcairn. Adams told Beechey that the Polynesian men determined that they would "put to death all the Englishmen, when at work in their plantations." Two men, Teimua and Niau, hid in the mountain. Titiahiti, one of two Polynesian men remaining at the huts, borrowed a gun from either Martin or Adams by claiming he was going to shoot hogs. Titiahiti then joined the runaways and then "fell upon Williams and shot him. Martin, who was at no great distance, heard the report of the musket and exclaimed, 'Well done! we shall have a glorious feast to-day.'"[13] Fletcher Christian was next, shot in the back while working in his taro patch. The mutineer-in-chief exclaimed, "Oh, dear," and died.[14] John Mills died after "two blacks fell upon him."[15] Isaac Martin and William Brown were shot, but they died only when Menalee took a maul to their heads.

Adams said he had taken a bullet through the shoulder. The bullet came out through his throat. His assailant tried to finish him off, but Adams survived because the gun misfired twice. Adams pulled himself to his feet and scurried off to hide. Edward Young, according to one version, was hidden by the women; another theory is that he was spared because, as a West Indies–born mulatto, he was darker than the others. McCoy and Quintal, whom the Polynesians hated for their cruelty, wisely fled to the mountain. When the sun set on Massacre Day, Adams, Young, McCoy and Quintal survived. Five whites had been murdered.

The Mystery of Fletcher Christian

Because Adams was unable to point out the location of Christian's grave to visiting navigators, and because he told significantly varying stories of how Christian died, some writers argue that Christian may not have died on Pitcairn, but escaped back to England. Sir John Barrow, in his *Mutiny of the Bounty* (1831), gave credence to this theory in a footnote which stated, "About the years 1808 and 1809, a very general opinion was prevalent in the neighborhood of the lakes of Cumberland and Westmoreland, that Christian was in that part of the county and made frequent private visits to an aunt who was living there." Barrow conceded that Christian's return could be mere gossip, except that, "In Fore Street, Plymouth Dock, Captain Heywood found himself one day walking behind a man whose shape had so much the appearance of Christian's that he involuntarily quickened his pace. Both were walking very fast, and the rapid steps behind him having roused the stranger's attention, he suddenly turned his face, looked at Heywood, and immediately ran off. But the face was as much like Christian's as the back and Heywood, exceedingly excited, ran also. Both ran as fast as they were able, but the stranger had the advantage and, after making several short turns, disappeared."[16] This story has never been put entirely to rest. Heywood neglected to call attention to the fact that any able-bodied seaman who was being chased by a naval officer in the Plymouth Dock area would be advised to run as fast as he was able to avoid impressment aboard ship. Others have suggested that Christian somehow returned to the Lake District where he met his friends Samuel Taylor Coleridge and William Wordsworth, and that Coleridge based his poem "The Rime of the Ancient Mariner" on Christian's adventure.

Christian's return is not a complete impossibility, but it is improbable. If a small ship had anchored at Bounty Bay, unseen or unreported to later visitors by Adams, and if Christian had somehow come aboard and told the crew he was the single survivor of a shipwreck, he may have convinced them to take him to South America and from there, in disguise, made his way home. However, if a crew had picked up a man on Pitcairn, it is unlikely the story would have been kept quiet for long. We will probably never know for certain exactly what happened to Fletcher Christian, but the very remote possibility of his escape makes a good story even more interesting.

The Pitcairn Island Civil War

H. E. Maude wrote that after the massacre, "The native men, coming from different islands and social classes, were soon engaged in disputes, particularly over the main spoils of victory, the women; while the women themselves, evinced increasing hostility towards them, hardly surprising in view of the fact that they had murdered five of their husbands and were endeavoring to kill two more."[17] Within a short time, Adams related, Manarii killed his fellow Tahitian Teimua. Manarii then ran to the mountain to hide out with McCoy and Quintal. McCoy or Quintal then murdered Manarii.

On October 3, 1793, Adams said, "the widows of the white men so deeply deplored their loss, that they determined to revenge their death, and concerted a plan to murder the only two remaining men of colour."[18] "From this time, the two remaining Blacks lived in a constant state of apprehent, had always a light burning and dressing up a figure, placed it in such a position as to have the appearance of a man keeping watch. They frequently went into the woods in search of McCoy & Quintal who had many narrow escapes. Once they found them asleep, fired at and missed them...." Teraura, Edward Young's bed mate, decapitated Titahiti with an axe, and Niau was killed by a gun fired by Edward Young. Young and Adams killed the remaining Polynesian male, Oha, in the woods. "These four Mutineers now in undisputed possession of the Island," Peard wrote, "divided the 10 women amongst them, or rather held them in common for the distribution was not strictly attended to...."[19] In four years, six Polynesian men and five mutineers had been murdered.

In December 1793, Young began to record events in his journal. Beechey read that the inhabitants "lived peaceably together, building their houses, fencing and cultivating their grounds, fishing," and performing other necessary chores. The women, however, regretted leaving Tahiti to live in on an isolated rock with degenerate ruffians. They determined to build a boat to return to Tahiti. Jenny (Teehuteatuaonoa) tore planks out of her house to contribute to the boat's construction. On August 15, 1794, when the boat was launched, "according to expectation [the craft] upset."[20] Looking back on the incident from the vantage of two decades, John Buffett, a later immigrant, observed that it was fortunate that the boat upset near shore "for had they launched out upon the ocean where could they have gone or what could a few ignorant women have done by themselves drifting upon the waves but ultimately have fallen a sacrifice to their folly."[21] Unable to leave their tiny world, the women remained "much dissatisfied with their condition." In November 1794, the men discovered a plot laid by the women to murder them. Unwilling to live without women, the men merely admonished them not to "give any cause even to suspect their behavior."[22] On November 30 the women attacked the men again. Once more they were pardoned.

Beechey found only one page in Young's diary for 1796, and concluded that peace had returned to Pitcairn, yet one may assume that the men spent some sleepless nights in fear of their throats being slit. The year 1797 saw mutual aid among the adults and a social life that included "dining frequently at each other's houses." The community seemed to have become tranquil. Tranquility was shattered when Will McCoy, who had previously enjoyed employment in a Scottish distillery, became bored and thirsty, altered his kettle into a still, and on April 20, 1798, "succeeded too well" in making liquor from the roots of the *ti* plant. After that McCoy and Quintal were frequently intoxicated. The liquor produced "fits of delirium" in McCoy and, during a seizure, he leaped from a cliff to his death. This dramatic event frightened — if only temporarily — the rest of the island's inhabitants into sobriety.[23]

In 1799 Quintal's wife Tevarua fell or leaped from a cliff to her death. Quintal then demanded Adams's or Young's mate and "he swore if they did not give him another, he would be the death of one or more of them."[24] According to Adams, he and Young decided their own lives were in jeopardy and that they had to kill him for their own safety. Adams told Captain Beechey he had split the quarrelsome Quintal's skull with an axe.

Peace at Last

The years 1794–1800 were apparently busy ones for the mutineers. When they weren't assaulting one another or defending themselves, six of the nine mutineers sired babies. None of the island children's names, neither first nor middle, were Tahitian. Perhaps John Adams was asked to suggest common English names for the children, as no name was to be repeated and few were biblical in origin. One wonders if Adams was reciting from memory the roll-call of his orphanage in London. Those six years saw the births of almost the entire second generation: Sarah McCoy, Alias Quintal, Dinah Adams, John Mills, Polly Young, Robert

Young, George Young, William Young, James Young, Edward Young, Dolly Young, Jane Quintal, Arthur Quintal, Rachel Adams, Edward Quintal, Catherine McCoy, Hannah Adams and, four years later, the last child of the first generation, George Adams. Midshipman Edward Young was the father of seven; he sired the most children of the mutineers and the name Young remains prominent among *Bounty* descendants. The third generation of Pitcairners entered the scene when Thursday October Christian's first son Joseph was born in 1806, only two years after the birth of George Adams.

Edward Young, "descended from respectable parents," and John Adams, "of a happy, ingenuous disposition," having seen thirteen men meet violent ends since the *Bounty* was burned, "resolved to train up their own children, and those of their late unfortunate companions, in piety and virtue."[25] To that end, Young taught Adams to read the Bible and the two instituted thrice daily services on the Sabbath. Beechey recorded that "At sunset they assemble for prayers." Every day they prayed before their early dinner "and at a early hour, having again said their prayers, and chaunted the evening hymn, they retire to rest; but before they sleep, each person again offers up a short prayer upon his bed."[26]

Adams told Beechey that on Christmas Day, 1800, Edward Young died of natural causes, probably asthma or consumption. Adams was the only Briton left on the island. According to Peard, Adams had begun to pray alone, and, according to his account, "this soon caught the attention of the children, and as he threw a sort of mystery around it, ... the children's curiosity became a thirst for knowledge. Each would separately beg of Adams to teach him a portion of prayer, and even buy his acquiescence, by working in his plantation and attending his crops."[27]

Pitcairn Island in 1825

Adams continued to instruct the children as best he could, and when they were able to support themselves, encouraged them to marry. Adams performed the marriage ceremony, using the only ring on the island for every couple. At some point the island ring was misplaced. In 1940, Mrs. H. E. Maude, wife of a British administrator, discovered it in an Adamstown garden. It can be seen in the Legislative Assembly committee chambers on Norfolk Island. Adams himself put on the wedding band when Captain Beechey married him and his long-time companion Teio, the mother of Adams's only son, George. His earlier consort, Vahineatua, was the mother of his three daughters, Dinah, Rachel, and Hannah.

The hamlet over which Adams presided, observed Beechey, "consisted of five cottages, built more substantially than neatly," but Adams, who had "retired from the bustle of the community to a more quiet and sequestered spot," had a house on the periphery at a higher elevation.[28] Perhaps Adams sought refuge from the children's music, of which, Peard charitably wrote: "if not of the most harmonious and elegant kind, [it] had at least novelty to recommend it."[29] Houses were described as being large — forty to fifty feet by fifteen, and thirteen feet high. Pathways from the hamlet led to valleys where proprietors grew taro, bananas, yams, and plantains on their "plantations." A family's pigs, goats, and poultry were fenced in near each house.

The most arduous work that women and girls performed was the Polynesian industry of making tapa. An islander described the process:

First, the plants must be cut down and divested of their bark. Each bark is then peeled and the inner portion beaten out until it becomes soft, and the fibers separate. Washing is the next thing,

House of John Adams. **Drawing by Captain Frederick William Beechey, 1825. Beechey wrote that "Adams had retired from the bustle of the community to a more quiet and sequestered spot." Adams sought refuge from the children's music which "had novelty to recommend it." Published in Beechey,** *Narrative of a Voyage to the Pacific and Beering's Strait,* **1831.**

and this is repeated until every trace of the abundant sap is removed. By this time the substance has widened to five times its natural width, and has a beautiful lace-like appearance. It is then wrapped up in the large leaves of the appi (arum gigantum), sufficient being inclosed in the wrap to make a sheet. Being allowed to remain for a few days, it becomes soft and almost pulpy. Then it is ready to lay out in strips of the required length, one bark being laid over another until the proper thickness is obtained. The whole is then beaten out, two persons being required to do this, as they stand on the opposite sides of a large, long, and smoothly planed log, called a "dood-a" and with their heavy beaters keeping time with the utmost exactness.[30]

The finished product is then dried in the sun until it is sufficiently hard to withstand washing. It is then dyed reddish brown from the inner bark of the candlenut tree soaked in water.

Another use of the "dood-a" or doodwi tree was artificial light. As *The Pitcairn Miscellany* explained:

The green fruit grows in profusion on the slender Doodwi tree, and inside each fruit are two nuts. These are easily cut from the soft flesh of the fruit and are stored and dried until ready for use when the hard outer husk of the nut is broken open and the combustible seed within exposed. These have the texture and feel of a peanut, are about the size of a walnut, and are even edible in small quantities. When properly aged and dried, these are skewered onto a Ni-au (the firm, narrow stalk of the coconut leaf) one on top of another, until a dozen or so are firmly fixed into place. Three or four of these stalks, similarly loaded, are bound tightly together with Pulau bark; and you have ready to light a torch that will last for hours.[31]

These lights were difficult to extinguish, even in stormy weather when they were used by women at Bounty Bay guiding men in from the sea in their longboats.

Two New Permanent Residents

Beechey met two other British men who had settled on Pitcairn. On December 10, 1823, John Buffet, age twenty-six, a shipwright from Bristol who had become a sailor, and his friend and shipmate John Evans, a Welshman, had arrived aboard the British whaling vessel *Cyrus*. Buffet had already lived through a lifetime of sea adventures. He had been shipwrecked eight years previously while serving aboard the *Penelope* in the Gulf of St. Lawrence; forty-two men were killed, but Buffet survived. Then, sailing from Jamaica to St. John, New Brunswick, aboard the *Weasel*, he was shipwrecked on Scituate Beach near Boston. Again he survived and sailed in 1821 to Canton and Manila. His ship was wrecked in a storm, so he signed aboard the *Lady Blackwood*, bound for Valparaiso. The *Lady Blackwood* was damaged severely in a typhoon. From the Philippines Buffett signed aboard a ship bound for Oahu in the Sandwich Islands and then for California.

Sailing from California aboard the whaling vessel *Cyrus*, John Buffett and John Evans arrived at Pitcairn. Buffett explained, "The inhabitants being in want of some person to teach them to read, and write, the Captain asked me if I should like to remain there. I told him I should, and was discharged and went on shore. At this time there were about fifty inhabitants.... I had escaped many dangers," Buffett related, "and those dangers were the means of causing me to think of a future state, or, if I should express my desires at that time to become religious ... and I now thought [Pitcairn] the most eligible place in the world, a place free from temptation and with no hindrance to prevent a man becoming a christian."[32] Captain John Hall of the *Cyrus* and John Adams both granted Buffett permission to stay. Shortly after the *Cyrus* had sailed out of view, Buffett's nineteen-year-old shipmate John Evans emerged from a hollow tree in which he had hidden. Adams had no choice but to allow Evans to remain on the island.

Buffett married Dolly (Dorothy) Young, Edward's daughter. Once married, Buffet soon found some of the temptation he had come to Pitcairn to escape. He sired two children in an adulterous relationship. The children's paternity could not have remained a secret in such an intimate community, and in 1833 a hint of Buffet's profligacy leaked out from the island known for its piety. Captain William Waldegrave of H.M.S. *Seringapatam* wrote in an article in the *Royal Geographical Society Journal*, explaining that when he physically counted islanders, he counted eighty-one. When he asked islanders their number, the answer was seventy-nine. The discrepancy of two was accounted for when a Pitcairner confessed to having not included the names of two children or identified their parents because, "It would be wrong to tell my neighbors' shame."[33] In 1834, a visitor stated that Mary, daughter of Fletcher Christian, "a young and interesting female," was the sole spinster because she "expresses great aversion" to Pitcairn men; "but, unfortunately, her antipathy has not extended to Europeans, and a very fair infant claims her maternal attentions."[34]

Evans married John Adams's daughter Rachel, who was several years older than he. Each man integrated into the life of the community. "I soon commenced school keeping, the children attended regularly and some of the young men also to learn to write, &c," Buffett related.[35] He was able to teach the children manual arts such as carpentry and to make curios from local woods to barter with visiting ships. In addition, Buffett also began to record island events in *The Pitcairn Register*.

Beechey learned that once the killing had stopped, the islanders lived in exemplary harmony under Adams's puritanical leadership. They produced clothing and artificial light, built substantial homes and raised sufficient food to sustain themselves. They sang poorly and played well. So long as John Adams lived, they had every reason to believe that Pitcairn would remain a utopia.

CHAPTER 10

Death of the Patriarch

George Hunn Nobbs Is Rowed Ashore

On November, 5, 1828, Buffet recorded in the *Register*, "George Nobbs came on shore to reside." Nobbs would be the most important single figure in his adopted community for over a half century. Nobbs, age twenty-nine, turned up at Pitcairn aboard a bark with Noah Bunker, a mysterious black-bearded American in his mid-thirties. Bunker appeared to be gravely ill. No other crew were aboard. Nobbs told Buffett that he and Bunker had failed to procure seals and, unwilling to report to their ship's creditors, had elected to settle on Pitcairn.

Two and a half months later, on January 21, 1829, a Flemish merchant and pearl fisheries entrepreneur, Jacques Antoine Moerenhout, landed from the schooner *Volador*. As part of his tour of the island, he was taken to see the dying Bunker. Bunker lay on a mattress while a woman fanned him. "At my approach the sick man signaled to me with his left hand to sit down. His appearance contained something sinister." Moehrenhout noted Bunker's "thin and very pale face, a covered forehead, very large eyes and thick eyebrows, and upon his features, extraordinary in their entirety, could be read at the same time suffering and unusual exaltation of spirit, which while despairing of life, knew not to struggle against sorrow."[1] In spite of nursing by solicitous islanders, Bunker's condition worsened. Buffett explained that one evening, when nobody was watching him, "Capt. Bunker got up, went to the precipice and jumped off. After searching for some time we found him on the rock with one arm

George Hunn Nobbs, 1799–1884. A sailor of fortune, Nobbs arrived on Pitcairn in 1828. He taught school and held church services. He was ordained in 1853, and emigrated to Norfolk Island in 1856. He was the father of 10 children. Daguerreotype by Kilburn, 1853. Engraved by H. Adlard.

and leg broken.... The distance he jumped was about 100 feet, but he told us he did not reach the bottom the first time. He said he tried to strike a projecting rock with his head and missing it he jumped to the bottom. When we found him he entreated us to kill him or remove him so that he might jump into the sea, saying it was no harm to put him out of misery." Bunker was put back to bed, but, "Soon after a whaler arrived and the Capt. sent on shore some laudanum for him. One day, no one being in the house but a boy he asked him to draw his trunk to him, which he did, taking the laudanum he drank it all, and died in consequence."[2]

Moerenhout stayed with a Pitcairn family and when he had gone to bed, the family said their prayers. "*Quel peuple! J'étais vraiment dans un autre monde!*" (What a people. I was truly in another world.)[3] Moehrenhout went on to write *Voyages aux Îles du Grand Océan*, a narrative of his adventures in the South Pacific. He became French consul in Tahiti and the United States consul for all of Polynesia.

Nobbs was born in Ireland in 1799. He claimed to be an illegitimate son of the Marquis of Hastings; Nobbs's mother, he said, was the daughter of an Irish baronet. After his parents gave him up, he was raised in county Durham by a family named Nobbs, whose name he took. At age twelve, he entered the Royal Navy and from then until the day he reached Pitcairn, he had never found it difficult to find adventure. He sailed on the *Indefatigable* to Sydney and Van Diemen's Land with a load of prisoners; he sailed off the coast of South America aboard a privateer seeking royalist vessels in the service of Latin American revolutionaries; he raided Spanish shipping in the Philippines, netting two thousand dollars as his share; he was captured by the Spaniards in Chile, and was among the last four men scheduled to be executed when the four were, in the final minutes, exchanged for prisoners. He later served in the Chilean navy under Lord Cochrane during Chile's war of independence from Spain. In Sierra Leone, he was aboard a ship on which seventeen died from tropical diseases and four lived. When he learned about Pitcairn, he determined to settle there and leave behind his perilous existence. After more travails in South America, Nobbs met Noah Bunker. He and Bunker somehow — their story varied — acquired an eighteen-ton bark in Callao, Peru's chief seaport, and from there sailed to Pitcairn.

On October 18, 1829, a year after his arrival, Nobbs married Fletcher's grand-daughter, nineteen-year-old Sarah Christian, described as "one of the prettiest natives."[4] By this time Buffett had lost the respect of at least some Pitcairners for committing adultery and fathering two illegitimate children. Buffet obviously felt inadequacy and further humiliation when the better-educated Nobbs started a school to rival his own school. Nobbs also began to conduct Sunday services. Until Nobbs supplanted Buffett as keeper of the *Register*, spiritual leader and sole schoolmaster, Moerenhout wrote, "I was very surprised to see that now they were going to hold services in two different places; and it was not long before I gathered that George Nobbs had already succeeded in making a split among these people who, before his arrival, had lived together in harmony."[5] A visitor noted, "there are some who already think that Nobbs ... affects a superiority over them ... and has created a division amongst them," and that Buffet and Evans were "jealous of the new comer."[6] At last, Buffett conceded, "Mr. Nobbs, being a good scholar, and my family increasing, I gave up school teaching, he succeeded me."[7]

Death of John Adams

The isolated community suffered an incomparable blow with the death of John Adams. His death was probably precipitated by the arrival within a short time in early 1829 of two ships, both bringing disease. One story states that when Moerenhout arrived aboard the *Volador* on January 21, John Adams went aboard, where he remained several days. Buffet thought that Adams's illness was precipitated because he had gone onboard and "the sun being very warm, and he being much on deck without a hat, the sun affected his head. After coming on shore he became worse...."[8] The *Volador*'s carpenter had already died of disease and many islanders had become ill. The whaler *Independence*, which arrived at Pitcairn January 26, offloaded four men who had high fevers; these men remained ashore a few hours while islanders cared for them. Every crew member of the *Independence* had the fever and several had already died.

Adams returned to his home ill from his visit with Moehrenhout. After five weeks, he died. Captain Waldegrave of H.M.S. *Seringapatam* wrote on his visit in 1830, "John Adams died in March, 1829. During his life all obeyed him as a parent,—'Father' was his only title. Shortly before his death he called the heads of families together, and urged them to appoint a chief; but they looked up to him whilst living, and have appointed none since his death."[9] The island *Register* and his grave record his age as sixty-five, but according to his birth records in London, he was seventy-two. Adams's grave, the only identifiable resting place of a *Bounty* crew member on the island, is inscribed "In Hope." His wife, Teio, died six weeks later and is buried with him. So many pieces of his wooden grave marker were whittled off by visitors, that a stone marker stands atop the grave today.

With the death of Adams, their key to the outside world and its myriad mysteries, the islanders were like children without a father.

A Portrait of the Islanders in 1830

Lieutenant Orlebar, arriving on March 15, 1830, aboard H.M.S. *Seringapatam*, described being brought in by islanders in a longboat: "The passage was most intricate, leading as it were through the centre of the roaring surf; borne on the bosom of a wave that topped so fearfully as to threaten each moment to overwhelm us, his cry of "Pull away, pull away, boys" shewed that even to them 'twas a dangerous task: we spun with the rapidity of an arrow among rocks covered with foam, and one hard bump displayed us for a moment on the very pinnacle of one, when half a dozen of the tall natives, who were observing us, sprang to our assistance, and watching the surf which again rolled toward us, launched us onward and in a moment we grounded on the beach, under the shade of a large tree."

When Orlebar and his captain, William Waldegrave, climbed to the village, "the men sprang up to the trees, throwing down cocoa-nuts, and tearing off the husks with their teeth, offered us the milk. When we had rested they took us to their cottages, where we dined and slept."[10] Waldegrave explained that grace was offered before and after meals and that "Should any one arrive during the repast, all ceased to eat — the new guest said grace, to which each repeated Amen, and then the meal continued."[11] Waldegrave claimed to have been shown Fletcher Christian's grave. No such grave has since been identified.

The *Seringapatam*'s crew unloaded supplies provided by the British government: sailor suits for men and dresses for women, as well as shoes, farm implements, iron tools and other items. In return, there was little of value Waldegrave could take away. He noted, "Ships may obtain fire-wood at Pitcairn's Island in abundance, with a certain quantity of yams, cocoa-nuts, and plantains, but not a large supply; poultry, pigs, they object to part with; it would be impossible to water a man-of-war, as the water is to be carried from Brown's well on the shoulders of the natives." Captain Waldegrave brought his ship's chaplain ashore to perform services. Kitty Quintal challenged Captain Waldegrave when he said, "I have brought you a clergyman."

"God bless you, God bless you!' was the universal answer. "To stay with us?"

"No!"

"You bad man, why not?"

"I cannot spare him, he is the clergyman of my ship. I have brought you clothes, which King George sends you."

"We rather want food for our souls."

When Waldegrave visited Nobbs's classroom he heard a pupil "say part of the catechism, and answer several questions as to his knowledge of the redemption in Christ, and of the different habits of the Jews, their sects and diseases, perfectly, clearly and distinctly showing that he understood their meaning." Waldegrave wrote, "The children were fond and obedient, the parents affectionate and kind towards their children — we did not hear a harsh word used by one towards another."[12] Of both children and adults, the captain wrote, "One of the remarkable circumstances is the correctness of their language and pronunciation. The general language is English; their divine service, also is in English, but they frequently converse in Otaheitian, the language of their mothers."[13] Curiously, Lieutenant Orlebar of the same ship on the same visit recorded a distinctly different impression: "We found ourselves frequently at a loss to understand their English, and they perhaps more so to comprehend ours:— for their wants and occupations are so confined, and the simplicity of their ideas requires but few words of expression, that only the most common and simple seem known among them."[14] Waldegrave was probably referring to the spoken English of pupils under Buffett's and Nobbs's instruction, while Orlebar had been listening to adults who had never had the benefit of formal schooling. The work of Buffett and Nobbs had obviously improved spoken English since the earlier reports of visitors who found language fractured and uncertain.

The unworldly islanders were waiting victims for anyone of evil intent whose ship stopped in the cove. Lieutenant Orlebar was told that, "some of the young men went a short time back in a schooner to an island some hundred miles off for pearls [probably one of the Gambiers], and from their good diving obtained for her an excellent cargo; in return for which the master of the schooner only gave them a check shirt and trousers apiece, so that here even they are exposed to the roguery of man."[15] Their vulnerability had been one of John Adams's chief worries about his community's fate when he was no longer present to guide and protect them, which is why he felt a strong leader necessary for their survival. Yet, Adams did not name Nobbs as his successor.

Lieutenant Orlebar and Captain Waldegrave each offered his own assessment of the rise of George Hunn Nobbs. Orlebar wrote that "there are some who already think that Nobbs being tolerably well-informed and versed in ways of the world, affects a superiority over them, which is extremely hurtful to their strict notions of independence and liberty of action, and has created a division amongst them, further fomented, I think by the arts of two other Englishmen who are jealous of the new comer."[16] Waldegrave observed that Nobbs sought to fill Adams's position. "Nobbs claims exemption from labour as pastor; by law he is to be maintained by the community. His information is superior to the natives, therefore he wishes to become the chief,— in which he will be disappointed; they do not like a superior."[17]

Jane Quintal, Marooned and Married

Dr. Bennett told the story of Jane Quintal, the first woman of the second generation to leave the island. It so happened that in 1829, Frederick Bennett's brother George had touched at Rurutu in the Austral Islands, now part of French Polynesia. The first missionaries had arrived at Rurutu only eight years previously. George Bennett had written, "On the beach I was accosted by a tall, fine, half-caste woman, dressed in neat European clothing. Her manner was artless, and she spoke the English language with correctness. She informed me that her name was Jane Quintal, of Pitcairn's Island. 'You have heard of Matthew Quintal?' she said: 'I am his daughter.'" When George Bennett asked why she had left, Jane replied, "It is, sir, but a very small island; quite a rock," and because "There are no husbands there," Jane explained, "I married a native of this island." Pointing to a child, she said, "This is my son. I was obliged to get married, they are so very particular; all missionaries. I could not talk to any male creature when single, so I got married."[18] There is more to Jane's story than she revealed. In 1826, a seaman on the whaler *Lovely Ann* had taken her with him as far as Rurutu and then sailed on without her. Jane had been marooned.

Nevertheless. Jane was fortunate to have left Pitcairn before the community underwent the greatest loss of life since the island was settled.

CHAPTER 11

Fatal Tahitian Sojourn

The Proposal for Migration

Four years before he died, Adams told Captain F. W. Beechey that he was concerned that Pitcairn's 1,100 acres, little of which was arable, would be insufficient to support the community of sixty-six and their future progeny. Adams was concerned about deforestation which deprived residents of building material and led to soil erosion, and periodic droughts. Adams worried that the naive community would be prey to unscrupulous visitors such as marauding whaling crews.

Beechey wrote: "The idea of passing all their days upon an island only two miles long, without seeing any thing of the world, or what was a stronger argument, without doing good in it, had with several of them been deeply considered. But family ties, and an ardent affection for each other, and for their native soil, had always interposed to prevent their going away singly.... Adams having contemplated the situation which the islanders would have been reduced to, begged, at our first interview that I would communicate with the government upon the subject, which was done...."[1] Beechey had written to Sir John Barrow, second secretary to the Admiralty.[2] Beechey told Sir John that Pitcairn was dangerously overpopulated. Barrow was keenly interested in Pitcairn and would soon write the first classic account of the *Bounty* mutiny. Ironically, instead of sending a company of men to bring Adams back to England for trial before hanging, the Foreign Office, Colonial Office, colonial governors' offices, and the diplomatic service, not to mention ardent missionaries, all together set to work immediately and efficiently to make the mutineer's wish a reality. The questions that remained were: Where would they go, when, and how many ought to be removed?

Adams had confided to Captain Beechey his hope that the islanders would be removed to Tahiti, New South Wales, or Van Diemen's Land. Barrow presented the request to the Colonial Office, recommending that "this fine race of men, so much improved by the Spice of Otaheitian blood in their veins," be relocated to New South Wales.[3] Had the islanders moved to spacious lands of their own in Australia, in an area separate from the convicts and their keepers, they may have never returned to Pitcairn. Abandoned, Pitcairn may have become an isolated French military outpost, a cell for high-risk prisoners, a monastery, a mid–Pacific victualing station for brave whalers willing to risk passing through the rocks, or — more probably — the lonesome home of an occasional Robinson Crusoe.

The Decision for Tahiti

Henry Nott of the London Missionary Society had come from Tahiti to London at the time that authorities were deciding where to relocate the islanders. Pomare's government feared a takeover by France. Nott brought a letter from the advisors of seven-year-old Tahitian king Pomare III (r. 1821–27) asking for British protection of his realm and for permission to fly the Union Jack. Learning about the situation of the Pitcairners, Nott recommended Tahiti as a home for the population, with the expectation that the pious Pitcairners would serve as a useful adjunct to the London Missionary Society volunteers. These volunteers had been laboring with frustration to make conversions. Nott also expected that the British government would accede to the Tahitians' request for protection in return for lands to be given to the Pitcairners. Nott's suggestion made sense initially in that the Pitcairners had blood relations in Tahiti; in fact four Tahitian women, consorts of the mutineers, were still living.

The following year Nott returned to Tahiti with a note, dated March 3, 1827, to King Pomare III from foreign minister George Canning, stating that "His Majesty has ... given orders that a ship shall be employed for conveying them ... to Taheite (sic) [if you are] willing to receive them into your Dominions. The British Gov persuades Itself that you will not refuse your consent to this arrangement, as the modest and amiable manners of these people, and their moral and religious sentiments are such as to have excited a strong feeling in their behalf, in the minds of HM's Officers who have visited Pitcairn's Island, as well as on the part of the British Nation at large."[4] By the time Nott was able to deliver the note, King Pomare III had died and his sister succeeded as Pomare IV. The queen's advisors replied, "The queen desires

This bucolic scene in Tahiti may have been similar to what Pitcairners saw during their tragic stay in 1831. The pious immigrants were affronted by the Tahitians' sexual morals and sickened by diseases to which they had no immunity. Photograph by Robert Kirk.

me to say, that they shall be kindly received, and well treated whenever they shall arrive on these islands."[5] Shortly after that John Adams died.

When they read Captain Waldegrave's account of his visit, Barrow and Nott began having second thoughts about removing the Pitcairners. Waldegrave had concluded, "Eleven twelfths are uncultivated. Yet population increases so rapidly, that in another century the island will be fully peopled. I think one thousand should be its limit of inhabitants."[6] Sir John Barrow wrote, "It is sincerely to be hoped that such removal will be no longer thought of.... The breaking up of this happy, innocent, and simple-minded little society, by some summary process, and consigning them to those sinks of infamy on New Holland or Van Diemen's Land, or to mix them up with the dram-drinkers, the psalm-singers, and the languid and lazy Otaheitans, would, in either case, be a subject of deep regret to all who take an interest in their welfare; and to themselves would be the inevitable loss of all those amiable qualities which have obtained for them the kind and generous sympathy of their countrymen at home."[7] A little more than a century later, H.E. Maude commented on the bureaucratic process that carried the program forward inexorably: "One would think that such unequivocal recantations might have halted proceedings, at least until further inquiry had been made. But it was too late; the machine was in full swing and nothing could now stop it."[8]

1831: *Lucy Ann* and *Comet*

In 1831, the Admiralty sent *Comet* as escort to the transport bark *Lucy Ann* from Sydney to remove the entire population of Pitcairn Island to Tahiti. To help them settle on Tahiti, the British government supplied tools and clothing. When the two ships arrived on February 28, Captain Sandilands of *Comet* assembled heads of all families, and "fully explained to them that they were perfectly at liberty either to remove to Otaheite or remain where they were...."[9] Those who were willing to go wanted assurance of being returned to Pitcairn if they disliked their new home. Sandilands was unable to make such a promise. By the next morning, after what must have been a sleepless night for some, the people reached a consensus. The consensus was influenced by several factors. Pitcairn suffered at that particular time from a lack of rain. The young islanders had a curiosity about what lay beyond the ever present watery horizon. They had some desire to meet relatives in Tahiti. They did not want to be split up. Buffett stated, "Some concluded to remain on the island, but from the persuasions of those who were going, and more or less nearly related, it also being a time of drought, they finally all concluded to leave."[10] Most of all, they did not want to displease the Admiralty, their protectors, who had spent time, money and effort thus far in their behalf.

"The whole immediately commenced preparations for embarking," wrote Sandilands, "by carrying down to the landing-place potatoes, yams, fruit, and household goods, which were continued to be embarked on board the ships until the 7th, on the morning of which day all the inhabitants were embarked without accident on board the *Lucy Ann*, being eighty-seven in number, men, women and children."[11] It was two years and two days following John Adams's death. The community members who were removed to Tahiti were young. Of the men, Thursday October Christian, forty-four, was the oldest. Nine of the forty-eight men were in their thirties, five in their twenties, and the rest teenagers, children and infants. Seven women were in their thirties, four in their twenties, and the rest younger.[12] The majority—who were children—had the decision made for them by their elders. One child, Lucy Ann Quintal, was born enroute and named for the ship.

Tahiti in 1831

Author David Howarth stated of the island paradise before it was revealed to the world by Carteret, its "discoverer," in 1767, "Tahiti was a small civilization perfectly in balance."[13] Unfortunately the balance was easily upset by the coming of Europeans. Two European innovations in particular upset this balance: the ideas — totally novel to the inhabitants — of sin and of private property. Moreover, the introduction of firearms overturned the political status quo and led to the island's being ruled by a single king.

Tahiti had been changed considerably since the *Bounty*'s first stay, not only by muskets, but by missionaries, whalers and beachcombers. The London Missionary Society had been founded in 1795 to propagate the gospel in heathen lands. Returning seamen reported that Tahitians certainly answered the description of "heathen." Reports from returning sailors had it that Tahitians were living dissolute lives; therefore, these evangelicals targeted Tahiti for reform. As a result, Tahiti and its sister islands would fall under strong British missionary influence until the 1840s when their queen capitulated to threats and surrendered her people to French "protection."

In 1797, thirty-nine L.M.S. members had sailed to Tahiti on the *Duff*. They were for the most part skilled workers — butchers, carpenters, and harness makers. They included six wives, three children and four clergy. Men arrived in the hot humid climate dressed in top hats, frock coats, boots, and trousers — all black. Women wore long dresses and bonnets. These well-intentioned volunteers had no interest in anthropology, archaeology or science; rather, as David Howarth writes, "They set to work with awful determination to ... reduce [the Tahitians] to the misery of the poor in England, to whom the message of preachers could be joyful news."[14] They called one another *Brother, Mister, Missus*, or *Reverend*. It was as if these were their first names.

Tahitians were baffled as to why these heavily dressed somber men and women had come to their shores. Tahitians offered missionary men girls, but the men refused all sexual enticements. Missionaries stressed the virtues of hard work, but could not convince the people of its benefits, because little hard work needed to be done. The missionaries did not know the Tahitian language. As one might anticipate, there were, initially, no takers among Tahitians for the austere set of tabus offered by the serious visitors.

To estimate how many Tahitians needed saving, several of the missionaries walked around the island surveying the population by counting houses. Their informed guess was sixteen thousand, considerably less than Cook's two hundred thousand a generation earlier. Anthropologist Bengt Danielsson estimated the number present at the time of discovery in 1767 as a hundred and sixty thousand.[15] Whatever the pre–European number, imported disease, guns, and alcohol had done their work. To make matters worse for the cause of the L.M.S. volunteers, between 1800 and 1810, usually forty to fifty beachcombers — deserters from ships and escapees from Botany Bay — were living on Tahiti. Some of the more enterprising among them served as mercenaries for tribal chiefs in the island's wars.

By 1809, the L.M.S. mission had clearly failed. All but three missionaries left. Two remained because they had married Tahitian women. By 1811, the missionaries who remained had learned Tahitian, and translated the Bible for their potential converts. In the same year, Chief Tu sagaciously demanded to be baptized. The missionaries now allied with Chief Tu of Matavai Bay against his adversaries. Tu's subjects soon called themselves Christians whether or not they had any understanding of the religion. Thus Tu was able by 1815 to consolidate power over the island. Tu (Pomare I) died in 1803 and his son, Pomare II, became supreme chief (r. 1803–21). To please his missionary allies, Pomare II built a seven-hundred-foot cathedral. It was longer than Westminster Abbey and a stream ran through it. This, the largest edifice in Polynesia, could hold a congregation of six thousand. Tahitians had always been restricted by tabus, but now Pomare II proclaimed the Ten Commandments as a new set of tabus. In 1818, Rev. John Williams of the L.M.S. came to Papeete. Williams became, in effect, prime minister for Pomare II, thus helping him consolidate and maintain power.

Two Tahitis were in evidence at the time the Pitcairners arrived. One was centered on a ribald waterfront catering to the most prurient interests of single young mariners. The other was found in a hinterland, patrolled by morality police. In the hinterland, men's and women's heads had been shaved of long, beautiful hair. Girls no longer wore a flower behind an ear to signify eligibility. Women wore mother hubbards from their chins to the ground. Like the Pitcairn men, whose dress appeared ludicrous to visiting crews, Tahitian men went to church in jackets without proper pants, pants with jackets but no shirts, and most without shoes. Houses were increasingly made of timbers and were no longer open to breezes. People now slept in beds.

Human sacrifices and cannibalism were now punished. The morality police enforced strict Sabbatarian laws. Liquor, dancing, kite flying, flute playing, music (except religious music), and prostitution were banned seven days a week. To circumvent the ban on liquor, Tahitians set up stills in the forests. To evade the ban on prostitution and premarital sex, couples met clandestinely. Dances were performed surreptitiously. Playing drums and the nose flute had to be done out of earshot of the morality police; these toughs dressed in cast-off European military jackets and roamed the woods looking for anyone doing anything of which the missionaries might disapprove.

By 1825, six years before the Pitcairners arrived, nearly all Tahitians had been baptized. Yet, as Herman Melville pointed out in *Omoo*: "Instead of estimating the result of missionary labors by the number of heathens who have actually been made to understand and practice (in some measure, at least) the precepts of Christianity, this result has been unwarrantly inferred from the number of those, who, without any understanding of these things, have in any way been induced to abandon idolatry and conform to certain outward observances."[16]

In 1827, when Aimata was declared Queen Pomare IV, the population had fallen to an estimated six thousand. Missionaries said people died due to their sins, but the causes of death were tuberculosis, alcoholism, smallpox, typhus, dysentery, diphtheria, pneumonia, rotted teeth and the mental depression that occurred when they were wrenched out of their lifestyles and norms.

Innocents Abroad

After seventeen days in transit, the migrants arrived. The Pitcairners may have been satisfied to live among Tahitians whose desires were suppressed by morality police, but they were stunned by the irreverent Tahiti they were unable to ignore when *Lucy Ann* and *Comet* brought them in to Papeete's ribald waterfront. All ships anchored there, and when they did the crews were willing to trade firearms for what they wanted from the islanders. They wanted women, alcohol and food.

Papeete had become a European/American town. European houses, churches, a prison, and American and British consulates with clipped lawns were located near the sea front. A modest royal palace was erected in which the eighteen-year-old monarch lived. In work gangs, people convicted of love-making or other criminal acts built a road around the island, starting at Papeete's seaside Boulevard Pomare.

The Pitcairners' hosts were most generous. Captain Sandilands wrote that, "a feeling of great regard was manifested by the Otaheitians to these People, endeavoring with great diligence to find out those who were their relations, in which they were successful. In one instance, a Woman came a considerable distance and discovered in one of the four remaining Otaheitian Women, a Sister."[17] The Pitcairners were provided lodging, food, land, tools and clothing.

The good intentions of their hosts notwithstanding, the move for the Pitcairn community was a disaster from the start. John Buffett wrote, "Before the *Comet* sailed from Tahiti, the Pitcairners made applications to the Captain to take them back, which he could not."[18] First, the pious newcomers were shocked when, on their arrival, some fifty scantily-clad women climbed aboard to form fast and profitable relationships with *Mary Ann*'s crew. To the Pitcairners, Tahitians lacked Christian morality. H.E. Maude commented that Pitcairners "on the question of morals," were "probably the strictest and the Tahitians the least restrictive to be found anywhere at the time." All but three of the emigrants were Polynesian or part Polynesian, yet the Pitcairn Islanders considered themselves English — and they were racists. According to H.E. Maude: "For them miscegenation obviously meant assimilation, and the only race they were prepared to be assimilated into was the European, to which they felt they rightfully belonged."[19] As members of the Church of England, speaking English rather than Tahitian, literate, and living in clapboard houses, they considered themselves superior to Polynesians.

Because of a tribal war, the newcomers could not be settled immediately on the lands promised them, which, according to Buffett, were "very small in comparison with Pitcairn's."[20] When peace came, they were lodged temporarily with Tahitian families, families characterized by Moerenhout as "the most corrupt people of the island."[21] The guests wanted desperately to go home.

Soon, repatriation became a matter of life and death. Waiting for their new homes, they were housed at Papeete in a single building belonging to the queen. Living together in close quarters undoubtedly helped to spread among them a cocktail of diseases brought to Tahiti by visiting mariners. Like the Tahitians who had lost an estimated twenty-nine out of every thirty people since 1767, Pitcairners succumbed. *The Pitcairn Register* recorded that six weeks after arrival, Thursday October Christian — the oldest — was first to expire. Four days later baby Lucy Ann Quintal — the youngest — died. Four days after that Vahineatua, a native of Tahiti and consort of mutineer John Mills, died. Sixteen Pitcairners died between April and November, nearly a fifth of the population.

Return to Pitcairn

On April 24, 1831, *The Register* stated, "John Buffett and family. Robert Young. Joseph Christian. Edward Christian. Charles Christian 3d. Mathew Quintal and Frederic Young sailed from Tahiti in a small Schooner but owing to adverse winds the aforesaid persons landed on Lord Hood's Island the Schooner returned to Tahiti." On June 3, while languishing on Lord Hood's, known today as South Marute Island in the southern Tuamotus, eighteen-year-old Edward Christian died on that hot, low spit of land. After three weeks the stranded men were rescued by Captain Arnaud Mauruc of the French brig *Le Courrier de Bordeaux*. They were home again by June 27, after an absence of just over three and a half months. *The Register* noted, "during our absence the hogs having gone wild destroyed our crops. After returning we employed ourselves destroying the hogs &c."[22]

The Pitcairners who remained on Tahiti hired American William Driver of the schooner *Charles Doggett* to take them home. Driver wrote, "at Tahieta latter part of July, 1831, found at Boby Atti [Papeete] village 65 of the inhabitants of Pitcairn island. Ten sickly looking despondent creatures huddled together in a large thatch house, where twelve their number had died of a sort of Typhoid or Ship Fever."[23] Captain Driver returned the remaining sixty-five émigrés on September 4, aboard his ship which had been bringing bêche de mer and tortoise shell from Fiji. Driver asked five hundred dollars for their transportation. Their nineteen-day voyage was paid for by a subscription taken up among Tahiti's European colony and by Pitcairners who sold artifacts, including the *Bounty*'s copper bolts, which they had carried with them into exile. The islanders also sold their blankets to Tahitians. The blankets may well have been ridden with lethal disease.

In the Process of Restoration, 1834

When this second group arrived home, five more died. The survivors were demoralized by death and illness. As they regained their health, they set about restoring their homes and fields.

By March 1834, when Dr. Frederick Debell Bennett arrived aboard the *Tuscan*, he noted a well ordered community. In his *Narrative of a Whaling Voyage*, Bennett described Adamstown: "The northern side of the island, or that occupied by the settlement, offers a very picturesque appearance; rising from the sea as a steep amphitheater, luxuriantly wooded to its summit, and bounded on either side by precipitous cliffs, and naked and rugged rocks, of many fantastic forms. The simple habitations of the people are scattered over this verdant declivity, and are half concealed by its abundant vegetation. They are neatly constructed of plank, thatched with leaves, ... and provided with windows to which shutters are affixed." Inside, "the furniture they contain is scanty and of the rudest description; nevertheless, every thing about them denotes great attention to cleanliness and order." Outside Bennett saw "cattle-sheds, pigsties, and other outhouses, herds of swine and goats, and many European implements of agriculture...." Bennett noted of the people, "So strong a personal resemblance obtains between the members of a family that it is no difficult task to distinguish brothers and sisters."[24] Bennett found older adults — those taught by Adams — "indifferently educated; scarcely any of them being able to write their own name, though most can read." He noted that due to Nobbs's teaching, children "exhibit a proficiency in the elements of education highly creditable both to their own intelligence and to the exertions of their teacher."[25]

Although Nobbs was acknowledged a superior teacher, he was not accepted as leader by all of the islanders. John Adams could never be replaced as their father. It was unfortunate that the community did not have strong leadership at that moment in its history, because a sociopath was sailing toward Pitcairn to dominate them.

CHAPTER 12

"The Mussolini of Pitcairn"

"Captain" Joshua Hill

Their "father," John Adams, was dead. The community had no leader who commanded universal respect and provided a measure of control. By some reports morality was deteriorating. George Hunn Nobbs wrote, "A short time after our return to Pitcairn's Island, some of the natives (Edward Quintal, William Young, and Fletcher Christian), determined to recommence distilling rum — a practice they had become accustomed to in John Adams's time. [I] remonstrated with them on the impropriety of their conduct, but to no purpose; the answer they gave ... was, 'We are our own masters; we shall do as we like; no one shall control us.'"[1] The distillers were unaware that a tall and powerful sixty-year-old Englishman was on his way to Pitcairn. His purpose was to become their master and to control them.

The Englishman, Joshua Hill, was born April 15, 1773. He had read or heard about the tiny colony, and targeted the remote Pitcairn populace as people he would like to control completely. He was in a sense their stalker. From 1828, he corresponded with British government officials, seeking appointment as administrator over the Pitcairners. When Hill learned that plans had been made to remove the entire population to Tahiti, he volunteered a ship for the project, but authorities rejected it as too small. British officials regarded Hill as a well-intentioned individual who wanted to help the Pitcairners, but gave him no appointment. Undaunted, in 1830, Hill left England as a private individual en route to Tahiti to claim control over the immigrants in their new home.

When he arrived at Papeete in 1831, the islanders had already returned to Pitcairn. While waiting for any ship that would take him to Pitcairn, he commandeered the home of the absent George Prichard of the London Missionary Society. When missionary Prichard returned, Hill congratulated him for Prichard's good fortune in having been selected to host him. Hill confided to Prichard that he was sent on a secret commission from the British government to affect the future of all of the islands in the South Seas. Prichard apparently believed Hill's claims. So did Queen Pomare IV, with whom he arranged an audience. Prichard paid all of Hill's expenses, including laundry bills, while Hill waited at Papeete. At least one skeptic, the Belgian Jules-Antoine Moerenhout, saw that Hill "exhibited a puerile vanity; a bombastic pride; a dangerous fanaticism; and an implacable hatred of any one who dared to oppose his plans in any way whatever."[2]

On October 28, 1832, the bark *Maria* brought Joshua Hill from Papeete to Pitcairn Island. The dazed islanders had had scant experience with people who lied to further their own purposes; they were ripe prey for a charlatan. Calling himself "Captain" or "Lord" Hill, he presented papers, consisting of copies of letters he had addressed to government functionaries on the topic of Pitcairn. Buffett wrote, "He informed us that he was sent by the British Government to adjust the internal affairs of the Island." Buffett stated that Hill "demanded all the fire arms to be given up to him, one of which he kept loaded near him...."[3] Schoolmaster George Hunn Nobbs recalled bitterly of Hill's claims, "Believing these things to be true, [I] gave Mr. Hill an apartment in [my] house, and used every means to make him comfortable; but before one month had expired, Mr. Hill had succeeded by villainous misrepresentation, atrocious falsehoods, and magnificent promises of presents, to be obtained through his influence from the British government and several British of Mr. Hill's acquaintance, in ejecting [me] from [my] house."[4]

The tyrant's next proclamation was prohibition of alcoholic beverages; Hill immediately set about destroying *ti*-root stills. Hill named himself "President of the Commonwealth of Pitcairn." Island historian Rosalind Amelia Young was to describe him as "overzealous, revengeful and tyrannical."[5] Novelist James Norman Hall called him "The Mussolini of Pitcairn."[6]

Joshua Hill. This sketch by sailor George Eliot is the only known likeness of Joshua Hill. Eliot inscribed his drawing: "Hill. The self-constituted King of Pitcairn — An Imposter." Hill appeared on the island in 1832 without official authorization and ruled as dictator until he was removed by Captain Bruce of *HM Imogene* in December 1837.

Captain Fremantle, a True Believer

Hill augmented his credibility by soliciting the approval of a representative of the Royal Navy, Captain Charles H. Fremantle. When on January 10, 1833, Captain Fremantle of H.M.S. *Challenger* arrived, Hill showed the ship's master his lengthy résumé, which read in part, "I have lived a considerable while in a palace, and had my dinner parties with a princess on my right, and General's lad on my left. I have had a French cook, a box at the opera.... I have (at her request) visited Madame Bonaparte, at the Tuileries, St. Cloud, and Malmaison.... I have had the honor of being in company; i.e., at the same parties, with both his late Majesty George IV then Prince Regent, and his present Majesty William IV then H.R.H. Duke of Clarence, as well with their royal brothers."[7]

Hill complained to Fremantle that when he had arrived at Pitcairn, on a Sunday, the inhabitants were intoxicated and that Nobbs was too drunk to perform church services. Accepting Hill's account, Fremantle wrote in his log that the islanders were "not improved by their visit to Otaheite, but on the contrary ... were much altered for the worse, having, since their return, indulged in intemperance to a great degree, distilling a spirit from the tee root, which grows in great quantities on the island." Hill said he had "found the island in the greatest state of irregularity."[8] Hill convinced Fremantle that he had saved the community from alcoholism and other forms of debauchery. Fremantle wrote that he hoped the islanders "do not return to the use of that spirit which they have the art of distilling. I obtained a specimen of it; it is not unlike whiskey, and very good."[9]

What Hill told Fremantle and what the captain observed for himself differed considerably. Fremantle concluded that the people have "lost much of that simplicity of character which has been represented of them by former visitors." On the other hand, his observations showed them to be "still a well-disposed, well-behaved, kind, hospitable people, and if well advised and instructed, could be led to anything." Believing what Hill told him about teacher Nobbs, Fremantle made no effort to reconcile the discrepancy between Hill's assessment of the schoolmaster as a drunken sot barely able to function, and his own notation of fifty-three islanders under twenty who, he wrote, have been "well instructed, many of them capable of reading, and nearly on a par with children of the same age in England."[10] In spite of signs that Hill had exaggerated or fabricated his assertions, Fremantle reported to his superiors, "I gave him all the assistance in my power to support him in his situation; the other Englishman [Nobbs], who had clearly proved himself by his conduct to be unfit for it, I recommend to quit the island, which he promised to do."[11]

Fascism — Pitcairn Style

Hill named six credulous young island men as his assistants, giving them titles of "councilors" and "cadets"; they provided muscle to enforce his rule. Hill censored all books which arrived on the island. John Buffett explained, "He has framed laws and built a prison; and should any of the natives refuse to obey him, let his proposals be ever so unjust, he tells them he will send to England for a governor and a regiment of soldiers. By such means he has persuaded the natives to sign a petition to Government to deprive us Englishmen and our children of our lands."[12] Hill soon gained the islanders' obedience. Buffett explained that "it was from fear partly, and hopes of gain. He told them if they did not obey him, he would write to Government and a ship of war would be sent to chastise them," and if they did obey, he would write a request to the government to send them whatever wants they were to list. Moreover, Hill stated that all previous gifts sent to the island, from all sources, had been sent at his request.[13]

Hill saw Evans, Buffett, and Nobbs, the residents most likely to see through his bombast, as his competitors. He began a concerted attack designed to drive what he termed these "lousy foreigners"[14] from Pitcairn. Hill tried to persuade Rachel Evans to leave her husband, John. He informed Nobbs that Hill himself would dictate curriculum and the method of teaching in the school; when the teacher refused, Hill fired Nobbs from the school.

On March 3, 1833, Hill wrote to the British consul at Valparaiso that, "I have experienced considerable trouble by the presence of two or three foreigners ... residing on the island; and till they are compelled to leave it, there will no peace upon Pitcairn's." A month later

Edward Quintal wrote to George Prichard in Tahiti, "Our good friend, Captain Hill, has been, and is doing all in his power for our general welfare; and I am sure his plans are well calculated to insure both our present and future happiness."[15] Nobbs complained, "As soon as a ship appeared off the island, a canoe was dispatched on board, forbidding the officers and crew coming to our houses, and we were threatened with stripes if we offered to go on board."[16] Hill ordered Buffet publicly flogged for adultery, an offense committed before Hill arrived. Hill next deprived Buffet's, Evans's and Nobbs's children of their land inheritance. *The Pitcairn Register*, maintained by Nobbs, omits any reference to Hill; in fact, the perennial litany of marriages, births, deaths, and ship arrivals is left unrecorded from December 1833 to April 1835.

Exiles

John Evans complained, "Mr. Hill and his colleagues were continually threatening the life of someone or other ... and had it not been for the opportune arrival of ... Stavers, murder would have been committed."[17] Evans referred to Captain R. T. Stavers of the British whaling ship *Tuscan*, which arrived on March 7, 1834. Dr. Bennett who was aboard the *Tuscan* observed that Joshua Hill's presence "had roused the worst passions of this hitherto peaceful race, and had divided the island into two factions ... with a rancour little short of open warfare." Bennett concluded, "The fraternal equality that had hitherto existed in their society was thus destroyed"; and "many of them asked to sail to Tahiti on the *Tuscan* to escape the unpleasantness that prevailed." Evans, Buffett and Nobbs, "who had suffered so much persecution during the late unhappy discords "were "glad to avail themselves of a passage to Tahiti."[18] The three exiles left their families behind.

At Tahiti, Captain Thomas Ebriel, whose bark *Maria* had brought Hill to Pitcairn, offered to take the three men to Lord Hood's Island in the Tuamotus, about a hundred miles north of Mangareva. Lord Hood's had been named by Captain Edward Edwards in 1791 when he discovered it in the Tuamotu Archipelago while searching for the mutineers. From Lord Hood's on June 12, 1834, Captain Ebriel brought the exiles home to pick up their wives — Dolly Buffett, Rachel Evans, and Sarah Nobbs — and their children. George Adams, having fallen out with Hill, went with them. The exiles knew by then that Lord Hood's Island was unsuitable for long-term habitation, so Ebriel took Evans and Nobbs and their families to Mangareva in the Gambier Islands. Buffett and George Adams returned to Tahiti. That Buffett, Evans and Nobbs opted to stay in the South Pacific and did not return to England is an indication of their faith that the authorities would come to realize that Hill was a fraud and depose him.

While in Mangareva, Nobbs and Evans witnessed the mass conversion of the islanders by Roman Catholic priests. On July 16, 1834, the ship *Peruvian* brought Father Honoré Laval and Father Caret of the Belgian Congregation of Picpus, as well as Father Colombian Murphy and a Polynesian interpreter from Rapa. In 1835 came Bishop Rouchouse and Father Cyprien Liausu accompanied by other priests and lay preachers. When Captain Morshead of H.M.S. *Dido* called at Mangareva in November 1835, he "found the French Protectorate flag flying on shore, and five French families, but no one in any official capacity. There are three Romish priests on the islands, Father Cyprien being at their head, who holds the king and natives in the most perfect subjection, both temporal and spiritual." Morshead arrived soon after an epidemic had killed several hundreds. The Polynesians had built several houses and "a handsome Romish church 200 feet long, with a double row of columns inside, and capable of containing a thousand persons." On the side of Mount Duff, Captain Morshead visited "a convent containing one hundred nuns and sixty children, whose interval between prayers and penance is filled up by trundling a distaff, and spinning native cotton, to supply a factory with a dozen hand looms at work."[19]

In 1836, Laval and Caret sailed to Tahiti with the intention of converting the people of the Society Islands to Roman Catholicism. When Queen Pomare, on the advice of missionary George Prichard, evicted the priests, the French claimed their nation had been insulted and used the incident as an excuse to intervene militarily. King Louis Philippe's government sent warships. In 1847, Queen Pomare was forced to agree to Tahiti's becoming a French protectorate.

Back on Mangareva, by 1839, Father Laval claimed to have baptized 1,568 people of the Gambier Islands — chiefly Mangareva. During his thirty-seven year ministry at Mangareva, Laval oversaw the erection of an astonishing 116 stone buildings. The work of the islanders in erecting these buildings was arduous. Building took time from planting, harvesting and fishing. The islanders were induced to dive for pearls to finance the ministry and its grandiose projects. Mass starvation resulted. During Laval's reign, the population fell from an estimated nine thousand to five hundred. In 1871, as a result, Bishop Monsignor Haussen removed Laval to Tahiti. There, he was declared insane. Laval died in 1880. The occasional tourist who arrives in Rikitea, Mangarava or in nearby Taravai marvels at the European-style churches and other buildings. These noble edifices, and the many graves, remain Laval's monument.

From exile the three aggrieved refugees petitioned the British naval command in Valparaiso, Chile, to send a ship to Pitcairn to forcibly remove Hill. Buffet detailed Hill's outrages in his appeal: "After Mr. Hill's beating me over the head, breaking it in two places, likewise my finger, I was suspended by my hands in the church and flogged until I was not able to walk home and [was] confined to my bed for two weeks...."[20] Evans complained that when he had asked Hill for a copy of the law depriving him of his lands, Hill "flew into a violent rage, and shortly after, your petitioner was dragged to the church, underwent a mock trial, no witnesses being allowed and received one dozen lashes with a cat-nine tails...." Evans said he had been confined to bed for ten days as a result.[21] Nobbs's letter to the British authorities in Valparaiso claimed he had been "in continued alarm for the lives of himself and family." When "several of the natives protested against his vicious conduct, Mr. Hill threatened to give them a flogging, and promised that soldiers would come from England and enslave them on their own land."[22]

A Dictator's Downfall

Island historian Rosalind Amelia Young wrote that Hill overreached his authority when he sought to punish two women whom he accused of spreading rumors about him. He called together his elders, sub-elders and cadets and the women. Leading the group in prayer, Hill pleaded, "If these women die the common death of all men, the Lord hath not sent me." Nobody in the room except Hill said "amen," thus signifying for the first time an outward display of public disapproval. Raging at the group, Hill "stood revealed before his followers in his true character, overzealous, revengeful, and tyrannical"[23]

When Joshua Hill threatened to execute twelve-year-old Charlotte Quintal for stealing yams, even his staunchest apologists began to regret his authority. When Arthur Quintal, Charlotte's father, physically defended his daughter's life by pushing the dictator to the floor and pointing a sword at him, Hill's reign was essentially over. Hill was allowed to live in the school house, lonely and without influence.

The islanders sent out letters on a passing ship, petitioning for Buffet, Evans and Nobbs to return. On September 16, 1834, Captain Charles Kendal of the American brig *Olivia*, on which Buffett had worked as a hand during his exile, brought the Buffett family and George Adams back to Pitcairn. At the request of the community, Kendal returned Evans and Nobbs on October 13, 1834. Hill protested but was essentially powerless to prevent their return. Rosalind Amelia Young stated that though the Buffett family arrived in good health, the Nobbses and Evanses "were extremely emaciated, owing to the poor food on which they were obliged to subsist" in Mangareva.[24]

On January 10, 1837, with the arrival of the British warship *Actaeon*, Hill was exposed once and for all as a charlatan. Hill had claimed to be a close cousin and intimate companion of the Duke of Bedford. Coincidentally, Lord Edward Russell, commander of the *Actaeon*, was the duke's son. Russell said he had never heard of Joshua Hill. Lord Russell had no specific orders to take Hill away. He ordered Hill to leave the island as soon as a ship was available to transport him.

On December 6, 1837, H.M.S. *Imogene* under command of Captain H. W. Bruce arrived. Captain Bruce wrote a detailed report to the Admiralty, calling their attention to the dissension on the island: "Most of the native men immediately came on board in their canoes though blowing fresh, with a tumbling swell, being rejoiced at the sight of an English Ship of War 'from home,' as they term England. They are a very kindly hospitable, and strikingly virtuous and correct, though among the natives it is to be regretted that two cases of deviation from the course of strict morality, have, not long since, occurred; and I am sorry to find that among the three English settlers, there have been cases perpetrated of deep, base, and disgraceful profligacy...." Captain Bruce recommended that a "competent Religious Instructor" and "a duly authorized person of character, intelligence and ability to preside over them and their interests...." be sent to the island. Without these men, "I should much fear that the approaches of depravity and wickedness will scarcely be effectively repeled from the state of society which affords so many temptations."

Bruce wrote, "I brought [Hill] away at his own request; he had made himself very obnoxious to the natives, having assumed a power and control over them," and although "his conduct was marked by the strictest moral integrity, his absence would result in harmony."[25] Hill apparently arrived aboard the *Imogene* in Valparaiso. He emerged later in England with a monetary claim against the government for six years' services rendered at Pitcairn.

H.M.S. *Fly* and British Protection

With Hill removed, peace returned to Pitcairn. George Hunn Nobbs was restored to his roles as *Register* keeper, unordained pastor, and schoolmaster. Nobbs recorded in his neat handwriting that on November 29, 1838, H.M.S. *Fly* arrived under the command of Captain Russell Elliott. According to a Pitcairn government history, "The dictatorship of Hill and increasing visits by American whalers ... brought the islanders to recognize their need for protection, and they prevailed upon Captain Elliott of H.M.S. *Fly* to draw up a brief constitution and a code of laws."[26] Captain Elliott may have wondered if he were overstepping his authority as commander of a rather minor sloop in committing the Royal Navy to

Circa 1850

The church and school, from a painting by Lieutenant Conway Shipley, 1848. John Adams, John Buffett, and then George Nobbs taught the children. In 1838, Pitcairn was the first entity in the British Empire to mandate compulsory education. Visitors reported the church to be filled with worshippers nearly every hour on Sundays.

protecting an entity which the British government had never claimed. For all intents, Pitcairn was a separate nation. Elliott's decision to take on an impecunious client for the empire could ostensibly be justified at the time by John Stuart Mill's dictum that the imperium, with its naval arm, ought to dedicate itself to "the service of others, than of itself."[27]

Islanders told a visitor that immediately before the *Fly*'s arrival, "half the ruffian crew of a whale ship were on shore for a fortnight, during which time, they offered every insult to the inhabitants, and threatened to violate any women whose protectors they could overcome by force, occasioning the necessary concentration of the men's strength for the personal protection of the females, and thereby great damage to their crops, which demanded their constant attention; taunting them that they had no laws, no country, no authority that they were to respect...."[28] Missionaries called whaling crews "boisterous, pleasure-seeking rabble" whose minds were focused "no higher than the grogshop and the brothel."[29] Islanders feared the return of those same men or another crew with evil intentions. The islanders were wise to ask for royal naval protection; Nobbs's *Register* tells us that from 1823 through 1838, seventy-one ships had stopped, some sending personnel ashore. The average was 4.43 ships each year.

The "constitution" signed aboard the *Fly* on November 30, 1838, provided that a magistrate be chosen annually on January 1, by islanders with over five years' residency — both male and female at least age eighteen — to carry on the community's administration. "There must be a school kept, to which all parents shall be obliged to send their children, who must previously be able to repeat the alphabet, and be of the age of from six to sixteen." George Hunn Nobbs, according to the law, was to preside over the school from seven in the morning until noon, Monday through Friday, and be paid a shilling per child per month — or the equivalent in yams, potatoes or plantains.[30] Thus Pitcairn became the first component of the British Empire to mandate female suffrage and the first to require compulsory education.

Notwithstanding the fact that he had served as chief elder to dictator Hill and had "stood by Hill to the last, when everyone else had deserted him," the first chief magistrate, elected unanimously, was Edward Quintal, "whose strong common sense and really excellent abilities recommended him as the fittest person to be nominated."[31] Quintal solemnly swore to "execute the duties of magistrate and chief ruler of Pitcairn's island ... by dispensing justice and settling any differences that may arise, zealously, fearlessly, and impartially; and that I will keep a register of my proceedings, and hold myself accountable for the due exercise of my office to Her Majesty the Queen of Great Britain, or her Representative. So help me God."[32] Captain William Waldegrave of the *Seringapatam* had written during his visit in 1830, "In time Edward Quintal, the best understanding in the island, will be chief; he possesses no book but the bible, but such knowledge has he drawn from it that he argues from facts stated therein, and thence arrives at conclusions, which will in time place him much above his fellows."[33]

Twelve years later, Walter Brodie, an Englishman stranded on Pitcairn, noted, "Many might suppose that the honour of the magistracy would be anxiously sought after; but such is not the case. Most of them, to use their own expression, would sooner give the whole community a feast, than be raised to so troublesome a dignity."[34] An elected councilor and a councilor appointed by the magistrate were to assist the magistrate. The captain of any Royal Navy ship that stopped could overrule the chief magistrate on behalf of Queen Victoria's government. Pitcairners consider their community part of the British Empire from 1838.

Laws for Dogs, Pigs, Goats, and Cats

With advice from the community, Captain Elliott wrote laws; these laws show us what was on the Pitcairners' minds in the late 1830s. Initial legislation focused largely on animals. Brought on the *Bounty*, goats had proliferated wild, providing meat, but also destroying young trees. The chief threat to goats was dogs; therefore, if a dog chased a goat, the owner of the dog paid a fine of a dollar and a half— an appreciable sum. Dollars were used rather than British pounds because most of the ships that stopped for food and water were American whalers. Because rats remained a menace, a law stated: "If any person under the age of ten years shall kill a cat, he or she shall receive corporal punishment. If any one, between the ages of ten and fifteen, kill a cat, he or she shall pay a fine of twenty-five dollars; half the fine to be given to the informer, the other half to the public. All masters of families convicted of killing a cat shall be fined fifty dollars...."[35] These were enormous sums.

If a swine were caught doing damage to a resident's crops, the farmer could keep the offending swine or he could collect damages from the owner. Anyone who killed white birds was fined a dollar for each bird slaughtered. Some laws applied to the most esoteric circumstances: "Any person without a pig-sty and wanting one, is allowed to cut green logs to make it with, if dry logs are not to be found." In another matter, "Squid ... is not allowed to be taken for food from off the rocks at the north end of the island, excepting by the owner of the rocks; but any one may take it for bait, when going fishing."[36]

In regard to all-important trade with whaling ships, it was forbidden to sell alcohol to crews or for crews to furnish strong drink to Pitcairners. Moreover, "No females are allowed to go on board of a foreign vessel, of any size or description, without the permission of the Magistrate; and in case the Magistrate does not go on board himself, he is to appoint four men to look after the females."[37]

Elliott's laws promoted sustainable ecology. Before cutting down a tree, even on one's own property, it was essential to obtain the magistrate's permission. Miro and purau wood were protected to the extent that their cutting was forbidden. These laws were to serve the islanders for the next forty-five years.

The decade that ended at the time the laws were enacted had been momentous for the community. They had lost their "father" and spiritual leader, John Adams. They had undergone what was for them a wrenching experience, the removal to Tahiti. On their return, mourning the loss of family members to disease, their polity was comandeered by a bombastic charlatan. By 1838, they saw clearly that their best interest was to give up their sovereignty by inviting British naval captains to rule over them. It proved to be a wise move. The next decade and a half would be better, though not without significant challenges. The next decade can be termed a Silver Age in the island's history.

CHAPTER 13

A Busy Port of Call: 1839–1849

The Whaling Industry

In the nineteenth century ships' crews came to the South Pacific Ocean from America and Europe to hunt sea otters, fur seals, sandalwood, bêche de mer, and whales. Pitcairn had none of these in any abundance, but the island became a victualing station for ships' crews. In the quarter century after the inhabitants' return from Tahiti, more than 350 ships stopped at Pitcairn. Most of these were whaling vessels.

American whalers, often absent from New England for three to five years at a time, made up the greatest number of these crews. Whalers sought to kill bowhead, right, humpback and gray whales, but sperm whales were most sought after. The sperm whale measured thirty to seventy feet and weighed thirty-five to sixty-five tons. The sperm whale could yield two thousand gallons of lubricating and illuminating oil, teeth, spermaceti (a fine oil), and ambergris — valued for its aroma. Men would lower whaleboats measuring twenty-eight by six feet and row as near to a whale as anyone would dare and throw harpoons into its side. New Englanders had hunted whales in the Atlantic from the founding of their colonies in the early seventeenth century and had become among the most proficient whalers in the world. Whaling flourished in the Pacific from about 1820 to 1860. In 1846, the American whaling fleet in the Pacific consisted of 736 vessels.[1] The whaling industry employed New England farm boys, water-front derelicts, and seasoned seamen; crew members included North American Indians, free Afro-Americans, and South Sea islanders.

Desperate for fresh food and water, crews often clashed with indigenous populations on islands which had never before been visited by Caucasians. Often a crew was attacked in revenge for atrocities perpetrated by a totally different ship's crew. For their part, the whalers took revenge against "the race and not individuals," killing indiscriminately.[2] These encounters were time consuming, sometimes deadly, and generally unproductive, and led whalers to seek reliable sources of supplies. Until the British restricted foreign vessels, the Bay of Islands ports in New Zealand's North Island were frequented by American whalers, as was Papeete in Tahiti; later Lahaina, Hilo, and Honolulu in the Sandwich Islands were the main ports. Some captains avoided Lahaina and Bay of Islands because to allow their crews ashore invited "desertion, venereal disease and mayhem."[3]

Pitcairn Island was enroute from Cape Horn to Pacific whaling grounds, and captains

PITCAIRN'S ISLAND.

View of Pitcairn, mid-nineteenth century. The island looks very similar today from a distance, but today there are fewer large trees. One can readily see that the terrain is steep and that flat land is at a premium. Courtesy of the Pitcairn Island Study Center, Pacific Union College, Angwin, California.

valued islanders who could trade using the English language and who were known for their scrupulous honesty. Pitcairners did not raise prices on their food and water to take advantage of starving crews, even when they themselves were suffering shortages. Captains looked forward to trading at Pitcairn because their men could not obtain alcohol or the sexual services of women on the island. Pitcairn was probably the only place in the Pacific that offered similar advantages to captains. Whalers such as the *Navigator* and the *Rose* out of Nantucket came at least six times each.

What is known about Pitcairn in the 1840s comes largely from reports of British naval officers, whaling captains and crews, and other visitors; some reports have been published and others preserved. *The Pitcairn Register*, maintained by George Hunn Nobbs, continued to provide a carefully maintained record of births, deaths, ship arrivals, and other significant events. We know much about this period through the writings of islander Rosalind Amelia Young; she lived on Pitcairn Island in the generation immediately following and learned about island life in mid-century from her elders. During the 1840s, according to Young, "Scarcely anything occurred to disturb the tranquil round of life that the inhabitants enjoyed, and day after day passed along in quiet monotony, broken only by the arrival of some passing ship."[4] Rosalind was right about the monotony, but she neglected to add that it was periodically broken by compelling events. The first of these was the visit of the former president of Chile.

H.M.S. *Sparrowhawk*

In 1839, thirteen ships stopped, more than in any single previous year. On November 9, 1839, H.M.S. *Sparrowhawk* under Captain J. Shepherd stayed long enough for officers to come ashore. In the ship's boat with Shepherd came the highest ranking dignitary to visit

Pitcairn to that time, General Ramón Friere, the former dictator of Chile. Having helped José de San Martín liberate Chile from Spain, Friere was instrumental in overthrowing President Bernardo O'Higgins in February 1823. O'Higgins, too liberal for the tastes of Santiago's wealthy classes, sailed to Peru and Friere assumed the presidency. Friere named his own cabinet, dismissed the congress and ruled by decree. He was overthrown in 1827 by still another dictator, Francisco Pinto. Enroute to Sydney, Friere had come to visit Nobbs, whom he had known eighteen years previously while Nobbs served under Admiral Thomas Cochrane in the wars for Chilean independence.[5]

Lieutenant James Lowry of H.M.S. *Sparrowhawk* found 102 people, "a great part of them children, and as fine a race as ever I saw. Some of the girls and young women were very pretty, and would be considered beauties in Old England, all were good-looking."[6] Lowry noted that girls married at fourteen or fifteen and the men under twenty. "There is not such another happy little community in the world," Lieutenant Lowry wrote.[7] Lowry knew of "only one old maid on the island, and she is now nearly fifty, and is as cross and crabbed as any old maid need be; she rails against the early marriages heartily."[8]

"A Serious Altercation"

According to *The Pitcairn Register*, the "monotony" was broken on May 2, 1840, when "A serious altercation took place between Edward Quintal sen. and John Evans sen.;— the latter receiving several bruises on the head, back and throat and several scratches on the breast." Observers noted Quintal's lingering animosity toward Evans, Buffett and Nobbs, the three outsiders. Evans could not have forgotten Quintal's position as physical enforcer under Joshua Hill's dictatorship, leading to Evans's exile. These seething hatreds served to mar what was otherwise an idyllic society. However, the fact that Nobbs troubled himself to preserve details of this bout in the *Register* is an indication that it was a unique — or at the very least rare — instance of physical violence between Pitcairn men in what Lieutenant Lowry had proclaimed the happiest community in the world.

Mr. Heath of the L.M.S.

Throughout Polynesia — in Tahiti, Hawaii, New Zealand, Samoa, Tonga, the Cooks and in lesser island groups — nineteenth-century missionaries came and lived for decades, converting heathen. Pitcairn never had a long-term missionary presence because it had no heathens in need of conversion. On November 9, 1840, the missionary packet *Camden* under Captain Morgan arrived, bringing Rev. Mr. Heath of the London Missionary Society. Mr. Heath was rowed ashore and preached a sermon in the afternoon "which was listened to with breathless attention."[9] During his four-day stay, Rev. Heath examined the fifty-one children at school for their attainments, gave a Bible to each household, and upon his return to England, sent to the community more religious publications, school texts, and school supplies.

H.M.S. *Curacoa*

H.M.S. *Curacoa* arrived on August 18, 1841. Not only did the ship's surgeon, Dr. Gunn, treat a score of influenza victims, but the crew was able to pull up part of the *Bounty's* timbers. Islanders carved curios from the oak hull to send to friends in England and to sell aboard visiting ships. For her part, Isabella, widow of mutiny leader Fletcher Christian, sent a piece of tapa cloth to the widow of midshipman Peter Heywood. Four years later the islanders were "employed fishing up two of the *Bounty*'s guns ... and ... on Saturday last one of these guns resumed its original vocation; at least the innocuous portion of it, to wit, belching forth fire and smoke, and causing the island to reverberate with its bellowing: the other gun is condemned to silence having been spiked by someone of the *Bounty*'s crew."[10]

John Buffett Remembers

In 1845, John Buffett sought passage from Pitcairn in order to visit friends and family in England, but he got only as far as the Sandwich Islands. Unable to find passage onward, he returned in frustration to Pitcairn aboard the whale ship *Hannibal*. His brief layover in Hawaii is important because, while waiting for a ship, he gave a long interview to the proprietor of *The Friend*, a periodical published in Honolulu. He was able to relate events that occurred during his residence of two decades on Pitcairn and events which occurred before his arrival, about which he had been told by Adams and the Tahitian women who had landed in 1790. This interview added to knowledge of early island history.

Buffett said that when he met Adams in 1823, Adams was "a man about 5 feet 6 inches high, stout made and very corpulent, he was dressed in a shirt and trousers."[11] Buffett explained the strained relationship between Mr. Christian and John Adams and the reverence with which Christian was regarded by other islanders:

> John Adams informed me that on one occasion he found the consequence of not showing him respect! The case was this; having allowed the hogs to run at large, it became necessary to fence in the cultivated land, and each man had his portion to keep in repair. Adams' part being out of order he was called upon to put it into repair which he refused to do. Christian told Adams that if he caught his hogs coming through the fence he would shoot them. Adams replied, "Then I will shoot you." He had no sooner made this reply than they seized and bound him, and sentenced him to be set adrift on a plank in the ocean, which sentence would have been put into execution had it not been for Christian.[12]

Buffett gave Adams full credit for training the second generation in morals and religion, but Buffett repeated what Will McCoy's son had told him: "They could not believe for some time that Adams understood what he read, but they thought (to use his own words) 'he spoke out of his own head.'"[13] All but two or three of the first generation could read; they owed their ability to the recently literate Adams.

Storm

On April 16, 1845, the "monotony" to which Rosalind Amelia Young referred was broken still again. "By midnight a perfect typhoon raged above and around us; the whole concave of the heavens was in a continued blaze and the roar of the thunder ... was incessant," wrote Nobbs in the *Register*. The following morning an islander told Nobbs that "a part of the island had given way and was going into the sea." The wind and rain had uprooted trees and shrubs and caused an avalanche. Nobbs saw thick mud gliding into a valley. Three hundred coconut trees had been uprooted and washed into the Pacific. Four thousand plantain trees were lost. Looking down into the landing at Bounty Bay, the islanders were horrified that boats and boat houses had vanished. Rocks had slipped into the harbor so that a passage no longer existed. A thousand yams awaiting harvest had disappeared. Landslides disrupted fishing. "The fact is," commented Nobbs, "from this date until August we shall be pinched for food."[14]

1848: *Calypso*

On March 9, 1848, HM corvette *Calypso* sailed to Pitcairn and its commander, Henry Worth, came ashore, bringing back John Buffett from the Sandwich Islands. Also aboard were gifts: two whaleboats, a corn mill, a medicine chest and other items. According to the *Shipping Gazette* of Sydney, May 26, 1848, Worth said, "I examined their laws, added a few to them, assembled them in church and addressed them. It was really affecting to see these primitive people, both old and young ... looking up to me, almost devouring all I said, with eager attention, and with scarcely a dry eye amongst them. I found a moisture collecting in my own which I could scarcely restrain.... Crime appears to be unknown, and if there is really true happiness on earth, it surely is theirs."[15] Worth concluded, "I would rather have gone there than to any part of the world. They are the most interesting, contented, moral and happy people that can be conceived."[16]

Dividing the Land

Men and unmarried women spent their time cultivating their gardens and plantation areas uphill from Adamstown. Because Fletcher Christian had adopted the English legal fact of private property rather than the Tahitian custom of communal property, disparities in holdings had become significant by the 1840s. After Christian divided the land in nine portions among white men, their children then divided the land once more among themselves. The third generation again divided their inheritances. As Captain Wood of H.M.S. *Pandora* explained in 1849, this on-going division "led to evils they did not anticipate; for instance, one of the original settlers had a family of eleven; his ninth was therefore divided into eleven parts. Again, one of his daughters married and has a family of eleven so that her children will have but the eleventh of her eleventh portion; whereas, another of the first lot, who has only one son and daughter (the latter of whom survives unmarried), left by the same rule the whole of his ninth to her, so that she now has much land as twenty-two of the first named family."[17]

Happy Birthday Queen Victoria

Various visitors observed that Queen Victoria had no more loyal subjects than the descendants of the mutineers. On May 24, 1848, for the first time, the islanders celebrated Queen Victoria's birthday. They dressed in their best Sunday clothes, put on shoes, and assembled near the church. George Hunn Nobbs headed the organizing committee and arranged that the *Bounty*'s old gun, dredged up from the bay three years previously, fired a salute to Her Majesty. Men fired their muskets into the air. A bell, given to the islanders by the crew of

H.M.S. *Basilisk*, was rung continuously while "cheer after cheer rang from the throats of the whole community...."

Nobbs wrote a song suitable for the celebration, sung to the tune of "The Girl I Left Behind Me." The community members sang:

> We'll fire the gun, the *Bounty*'s gun,
> And set the bell a-ringing,
> And give three cheers for England's Queen,
> And three for Pitcairn's Island.[18]

The day concluded with a public dinner, various sports, and dancing to the music of a drum and tambourine.

A Description of the Islanders in 1849

On July 9, 1849, Captain James Wood arrived in command of HM brig *Pandora*. Wood was impressed by the "simple minded hearty good will with which we have all been received." The arrival of a ship, whether whaler, trader or Royal Navy vessel, was a major event. Wood noted that the people "gave themselves up with the most complete and childish joy to seeing a man-of-war off their island," and he saw his officers "decorated with garlands, not only round their hats but their necks."[19] On greeting the ship's company, the first question the residents asked was about the health of Queen Victoria. When satisfied that the monarch was well, they got on with trade, giving curios and food for textiles, used clothing, soap, illumination oil, and metal goods.[20]

Captain Wood described what he perceived to be the idyllic life of the inhabitants: "They rise before the sun, eat when hungry, sleep when tired, and in fact are barred by no rules as to the disposal of their time, except on Sunday when they attend church twice. On that day alone Mr. Nobbs winds his watch and sets it, so as to ensure punctuality; but he prefers the sun as a guide."[21] Wood noted that before meals, "in the midst of their laughter and glee, before they touched any thing they joined their hands, and in a devout and unaffected way prayed for a blessing on their food. This is their invariable custom, and like much we saw there, read a lesson to us all which we shall not easily forget."

"The young people," he wrote, "are generally good-looking, some of them very pretty; all of them have good eyes and teeth, and the most engaging expression of countenance I ever saw...." The islanders were not given to sartorial elegance: "Their dress is as varied as their methods of obtaining it," Wood observed. [T]he hair, which is very long (a dark brown or black), is kept clean, neat, and very glossy by the aid of cocoa-nut-oil, which they contrive to scent very agreeably with the orange blossom. It is turned up behind in an ingenious manner, which needs no comb or other aid to keep it in its place."

Occasionally a ship arrival allowed islanders to trade for European clothing, and when that was possible, women's dress was transformed. Intermittently exposed breasts were now encased in modest English blouses. "The women wear a full petticoat," noted Captain Wood, "and above that a loose gown, with a handkerchief thrown over the shoulders. A wreath of flowers is often worn round the head." Men's dress was practical for their work, which often took them to the Landing and onto boats. "The men wear short trousers, the legs of which are cut off two or three inches above the knee. A shirt, and a cap or hat, complete their costume. They seldom wear shoes or stockings, except on Sundays."

George Hunn Nobbs took Captain Wood in a number of homes. Wood wrote:

They are all lodged alike; the houses are built of wood, and show progressive improvement in the mechanical part of them which would not disgrace an European tradesman. They consist of one long room, divided by two or more partitions, and are raised upon huge sleepers placed upon large stones, to clear them some two or two and half feet from the ground ... their roofs have a moderately high pitch, and are formed of the pandanis leaf, which being bent over a long light stick forms a kind of board. Several of these laid nearly close form an excellent thatch, lasting from five to seven years. The side opposite the windows is occupied by bed-places, which are similar to the sleeping-berths in the old packets.

Bed clothes were all made of tapa and most homes were decorated with prints or mirrors on the walls.

Work and sports provided exercise, Wood noted, which, with their diet, accounted for the islanders' healthy lifestyle. Children were taught to swim from an early age and they learned to "thread the difficult passes of the rocks like so many young goats," barefoot like the adults. Visitors marveled at the strength of the healthy men and women. In 1843, Lieutenant Edward Belcher wrote that George Young and Edward Quintal were able to carry "without inconvenience" a kedge anchor, two sledge hammers, and an armourer's anvil, "amounting to upwards of six hundredweight." Quintal once carried a twenty-eight-foot boat by himself. Captain Wood remarked that an eighteen-year-old woman normally carried a hundred pounds of yams "over hills and precipitous places"; and that a sixty-year-old resident carried the *Pandora*'s six-foot-tall surgeon up three hundred feet from the Landing to the Market Place. Captain Wood made it up the slippery slope of the Hill of Difficulty only with the help and support of "Jemima Young, a stout and good-natured girl, who seized my arm and almost carried me up without the aid of my feet, and this without any apparent effort on her part."

Ship's officers normally visited the school as part of their island tour. The building, fifty-six feet by twenty feet, and filled with slates, books and maps, was described by Wood as "furnished with cross-benches, fitted with ink-stands, etc,; and at the upper end a square compartment is formed by the benches, and a table and seat for the master, and against the end is the pulpit or reading-desk for the school-room is the church on Sundays."[22] In 1847, a student described his academic week to a ship's captain:

We attend school five days in the week, five hours each day. Our routine of school duties is as follows:— namely, commence with prayer and praise; conclude with the same. Monday [Tuesday and Thursday], recital of weekly tasks, reading the Holy Scriptures, writing, arithmetic, and class spelling. Wednesday, reading in history and geography, transcribing select portions of Scripture, &c. And on Friday, which is the busiest day of the week, transcribing words with their definitions from Walker's dictionary; read hymns, or rather devotional and moral poetry; repeat Watt's and the Church Catechism; arithmetic tables, &c, &c.; and emulative spelling concludes the whole.[23]

A description of the school's master, George Hunn Nobbs, survives from the mid–1840s; it was written during the visit of seaman John A. States aboard a whaler. States saw Mr. Nobbs as "a sleepy looking little old man, dressed out in black pants with pumps, and white cotton stockings, a sack coat of drab and all surmounted with a belltopped beaver, the brim of which was about half an inch wide; he never took notice of any of our crew, but made himself acquainted with our officers, thinking I suppose, that a foremast hand was not worthy of notice."[24] Because parents paid a shilling a month in produce or labor for each child in school, some named schoolmaster Nobbs as their child's godfather, a relationship which won them exemption from fees.

Another visitor, Rev. William Armstrong, wrote in October 1849, "It has never been my lot to witness a community more entitled to admiration and respect...."[25] Captain Wood of HM *Pandora* wrote, "I must say in common with all on board, I felt more regret in parting with the Pitcairn Islanders than I had in parting with any one since leaving England."[26]

A Tradition Invented

On January 23, 1850, the sixtieth anniversary of their ancestors' burning George III's ship, the islanders observed the first "*Bounty* Day." "At daylight," Nobbs recorded, "one of the *Bounty*'s guns was discharged and wakened" the entire island. Following divine services and the reading of letters of congratulations from Her Majesty's government, and following a community dinner, all assembled to give "three cheers for Queen Victoria, three for the Government at Home [London], three for the Magistrates here, three for absent friends, three for the Ladies and three for the community in general...."[27] So enjoyable was the holiday that the islanders vowed to do it again in 1851. They have continued to celebrate *Bounty* Day on or about January 23, nearly every year.

Six months later the final living tie to the mutiny was severed with the passing of Susannah [Teraura], the last surviving *Bounty* passenger. She had been Edward Young's consort. She had given birth to Mathew Quintal's child. Susannah later married Thursday October Christian, first born of the second generation, sixteen years her junior. She bore Thursday October six children. Susannah had lived on Pitcairn Island for sixty years.

If the commune of innocents that flourished under the paternal guidance of John Adams may be characterized as Pitcairn's Golden Age, certainly the period of the 1840s and early 1850s that earned lavish praise from all visitors for the inhabitants' honesty, piety, and genuine humility was the island's Silver Age. One crew member told an admiral, "Sir, I expect if one of our fellows was to misbehave himself here, we should not leave him alive."[28]

But all was not and could never be perfect on Pitcairn Island. In its Silver Age, disease and accidents continued to be scourges that marred the islanders' arcadian existence and reminded them of their isolation and mortality.

CHAPTER 14

Emergency Ward

Whalers and Disease

Pitcairn Island in the mid-nineteenth century had no emergency ward, but if one had actually existed, it would have been a busy place. When there were no outside visitors, the Pitcairners were generally a healthy community. They consumed a largely vegetable and fruit diet with occasional protein from fish, pigs, and goats. In their daily work and play they had plenty of exercise. Fresh air, lack of stress and the security of close family relationships kept most well. But, the 1840s saw the arrival of many more ships — forty-nine in 1846 and forty-seven in 1849, with an average of seventeen per year from 1841–50. Most were whalers. Most whalers were American. On the one hand, more ships meant more trade and an improved standard of living. On the other, crews had a deleterious effect on the islanders. When they brought money, tools, clothing and other useful objects, they also brought disease.

Isolated as they were, three hundred miles from another human community, the islanders had little immunity to whatever flu-like disease was current. Tightly packed ships served as incubators for germs that affected crew members and their officers. Disease was rowed ashore and island families took turns having the ship's captain stay in their homes; they considered hosting him an honor; other families provided sleeping space for a ship's other officers. Crew were not usually welcome ashore. Entire Pacific island populations were affected by these same diseases and, in addition, for many in those indigenous communities, by venereal disease as well.

Little help was available from professional physicians. Although French and British naval ships had, according to law, to carry doctors, Americans, according to whaling industry historian Granville Allen Mawrer, "were made of sterner stuff." Every seaman on well organized whalers had an amount deducted from his wages as a contribution to the ship's medicine chest. To make dispensing easier for captains, each medicine in the chest was numbered instead of being identified by its baffling Latin or Greek name. The captain could read what number and in what quantity to administer for specific symptoms. Thus, crews were dependent on an untrained man deciphering the correct portion of the correct medicine for the malady. One can only hope that the story of the captain who had run out of number 9, and went ahead to combine equal amounts of 4 and 5 to make up for it, is apocryphal.[1]

The first mention in the *The Pitcairn Island Register* of disease on the island was recorded in the winter of 1841. Schoolmaster George Hunn Nobbs wrote: "The number of sick continue to increase[;] there are more than fifty cases — there is not a sufficient number of persons in health to dig the yams out of the ground (this being the harvest time).... The school house is shut up.— And almost every house has the appearance of an hospital. Truly the hand of God is upon us, O Lord in wrath remember mercy." And five days later, on a Sunday, he wrote: "But no service this day the number of sick continues to increase although there are a few convalescents, the epidemic is fever attended with a distressing cough."[2] Four days later Nobbs reported the death of a resident. Two weeks after that influenza claimed the life of Isabella, next to last survivor of the original settlers who had arrived aboard the *Bounty*. Though Isabella's age was uncertain, she assured interviewers that she recalled perfectly Captain Cook's first arrival at Tahiti in April 1769.

The following year, 1842, brought thirty-one ships, and in early January of 1843, Nobbs reported fever that begins "with a slight shivering, succeeded by violent pain in the loins and head and much febrile heat — emetics and application of warm water to the feet, hands and loins are the principal remedies applied, and under the Divine blessing, have been attended with beneficial results."[3] Nobbs himself was so ill that school was discontinued for the duration.

On July 30, 1844, the surgeon of HM cutter *Basilisk* vaccinated sixty islanders in an attempt to protect them from disease, but within two weeks Nobbs noted, "All our hopes concerning the vaccination are at an end, it has turned out a complete failure." And so it went. Nobbs wrote of disease exacerbated in 1844 by weeds that "overrun the island, worms [that] infest the potatoes and there is a comet in sight."[4] By the following year, Nobbs felt able to account for influenza outbreaks:

> I do not think the fever was infectious; and though in the space of six days not less than sixty out of one hundred and twenty two were attacked yet I attribute it solely to the peculiar state of the atmosphere: whenever we have been visited by this epidemick the circumstances, as respects the weather have been invariably the same. A long drought succeeded by two or three weeks of wet; and the wind settling into the north west; in fact a north west wind is always the precursor of rheumatism, catarrh, and slight febrile affection.

Nobbs, who prided himself in acting as doctor as well as teacher, even when he was himself contagious, went on to counsel against bleeding; rather, "vomits are the sovereign remedy for certainly no community of persons secrete greater quantities of bile than the inhabitants of this island."[5]

In a *Register* summary of the year 1849, Nobbs recorded that, "The inhabitants, with scarcely an exception have suffered severely from sickness during the months of August, September and October. The school was discontinued, the children were too sick to attend and the teacher (thank God efficiently) was employed in ministering from house to house." The influenza "was more severe and considerably modified from that of former years — violent spasms in the stomach and epigastric regions were frequent in all stages of the complaint."

Whether crew members came ashore or islanders visited the ships to trade, the results were the same. Finally, in 1849, Nobbs seemed to see for the first time a connection between the meeting of diseased sailors, packed closely together for long periods, and islanders devoid of immunity to whatever flu was current in any given year. Nobbs wrote on August 30, 1849, "The major part of the inhabitants are sick — probably they have received an accession of disease from the bark *Elizabeth Archer* from Sydney which touched here a few days since: some of her passengers were unwell at the time and our epidemic has assumed a different type." Nobbs went on to express delight at "the wonderful occurrence" of so many ships arriving—

many on their way to the California's Sierra Nevada range to take part in the gold rush that began in 1848.[6]

Even when the islanders began to suspect the origin of their sicknesses, they could hardly have afforded to forbid the arrival of ships. Pitcairners spent their spare time carving, weaving and plaiting souvenirs to trade. They cut fire wood, hauled water, and grew food specifically to barter for goods which had become necessities. Ships then, as today, are Pitcairners' umbilical cord to the rest of the world and source of all that is not available in their limited environment.

Infant and Child Mortality

As was true through much of the rest of the world in the nineteenth century, a number of babies on Pitcairn died shortly after their birth. Nobbs inscribed in the *Register* in 1839: "Decr 3rd Margaret McCoy delivered of a male child which died shortly after birth Decr 4th The above mentioned infant interred."[7]

Accidents

Accidents occurred to a number of Pitcairners. Accidents were the banner headlines of Nobbs's *Pitcairn Island Register*. Accidents loomed so large in their lives that Pitcairners named geographical locations for fatal and serious mishaps: Where Dan Fall, Johnny Fall, McCoy's Drop, Tom Off, Where Dick Fall. In addition, one can hike to Where Freddie Fall, Break im Hip, Where Warren Fall and, finally, Oh Dear.[8]

People who toppled into the sea while balancing on precarious precipices were not the only victims of accidents. The *Register* gives us a summary of some incidents. A hazard of the South Seas is falling coconuts; one conked George Nobbs' wife on the head in 1840, causing a contusion. Two weeks later Moses Young fell forty feet from a coconut tree, "and was but slightly injured."[9] Lockjaw claimed John Quintal in 1838; he had punctured his foot while attempting to catch a goat. In 1842, George Adams fell from a tree, injuring his back severely, and two months later fifteen-month-old Stephen Christian was "dreadfully scalded" when he overturned a pot of boiling water.[10] Four years later Levi Quintal, age one and some months, caught his clothing on fire in the cook house and died of his burns during the evening.

The accident most painful for George Nunn Hobbs to record took place on February 20, 1847. While his son, Ruben Nobbs, "was out in the mountains shooting goats his foot slipped and he let fall his musket which exploded and wounded him severely," the father wrote. "The ball entered a very little below the hip joint and passing downwards came through on the inside of the thigh about half way between the groin and the knee." On the following day, "the men and grown lads have formed themselves into three watches to attend his wants by day and night. It is most gratifying to his parents to see the esteem in which their son is held." The surgeon from H.M.S. *Spy* pronounced that there was little danger to the boy, although "a narrower escape from death never came beneath his notice."[11]

In 1847, one-year-old Emma Young fell into a fire and was badly burned. Mathew McCoy was severely bruised later in the year when his canoe broke up in violent surf on the west side of the island. In 1848, William McCoy stepped on "a small pointed stick which entered among the sinews of the third and fourth toes and broke off considerably below the surface." Nobbs injected laudanum into the wound and applied a poultice made of bread. McCoy's pain was so bad, and no anesthetic being available, Nobbs was unable to extract the wood. "Things went on in this train several days — the patient suffering severe pain in his foot, his groin and the lower part of his belly."[12] McCoy began to experience pain in the back of the neck and stiffness in his jaws. Eleven days after the accident his jaws tightened and closed. He died the same day of lockjaw, age thirty-eight. Something similar happened to five-year-old William Wilburn Quintal, who died after stepping on a thorn; the infection led to lockjaw.

In 1849, Arthur Quintal fell from a rock, injuring his ribs badly, but as he did not die from the fall, no geographical location is named for him. In 1853, three men out fishing in a whaleboat were seriously injured when a gun discharged accidentally.

In January 1853, during a visit of H.M sloop *Virago* sailing from Callao, Peru, tragedy struck three men. Aboard was B. Toup Nicolas, Esq., British consul at Raiatea; he recalled that "we were about to get under weigh, when our attention was arrested by the firing of the *Bounty*'s gun in farewell salute. Scarcely had the sound died away, when it was succeeded by what we at first took to be cheers; but which, alas! proved to be shrieks from the women and children along the cliffs.... [w]e could see women carrying two forms along the cliffs towards the houses, by which feared that some fatal accident had occurred."[13] Rosalind Amelia Young explained that "The ramrod used on the occasion was an old, smoothly-planed rafter made from the wood of the cocoanut tree, very hard, and which had been used in building. Unknown to those in attendance was a nail in the rafter. This, coming in contact with the gun, already heated by the sun, caused the powder to ignite before all was ready."[14] Nobbs wrote: "Matthew McCoy was blown away several feet from the gun, his right arm dreadfully shattered, his body burnt in several parts and his whole system received a most severe shock. Charles D. Christian was badly wounded in both legs and also slightly burnt. William Evans received a violent shock and was slightly wounded and burnt."[15] Surgeons from the *Virago* hurried back to shore and amputated McCoy's arm; he died within a few hours. The other two men survived. The crew took up a collection and were able to donate thirty pounds to McCoy's widow and children.

Later the same year Sarah McCoy broke her collarbone and fractured her jaw in a severe fall. In 1853 Macy Quintal threw a knife into his brother's right side, but the boy healed and survived. The next year Frederick Young suffered a cut from a chisel on his foot. Thinking nothing of it, he went fishing and walking. The following day Frederick suffered stiffness in the neck, spinal pains and muscle contractions. Nobbs, acting as physician, recorded, "ten grs of calomel combined with two of opium was immediately administered to him the wound was probed very gently, & a bit of lint wetted with turpentine was inserted and a pumpkin posit placed over all as an emollient." Nobbs's care notwithstanding, "the spasmodic contractions increasing in frequency and force so much so that at times he would start from a recumbent position to a sitting one without the slightest premonition."[16] Nobbs finally placed the wounded foot in a bath of wood ashes and very hot water (as hot as was bearable) for forty minutes, during which time Frederick fainted only twice. At this point, the 1790–1854 *Register* ends.

Like people throughout much of the nineteenth-century world, Pitcairners suffered due to ignorance of both cause and treatment of diseases. They were dependent on visiting ships for practicing physicians; on the other hand, many physicians before the twentieth century hastened the death of their patients, so the lack of a full-time professional may well have been a blessing for at least some. Islanders suffered accidents because so much of their land was perilously steep, because they went everywhere without shoes, because of boating accidents, because of gun accidents, or because of the law of gravity's application to weighty coconuts. Disease and accidents were the price they paid to live on lovely, lonely Pitcairn Island.

CHAPTER 15

Before the Separation

Stranded

The most memorable visit of the forty-seven ships that came to Pitcairn in 1850 was that of the bark *Noble*. On March 24, it hove to only briefly for food and water. The *Noble*'s passengers were eager to dash into California's Mother Lode to make their fortunes by plucking large gold nuggets out of streams. Passengers Walter Brodie, Albert Taylor, Samuel Vaile, Hugh Carleton, and Frenchman Charles Baron de Thierry came ashore to see what life was like among the 156 inhabitants. When they looked beyond Bounty Bay they were astonished to watch the *Noble* sail off without them. Months later, after he had made his way to California, Walter Brodie confronted the ship's master, Captain Parker, when the *Noble* anchored in San Francisco Bay. Parker claimed that weather conditions at Pitcairn made it inconvenient to wait for the five men to reboard. Brodie found that a poor excuse.

Through the Eyes of Walter Brodie

The five were marooned, their only "worldly possessions consisting of the clothes we stood up in...."[1] Brodie decided to make the best of the situation. During his two-week stay Brodie learned all he could about Pitcairn Island and its residents, and when he returned to England after an arduous journey by way of San Francisco, Panama, Havana and New York, he wrote a book —*Pitcairn's Island and the Islanders in 1850*. To reward his hosts for being "the most moral and religious island in the world, and amongst the most kind-hearted, hospitable, and generous islanders ever met with," Brodie attached a notice to each book inviting purchasers to donate money for extra copies to be sent to Pitcairn. Islanders were to sell these donated copies to passengers and crew of visiting ships and use the profits for their own benefit.[2]

Brodie's description offers the most complete and discerning view of the community at mid-century that is available. Brodie wrote that after "ascending a very steep hill at an angle of forty-five degrees, which was very slippery after the rain ... and then getting over a style, which was placed to prevent the cattle from approaching the settlement, we came to the market-place, a small open space surrounded by cocoa-nut trees; and a few hundred yards farther, came to the village, to which the inhabitants have not at present given a name."[3] Brodie found a community that was "the realization of Arcadia, or what we had been accustomed to suppose had existence only in poetic imagination — the golden age; all living in one family, a commonwealth of brothers and sisters...." Brodie wrote that "there never was, and perhaps never will be, another community that can boast of so high a tone of morality, or more firmly rooted religious feelings," than the Pitcairners.[4]

Brodie noted that, as in many Polynesian communities, "The children appear to be more nursed by their relations than by their mothers, which makes it often difficult to distinguish the married from the unmarried," except that "A wreath of flowers round the head denotes their being unmarried."[5] "In the course of conversation with some of the girls, whilst feasting upon cocoa-nuts, I spoke to them about their beauty; when one of them observed she did not think I was an Englishman. I asked with some curiosity what could have led her to such a conclusion, and was informed by the fair damsel in question, that I flattered too much to be British born."[6]

Brodie described houses forty to fifty feet long, fifteen feet wide and thirteen feet high. The only piece of glass on the island, a port taken from the *Bounty*, served as a window in George Hunn Nobbs's house. Brodie attended divine services twice on Sunday in the church-schoolhouse that could seat two hundred. Mr. Nobbs presided and held a Bible class every Wednesday evening in his home. As did many other visitors, Brodie noted that everyone thanked God before and after each meal.

Although the island was luxuriant, Brodie found agricultural methods primitive and the farmers "totally unversed in the mysteries of subsoil ploughing, and ignorant of the virtues of guano, all their field-work is performed with the hoe...." Nevertheless, they produced abundant food. When a vessel arrived, school was dismissed and everyone collected food and curios to trade. Then, "the provisions that she may require are brought — Mr. Nobbs taking an account of what each family contributes. As all are entitled to share alike in the benefit of trade, no one is suffered to bring more than his proportion of the gross quantity required...."[7] For their families' profits, men made walking sticks and wooden boxes, while women plaited hats and baskets from pandanus leaves. "They sell as many of all the above as they can make, every person coming on shore wishing to carry away some memorial from this interesting island."[8] To reach the visiting ships, "they seldom go off to a whaling vessel in a boat — using a canoe generally...."[9] Brodie noted twenty canoes; canoes were used for fishing as well. Each held two people and were light enough to be carried to and from shore by one man.

Learning to Sing

Another stranded passenger, Mr. Carleton, gave the people much-needed singing lessons. John Adams had taught his flock to sing what church hymns he recalled, but the results were monotonous because Adams knew only one tune. When John Buffet arrived in 1823, he introduced a few more tunes. Yet, "The effect produced by the congregation, singing without regard to time or tune, was so discordant and jarring that Mr. Carleton, the supercargo, declared the sounds grating upon his ears." According to Rosalind Young, he complained to John Buffett. Buffett asked him to try to train a group of singers. Fortuitously, Baron de Thierry produced a tuning fork he happened to have at the time in his pocket. Carleton began his arduous task immediately and trained twenty-six females and thirty-one males every evening. A song they began vocal training with went:

> "My wife's dead, so here her lie;
> She's at rest, and so am I."

Rosalind Young judged that in a short time they succeeded in producing good music "beyond their highest hopes."[10]

Brodie recalled that one evening, "At 8 p.m. Carleton gave an extra singing-lesson.... Edward Quintal brought a fiddle; he had picked up some hornpipe and reel tunes by ear on board ship, which he really played with great spirit, and the true artistic twang, not omitting the stamp and wriggle, or the grind upon the fourth string. Some of the islanders danced very well, not waltzes certainly, but reels. The women never dance." After hours of singing, dancing, blind man's bluff, "and other innocent games, in which the ladies joined," the guests departed at two in the morning.[11]

After only two weeks' instruction, Brodie "heard them ... singing among themselves in the open air trios and quartettos for the most part performed in chorus, during the greater part of the night." In fact, when Carleton departed with Brodie, they were "sufficiently advanced to be able to pursue the study [of singing] without assistance."[12] For years afterward, the singers repeated the songs Carleton had taught them. Admiral Fairfax Moresby's son and secretary, Fortescue Moresby, wrote in the early 1850s that "really I have never heard any church singing in any part of the world that could equal it, except at cathedrals...."[13] Another visitor wrote in 1852: "I doubt much whether any church in England, excepting cathedrals, can boast of such a good choir."[14] When in 1853, the islanders sang "The Sailor-Boy's Early Grave" to B. Toup Nicolas, Esq., British consul to Raiatea, Nicolas wrote that "The voices of the Islanders are both powerful and sweet; and the thrill of rare and unexpected pleasure I experienced on hearing them sing the above song, was never surpassed, not even when listening to Jenny Lind."[15]

Their descendants have continued to make the most of Carleton's training, serenading departing passengers and crews with sweet and sentimental songs:

> Now one last song we'll sing
> Goodbye, goodbye
> Time moves on rapid wings
> Goodbye, goodbye, goodbye
> ...
> We part but hope to meet again
> Goodbye, goodbye, goodbye.

A Very Adventurous Baron

On April 11, Carleton and Brodie were rowed out beyond Bounty Bay and put aboard the next passing ship, the bark *Colonist*. The two men sailed to San Francisco with 120 passengers. Three others who had been stranded by Captain Parker of the *Noble*, including Baron de Thierry, were left in Adamstown. The baron told his life story to his island hosts. His story, unlike that of Joshua Hill, did not require embellishment. Charles was the son of royalist émigrés fleeing the French Revolution, and godson of King Charles X of France. His résumé included working as secretary to a Portuguese diplomat in 1815 at the Congress of Vienna; serving in Britain's 23rd Light Dragoons; and being an attaché at the French embassy in London. In 1819, de Thierry was studying theology at Oxford, followed by law at Cambridge. To recoup the fortune his family lost in the French Revolution, he purchased — or at least was convinced that he had purchased — forty thousand acres in New Zealand; he proposed a grand scheme to bring British colonists to New Zealand, only recently penetrated by Caucasians. He gave himself the impressive title "Sovereign Chief of New Zealand."

Rebuffed by the Colonial Office, he then proposed to the Dutch and the French governments to found a colony in New Zealand for their citizens, nominating himself as viceroy. France and the Netherlands either rejected or ignored his proposals; instead of being appointed viceroy, he was imprisoned for bankruptcy. On his release, he spent several years in the United States before drifting between Caribbean ports. While in the Caribbean, he announced plans to cut a canal through Panama. Those plans came to nothing.

In 1835, the baron sailed to Nuku Hiva, principal island of the Marquesas, proclaiming himself king of that cannibal realm. Rejected there as well, he moved on to Tahiti and then to New Zealand, where he earned a meager living teaching music in Auckland — which explains the tuning fork he produced from his pocket for Carleton's use.

All of the baron's grandiose schemes having failed, he decided — like tens of thousands of other men — to make his fortune in the California gold fields. In February 1850, he sailed from Auckland on the *Noble*, and was stranded in Adamstown until April 26, when the brigantine *Velocity* took him to San Francisco.

The *Illustrated London News* identified de Thierry as "the original possessor of the Franco-Granadino Privilege, for the Inter-Oceanic Railway [in Panama], afterwards Sovereign Chief of the Marquesas, and King of the Sandwich islands." The article continued, "His Majesty was reported to have been devoured by his subjects, but we hear that he has escaped that fate, and is now living with his family in California, giving instruction in music...."[16] This dreamer of magnificent dreams shortly thereafter sailed from California to Hawaii, where he served briefly as French consul general. In March 1853, he found his way back to Auckland to eke out a living teaching music. He would die there in 1864, age seventy-one, his stay at Pitcairn Island having been but one of his more colorful experiences.

A Baby Named William Ward Dillon

Masters and commanders of British warships appeared to the rock-bound residents as symbols not only of authority but of freedom — men who could roam the world at will, in charge of their own and their crews' destiny and destination. Some islanders honored them in significant ways for bringing gifts and medical attention. For example, on July 25, 1851, William Ward Dillon, commander of HM schooner *Cockatrice*, sailing from Tahiti to Valparaiso, brought donated women's clothing to Pitcairn Island. Apparently islander Caroline Adams, granddaughter of Mathew Quintal, was able to augment her wardrobe with European dresses during the resulting shareout. On November 10, Caroline addressed her "Dear Friend," Captain Dillon of the schooner which she mistakenly wrote as "*Cockataine*." After an effusive thank you for transporting gifts, including dresses for the community, she wrote, "I must also, before I close my letter tell you that I have a little boy lately, named William Ward Dillon after you, and I sincerely hope he may prove himself worthy of the name[;] he is at present to all appearance well and healthy." William was born October 28, and lived until 1912.[17] William was one of several island males named for sea captains. What is most interesting about Caroline Adams's letter is that its spelling and grammar are perfect and the handwriting easily decipherable. Caroline's letter suggests that schoolmaster Nobbs educated his pupils well.

A Trip to Henderson Island

Getting away from their confined living space was only a dream for all but a few until November 1851, when a visiting ship, the *Sharon* from New Haven, Connecticut, under command of Captain James Johnson, took thirty-eight inhabitants to Elizabeth Island, now known as Henderson. It was the first visit of the islanders to Henderson. The voyage lasted three days. Pitcairners found the soil there to be "very scanty, and totally unfit for cultivation." They found shells deposited all over the island which, with "thickly scattered pieces of coral," made walking dangerous. They also found the skeletons of eight stranded seamen, and pieces of wreckage from their vessel nearby.[18]

Admiral Moresby Comes Ashore

On August 8, 1852, H.M.S. *Portland* arrived, commanded by the highest-ranking naval officer to come to Pitcairn, Rear Admiral Fairfax Moresby. The admiral served as commander of Britain's Pacific Station at Valparaiso from 1850–1853.[19] Longboats brought the ship's band ashore and the community heard their first truly coordinated instrumental music. According to a report in The *Illustrated London News*, "their delight was very great." After the band played *God Save the Queen* at the islanders' request, they played marches and polkas, which "called forth the remark that such tunes seemed scarcely proper for Sunday."[20]

The admiral's son, Mathew Fortescue Moresby, serving as his father's secretary, observed: "Never were seen so many happy smiling faces, all eager to look at the first admiral that came to their happy island; but not one tried to push his way.... If we said a kind word to any of them, they looked so happy and pleased! ... There is not one in whose face good humour, virtue, amiability, and kindness does not beam."[21] In all probability the former Esther Nobbs and Abraham Quintal brought their month-old son, Fairfax Moresby Quintal, born on July 13, 1851, for the captain to admire.

On August 11, at one in the afternoon, Admiral Moresby ordered the royal standard hoisted aboard the *Portland* and a twenty-one-gun salute fired. Although dazzled by the naval display, the islanders were at the time suffering from malnutrition due to a severe drought that resulted in a scant harvest. Admiral Moresby ordered that ship's stores be sent ashore to tide the people over until their next harvest. The *Illustrated London News* commented, "They are badly off for clothing, which they purchase from the whaling vessels that occasionally touch there; their money is derived from the sale of their surplus yams, &c.; but, owing to the small size of the island ... together with the rapid increase of the population, they must in a very few years withhold from ships all supplies, except water."[22]

Admiral Moresby also made a valuable suggestion for the islanders to inform captains of approaching ships whether or not it was safe for them to come ashore. Adopted in 1853, the signals included a plain white flag, which was an invitation to land; a white flag above a red flag told the captain to come around to the western cove. A red flag alone signified danger in landing at any point. Moresby's system was used until the introduction of Morse code in the early twentieth century when resident Andrew Young used a shuttered lamp to send signals to ships.

Admiral Moresby became among the best friends the community ever had. Writing on August 12, 1852, from his flagship *Portland*, he praised "the spirit of order and decency that animates the whole community, whose number amounts to 170.... Of all the eventful periods which have chequered my life, none have surpassed in interest, and (I trust and hope) in future good, our visit to Pitcairn...."[23]

The admiral's son Fortescue found himself the object of attention of the island's young women: "I was generally accompanied by one or two with their arms round me; and most as often by three or four." These girls "could not restrain such expressions as the following, all the time clinging round us and looking up into our faces: 'Ah, I do love the English so!'; 'How good, how kind you are to come and see us!'; 'Oh, I do love you so!' and it was evident to see the pleasure that was in their good hearts by their faces." Common seamen were not allowed on the islands by Royal Navy captains, so the young midshipmen and officers had the company of the girls to themselves. Young Fortescue, on leaving, confessed, "I broke down, and am not much ashamed to say (I kissed them all round) I cried as much as they did." Showing affection, "One big stout fellow came and said, 'God bless you, sir!' and gave me a kiss."[24] Returning to England, Fairfax and Fortescue Moresby became patrons of the island, inviting donors to contribute to a Pitcairn Fund. The fund eventually collected enough money to provide the islanders a whaleboat and farm implements.

A major purpose of the admiral's visit was to take George Hunn Nobbs to Valparaiso so he could be transported to England for ordination. The Pitcairn population had long felt the need of an ordained Church of England minister. Admiral Moresby loaned the islanders his own ship's chaplain, Mr. Holman, to serve in Nobbs's absence. Holman was popular during his stay and after he left, three babies were named Rebecca Holman Ascension McCoy, Elizabeth Holman Adams, and William Henry Holman Christian.

A Plea to Queen Victoria

When Admiral Moresby took Mr. Nobbs on the first leg of his journey to England, Moresby carried gifts to Queen Victoria from the islanders and a petition for annexation. The community "ventured to present" Her Majesty with a small chest of drawers made of miro and breadfruit wood. The islanders stated they would consider it "a great favour if your Majesty would condescend to except [*sic*] of it; as a token of our loyalty and respect to our gracious Queen." The petition requested that "your Majesty's government would grant us a document declaring us part of your Majesty's dominion."[25]

Pitcairners sought protection because, in 1849, a French officer disembarked from the brig *Fanny* which was transporting gold seekers from New Zealand to California. The Frenchman asked Nobbs if the islanders had heard of President Louis Napoleon Bonaparte of the French Republic, and when Nobbs acknowledged that they had, the visitor invited the islanders to become French subjects. The officer produced a treaty from his pocket that, when signed by Pitcairn's representatives, would make the island a French colony. Nobbs told the Frenchman that the people were loyal to Queen Victoria and could not entertain his offer. The Frenchman apologized and sailed to California.

Ironically, at a time when the French were wresting Polynesian islands from chiefs who ruled them, and fighting to take over New Caledonia in Melanesia, here was a South Pacific colony begging Westminster for colonial status. The British government rejected the community's petition. The timing was bad. James Morris explained: "Still the British as a nation were not conscious expansionists.... Painting the world red was not a popular purpose." Free trade allowed British industry and commerce to flourish and British investors did not need for their government to dominate a place in order to make a profit. As a result, "empire building" remained "fitful, unpremeditated" and "often reluctant."[26] The Empire had grown rapidly as a result of the Napoleonic Wars when Britain took Cape Colony, Ceylon and other far-flung real estate, and now the British felt that their widespread possessions were a financial burden and a burden on the Royal Navy. The Royal Navy might take some responsibility for the well being of Pitcairners but the government had no intention of proclaiming their formal annexation of Pitcairn Island, at least not yet.

An Audience with Prince Albert

Because Church officials had agreed, in this singular case, to shorten the time needed for ordination, Nobbs was able to complete his requirements and be ordained on November 30, 1852. Church of England officials designated Nobbs "Chaplain to the Inhabitants of Pitcairn's Island." Rev. Thomas Boyes Murray recorded that, after Nobbs had been ordained, Nobbs went to Osborne House on the Isle of Wight for an audience with Prince Albert. Rev. Murray, to whom Nobbs related his meeting with the Prince Consort, wrote that after Albert asked many questions about Pitcairn, Nobbs "humbly begged to be allowed to pay his duty in person to the Queen, and it having appeared that her Majesty had expressed her readiness to receive him, the Prince was pleased to present him to Her Majesty.... The Queen, who was most gracious and condescending in her demeanour towards him, was pleased to present him with her portrait."[27]

The Society of the Propagation of the Gospel awarded Nobbs an annual salary of fifty pounds, which made him enormously wealthy by Adamstown standards. Returning to Valparaiso, the Reverend Nobbs was reunited with his crippled son, Ruben, who had gone to Chile to assume a clerical job because, after his rifle accident, he had been unable to support himself in Pitcairn's rugged terrain. Ruben now returned with Reverend Nobbs aboard Admiral Moresby's flagship, H.M.S. *Portland.* On his return journey, George Hunn Nobbs wrote a "national anthem" for his adopted community:

> Mid the mighty Southern Ocean
> Stands an isolated rock
> Blanched by the surf's commotion,
> Riven by the lightning's stroke.
> Hark those strains to heaven ascending,
> From those slopes of vivid green,
> Old and young their voices blending—
> God preserve Britannia's Queen!

After an absence of nine months, Nobbs returned as a priest missionary.

H.M.S. *Virago*

On January 24, 1853, the British consul at Raiatea debarked at Bounty Bay from H.M.S. *Virago,* the first steamship to call. "From the landing place," wrote Consul B. Toup Nicolas, Esq., "we scaled a kind of zigzag goat path for about two hundred yards, which brought us to the 'market place.' But, instead of buildings, benches, butchers' shops, and all that constitutes an English market-place, one must fancy a floor of shrubs, and a roof of cocoa-nut trees; a small space of a few yards being cleared away: and on this the different families bring their stock for sale, when any merchant-vessels call at the island for provisions."[28]

Captain Prevost of the *Virago* welcomed everyone aboard and took all but six members of the community on a circumnavigation of their island. That evening, Nicolas recalled, "the Islanders again sang the songs we were never tired of hearing; and we amused them by dancing among ourselves, and playing at leap-frog, blind-man's bluff [*sic*], &c., at which they laughed heartily."[29] This isolated idyllic existence would soon be disrupted by a move away from Pitcairn and the eventual separation of island families.

CHAPTER 16

The Move to Norfolk Island

A Growing Population

The annual addition to the community of seven to nine souls through births was common in the 1840s and early 1850s. The population had grown from 71 at the time of the return from Tahiti in 1831, to 187 by 1855.

On July 28, 1844, H.M.S. *Basilisk* called under the command of Henry S. Hunt, Esq. The captain decided several cases presented by local leaders for adjudication and made suggestions "for the improvement of the moral and religious observances of the community...."[1] Because of the population increase, Hunt recommended that the people be removed to another location; he mentioned the Bonin Islands. Six hundred miles south of Tokyo, some of the twenty-seven Bonins had already been colonized in 1830 by people from Europe and from Hawaii.

Moving off of Pitcairn made sense to many in the burgeoning community. They feared increasing isolation as the number of ships' visits fell from forty-eight in 1846, to seventeen in 1847, to only nine in 1848. "This is accounted for," Walter Brodie wrote in 1851, "by the whaling vessels, by which the islanders obtained the most of their clothing and other necessaries, leaving the South Seas."[2]

An Invitation from the Sandwich Islands

When he arrived on July 9, 1849, Captain James Wood of the brig *Pandora* returned John Buffett to Pitcairn; Buffett had gone to Oahu in January, hoping to find passage to England. While in Honolulu, John Buffett met with Hawaii's foreign minister, Robert Crichton Wyllie. Wyllie had come to Hawaii as secretary to Britain's consul general, William Miller. Wyllie entered the service of King Kamehameha III in 1845, and served as foreign minister to 1865, making treaties with European powers to confirm Hawaii's independence. When Wyllie learned that a proposal had been made to relocate some of the Pitcairners, he invited two families, or about twenty people, to settle in Kauai, one of the Hawaiian Islands.

Buffett discussed Wyllie's proposal with William Miller, still Britain's consul general in Honolulu.[3] With this British official's concurrence, Buffett agreed to take Wyllie's proposal back to the Pitcairners.

Wyllie was able to offer available land because Kauai had lost population due not only to disease but to King Kamehameha III's demand that Kauians cut sandalwood for export to China. Kauians collecting sandalwood "in 1830 in very cold weather ... were often driven by hunger to eat moss or wild, bitter herbs...." As in Mangareva, islanders had insufficient time and energy to plant and maintain gardens while cutting and hauling trees. "Working in damp forests, where the good trees were farther away and smaller in size, did much to wear down the stamina of the natives, and contributed to the gradual decline of the Hawaiian population."[4]

Nobbs wrote in the *The Pitcairn Island Register* for July 10, 1849, that "Captain Wood brought with him letters from Consul General Miller and several other persons offering to provide land &c. for any families who wish to emigrate. Captain W. assembled the inhabitants at the school house and on the letters being read informed them that he would remain on shore till the afternoon of the next day in order that they might have time to deliberate...."[5] After deliberation and discussion, the islanders respectfully declined the offer. As long as they thought they could remain on Pitcairn Island, they intended to do so. Kaui might have made a number of them a good home but none were ready to leave. Had the islanders accepted and settled Kaui, Britain may have claimed sufficient reason to make the Hawaiian archipelago a possession.

Thirty-three days after Captain Wood left, Captain E. G. Fanshawe of HM corvette *Daphne* delivered a bull, cows and rabbits. Fanshawe reported, "I could not trace in any of them the slightest desire to remove elsewhere. On the contrary, they expressed the greatest repugnance to do so, whilst a sweet potato remained to them; a repugnance much enhanced by their emigration to Otaheite about eighteen years ago."[6]

In January 1850, John Buffett wrote to Consul General Miller, stating that "the inhabitants will not remove until driven by necessity; that time, I presume is not very far distant. The number at present is — males, 76; females, 79. Ten births last year, and one death — an infant. About ten couple are now marriageable, and the increase will be rapid." George Hunn Nobbs, on the same day, wrote to Consul General Miller that, "although the necessity exists, and its imperative demands cannot be much longer avoided, such is the affection existing between the members of this unique society, that they are intent only upon putting off the 'evil day' of separation."[7]

To Go or Not to Go ... and If So, Where?

In 1850, the stranded Baron de Thierry lectured the islanders "on their helpless situation," and "the uncertainty attending the arrival of vessels." The baron pointed out their scarcity of water and food. De Thierry concluded: "Whichever way I look, in whatever light I view your case, I see nothing left for you but removal, and that, too, as speedily as possible." He advised them to apply to Britain's colonial secretary for removal to Norfolk Island. Norfolk, 930 miles northeast of Sydney, was a British prison colony but authorities were moving the convicts away and the island was to be abandoned.[8] In 1851, Walter Brodie expressed concern that "the fast increase of population is now becoming such, that what they are able to grow they will require for themselves. Consequently, they will have none for export, which will be a double privation,—first, in having nothing to trade with the shipping for clothing; and secondly, on account of having nothing to sell to the shipping. Shipping will never call there; they will be completely out of the world, excepting being now and then visited by a British man-of-war."[9]

If they did have to move, they did not want to separate; the community members decided they would move as a whole or not at all. If they did have to move, neither the Bonins, Societys nor Kauai were acceptable to them. They wanted the advantage of an uninhabited island so they could continue to govern their own local affairs and maintain their privacy as a community. Moreover, islanders feared having to "succumb to the dictates of those against whom an instinctive dislike has been implanted in their breasts." This reference was to the French. Nobbs wanted a home where they could all "worship God without molestation"—certainly within the Protestant faith.[10]

Walter Brodie commented, "Juan Fernandez is where they want much to go, which might be obtained from the Chilean Government, and they would in that case be under the eye of the [British] Admiral of the Valparaiso station, these islands being only 250 miles from there."[11] Juan Fernandez, Pitcairn's nearest inhabited neighbor to the east, may well have been acceptable to the islanders. It is situated at latitude 33° 37' S, 79° 50' W. Chile seemed to have no permanent purpose for the islands. Chile occupied and then abandoned thirty-six-square-mile Mas a Tierra from time to time. Since the Spanish settled there in 1592, it had served as a prison colony and sometimes it was wide open to passing ships and resident beach-combers, including Alexander Selkirk in 1704. In 1834, Richard Henry Dana, author of *Two Years before the Mast*, was enchanted with this, the first land his feet had touched after 103 days out of Boston enroute to Mexican California. From 1837 to 1842, the penal colony was again abandoned because of the expense of bringing in supplies. Chile, however, was unwilling to cede the Juan Fernandez Islands to the British Empire. Chile was wary of any powerful nation having a base at Mas a Tierra.

The Decision for Norfolk Island

In 1853, Fortescue Moresby observed that all the men on Pitcairn Island "looked ill and poor; which they told us, was the effect of the long drought having disappointed them in their crops. This had caused not quite a famine, but so near it, that for months they had been reduced to pumpkins, berries, cocoa-nuts, and beans for their existence."[12] George Hunn Nobbs was more specific when he wrote, in July 1853, that the people had undergone "for some weeks almost actual starvation; their only resource being half-grown pumpkins." Nobbs related that his wife had told him that "younger children would wake up about midnight, and cry for hours from sheer hunger."[13]

Illness and malnourishment motivated Magistrate Arthur Quintal, and his councilors Thomas Buffett and Edward Quintal, to write Admiral Fairfax Moresby on May 18, 1853: "As regards the necessity of removing to some other island or place, it is very evident that the time is not far distant when Pitcairn's Island will be altogether inadequate to the rapidly increasing population; and the inhabitants do unanimously agree in soliciting the aid of the British Government in transferring them to Norfolk Island, or some other appropriate place...."[14]

On the advice of Admiral Moresby, the British government offered to relocate the Pitcairners to Norfolk Island, more than 4,000 miles away. John Buffett wrote in a Honolulu periodical: "Our sincere friend and benefactor, Rear-Admiral Moresby, has interested himself in our behalf. In England, funds have been raised to the amount of £500, which is invested at 3 1/2 per cent, for the benefit of the islanders. We have received official letters that allotments of land will be given us on Norfolk Island, after the removal of the convicts."[15]

Norfolk Island's Grim Past

Norfolk Island had undeniable advantages for its potential settlers, but its landscape was littered with reminders of a sanguinary past. Captain James Cook, aboard the *Resolution*, discovered the uninhabited island in 1774, and described it as a "paradise." He named it for the ninth Duchess of Norfolk, one of his patrons. When, in 1788, Captain Arthur Philip brought the first convicts — eleven shiploads — to Sydney Cove, he was instructed by Lord Sydney to found a colony also at Norfolk Island. The British were eager to settle it to forestall French occupation. The British wanted this thirteen-square-mile lonely island as a source of food for the infant New South Wales colony; of equal importance, its tall Norfolk Island pines were earmarked as masts for His Majesty's ships and its flax for the production of sails.

Lieutenant Philip Gridley King led the first expedition to Norfolk. King transported nine convicts, eight free men and six women, all sailing aboard H.M.S. *Supply*. Like Pitcairn, Norfolk had no easy place to land. King's ship's master finally found an opening in the reef large enough to admit the *Supply*'s boats but not the ship itself. Once ashore, the company of men and women busied themselves building a road and a settlement. They felled trees and planted fruit and vegetables.

By 1790, 150 prisoners and staff were working on Norfolk. Soon there would be hundreds more, mostly miserable men and women sentenced for crimes of every magnitude from theft to murder. Norfolk Island pines proved inadequate for masts and the flax inappropriate for sails. Without apparent economic advantage to the navy, authorities found it too costly to run. In 1813, after a quarter century of man-killing labor to make Norfolk habitable, the prison colony was abandoned. The convicts were moved to Van Diemen's Land to toil under equally harsh conditions.

In 1826, because jails in Britain were overcrowded, Norfolk Island was resettled once more as an isolated prison colony. To be sent there constituted "the extremist punishment short of death."[16] R. B. Nicolson wrote that Norfolk's "lovely pine-clad hills had about them a darkness, a quality of brooding sorrow that seemed to rise from the suffering of men for whom the final horror was no longer the gibbet, but a degradation and inhumanity almost unimaginable."[17] A commandant's wife wrote of the prisoners' fate: "During the twelve months that we were on the island, one hundred and nine were shot by the sentries in self-defense and sixty-three bayoneted to death, while the average number of lashes administered every day was six hundred."[18] Victims who fainted from the flogger's blows were allowed to rest for a short time until they had recovered sufficiently to continue to receive the number of lashes promised. The flesh normally split after four blows and it was not uncommon to find survivors with no flesh on their backs.

When a group of these prisoners was sent to Sydney to give evidence in a trial, the judge wrote: "Their sunken glazed eyes, deadly pale faces, hollow fleshless cheeks and once manly limbs shriveled and withered up as if by premature old age, created horror among those in court. There was not one of the six who had not undergone from time to time a thousand lashes each and more."[19] Fifty lashes were laid on for smiling while on the chain gang, not walking fast enough, having a pipe, taming a bird, or singing a song. In 1834, when prisoners rebelled, many were shot and 162 locked in cells. In his narrative of penal colonies in Australia and Norfolk, descriptions that plumb the very depths of evil, Robert Hughes explained: "cruelty is an appetite that grows with feeding, and few people receive an epiphany of their own sadism in the abstract; they must see their victims first."[20] Sadism flowered exuberantly in governors and jailers alike at Norfolk.

View of Kingstown, Norfolk Island, in 1848. Abandoned as a prison, it was given to the Pitcairners, who arrived in 1856. In 1858, two families returned to Pitcairn and others in 1864. Mutineers' descendants still live on Norfolk. From an engraving published in Reverend Thomas Boyles Murray, *Pitcairn: The Island, the People and the Pastor*, London, 1860.

William Bernard Ullathorne, vicar general at Sydney, visited the hapless prisoners in his capacity of Roman Catholic priest. Father Ullathorne wrote: "I have to record the most heart-rending scene that I ever witnessed. The turnkey unlocked the cell door and ... then came forth a yellow exhalation, the produce of the bodies of the men confined therein. I announced to them who were reprieved from death and which of them were to die. It is a literal fact that each man who heard his reprieve wept bitterly; and each man who heard his condemnation of death went down on his knees and, with dry eyes, thanked God they were to be delivered from this horrid place."[21] Ullathorne later testified before Parliament of the evils of transportation to the prison colonies.

When reformers attempted to ease the regimen and punishments, hard-liners cried out and the punishments were reinstated. Finally, in 1854, when bishops protested loudly enough, the Norfolk colony was shut down by Order in Council. The prisoners were transferred to Port Arthur in Van Diemen's Land. In 1855, the bloodied piece of imperial real estate was placed under control of the governor of New South Wales.

At 29° 05' S, 167° 59' E, Norfolk was cooler than Pitcairn. Pitcairn's peak was only a hundred feet higher than Mt. Pitt on Norfolk; other than the elevation and the tortuous entry, there was little resemblance between the two islands. A Norfolk resident of three years, Rev. F. S. Batchelor, wrote a description for the Pitcairners: "The island is about twenty miles in circumference, with an average breadth of five or six miles. It is beautifully diversified with hills and dales ... and these low lands are exuberantly fertile." Reverend Batchelor went on to enumerate a vast variety of vegetables and fruits on the "Thousands of acres [that were] in high cultivation; and much more of the island can be speedily reclaimed and made available for any purpose. Fortunately, too, there are a number of capital stone-built houses, really large and handsome buildings, which would not disgrace our large cities, and plenty of store-houses, granaries, barns, &c., with a neat chapel capable of holding a thousand persons." All of these had been built by convict labor. "Besides tools and other implements of husbandry, now in use by the convict population, there is a capital stock of cows, sheep, horses, pigs, and poultry, which would be invaluable to a new community."[21] Rev. Batchelor's description of teeming fish and wildlife made Norfolk difficult for Pitcairners to resist, especially when offered as a gift from the Queen. Just as Pitcairn had answered every need of the mutineers, Norfolk seemed to answer every need of their descendants.

Captain Fremantle's Question

On August 17, 1855, Captain Stephen Fremantle arrived at Bounty Bay aboard H.M.S. *Juno* on orders from Sir William Denison, governor of New South Wales.[22] Assembling the adult population at the church/school, Captain Fremantle explained that he had come to receive their answer on whether they would move as a community to Norfolk Island. Every Pitcairner was painfully aware that if anyone stayed behind, families would be separated. When they met again the following evening, 153 out of 187 expressed willingness to go. But there were some, as Fremantle explained, "whose attachment to Pitcairn was apparently too strong to reconcile them to the thoughts of abandoning it." Fremantle felt that "the lamentable migration to Tahiti in 1831" was "still fresh in the recollection of the older and more influential part of the community...."[23] The most intractable holdout was George Adams, born to John Adams in 1804. He was reluctant to transport his ill three-month-old grand-daughter, Phoebe Adams, aboard ship. George Nobbs advised Adams that the infant would not survive the voyage. When Adams was at last convinced to go, he took a small coffin with him. Phoebe would survive the voyage, only to die shortly after being settled at Norfolk.

Nobbs explained that the minority gave in when Fremantle pointed out that the remaining few "would probably find themselves very much isolated, without grown-up men sufficient to work the plantations, or to man the boat, and without the means of controlling the crews of whalers, which now frequently call off the island...." Worse, "the rising generation might not imbibe or retain those pious and moral principles which are now universal."[24] Reluctantly, all agreed to move away from the home they had always known. Nobbs wrote, "I regret that too much coaxing and persuading has been used...."[25]

On February 16, 1856, Governor Denison wrote to his brother, Evelyn, Viscount Ossington:

> Captain Fremantle, who went down in the *Juno* to ascertain the wishes of the Pitcairn Islanders as to their transfer to Norfolk Island brings me a most wonderful account of their simplicity, single-mindedness, &c. We are going to put them on an island provided with cattle, which they have never seen, sheep of which they know not the use, machinery, such as mills, &c., of the application of which they can have no conception. It would be a curious and interesting occupation to watch the development of their ideas under these very novel circumstances.[26]

1856: Pitcairn Abandoned

All of the families had at last resigned themselves to the fact that the move was in their best interest. They embarked on May 3, 1856, aboard the *Morayshire*, under command of Captain Joseph Mathers. This immigrant transport had been sent by Governor Denison.

Many of the 194 passengers suffered "the most alarming cases of sea-sickness that ceased not from island to island."[27] On June 8, they arrived at Norfolk, where they were disembarked. Most bore the names of mutineers: forty-eight were surnamed Christian; forty-eight, Quintal; twenty-one, Young; eighteen Adams; and sixteen, McCoy. With them came twenty Buffetts; thirteen named Nobbs; and eleven named Evans.

Governor Denison sent to Norfolk 45,500 pounds of biscuits, flour, maize, rice, other groceries and milk. He sent twenty-two horses, ten swine, an indeterminate number of chickens, six thousand pounds of hay, and five thousand pounds of straw. All of this was intended to tide the newcomers over until their first harvest. Seven former convicts were hired to remain on Norfolk to look after livestock.

Each family received a fifty-acre plot. The island already supported large numbers of cattle, sheep and horses. Lemons, guavas, peaches, figs, grapes, loquats, quinces, mulberries, pomegranates and watermelons flourished in the rich soil. Thick groves of Norfolk Island pines sheltered parts of the island, but George Hunn Nobbs wrote in his diary, "There are two things in which we feel disappointed, to wit, the paucity of wood and water, there is scarcely a tree in sight from the settlement ... and all the water has to be raised from a few dangerous wells, sixty or seventy feet deep."[28] Neither of these two scarcities was to limit significantly the overall utility of the island as a permanent home.

In September, 1856, Nobbs described their new life to Reverend Thomas Boyles Murray in England: "The astonishment of the people, on viewing the magnificent structures of Norfolk Island, is said to have been great; and they were much amazed and delighted at the sight of a horse,—a creature which they had never seen before.... [T]he islanders have commenced farming and gardening operations; and they have probably discovered ... that labour, and plenty of it, will be necessary to advance their welfare and happiness."[29]

The islanders cast lots for the dwellings, some of which were larger than others, and the process having been completed, each family took up its new home with no demonstrations of envy for their luckier neighbors who acquired roomier houses. George Hunn Nobbs set up classrooms for the children in the former prison barracks. In addition, Nobbs continued to act as minister.

In 1864, tragedy struck two families. Anglican Bishop of Melanesia John Coleridge Patteson invited two former Pitcairners, Edwin Nobbs and Fisher Young, to join him aboard the missionary vessel *Southern Cross* to proselytize among Melanesians in the Santa Cruz Islands. This was the archipelago in the Solomons that Captain Edward Edwards of the *Pandora* had combed looking for mutineers. Although he had been treated well by the Santa Cruz Islanders two years previously, Patteson still took the precaution of landing alone and leaving Nobbs, Young and two Englishmen aboard to await further instructions. After sitting in seeming friendship with islanders in their village, Patteson swam back to the ship, but by the time he reached it, hundreds of fierce Melanesians attacked. Nobbs and Young both received arrows, Nobbs wounded in the chest and Young in the wrist. The question was: Were the arrows poisoned? Five days later, Fisher Young said to the bishop in the ship's cabin, "I can't think of what makes my jaw so stiff." His body became "rigid like a bar of iron, with fearful convulsions and spasms...." Five days after Young died, Nobbs also contracted lockjaw. Both men were buried at sea.[30] On September 20, 1871, when Bishop Patteson visited Nukapu in the Santa Cruz Islands on behalf of the Melanesian Mission headquartered at Norfolk Island, he was clubbed to death by irate islanders. The Santa Cruz Islanders were angry because white "blackbirders" (slave-catchers) had treated their people harshly while taking men away to work in fields in Fiji and Queensland.

Homesick

On May 16, 1856, Governor Denison wrote to Lieutenant Gregorie on Norfolk Island to advise him that "the arrangement of the land is subject to be revised and amended if necessary by the Governor of New South Wales, to whom all the arrangements connected with the settlement of Norfolk Island have been entrusted by Her Majesty."[31] Governor Denison, without asking the Pitcairners, had sanctioned the establishment of a Melanesian Protestant mission on part of Norfolk. The former Pitcairners felt betrayed when they had to share Norfolk with outsiders, having been offered it for their own exclusive use. Homesickness and a sense of betrayal motivated some émigrés to return to Pitcairn. Many were homesick for Pitcairn's wild beauty and warmer weather. They felt they had lost the precious autonomy they had been promised.

Finally, a drought threatened agriculture. John Buffett's diary for January 1, 1858, stated, "We have now entered a new year, our prospects are something better than at the commencement of last, and we have a tolerable stock of sweet potatoes in the ground, and have been enabled to supply some whalers, but from long drought we have been unable to plant for some months, and those that are planted are suffering from want of rain. Our maize crops are not near so good as last year and some patches are lost for lack of moisture. A great many of our community are wishing and striving to return to Pitcairn's, still I trust that He who feedeth the fowls of the air will not suffer us to want, unworthy as we are."[32]

Nobbs, Buffett and Evans were not among those who would leave Norfolk Island to return to Pitcairn to stay. Reverend George Hunn Nobbs died on Norfolk in 1884, age eighty-five; at the time of his death, he left seven children from his wife Sarah, sixty-five grandchildren and nineteen great-grandchildren. The former shipmates John Buffett and John Evans, who had come to Pitcairn in 1823, would remain on Norfolk Island and outlive Nobbs. John Buffett died in May 1891, and John Evans died in December of the same year.[33]

CHAPTER 17

Return to Pitcairn

A Tearful Separation

In 1858, sixteen émigrés left Norfolk Island. Rosalind Amelia Young, one of the passengers, recalled, "A much larger party had at first decided to return, and had already conveyed their goods on board the vessel that was to bear them away, but the tears and persuasions of the friends from whom they were about to part were more than they were able to resist, so they did not leave, as they had at first intended."[1] John Buffett wrote that on November 27, eighty people were packing their goods and carrying them to the pier, "but when the separation drew nigh the affection for each other was so great that they concluded to remain and agreed to pay £300 to remunerate the Captain for the loss of time."[2]

The sixteen who sailed were led by two brothers, Mayhew and Moses Young, who were the grandsons of both Fletcher Christian and Edward Young.[3]

Mayhew, born in 1823, was joined by his wife Margaret, the widow of Matthew McCoy. They brought their infant daughter and six children by Margaret's first marriage. Three of Margaret's daughters remained on Norfolk. Moses Young was born in 1829. With him came his wife, Albina, and their five children. Some thought that Moses was an appropriate name for the leader of his people on this momentous journey. The families boarded the brigantine *Mary Ann* for their promised land, Pitcairn Island.

Some time later, the *Mary Ann*'s Captain Wilson wrote an article which was printed in the May 26, 1860, edition of the *New York Tribune*, in which he pointed out that at least some of the islanders had planned to return even before they left in 1856. "They took such steps as appeared to them likely

Moses Young, 1829–1909. Polly Christian, impregnated by her half-brother, Edward Young, tried to conceal her baby with pandanus fronds; thus, the baby was named Moses. In 1858, Moses led two families from Norfolk back to Pitcairn. Printed in *The Graphic*, November 22, 1879. The artist, who visited aboard *H.M. Opal*, is unknown. This engraving appears on a 1994 Pitcairn stamp designed by Jennifer Toombs.

119

to preserve the place (Pitcairn) in the same condition in which they left it. They killed all pigs and dogs, so that the former might not destroy their gardens, nor the latter hunt down the goats and sheep upon the island. They posted notices on the doors of their houses requesting visitors not to harm them as the owners were merely gone for a short time, and would undoubtedly return."[4]

The sixteen immigrants returned in time to witness two boats with well-armed crews approaching the Landing from the French vessel *Joséphine*. France had been about to occupy Pitcairn in the name of Emperor Napoleon III. Pitcairn Island would have become *Île de Pitcairn*, but the *Joséphine*'s crews apparently had difficulty maneuvering boats between the rocks into the inner cove's placid waters; they gave up in frustration and returned to their ship, depriving *Polynésie Française* of an isolated if spectacularly beautiful island.

The Young families saved their island from Napoleon III, but they were too late to save their houses from destruction. When they climbed to Adamstown, they were astonished to find that vandals had torn up some houses and burned down four others. The vandals' identity and motive were soon discovered, etched with a metal object on a slate in the school house. Some months later, when the whale ship *Hiawatha* deposited a sailor on the island, the man was able to fill in more of the story. Still later the islanders received a copy of the periodical *The Friend* from a Rev. Damon in Honolulu. An article in *The Friend* explained in full what had happened. The crew of a shipwrecked vessel had used houses to supply lumber to build a boat to escape. The wrecked vessel was the *Wild Wave*, under command of Josiah N. Knowles.

The Crew of the *Wild Wave*

"On Tuesday, February 9th, 1858," wrote Captain Knowles in his diary, "I sailed from San Francisco on the ship *Wild Wave*, a fine clipper of 1500 tons, with a crew of thirty all told, and ten passengers." At one in the morning on March 5, "the lookout reported "breakers under the lee.... So close was our proximity to the rocks and so great our speed, that it was impossible to avoid running upon them, and in less than five minutes the good ship was on a coral reef, full of water, and the sea breaking all over her." At dawn, Knowles realized they were at Oeno Island, which had been placed incorrectly on his ship's charts. Knowles evacuated all hands and passengers onto the "dreary waste of sand," but found sufficient water, birds' eggs and fish to supplement food that was rescued from the ship.[5] Fortunately Captain Knowles kept a careful diary to chronicle the ordeal. *Harper's Weekly* noted that Knowles rescued in addition fifty thousand dollars in gold, "which last the captain prudently landed without knowledge of his crew." "The true seaman," *Harper's* cautioned, "is honest and reliable; but the beach-combers, who chiefly man the ships now trading in the Pacific, are a set to whom no species of crime comes amiss...."[6]

Knowles reasoned they could either wait for rescue at Oeno or attempt to sail to Pitcairn and ask to be returned to civilization aboard a visiting whaler. On March 13, Knowles wrote, "I mustered all hands on the beach and I selected my boat's crew, consisting of my mate [Mr. Bartlett] and five men. At noon, having on board all our provisions, we set out for Pitcairn's Island." Ingeniously, Knowles took caged sea birds with him from Oeno, planning to attach notes to their necks to inform crew members left on Oeno of his progress toward their rescue; he would release the birds when he reached Pitcairn, trusting the birds would return to their nests.

Two days later the small party reached Pitcairn and with some difficulty unloaded their effects at Bounty Bay. Knowles was astonished to find the ship's boat on which they arrived had broken against the rocks and "not a vestige of her was in sight." Knowles was even more astonished to find the island utterly deserted. He found notes in abandoned houses informing any arrivals that all of the inhabitants had moved to Norfolk Island. Knowles was disheartened when he realized that without inhabitants, whalers would find no reason to stop. Fortunately, the boat crew found plenty of food — fruit, chickens, goats, sheep and cattle. Knowles later complained of eating goat nineteen times in a single week, "the monotony being varied only by chicken and fruit." They cleared out a house to live in, noting that the houses "have berths like those of a ship, which are filled with dried leaves, making a bed, but more comfortable than bare rocks."

Impatient of rescue, on April first the men began the arduous task of building a boat with the goal of sailing to an inhabited island of French Polynesia. Fortunately, they found sufficient tools left behind — axes, hatchets, planes, chisels, a hammer and gimlet. They were able to cut timbers and hew planks, supplementing them with planking they ripped from homes. Knowles admitted to his diary of being unused to this "very tedious work" when "I could do but little and got very tired, Was glad to lie down." Eventually, "My hands have hardened to the work by day and I am now able to swing my axe for hours without inconvenience of pain." By early May the men made sails of every piece of fabric they could find. "We even burned houses to get nails, but hardly got enough then." On May 27, we "set fire to a house today to obtain nails for our boat," and soon noticed "smoke pouring over the hills," and found "not only one but four houses had been destroyed." On July 4, Knowles "wrote several letters, intending to leave them on the island, giving an account of my adventures, etc." Because part of the boat's hull had splintered and had to be caulked, three men opted to stay on Pitcairn rather than face the possibility of drowning.

On July 23, having christened his boat the *John Adams*— in honor of the second president of the United States — and decorated her with the American Stars and Stripes made from red cloth found on the church pulpit, blue calico from a bed quilt, and pieces of a white bed sheet, Knowles and two others set off, intending to touch at Oeno to rescue the rest of the shipwrecked crew and passengers. Due to adverse winds, they were blown hopelessly off course, and by August 4, they reached Nuku Hiva in the Marquesas, where "to our great joy and surprise there lay at anchor an American man-of-war, the only vessel in the harbor." It was the *Vandalia*, and its captain took Knowles and his men to Tahiti. Then the *Vandalia* reversed course to rescue everyone on Oeno before sailing on to Pitcairn to pick up the three crewmen. Meanwhile, Knowles found passage to Honolulu, San Francisco, Boston and finally home to Brewster, Massachusetts, where he was reunited with his wife, baby, and mother.[7]

Reconstruction

The Young brothers and their families set about rebuilding their homes. They were able to concentrate on construction because, due to adequate rainfall and the fact that crop land had lain fallow, agriculture required little effort. Two of the older children, regretting having been pulled out of formal classes at Norfolk, set up a school in Nobbs's former study. They found books and slates in the old school and taught seven or eight children reading, writing, arithmetic and spelling. Because the school was entirely voluntary and because the young instructors had little authority, they succeeded in imparting only a little basic education to their pupils.

In 1860, the Young families were visited by H.M.S. *Calypso*. The brothers told ship's officers that they had left Norfolk "because they did not consider Norfolk Island as their own ... that a school-master and miller had been placed among them, who were not of them ... and that their own magistrates, formerly only responsible to the people themselves, were now held responsible by Government for the performance of certain obligations by the people ... and that they had a longing to be back to the island, where nobody could interfere with them, however good and kind the intention, and however necessary, perhaps the interference."

Captain Montrecor of the *Calypso* described the community in a letter dated October 7. After Montrecor and his officers had "clambered up the ascent," they noted that the church and school were "sadly dilapidated," and all but the two occupied houses remained without roofs. The two occupied houses "were neat and clean, resembling in the interior the cabin of a merchant-ship, with a row of six bunks on one side." The ship's chaplain questioned the islanders and ascertained that they continued religious services after their return; they worshipped twice on Sunday in addition to two daily observances among family members. In fact, the two families met on Sundays in one of their homes, conducting services according to the Church of England liturgy and the *Book of Common Prayer*.

Officers noted healthy pigs, goats and poultry, both domesticated and wild, as well as wild cattle which had increased during their absence. So well supplied, in fact, were the two families in food that they told Captain Montrecor that it wasn't even necessary to plant crops, because "bread-fruit, taro, and peas grew wild and in abundance," and that there were animals "enough to supply them with flesh and fowls for years."[8]

Although they did not want for food, they were starved for items taken for granted in the industrial world. The *San Francisco Call* reported that when the British bark *Parsee* called out of Port Chalmers, New Zealand, eight islanders, mostly women, climbed aboard. The women wanted jewelry, castile soap, and cologne. "One young fellow was particularly anxious to secure a pair of sleeve-buttons; so pleased were the visitors with having been presented with some of these gewgaws that they went ashore without the provisions and clothing they had been presented with." A crew member who was "so struck with the beauty of one fair damsel" had to be forbidden to accompany her ashore to "find a home with them."[9]

The Vandal Returns

In 1872, Captain Josiah N. Knowles, this time master of the *Glory of the Seas* out of Boston, returned to Pitcairn. Knowles saw the islanders approaching the ship in their canoes, "bringing a heavy cargo of fruit, etc., and some fowl and a gift of some sort from everybody on the island." He was quickly forgiven by the understanding and compassionate community for the destruction of much of Adamstown.

On February 19, 1873, Knowles made a third visit, aboard *Glory of the Seas*. This time he spent an hour ashore. Knowles wrote that he was greeted as a long-lost friend: "On the rocks at the landing stood about twenty-five or thirty women and children, all of them barefooted.... As soon as the boat came in they rushed out to me and would have taken me on shore in their arms but I took the hand of one buxom lass and sprang on the rocks dry-shod, and on the very rock which I built my boat on." Knowles wrote that he "went into all the houses. They did not look as if they had many luxuries, nor as if they were very industrious, but it had been a dry season and they were short of most everything. Went into my house. It looked as natural as could be. Everything just as I left it...."[10]

A Close Encounter with Blackbirders

The tiny undefended community was vulnerable to evil intentions of any passing ship's captain or crew. In 1863, the bark *Rosa y Carmen*, previously unknown to the islanders, appeared suddenly at Bounty Bay. The crew were blackbirders, men who sold Polynesian islanders into slavery to mine guano deposits on rocks off the Peruvian coast. Two canoes from the island brought Captain Marutani ashore. Marutani has been described as "a terrible ogre with one eye." He was armed with a gun, revolvers and a bowie knife — "a swashbuckling martinet who brooked no interference with anyone, ashore or afloat." In December 1862, Marutani and seven other blackbirder captains had taken away 249 Easter Islanders. In all, blackbirders in the early 1860s were to abduct 1,407 Easter Islanders, over a third of the population.

After having grabbed a quarter of the population of tiny Puka Puka in the northern Cooks, and half the people of the Tokelaus, Marutani soon saw his anticipated profit diminish with an outbreak of deadly dysentery spreading among his human merchandise. Marutani dumped his three hundred sick passengers on Kermandec Island, six hundred miles northeast of New Zealand, to either die or recuperate. He attempted to cleanse his ship of the disease. The captain of the schooner *Emily* happened to be at Raoul Island in the Kermandec Group and described Marutani's human cargo: "The first launch load that was landed consisted of fifty-three men; only three could stand of the number, three were found dead on reaching the beach and the residue were hauled out of the boat in the roughest manner to be conceived and thrown on the beach, some beyond the surf, and others in it. Several were drowned where they were thrown, and eight died immediately after landed." All, according to the *Emily*'s commander, "were so emaciated and feeble that ... some [were] not able to crawl." An estimated half of the ship's prisoners died aboard ship or after arriving at Raoul Island.

By the time Captain Marutani reached Pitcairn he was desperate for human cargo. The Young families became suspicious when Marutani seemed dismayed that they spoke good English and that their skins were lighter than skins of full Polynesians. Nevertheless, the captain tried to persuade all of the islanders to visit his ship. When a boat crew returned Marutani to his ship, the Pitcairners came aboard and saw naked or nearly naked Polynesians ranging in age from children to middle age who were "sad, and their countenances bore the trace of much sorrow, and had a look of hopeless misery." The ship's hold was "unwholesome from want of fresh air, and many of the slaves were suffering from a distressing cough that shook their frames." Because they declined to remain aboard and because Marutani apparently realized that English-speaking people would be a liability to him, he was deterred from taking any of them to Peru.[11]

The Young families were lucky to have been spared. An estimated 3,600 Polynesians had been taken away from their islands. Blackbirders' captives died enroute to the guano mines and at labor in Peru. Worse, when the French chargé d'affaires in Lima complained loudly and bitterly about blackbirding, the Peruvian government finally outlawed it, and Peru's courts ordered the slaves freed and repatriated. They were brought back to any island convenient to the captains who had been paid by the Peruvian government to transport them. Once landed, they spread deadly disease among the alien populace of the island on which they were dumped. H. E. Maude wrote: "For Polynesia the Peruvian slave trade thus constituted genocide of an order never seen before or since in her history...."[12] These events occurred in 1862–64, at the time Lincoln was freeing slaves in the United States.

1864: Four More Families Return

Relatives in Norfolk had no word from those who had sailed to Pitcairn until they read an article written by a visitor who had been to Pitcairn in October 1862, aboard H.M.S. *Charybdis*. The writer described Pitcairn as a garden of Eden; this message probably caused some members of the Norfolk colony to think about the precipitous, lushly wooded paradise they had left.

On February 2, 1864, four more families returned on the *St. Kilda*, led by Thursday October Christian II. Thursday October II brought his wife, nine children and his wife's mother, Elizabeth Mills. Elizabeth was the daughter of mutineer John Mills. Elizabeth Mills and Hannah Young were the last living of the second generation. These two ladies each left behind children on Norfolk. Disembarking also were Robert Buffett and his wife, and Simon Young with his wife and eight children. New blood was introduced when Samuel Warren, a sailor from Providence, Rhode Island, came to Norfolk and married Agnes Christian, daughter of Thursday October II, the day before the *St. Kilda* sailed; Warren was accepted into the migrating community and Warrens were to remain prominent on Pitcairn Island. In all, twenty-seven came among this second group.

When the eager passengers arrived in Bounty Bay after dark, they sought to arouse the attention of the Young families by firing muskets and shouting. Alarmed, the Youngs thought themselves under attack. Parents hid their children as they tried to figure out what the invaders intended to do. In the light of morning after a long sleepless night the Youngs realized their long-separated relatives and neighbors had returned.

Rosalind Amelia Young, whose father was Simon, recalled that on close examination, "to the younger people the change from the island they had just left made a great impression, the dwelling houses and kitchens, in their ugly bareness and smoke-begrimed appearance, contrasting unfavorably with the neatly-built houses and tidy kitchens they had been accustomed to." On Norfolk they had become accustomed to "a long row of houses neatly standing side by side, facing a broad and well-paved street, [but] here were only a few humbly-thatched dwellings — only two of which were habitable — half hidden amongst the thick growth of trees which surrounded them."[13]

The Reconstituted Community

As soon as the newcomers were settled, the islanders set about sawing planks to erect a church in which school classes were also to be held. Simon Young was designated the teacher. In anticipation, he had brought some school books from Norfolk. He also taught the children to sing and organized a Sunday school. On November 26, 1866, the first letters arrived aboard H.M.S. *Mutine* from friends and relatives on Norfolk Island. They learned to their sorrow that two young Norfolk men, Edwin Nobbs and Fisher Young, who had dedicated themselves to missionary work among Melanesians, had been killed in the Santa Cruz Islands.

With more mouths to feed, Pitcairn was no longer an overflowing larder that required little labor. The whaling industry was in rapid decline and now the number of ships to call in any one year was seldom more than a dozen. The islanders experienced water shortages when all but two springs dried up. Their sweet potatoes were attacked by a blight and by worms. Breadfruit production declined. Farmers noted increasing soil erosion.

On November 9, 1866, Charles Wentworth Dilke, recently graduated from Cambridge

University, arrived aboard the steamer *Rakaia* on a world tour and reported that the first Pitcairner to climb aboard "rushed to the captain, and shaking hands violently, cried in pure English entirely free from accent, 'How do you do, captain? How's Victoria?'" A few minutes later Moses Young, the island magistrate, climbed aboard. Dilke described him as "a grave and gentlemanly man, English in appearance...." Captain Wright gave the islanders a bottle of brandy "for medicine, as the islanders are strict teetotalers.... One of the canoes was filled with a crinoline and blue silk dress for Mrs. Young, and another with a red and brown tartan for Mrs. Adams ... while the lads went ashore in dress-coats and smoking-caps." Six years after boasting to Captain Montrecor that they need not even plant in order to eat, they told Dilke "meat is scarce, so are fish. We have some sheep and goats, no cattle; and the hogs are diseased. There has been a failure with the yam crops, so that our principal food is sweet-potatoes and plantains. Oranges are plentiful, and bananas and pine-apples, etc., so that we make out pretty well in the eating line."[14]

Pressure to Return to Norfolk Island

In 1868, a delegation from Norfolk Island, headed by John Buffett, arrived at Pitcairn to invite the population to emigrate once again so that all families could be reunited. Expressing fear that they were so isolated they would lose their faith, Bishop Patteson sent a message warning them against "living apart from the regular ministrations of the church."[15] The families who had returned in 1856 and 1864 declined the invitation, although they would have regained extensive material advantages over living on Pitcairn Island had they accepted.

In 1872, James Russell McCoy and Benjamin Stanley Young, whose brother Fisher had been killed in the Santa Cruz Islands, sailed to Norfolk and were baptized by the bishop of Auckland. After a stay of three months, McCoy and Young returned with letters from friends and relatives imploring the Pitcairn residents to come back. The Norfolk Islanders sweetened the offer by promising free passage and generous grants of land to each family. The only condition was that all Pitcairners were to return together. The majority of Pitcairners were in favor of returning to Norfolk, but "a few families were determined to remain where they were, and there the matter ended."[16] In 1880, seven young people from Norfolk Island came to see their friends and relatives. It was the first communication between the communities since 1872. Pitcairners noted that their visiting relatives "were all slaves to the tobacco habit."[17]

Descendants of the Pitcairn Island emigrants still live on Norfolk Island and are able to speak to one another in a variation of Pitkern called, appropriately enough, *Norfuk*. Of the 1,828 people on Norfolk in 2006, roughly half were estimated to have the mutineers' genes. The entire population of Pitcairners have never again abandoned their home.

CHAPTER **18**

Shipwrecks and Hysteria

Hard Times

By the 1870s, whalers had stopped coming to Pitcairn for food and water. South Pacific whaling was in decline because in 1859 oil for illumination was discovered in Titusville, Pennsylvania, and judged a more easily obtained and less expensive source of illumination than whale oil. Moreover, Confederate raiders during the American Civil War had disrupted much of the New England whale industry. Fortunately, Pitcairn was now visited by mail steamers running from New Zealand to North America.

Except in periods of drought, the islanders were able to satisfy their own food needs and to grow a surplus to trade with the fewer ships that did stop. A period of prolonged drought occurred at the end of 1873 and lasted through nearly all of 1874. Islanders rationed their meager food supply, as they had no idea when the next substantial rains would occur. Insufficient food supplies were further strained in 1875 as a result of feeding survivors of a shipwreck that occurred on Bounty Day.

Wreck of the *Cornwallis*

When the *Cornwallis*, sailing from San Francisco to Liverpool, arrived on January 23, 1875, Captain Hammond and other officers came ashore, leaving the ship in charge of the first officer. The *Cornwallis*, owned by Balfour, Williamson and Company, had not been securely anchored and the 1,214-ton vessel "drifted shoreward, coming on swiftly and surely" until she "soon struck on some unseen rocks a few feet from the shore."[1] Everything aboard was lost except the ship's company, all of whom had time to row ashore. While islanders and crew tried to save the captain's gig and lifeboat in the raging surf, twelve-year-old George Tornlyn Young, son of Moses Young, was thrown into the sea by a savage wave and drowned.

Characteristically, islanders accommodated the shipwrecked company by giving up their own beds and sharing what little food they had. Three days later the American ship *Dauntless*, out of San Francisco, arrived and agreed to take the refugees to New York. The hospitable populace was saved from starvation.

Wreck of the Khandeish

Nine months later, on September 27, 1875, more unexpected guests arrived. They were survivors of the wrecked ship *Khandeish* from Liverpool. The *Khandeish* had run aground two days earlier on Oeno Island, and the crew arrived at Bounty Bay under favorable winds in the ship's longboat and gig. Islanders rowed out to meet them and accommodated them in their homes for fifty-one days. Rosalind Young reported that the crew "were soon like members of the families where each sojourned, taking part in the daily labors, and joining with them in their family worship, as well as attending all of the religious services that were held."[2] On November 19, the *Khandeish* crew was taken aboard the British ship *Ennerdale*. A great deal of sadness was expressed by both crew and Pitcairners as the *Ennerdale* prepared to sail. One crew member, Peter Butler, an American, remained on the island and married Alice McCoy. Butler wrote to relatives in San Francisco that he had found "the fairest of the fair maidens" on Pitcairn.[3] When Alice gave birth to Butler's twins, Butler left on the next ship out and never returned.

Hospitality given to the *Khandeish* crew brought welcome rewards. When the *Ennerdale* reached San Francisco, the story of the shipwrecked sailors and their generous hosts was given wide publicity. Newspapers painted a picture of poverty on Pitcairn, of welcoming and pious people dressed in cast-off clothing bartered from passing ships, unable to afford many necessities and most luxuries. San Franciscans collected goods to send: flour, cooking utensils, tinware, tableware, cutlery, pails, clothing, needles and thread. When they learned that for decades island school children had shared single copies of tattered books with pages falling out and words so worn as to be unreadable, San Franciscans sent school books.

When, on March 18, 1876, the ship *St. John* arrived from San Francisco with these gifts, for many, the most appreciated donation was an organ. Manufactured by Mason and Hamlin, the bulky instrument was transferred from the American vessel to a longboat, secured tightly, and rowed to shore. Once landed "it was lifted on the shoulders of a few strong men and borne by them up the steep path until they reached the thatch-roofed church...."[4] Islanders flocked to church, and accompanied by this new miracle instrument, sang "Shall We Gather at the River?" In addition to the organ, Captain Scribner of the *St. John* brought letters from the *Khandeish* crew thanking their hosts. From Oakland, California, Elders James White and J. N. Loughborough sent a box of Seventh-day Adventist literature on the *St. John* with a letter asking the islanders to read and consider its contents. This was the first information Pitcairners received about the new American church whose adherents worship on Saturday.

Rear Admiral Algernon Frederick Rous De Horsey

By the end of the 1870s, vegetables and fruits could be refrigerated aboard ships, and crews no longer needed to replenish their larders through barter at Pitcairn. Most ships now bypassed the island. Goods from the outside world became scarce. Therefore, islanders were gratified on Sunday, September 8, 1878, to see the approach of HM frigate *Shah* with eight hundred men aboard, under the command of Rear Admiral Algernon Frederick Rous De Horsey, commander of the British fleet in the Pacific from 1876 to 1879. De Horsey's report to the Admiralty of his visit included a candid account of the Pitcairn community.

The admiral was greeted by Chief Magistrate James Russell McCoy. McCoy was a great-grandson of Fletcher Christian and of Will McCoy. James Russell McCoy was born on

Pitcairn in 1845, and emigrated with his family to Norfolk. He was among those returning in 1858. A natural leader, at age twenty-five he was elected magistrate. In the thirty-seven years from 1870 to 1907, he was reelected for twenty-two single-year terms. British official H.E. Maude wrote that had it not been for Magistrate McCoy, morals may have deteriorated further. "Autocratic though he often was, he provided the firm rule that Pitcairn needed and probably saved the British Government from having to take drastic measures to deal with the local situation."[5]

Of the ninety residents that De Horsey and his officers met, the oldest was Elizabeth Young, age eighty-eight. The population consisted of sixteen men, nineteen women and sixty boys and girls. All professed to be devout members of the Church of England. Simon Young continued to serve as teacher and pastor. Arriving on a Sunday, De Horsey noted that observance of the Sabbath was "very strict," no work being done; nevertheless, "everything consistent with not neglecting Divine service was done to supply us with refreshments for the crew, the chief magistrate arguing that it was a good work, and necessary, as the ship could not wait." De Horsey wrote that nobody consumed alcoholic beverages, and residents had "very few vices." "The puerile simplicity of the laws is perhaps the best evidence of the good conduct of the people," he wrote.

At the school, Simon Young and his daughter Rosalind Amelia Young taught reading, writing, arithmetic, Scripture, history and geography. Girls also learned sewing, hat making and singing. De Horsey reported, "English is the only language spoken or known." He wrote that, "The Pitcairn islanders are, of course, entirely dependent upon their own resources. They grow sweet potatoes, yams, plantains, &c., and formerly plenty of breadfruit, but these are nearly all dying out. They have also bean, carrot, turnips, cabbages, and a little maize, pineapples, custard, apples and plenty of oranges, lemons and cocoanuts." To maintain their families the men worked hard tending their plots; raising goats, pigs, and chickens; building houses and canoes; and fishing. Women worked sewing and weaving pandanus hats and bas-

kets to barter, in addition to their arduous household and child-rearing tasks. The admiral observed that an average of one ship called at Pitcairn in a month and that refreshments were bartered for "flannel, serge, drill, half boots, combs, tobacco and soap."

"The islanders, at my invitation," the admiral wrote, "visited the *Shah*. No less than 68 men, women, and children, out of a total of 90, came on board, regardless of the difficulties of embarking, and the wind and rain. Their poor thin garments were nearly wet through, and many were seasick, but the pleasure of going on board one of their own country's ships of war outweighed all other considerations, and made them essentially happy."

When leaving, the admiral promised that, under his command, a ship of war would call annually. De Horsey told the lords of the Admiralty, "Her Majesty the Queen does not,

James Russell McCoy, 1845–1924. Beginning in 1870 when he was 25, McCoy served as chief magistrate for 22 one-year terms. McCoy is credited with enforcing the laws and giving purpose to the community. He was the hero of a Jack London story. Engraving printed in *The Graphic*, November 22, 1879, by an unidentified artist aboard *H.M. Opal*. McCoy is honored by a 1994 Pitcairn stamp issue designed by Jennifer Toombs.

I believe, possess in any part of the world more loyal and affectionate subjects than this little knot of settlers."[6]

Incidents of Mass Hysteria

Rosalind Amelia Young related a series of incidents that occurred to "younger" community members in the 1880s. A dozen suffered what Young termed "temporary insanity." The "young girl" who suffered delusions the longest was first afflicted in April 1884, and was not improved until early 1886. Symptoms included "seeing some object which greatly terrified him, or hearing voices calling to him, then gradually losing all recollection of former events, until the mind became an utter blank." Some victims claimed "distorted vision, that transformed every object into something different to what it was: grown-ups appeared to be children, and infants appeared to be adults. In almost every case the patient was calm and quiet; the power of speech seemed taken away, while the vacant stare showed that the mind had lost control over itself."

In 1881, a young temporary resident, the survivor of a shipwreck, "declared that during the night he saw his mother's coffin pass above him out of the window.... A few hours afterwards he became oblivious to everything that was going on around him, and ... was deprived of the power of speech." After a few days he regained his ability to speak, and began a house-to-house search for an unnamed friend who had been unjustly sentenced to jail; he was convinced his task was to rescue the friend. He believed at various times that he was a well-known personage. One night he wandered off to the opposite side of the island, where he was discovered "sleeping under an overhanging rock, wrapped up in his scout's blanket, for at that stage of his derangement he declared that he was Davy Crockett out on an Indian trail." "There has never been any satisfactory explanation of the cause that produced it.," wrote Young.Eventually the afflictions ceased.[7]

Mass hysteria is known clinically as *mass psychogenic* illness. Incidents including frenetic dancing in the Middle Ages and the hysteria attending the Salem witch trials are famous examples of those noted over the last six hundred years. Dr. Timothy F. Jones, writing in *American Family Physician*, related the story of a high school teacher, as an example of the phenomenon, who complained of smelling strong gasoline fumes in her classroom. Her pupils soon complained of her reported symptoms: dizziness, shortness of breath, headaches and nausea. A hundred people from the school rushed to local emergency wards. Five days later seventy people reported to emergency wards with similar complaints. According to the results of laboratory tests, there was no measurable evidence of gasoline fumes present anywhere in or near the school.

According to a study performed in the two decades after 1973, half of all reported outbreaks of psychogenic illness occurred in schools and ten percent in towns and villages. Females were affected disproportionately and incidents "frequently involved adolescents or children."[8]

Wreck of the *Acadia*

On June 13, 1881, the *Acadia*, sailing from San Francisco, smashed into the voracious coral that protects Ducie Island. The crew made their way in the *Acadia*'s boats to Pitcairn to wait for rescue. Each survivor was housed with a family. After the ship *Edward O'Brien* picked up the captain, first officer and two or three men on June 27; several men had to wait for nine months for a ship to come to take them away. When the opportunity came to leave, three crew members opted to stay on Pitcairn. They were Albert Knight, Albert J. Volk and Philip Coffin.

Volk soon married Mary Ann Young, and Coffin married Mary Florence Warren. Albert Knight, the *Acadia*'s carpenter, became engaged to Maria Jane Young, but her family demanded his removal from the island because Maria Jane had already promised her hand to a native Pitcairner. Chief Magistrate McCoy "soon had an opportunity, from a fancied insult to himself, to order the Englishman off the island. This act, unjust in itself, was carried out, and he left the island on the British man-of-war *Sappho*, in July 1882."[9] Three years later Chief Magistrate James Russell McCoy complained that Volk and Coffin were "useless interlopers"[10] who brought no skills but subsisted on their wives' property. When Albert J. Volk took Mary Ann Young to his home in Wales, only Philip Coffin remained.

As a result of Albert Knight's trying to take a young woman away from a resident to whom she was engaged, island officials yanked the welcome mat by officially banning further permanent settlers. The ban on immigrants was amended eventually to admit persons whose presence might be of benefit to the island. Rosalind Young judged that "as the island offered no inducement whatever to anyone outside of its own inhabitants as a desirable place for a home, there was no danger of any addition to the population from outsiders, and the law might have remained as it was originally written."[11]

One of the crew of the *Acadia* who had been taken off by the *Edward O'Brien* was to return as a permanent resident. He was Philip Coffin's friend and fellow shipwreck survivor, Lincoln Clark. Clark had remained on the island for nine months in 1881–82, waiting for passage home. After recovering from being stricken by the mass hysteria which had taken over some of the youth, he eventually returned to California. Following the death of his wife, Clark entertained fond recollections of his stay and decided that he wanted to spend the rest of his life on Pitcairn Island. He returned in 1906, and brought his sixteen-year-old son Roy. Both would remain for the rest of their lives. Thus, Pitcairn received an infusion of new blood as a result of the *Acadia* accident.

Off to See the World

A few adventure-seeking Pitcairners traveled widely in the last half of the century. Between 1859 and 1893, nine, including chief magistrate James Russell McCoy, ventured off the island to see other parts of the world. One unfortunate Pitcairn man, on reaching England, "was secured as a highly prized specimen of the human species." He was persuaded to travel from Liverpool to London, where, as resident of Britain's most isolated possession, he became an exotic exhibit in Westminster Aquarium. The unfortunate "specimen," his health impaired by his demeaning experience, was soon rescued by Reverend A. W. Drew, who took him to his home and cared for him until his health was restored.[12]

Wreck of the *Oregon*, 1883

As if the arrival of shipwreck survivors was almost to be anticipated, after dark on August 23, 1883, the inhabitants heard shouting from near the Landing and rushed down the

Hill of Difficulty to find a boat bobbing in the cove. The boat was packed with survivors from the bark *Oregon*. They had rowed a ship's boat from where the *Oregon* had been wrecked at Oeno reef. Hardy, the commander of the boat, had until the wreck served as first mate. Walker, the captain, had drowned in the surf at Oeno. Most of the crew were Chileans. Always gracious, Pitcairners hosted the survivors in their homes. Pitcairn men offered to sail back to Oeno with the crew to rescue other survivors. There, the new captain drowned when his boat capsized in the reef leading into the lagoon. Meanwhile, the *Leicester Castle*, a British ship, arrived and took the survivors to San Francisco.

Captain Doughty's Report

On March 18, 1884, Captain F. Proby Doughty of H.M.S. *Constance* visited Pitcairn, investigated the condition of the islanders, and reported his findings to Rear-Admiral Lyons, Commander-in-Chief, Pacific. Doughty offered his superior a picture of 1880s Adamstown: "The cottages, 17 in number, are scattered about; in some places two or three may stand near each other. Most have outhouses for cooking and storing wood, agricultural implements, etc. The church and schoolroom is a long wood style and rafter-thatched building, seating for 90 people being partitioned off at east end for the church, with a Communion rail dividing off the 'minister' and harmonium from the congregation. The school portion of the building has seating sufficient for the entire present community — 104 of all ages and both sexes. This building has five doors — three at side facing the sea, two on north side. There is a door through from schoolroom to church."

Doughty described minister Simon Young as "a simple-minded, honest-intentioned, inoffensive man, well up in years, quiet in manner, evidently respected." The captain found teacher Rosalind Young to be "capable in the matter of control, has a pleasant face and a very happy manner, and yet a quiet self possession that made me remark her," as well as "a quiet, kindly dignity."

Chief Magistrate James Russell McCoy "has much more of the Englishman in his features, colour, manner, and tone of thought than any of the other men now on this island of the original stock." McCoy expressed regret at the islanders' "ingratitude" in returning from Norfolk "after all the expense the Crown had been put to in clearing out Norfolk Island, leaving them the buildings, roads and 50 acres of land apiece." McCoy excused himself by stating: "I was young and simple; came back here with my parents."

Doughty expressed himself "unfavorably impressed by the ill-made clothing and dirty finery clothes sent them by well meaning friends at home." He singled out "pork-pie hats, tawdry ribbons, and brass, glass, and steel ornaments." Nor did he approve of their houses, which "do not seem so clean, the gardens are now ill-kept — nothing looks trim or in order.... In short ... all look much neglected." Doughty explained that since George Hunn Nobbs had left, the community had deteriorated and that "What these people want is an Englishman in love with their cause over them ... an English Governor of some sort or other...."[13]

Had the islanders' morality deteriorated from that of earlier decades or was Captain Doughty being overly critical of what he observed? If Doughty's impressions were correct, cleanliness of houses had deteriorated since the islanders had returned from Norfolk.

Two years later, Stephen Gundy, a crew member aboard H.M.S. *Pelican*, made two interesting observations; one shed light on patriotism, the second on morality. He wrote, "I noticed in several of the houses pictures of the Royal Family, not framed but nailed up on the wall so that a stranger entering could see at once." Gundy also noted, "I have read that the girls are supposed to be very moral and religious, but I cannot but take the word of mouth from Miss A. Young, also Mrs. McCoy, both of who said the people on the island are not so good as the outside world would make them to be."[14] Some were, it would seem, and some not. Their faith was soon to be renewed by conversion to Seventh-day Adventism, but their self-doubts as a pious community would be exacerbated by the first Pitcairn Island murders in a century.

CHAPTER 19

Pitkern and Place Names

Speaking Pitkern

It is not difficult to imagine that, in the early 1800s, the second generation of islanders, raised by Tahitian women and under the tutelage of fewer and fewer English speaking fathers, would have spoken Tahitian among themselves. In fact, the second generation children spoke Tahitian to their mothers, and the women spoke their native Tahitian among themselves, but the children learned English and spoke it among themselves and to visitors. Even before 1808, when the first visitor arrived, English predominated because it was the written language of the Bible and the *Book of Common Prayer* and thus served as the key to Divine law and eternal salvation. Tahitian, conversely, was the language by which pagan gods were served. English predominated because the children had come to think of themselves not as Polynesians, but as British. White skin had prestige as did the language of white-skinned men.

Second-generation Pitcairners' accents must have reflected the origins of their Caucasian fathers — London Cockney, Scots, Philadelphia American — and their vocabulary dialects from the north of England, Guernsey, Cornwall, and, in the case of mutineer Edward Young, St. Kitts in the West Indies. Probably John Adams's East-End London accent dominated. Some early visitors described the second generation's English as clear, while others were baffled to know what islanders were saying.

Today Pitcairners speak clear comprehensible English when dealing with visitors, but they speak a dialect among themselves that has been labeled Pitcairnese, or more properly Pitkern. Pitkern originated as a way for the mutineers and Polynesians to communicate; it was a hybrid pidjin using Tahitian and English words. Among the second and subsequent generations it evolved into a nearly complete language with English predominating and Tahitian sublimated. It was transported to Norfolk Island in 1856 and used there as well and is known as Norfuk.

The Pitkern pidjin dialect can sometimes — but not always — be comprehensible to outsiders who listen carefully and anticipate intent; for example when an islander responds "Es stolly" to the teller of a tall tale, he is saying, "It is a story, a fabrication." "No fet" means "It doesn't fit." "Em almos' daid for tired" is just as easy; the speaker signifies being very tired. "I'sa done a school" means "I have completed my formal education." She is "boney-boney," or very thin. "Larn" is to tell or explain, as in "You larn me how you feel."

"Wut a way you?" asks how you are. "Humuch people levan on Pitkern?" is not difficult to understand, and asks the number of residents who live there. "Humuch shep corl ya?" is almost — but not quite — within the grasp of non–Pitkern speakers; it translates as, "How often do ships come here?" "Foot yawly come yah?" asks one's intention in visiting the island. Perhaps the most descriptive of all is. "Want a beak for eat it," which expresses distaste for certain food — food fit only for birds.

"Wut wekle groos ana Pitkern?" may require translation and asks what foods are grown; once one knows that wekle is food he or she has a chance to decipher the question. One can make out the statement, "Ah could go ho-um and get I weckle," which means "I could go home to eat." "Stay well out" means, quite obviously, "Don't enter." "Cah smoke yah" means no smoking in this place. Knowing now that "cah" means "can't" is of little help in deciphering "Cah fetch," which means that something cannot be accomplished. "Wha you pick up a, boy?" asks a child where he learned something.

A stern admonition may be directed to children in or out of school who are not allowed to accompany the crews out to visiting ships; if they start down from the Edge toward the Landing, a concerned adult might demand, "Bout yawly orkal sullen gwen?" That means, "Where do you kids think you're going?" "Tomolla ha tudder one" means the day after tomorrow. A non-serious threat is "You'sa daid as a hatchet grown' fahs!" Children (or adults) doing something silly or absurd may be asked, "Fut you ally comey diffy and do daffy?"

Other expressions would require long residence in Adamstown or the services of a translator. Among these are "The sea is illi-illi," meaning the sea is hilly or very rough. "Yus plum how poo-oo" is beyond comprehension of aliens but is essential if you want to inform an islander that his bananas are green. And if you want to convey your intention of cooking food in banana leaves, you would say in Pitkern, "I gwen whihi up some wettles." Something that is "mono-mono" has a positive connotation while "huppa" has the opposite meaning. "Ikawa" means "I do not know"; "kai," from the Polynesian, is another name for "food." "Cooshoo" means good. "Lebbe side is" tells a person to leave something alone, or to leave it where it lies.

In 1996, the island council decided that Pitkern is a language and not a dialect. The tiny community has two official languages: English and Pitkern. One can hope that the introduction of television viewing does not serve to diminish the use of Pitkern among the islanders. Among the best advice one may be given on Pitcairn is "Dunt climb hem tree, bair you fall off." And if you pay no attention to the warning and fall from a tree or a cliff, a place name may be entered on the map to commemorate your tragic ending.[1]

Naming Places

Arriving at the Landing, and walking past the large "Welcome to Pitcairn" sign at the boat sheds, one must climb the Hill of Difficulty. Somebody — islander or visitor — had read John Bunyan's *Pilgrim's Progress*, first published in 1678, and noted that a protagonist named Christian found that the "narrow way" was the right way, but it led up a hill named "Difficulty"; the association with Pitcairn's precipitous trail was only too obvious and the name stuck.

The Hill of Difficulty is nearly unique as a literary allusion that has lent itself as a place name. Except for the Biblical origin of the name St. Paul's Rock, Pitcairn place names suggest that mutineers saw their island as a new independent world, not a replication of either Britain or Tahiti. Place names suggest events that occurred in Pitcairn's rich history. One is unable to find a King's Valley, or Queen's Peak, or Coronation Peak on an island map. Place names are almost all original. No part of the island is called Cumberland after Fletcher Christian's home, or Hackney after Adams's birth place, or Portsmouth or Plymouth after the ports the mutineers knew well. The village became known as Adamstown, in honor of John Adams, sometime after 1850; the exact date is uncertain. The Edge, Flatland, Hot Pool and a few other places are clearly descriptive and need no explanation.

In 1957, when Fred Christian showed marine photographer Luis Marden around, he explained the origins of some geographical names. "Oh Dear" on the coast was named because, "Well, native man wading 'long shore there drop his malu [loin cloth] in water. You know, that's all they wear, and he look down and say, 'Oh dear!'" The place name "Headache" on the western shore had a tragic cause according to Fred: "One man gwen fishin' 'long that place, when his boy say, 'Let's go back, my head hurts.' Before he get him back, he dead."[2]

McCoy's Drop dates from the time of the dwindling group of mutineers; Will McCoy so enjoyed the alcohol he distilled from *ti* root that, in a fit of delirium tremens, according to John Adams, he threw himself from a cliff into the sea. Bob's Valley was farmed by Robert Pitcairn Buffett when he returned from Norfolk. Howland Fall is a precipice from which Howland Christian slipped and fell 250 feet onto the shore rocks while gathering birds' eggs. O'er-Side-Lucas-fall marks the spot where nine-year-old Lucas Kipriano, a Mangarevan temporary resident, was chasing goats, slipped, and toppled ninety feet onto rocks to his death.

In the center of the island is a place still known as Polly. Here, according to local lore, Polly Christian, daughter of Thursday October II, came to give birth secretly to a boy sired by her half-brother, Edward Young. Although she wanted to keep the baby's birth from being known, and tried to conceal it in pandanus palms, the baby cried and was heard by others. Because of the circumstances of the baby crying among the branches, he was named Moses. Sadly, Polly died soon after, as did the baby's father when he migrated to Tahiti with the rest of the islanders in 1831. In 1858, Moses Young would lead a migration from Norfolk to Pitcairn.

Some places retain names of things that no longer exist: Big Fence, Down Fence, Down Rope, Old Fence, New Fence, Tithe House, White Cow Pen, and Market Place. The Park existed in the late 1890s. A more recent park is at Aute Valley and is named the Bernice Christian Memorial Park in honor of "Beanie," who was the oldest living woman on Pitcairn before she died in the 1990s. Pitcairners play various ball games there. Up-the-Image is where Fletcher Christian reportedly erected a scarecrow.

Roy Clark, who came to Pitcairn with his father Lincoln, explained the origin of other esoteric Pitcairn place names. "Bang on iron" is the site of the *Bounty*'s forge. Down Under Johnnie Fall is where, in 1814, second-generation resident John Mills fell from a cliff at age fifteen while gathering birds' eggs. Big George Coco-nut denotes trees belonging to second-generation islander George Young. Isaac's Stone is an offshore rock claimed by mutineer Isaac Martin, ostensibly as a place to sit and fish. Brown's Water is a spring near Adamstown probably discovered by William Brown, assistant gardener on the *Bounty*. "Up a side, Pugy'sa roll" recalls the place where Edwin Christian, nicknamed "Pugy," fell down the hill. No Boar is an area where islanders held a boar hunt but came home empty handed. A Polynesian who arrived on the *Bounty* was murdered at Timiti's Crack.[3]

In 1855, George Hunn Nobbs explained the sad origin of the place name Where Dan Fall. "Daniel M'Coy and his wife went to the north-west side of the island in quest of fish. After descending to the rocks, Daniel left his wife, and re-ascended, with the intention of passing the head of a small inlet of the sea, and then going down to the rocks on the other side. While doing so, he fell ... His wife without hesitation plunged into the heavy surf ...

and, landing on the opposite side of the inlet, found him on the rugged lava of the shore, a corpse!"[4]

Rachel's Coconut is where Rachel Adams apparently owned or picked coconuts. Aute Valley refers to the place where the aute plant grows. No Guts Captain refers to the burial place of a ship's captain who died at sea a few days before reaching Pitcairn. His last request was to be embalmed and buried on land. The ship's surgeon accommodated this request. The place name recalls that the skipper's innards had been removed as part of the embalming process.

Tedside is T'other side of the island from Bounty Bay, where a secondary landing is located, more remote and dangerous than Bounty Bay. Where Minnie Off refers to where Minnie Christian in the 1880s was swept from a shoreside rock; Skelly Warren grabbed a plank and, despite a fever, jumped in and saved the drowning woman. Both survived. Roy Clark confessed to not having a clue as to the origin of Allen's Stone, but it is a rock where Allen Christian, born in 1855, wrecked his canoe.

Big Belly is a large rock that resembled a "human form." Cabin refers to a small cave bordering a pool in the shore rocks; the cave has a hole shaped like a ship's porthole. Dog's Head is a foreshore rock that resembles a canine's head. Another rock has the memorable name Bop Bop. Rat's Hole is a sea cave, the opening of which is like a rat's hole. Tati Nanny is where Tati, a Tahitian chief, kept a female goat. Buffet's Harbour is where John Buffett fell asleep while fishing and fell into this "harbor." Up Ha Hollow is where a landslide had taken place. Sailor's Hide designates a valley below Christian's Cave where sailors were said to have hidden in an attempt to jump ship and remain on Pitcairn. Down the God is where the mutineers tipped Polynesian pagan idols into the Pacific Ocean.

In a similar vein, visiting physician Bob Kendrick observed in the mid–1980s that, "A map of Pitcairn is like a catalogue of odd anecdotes of events through the ages." After treating patients, he suggested place names such as "Where Jackie's Toenail Off," the road junction at "Tania's Tummyache," or "Where Dean Heave-up," and "Releene-Catch-a-Itch." "If there are not yet more places per square mile here than anywhere else on earth, I am sure it is a shortcoming that will be rectified with time."[5]

CHAPTER 20

Conversion, Constitution — and Murder

Seventh-day Adventism

In 1876, when Captain Scribner of the ship *St. John* had brought a trunk full of literature from the American Seventh-day Adventist denomination, some islanders read it with interest, but they felt that disassociating themselves from the Church of England in favor of an American creed would be tantamount to disloyalty to Queen and Empire. In addition, the Adventists' proscriptions against pork, crayfish and shellfish — ready sources of sustenance — caused them to reject Adventism and to continue to worship on Sundays. They would continue to do so until the arrival of lay missionary John I. Tay.

John I. Tay had gone to sea at sixteen. He took a Bible and a story of the *Bounty* mutiny with him. Having left sea-faring to work as a carpenter in Oakland, California, Tay was converted to the Adventist faith. He then determined to become an unordained missionary to Pitcairn, a place that had fascinated him since reading about its founding by the mutineers. Tay sailed to Tahiti, where he begged passage to Pitcairn aboard H.M.S. *Pelican*. He arrived on October 18, 1886. When he made his intentions known, the islanders allowed him to stay for five weeks.

Islanders' loyalty to the Crown and the Church of England required that Tay call up all of his persuasive skills to convince them of the logic of his belief. Tay was able to point out biblical passages which strengthened his argument for Saturday worship. Ironically, earlier Pitcairners had worshipped on Saturday from the time that Edward Young and John Adams conducted their first religious observances in the 1790s until 1808, when Captain Folger of the *Topaz* explained to an obviously agitated Adams that the mutineers had forgotten that the *Bounty* had lost a day when it proceeded eastward. When community members asked Tay to baptize them in the Adventist faith, Tay explained that because he had not been ordained, he was unable to perform the ceremony. He sailed from Pitcairn on November 20, aboard the yacht *General Evans*, bound for San Francisco. He promised to return and to see that the islanders were properly baptized.

Seventh-day Adventism has its roots in the teachings of Baptist preacher William Miller, an American. Between 1831 and 1844, Miller, a former army captain in the War of 1812, insisted that Jesus would return on October 22, 1844. Miller cited Daniel 8:14 as the basis for his prediction: "And he said unto me, Unto two thousand and three hundred days; then shall the sanctuary be cleansed." Miller's prophecy attracted thousands of believers in several countries. When Christ did not return on October 22, 1844, many Millerites experienced "The Great Disappointment," and abandoned their leader. Miller read relevant parts of the Bible again and concluded that the date was correct, but that he had misinterpreted the event. The correct event, Miller told those of his followers who had not left, was that on October 22, 1844, Jesus had begun to prepare a special ministry in heaven for his followers. Thus, the Second Coming was imminent but the date was as yet uncertain.

Among those who continued to believe in Miller's prediction were James and Ellen White and Joseph Bates. In 1860 a small group of adherents met at Battle Creek, Michigan, and chose the name Seventh-day Adventists for their church. Three years later they counted 3,500 members in North America. Before Ellen White died in 1915, her writings and speeches had helped to forge the modern Adventist movement. By 1900, church membership numbered 75,000 in the United States and abroad. Adventists believe that God saves mortals through their faith in Jesus. They are committed to the belief that the Bible, as a record of creation, is to be accepted literally — that God created the world in six days and rested on the seventh. Like the Jews, they calculate the seventh day to be Saturday. Because the New Testament relates that Christ washed the feet of his disciples and asked that his followers do the same, quarterly, in preparation for taking part in the celebration of the Lord's Supper, Adventists peform the Ordinance of Humility, pairing up to wash one another's feet.

When the Pitcairners became Adventists, they confirmed that the body is the temple of the Holy Spirit and as a result those Pitcairners who embrace Adventism avoid tobacco, alcohol, caffeinated beverages, pork, and scaleless fish. Some are vegetarians. Some of these dietary prescriptions no doubt account for the longevity and general good health of Pitcairners. Baptism is by immersion. The resurrection, Adventists believe, will manifest itself in Christ's arrival in a great cloud with all of the angels. The dead will arise and those with faith in Him will return with Him to heaven. Pitcairners tithe and give extra donations to finance proselytizing among the heathen, particularly those to be saved in the South Pacific islands.

Because of Tay's message, in March 1887, the congregation stopped using the Book of Common Prayer and began worshipping on Saturday. The converts dreaded the reaction of representatives of Her Majesty's government in the persons of officers aboard the next warship to arrive. When the next warship, H.M.S. *Cormorant*, arrived in December 1887, they must have been shaken by the profound disappointment expressed by the ship's officers. A *Cormorant* officer wrote of his visit to Pitcairn: "the simple islanders, ignorant of sophistry and the subtleties of scriptural deductions, listened attentively to the arguments of their fanatical visitor [Tay], who, taking the Bible as his standpoint, soon convinced them of the soundness of his views"[1] Although islanders rejected the Church of England, they most definitely did not abandon their loyalty to the Crown and Empire.

Her Majesty's Golden Jubilee

In 1887, Queen Victoria celebrated fifty years on Britain's throne. A much publicized Golden Jubilee in London was attended by crowned heads of Europe, many of whom were her relatives by blood and through her children's marriages. At Adamstown, months after the event had taken place, Captain J. T. Nichols of HM *Cormorant* asked the islanders how they intended to mark the Queen's Golden Jubilee. When they told Nichols that they had made no plans, he suggested they send gifts for the sovereign. The people of Pitcairn sent the queen a box filled with island crafts and an effusive letter of congratulations. In return, Victoria sent the islanders a box of commemorative coins, which were then distributed among the island women. Although they were abandoning the Church of England, the islanders had reaffirmed their loyalty to the Crown.

In 1887, the Crown reaffirmed the islanders' dependent and protected status by declaring the island a British possession under the British Settlements Act, proclaimed by Orders in Council. Nevertheless, Pitcairners date their membership in the British Empire from 1838, when Captain Elliott of H.M.S. *Fly* wrote their first constitution.

In further recognition of their loyalty, Queen Victoria gave the islanders three boats. The first was named the *Life-Boat* because within its structure were sealed tanks to keep it from sinking. The second was the *Drew*, which became known for its leaks. The *Ella May* was brought from California. Island craftsmen used the *Ella May* (a.k.a. *Belluga*) as a model for future boats. Some of these later boats were called *Winchester, Nuni, Ho-Ho, Helen Hare, George's Boat, Herbert's Boat, Parkin's Boat, Ronald Garvey, Boxhead* and *Reid Cowell*.

1890: Tay and the Vessel *Pitcairn*

Four years later, on November 25, 1890, lay missionary Tay returned aboard a ship christened *Pitcairn*. With him were Mr. and Mrs. Gates and Mrs. and Mrs. Read; Gates and Read were church elders. These Adventist missionaries and the ship were funded through American Adventists' contributions. The 156-ton *Pitcairn* was built in Benicia, California, for the particular purpose of transporting missionaries to convert South Sea islanders to their faith. Earlier the Adventists had purchased a schooner, the *Phoebe Chapman*; it sailed with Elder Cudney in charge but was apparently lost at sea.

The Adventists stayed at Adamstown only three weeks and in that short time 82 of the population of 126 received baptism; these were adults, as children are considered still too young to make the conscious decision to understand all of the Adventist beliefs. The missionaries were determined to bring the amenities of civilization to the isolated community. To prepare island girls for careers, Mrs. Gates set up a secretarial school, teaching shorthand and office procedures. As there were no offices on the island, those girls who enrolled soon dropped out. The missionaries inaugurated a short-lived literary society. Inspired by the missionaries, and to have an outlet for her literary ambitions, Rosalind Amelia Young handprinted the first issue of *The Monthly Pitcairnian*, dated December 14, 1892. Passed from person to person, or more likely read aloud to her friends, it contained Rosalind's poetry on its first page. The poem "Our Paper" concludes:

> Now list to the wonderful tidings
> We are starting a paper today
> A sign that at last is awaking
> The dawn of the mind's brighter day.

The paper contained poetry, moral and religious topics, news, "pleasantries" and an editorial by Elder Gates.

Adamstown was only the first of several stops for the ship *Pitcairn* on a long Pacific islands mission which intended conversion of Polynesians and Melanesians. Three Pitcairners — James Russell McCoy, his sister Mary McCoy, and Heywood Christian — sailed when the *Pitcairn* departed. They went to Tahiti, Raiatea, Huahine, Mangaia, Rarotonga, Aitutaki, Samoa, Fiji, Tonga and Norfolk Island. When the three Pitcairners returned to Bounty Bay aboard the *Pitcairn* on July 27, 1892, islanders learned that John Tay had died at Fiji.

The *Pitcairn* returned from California on February 19, 1893, bringing Miss Hattie Andre, a recent college graduate. She would be the island teacher, the first to be sent by Adventists. She recalled of her unceremonious disembarkation: "Someone threw me bodily over the railing down into the arms of another who caught me, and seated me in the rowboat to be rowed ashore."[2]

Between 1893 and 1896, Hattie Andre taught pupils age fourteen to thirty-nine. Meanwhile Rosalind Amelia Young taught seven- to thirteen-year-olds. These teachers were, according to the *San Francisco Bulletin* (as quoted by the *New York Times*), quite effective. "The children of the colonists," the paper reported, "are by no means lacking in book knowledge, for it is reported that in addition to their regular studies of reading, writing, and arithmetic, the Pitcairn youngsters absorb much of Shakespeare, Macaulay, and Carlyle."[3]

Islanders helped the missionaries build a mission house, named Shady Nook, so that Adventist visitors would have a place to stay of their own. Teachers sent by the Seventh-day Adventists taught in the island school until 1917 and from 1938 to 1948.

By 1900, the *Pitcairn* would make six voyages to the island before being sold in San Francisco. Several islanders would sail to California to attend Healdsburg College, an Adventist institution seventy miles north of San Francisco.[4]

An Island Historian

In January 1890, community members celebrated the centenary of the arrival of the *Bounty* mutineers. For the settlement's centennial Rosalind Amelia Young wrote:

We own the depths of sin and shame,
Of guilt and crime from which we came;
Thy hand upheld us from despair,
Else we had sunk in darkness there.

We, their descendants, here today
Meet in thy house to praise and pray
And ask thy blessing to attend
And guide us to life's journey's end.[5]

In 1893 the ship *Pitcairn* carried to an American publisher a manuscript by Rosalind Amelia Young. Her book, *The Mutiny of the Bounty and Story of Pitcairn Island, 1790–1894*, illuminates many of the events that occurred during her lifetime and before; in fact, it is a major source for events in the last quarter of the nineteenth century.

Rosalind Amelia Young, 1853–1924. With her father, Simon Young, Rosalind taught school on Pitcairn. The island's major literary figure, she wrote *Mutiny on the Bounty* and *The Story of Pitcairn Island* (1894) as well as poetry. From an engraving in *The Graphic*, November 22, 1879, by an unidentified artist visiting aboard *H.M. Opal*. In 1994 the Pitcairn Islands featured her on a stamp designed by artist Jennifer Toombs.

Rosalind concluded her history by cautioning the reader not to believe that Pitcairn was the pure sinless community of John Adams's time. "[I]t is certainly a mistake," she told her readers in the 1890s, "to think that ... no vice or sin of any kind mars the character or degrades the reputation of those who dwell so secluded from the world." Sin, according to Young, did indeed "have a kingdom on the little island."[6] In 1907, she left Pitcairn, having married a minister, David Nield. She settled in Auckland, New Zealand. Rosalind died in 1924 while visiting Pitcairn. She remains Pitcairn's principal literary figure.

A Cumbersome Constitution — 1893

Although the blueprint for government designed by Captain Elliott of the *Fly* in 1838 had served them well, it seemed to some that it was now inadequate. The islanders had been impressed by the energy and inventiveness of the Seventh-day Adventist missionaries, and attributed their own "social inertia to weakness in their leaders."[7] Some felt that a change in the process of local governance was what was needed.

On October 3, 1892, Captain Rooke of H.M.S. *Champion* arrived. Island leaders asked Rooke to help them write a new constitution. The document that resulted was a radical departure in that it provided for a legislative branch as well as executive. Pitcairners of both sexes eighteen and over were guaranteed the right to vote for a seven-member parliament "with power to legislate, to plan for the public good, to execute all decisions of the court, and to see that all public demands are attended to without unnecessary delay."[8] They also selected a magistrate; thus, legislative and executive powers were divided for the first time. In addition, the executive branch included a vice president and secretary. A judge constituted the judicial branch of government.

Rooke also helped the islanders revise their legal code. The code of 1893 focused less on problems with goats and cats than with human trespasses; clearly the islanders had lost some of the innocence that had endeared them to visitors in the early and mid-nineteenth century. The new code reflected the influence of austere Christian morality. Adulterers were penalized with a fine of ten to twenty-five pounds; if the court so ruled, one or both parties could be banished from Pitcairn. Fornicators got off easier, paying four to twenty pounds for their transgression, but if a child resulted, the father was sentenced to support the child "as long as it lives." Hiding to watch women bathe was costly as well, with a fine of two to four pounds. Malicious false gossip cost from ten shillings to a pound. Other fines were set for stealing, wife abuse "in any way," assault against "fellow human beings" or animals, threatening a human life, carrying concealed weapons, and killing or wounding a cat. If a dog were to kill a cat, the dog would be killed.

Other laws concerned damage to fields by chickens, damage to chickens by dogs, shooting goats, shooting inside Adamstown, or practicing medicine without the president's permission. Moreover, it was forbidden to take coconuts from T'Otherside — "unless accompanied by one or more of the members of parliament, on the first week of every month, on Sundays...." If the writers of the laws had not thought of every offense that could occur, they wrote an elastic law stating that even though an incident may not have been mentioned, if it were "contrary to the decency, peace and good order of the island," it shall be punished by a fine.[9]

Although it had minimal effect on daily life in the colony, according to the Pacific Order in Council of March 15, 1893, Pitcairn was to be transferred in 1898 to the control of the

High Commissioner for the Western Pacific. This official was stationed in Fiji. The High Commissioner delegated direct responsibility for Pitcairn to Mr. R. T. Simons, British consul at Papeete. Pitcairn would be the responsibility of the High Commissioner in Fiji until Fiji's independence in 1970.

On July 10, 1902, under Captain G. F. Jones, a crew of island men sailed in the cutter *Pitcairn II* to raise the British flag and put possession markers on the shores of Pitcairn's uninhabited neighbors, Henderson, Oeno, and Ducie. The markers read: "This island is a dependency of Pitcairn, and is a property of the British government." Since 1902, the colony as a whole is correctly designated *Pitcairn Islands*.

Shipwreck and Disease

In 1893 a shipwreck occurred that was to cause a health disaster for the Pitcairners. On April 24, the *Bowden*, commanded by Captain Law, ran up on Oeno reef. Law saved what he could from the wreckage, piling ship's stores on the beach. Then he and his crew made for Pitcairn in a longboat, arriving three days later. The captain and a few others found passage almost immediately on an American ship, which took them to England. The rest of the crew waited for a ship to take them to San Francisco.

In June, Pitcairners agreed to return to Oeno with some of the *Bowden* crew to salvage valuables. They made four trips by longboat. On July 28, the remainder of the *Bowden* crew found passage aboard H.M.S. *Hyacinth* bound for Coquimbo, Chile. Possibly in taking goods from the hold of the wrecked ship, the volunteers contracted typhoid fever, which they spread among their fellow islanders on their return to Pitcairn. Between August 26 and October 19, thirteen island residents died, including the most prominent among them, Simon Young, teacher and pastor. Among the thirteen were five children. The typhoid epidemic was the islanders' single greatest disaster since the relocation to Tahiti sixty-two years previously. When she wasn't nursing the sick, teacher Hattie Andre helped build coffins. When the epidemic had subsided, the population stood at a hundred and thirty-six.

In the Eye of the Beholder

Reports of Pitcairners' virtues or lack thereof often differed significantly depending on who was writing the report. On November 23, 1897, Captain Henry H. Dyke of H.M.S. *Comus* reported to the Admiralty on his investigation of the community. He was ashore only a few hours on November 3. Although he scarcely had time to walk around the village and meet more than a handful of islanders, he reported confidently that the 149 inhabitants were degenerating due to intermarriage. Perhaps he had been influenced by the resident teacher, an American missionary, who told Dyke that "the want of intellect among the young was simply appalling, and they had no hesitation in putting it down to this inter-marrying. In fact they [the teachers] had given up all hope of improvement, and intended leaving by the first opportunity." Dyke continued, "As to literature, they have little or none; in fact, they refused what was offered them." Captain Dyke concluded that the people "do absolutely nothing all day," and that "the morals of the community are not what they should be."

In a cover letter, forwarding Dyke's report, Rear Admiral H. Bury Palliser concluded that the island needed a governor because "these people have left their primitive ways and vice and crime are amongst them.... It seems to be the absence of discipline and incentive to work that is chiefly the cause of this lack of moral fibre."[10]

Thirty days after Dyke made his inspection, the four-masted bark *Silberhorn* arrived from Vancouver. An apprentice aboard *Silberhorn* recorded that two whaleboats approached as the ship entered Bounty Bay as the islanders sang "Rock of Ages, cleft for me, Let me hide myself in Thee." "Soft-spoken, very gentle men, they swarmed up to the deck," he wrote. "And if they'd hear us curse, they'd say, 'Oh, sir!' or 'Please, sir!' On the deck I heard Mac-Donald say, 'They're Jesus-lovin' bastards, aren't they?' ... Now, they were Jesus-lovers surely. No more religious people on earth."[11] In fact, the *Brooklyn Daily Eagle* had reported in 1899, "It has always been considered that these descendants of the old mutineers have been so blessed as to be able to live in absolute harmony — a 'Happy Family' ... and that the incursion of a clergyman would be analogous to the importation of coal to Newcastle."[12] Either virtue is in the eye of the beholder or the islanders had reformed miraculously in a short time.

A Double Homicide

On August 27, 1898, H.M.S. *Royalist* approached Bounty Bay from Sydney. Mr. Hamilton Hunter, judicial commissioner, was onboard to try Harry Albert Christian for the murder of Julia Warren and her child, Eleanor Linda Warren. In this particular instance, it seemed that Captain Dyke's worst fears had been justified. Julia and Harry had been lovers. Eleanor Linda was born August 14, 1895, and Harry was acknowledged as her father. Although the bodies were never found, Harry confessed to cutting Julia's throat and pushing mother and child off a cliff into the raging Pacific on June 17, 1897.

Officials accused Harry of the first murder on the island since the mutineers and the Tahitians did away with one another a century earlier. Harry, born in 1872, apparently had fallen in love with another woman on the island. His new love rejected him because of his involvement with Julia and his having fathered her child. Harry reasoned that the lady with whom he was now in love would accept him if Julia and Eleanor were no longer alive.

Hunter and a jury composed of Pitcairners found Harry guilty and sentenced him to death. Harry boarded H.M.S. *Royalist* for Fiji to be executed under the High Commissioner's direct jurisdiction. Enroute, Harry wrote to his family, "Dearest mother, father, and brothers and sisters, let us live so that we shall meet each other in the earth made new." From jail in Fiji he wrote, "I'm still in favour with the Lord. He is still with me and I can trust him in the time of trouble." He wrote again from jail asking forgiveness of the island congregation: "You all know what I have done, therefore I seek your forgiveness."

Harry Albert Christian was hanged on October 8, 1898, at Korovou Gaol. Following Harry's execution, a witness wrote to the murderer's father, Alphonso Christian: "He confessed full and free to the awful crime he had committed ... [and] I believe he fully repented of his fearful deed."[13] The crime and its circumstances, needless to say, further undermined Pitcairn's reputation as a pious and moral community.

Attempts to Trade with Mangareva

Rosalind Amelia Young wrote in 1894, "Our circumstances make it possible to exist, as far as the necessities of life are concerned, without the use of money, i.e., as far as food, fuel, water, and our houses are concerned, but for clothing, we depend upon the produce of our island, which we sell, when the opportunity offers, to a trader who calls here and brings us our supplies in that line."[14] The islanders reasoned that if they were able to cut out the "middle man" and trade directly with the outside world, they would realize a higher return for their labor.

Secondly, they wanted to begin the new century with regular boat service to their nearest inhabited neighbor, Mangareva. The necessity for being able to come and go at will was called to the attention of Chief Magistrate James Russell McCoy by Philip Coffin. Coffin had gone to San Francisco in 1899, but according to the *New York Times*, "It was not his intention to stay there, but he had the idea that it would not take more than a year to persuade some sea Captain to arrange to drop him on the island in passing that way. He was mistaken. For more than two years he staid [*sic*] in California, and then he succeeded in getting back to the Southern Pacific only after he had sailed to England."[15]

In 1899, the islanders purchased a cutter which they named *Pitcairn II*. Three Pitcairn islanders established themselves in Rikitea, French-controlled Mangareva's only town, as agents to promote trade. On the night of June 12, 1904, while every crew member of the *Pitcairn II* was asleep, a storm came on suddenly and capsized the ship. One man, Samuel Coffin, age eighteen, was drowned but the others were saved on the cutter's small boat. When the *Pitcairn II* sunk, islanders' dreams of maritime trade were temporarily sunk with it.

But they wanted to try again. The community accumulated 124 pounds, and, supplemented by the British government's donation of 150 pounds, they were able to purchase a sixteen-ton cutter which they christened *John Adams* in honor of the island's patriarch. The *John Adams* was soon found inadequate to sail the three hundred miles to Mangareva and was sold at a substantial loss.

Dreams of Mangarevan cash derived from pearl fisheries died hard, and, at the instigation of Adventist missionary Melvile Adams, the islanders began constructing the *Messenger*, a twenty-five-ton schooner. In January 1916, Herbert Young, who was given responsibility for the island's trade, wrote to Seventh-day Adventist headquarters in Australia that the islanders were working on a forty-five-foot-long trading vessel. With profits from produce sold in Mangareva, they would be able to pay their church tithes in cash rather than yams. Young explained the difficulties of building a boat without essentials such as ropes, or bolts, but that "a ship came along and provided those articles."[16] The resourceful workers manufactured nails out of metal objects donated by islanders. By using island materials and using volunteer labor, the total outlay for constructing the Messenger was calculated at fifteen shillings. The *Messenger* made eleven round-trip voyages from Bounty Bay to Rikitea.

In March 1920, nineteen islanders sailed the *Messenger* to Mangareva. It was the ship's twelfth voyage to Mangareva. George Warren was in charge. George had studied navigation and received his seaman's papers from the British Consul in Tahiti. From Mangareva, they sailed to Tahiti, but on the way home, the winds were against them. At the same time the *Messenger* sprang a leak because nails they had made from metal found on the island rusted and disintegrated. The ship was coming slowly apart. Unable to make land, and without food, the crew began to starve. George Warren said, "Floating on a leaky boat, without provisions, the few men left on board having to be at the pump day and night to keep the water from overflowing the ship, and working without food, we were growing weak and feeble."[17] Rescue boats from Pitcairn attempted to row out to the *Messenger* but were unable to reach it. When the islanders saw a steamship, the *Sassenach,* from the United States, passing, Magistrate Parkin Christian was able to persuade the captain to pick up the *Messenger*'s crew. Fred

Christian, who helped in the maneuver, recalled in the 1960s, "Before we reached Bounty Bay, the Messenger had sunk, and good riddance. She was a terrible job, with a heavy nose, and she went just as fast sideways as forward."[18]

Canoes

More successful than the *Pitcairn II*, the *John Adams*, and the leaky *Messenger* were island-produced canoes. Unique in design and construction, the canoes were based on those designed by Moses Young. The process began with the felling of a mango tree. At the building site, immediately behind the Public Square, each canoe was built in two halves, running lengthwise. The two sides were then laid next to each other. Suitable boards were then sawed and planed and fitted into the structure for the sides. Six-inch wooden pegs secured the pieces. The two halves were screwed together with four-inch screws, four inches apart. The canoe measured about eighteen feet long with a thirty-inch beam. Once planed, caulked and painted, the canoe would be used for several years in offshore fishing and meeting ships.

CHAPTER 21

Into a New Century: 1900–1928

Waited On by Laughing Girls — in Men's Clothing

The first event to occur at Pitcairn in the new century was the arrival of the four-masted bark *Silberhorn*, from Liverpool. On January 4, 1900, seaman Bill Adams got his first look at Pitcairn from the deck. Bill Adams wrote of his reception, "Ordinarily the people of Pitcairn were not given to making friends with seafaring men. Deeply religious, they feared contamination, and, excepting in case of shipwreck, allowed no sailors ashore; but with our Old Man and his wife they were friendly...." When Bill and others rowed Captain and Mrs. Gibson to shore, Gibson ordered, "You boys stay with the boat." "Oh, no sir!," contradicted the Pitcairn boat captain. Bill followed the skipper and his wife up the steep path, and at dinner he and his boat crew were waited on by "laughing girls...." "Hole by hole," he recalled appreciatively, "we let out our belts."[1]

A little more than four months later, the cargo vessel *John A. Briggs* stopped at Bounty Bay. The officers noted that two-thirds of the 150 inhabitants were women. These women for the most part wore male garb — "coats and trousers, in which comfort more than fit seemed to be aimed at."[2] The problem was that visiting ships were cargo vessels and the only clothing available was suitable for crew members. The *Brookly Daily Eagle* suggested, "Here's a Chance to Get Rich": "All that Is Needed Is to Take a Stock of Women's Clothing and Go to Pitcairn Island."[3]

1901: Commander Knowling's Report

On February 21, 1901, Commander George F. S. Knowling of H.M.S. *Icarus* landed and reported to the Admiralty his generally positive findings on island life. Chief Magistrate James Russell McCoy told him that thirty-five vessels had arrived on average each of the previous four years. McCoy reported that twenty-nine men, subject for service under the direction of the island parliament, were available for public works from 5 a.m. to 2 p.m. and as a result, "There is now a very fair road leading to the landing-place...." In addition, the men were building a new school and a whaleboat, "shooting of goats, &c." After their dinner at two in the afternoon, island men had time to perform their own gardening and other tasks. Women kept house and "many of them smooth and paint cocoanuts, plait and decorate mat bags, &c. The islanders' days' work often, to my knowledge ... would astonish many a British labourer, as it astonished, on more than one occasion, myself and the ship's company," Knowling wrote. Admiralty officials may have been puzzled by Knowling's assessment in that Captain Henry H. Dyke had reported only four years earlier that the people do nothing all day.

McCoy told Knowling that the people had been free of disease since a typhoid epidemic in 1894; in fact, Knowling reported, "Men, women and children, seem, without exception, in robust health, and full of vigour." Knowling added that "It was common talk, during our recent visit to both Honolulu and Tahiti, that the islanders were rapidly deteriorating in morals and physique, a condition of things which my officers and myself—after the best opportunities of judging—believe does not hold good at this time: and on the other hand, looking to the present flourishing state of the island and its people, it is difficult to understand how reports to their detriment can have got abroad."[4]

Another New Constitution and More Laws

Islanders soon found the parliamentary system cumbersome; the system devised in 1893 was more suitable to a nation than to a village. When the British consul at Papeete, R. T. Simons, visited in 1904, he advised them to readopt their previous form of government. They accepted Simons's advice and wrote a constitution that provided for a chief magistrate, a council consisting of two assessors, and an internal committee. The chair of the internal committee was elected by voters and its two members were appointed by the chief magistrate. An external affairs committee soon ceased to function due to lack of work. This constitution and laws remained in force with some amendments until 1940.

The laws enacted in 1904 with the promulgation of the constitution suggest that antisocial behavior had not abated and that additional problems had been recognized. Consul Simons reported that not only were the island judges "oftentimes incompetent to deal with the matters brought before them," but also "fornication, adultery, illegitimate children, petty thefts, brawls, bad language, etc.," were frequent and "it was disquieting to learn that the laws and regulations dealing with these offences had seldom been enforced."[5]

Errant dogs, goats and pigs remained an issue, but violence among humans had grown into a more important problem. Citizens had to be reminded in the new set of laws not to hit one another or to fire guns near homes or at their fellow citizens. In addition to penalties for the seemingly perennial pastimes of fornication and adultery, procedures were added for dealing with seduction of a girl under fourteen; the seducer was subject to a twenty-pound fine and possible imprisonment for a month. Performing an abortion was to result in "a lengthy term of imprisonment." Rape, which had not been provided for in earlier laws, required adjudication not by an island magistrate, but by the High Commissioner's Court for the Western Pacific in Fiji. Again, peeping toms paid ten to forty shillings for their view. Not only was the penalty for theft spelled out, but the law specifically mentioned penalties for parents "instigating their children under the age of 14 yrs. to steal produce or other goods." Caning and imprisonment in addition to a fine and the return of the goods were penalties designed to deter thefts. Law Number 20 stated, "No alcoholic liquors are to be imported into the island except for medicinal purposes." Thus, Pitcairn's "noble experiment," enforced by law, preceded the United States' unsatisfactory experiment with prohibition by sixteen years.[6]

Evidence exists of more lawbreaking than in past decades. In 1908, the Government

Secretary reported, "Crime is of frequent occurrence; of Law there is almost none, every man does practically as he sees fit — while the idea of restraint in any form, is abhorrent to them."[7] During the period 1904 to 1908, forty-three cases were heard in the magistrate's court. Thirty-five were criminal cases; of these, five had to do with sexual improprieties, seven with theft of a newspaper, coconuts, chickens, a goat, and pineapples — mostly by children; and five involved gathering coconuts or cutting down a tree. Persons were found guilty in nineteen cases. During the next eight years, 1908–16, 128 criminal cases were tried. The harshest penalty pronounced in that period was a month's imprisonment. A woman who was found guilty of having a child out of wedlock was fined five pounds. A man who tried to shoot himself in a suicide attempt was forbidden by the court to use firearms to shoot himself in the future.[8]

Under the constitution of 1904, the Internal Committee had the right to enact further laws, subject, of course, to review by the High Commissioner of the Western Pacific. These laws dealt with trading from island boats, performing public work, littering public roads, the control and protection of animals — chiefly goats — picking coconuts, starting fires (children were not to do it), and — of course — sexual impropriety. Propriety included covering up "from neck to knee" while swimming near the village between the Rocks and the Landing. In other parts of the island, bathers had also to cover up when members of the opposite gender were present.[9]

Attorney Donald McLoughlin concluded, "The overall picture of the Pitcairn islanders which emerges from the court records is that of a somewhat backward self-centered community of individualists, with most of the failings, other than that of addiction to liquor, to be found in any other isolated community in other parts of the world but certainly not degenerate or lawless as the observers during the early part of the century appear to consider them."[10]

In the first decades of the twentieth century Pitcairn was the subject of Britain's benign neglect. Administrators came infrequently and stayed for astonishingly short times. In late 1913, the British high commissioner from Fiji, and the British consul from Tahiti, arrived in stormy weather. When a longboat set out to bring them to shore, it overturned, smashing islander Walter Young against rocks, breaking his back. Two other men, badly injured, survived, but Young died a few hours later. Because of the First World War, 1914–18, and then difficult financial circumstances for Britain, from 1913 to 1937, no Royal Navy vessel visited the island. Pitcairn would have to wait for the completion of the Panama Canal in 1914 to find itself once more on Pacific shipping and passenger vessel lanes.

Mrs. Scoursby Routledge, Archaeologist

Visitors were rare during the First World War. Therefore, when on August 27, 1915, Mrs. Katherine Scoursby Routledge and her husband William came to Pitcairn from Easter Island aboard their steamer *Mana*, they were welcomed ashore. They had spent seventeen months on the Chilean dependency, once home of an enigmatic and resourceful Polynesian people. Easter Island is Pitcairn Island's nearest inhabited neighbor to the east. An amateur archaeologist and yachtswoman born in 1866, Mrs. Routledge studied and mapped the giant heads called moai that once stood looking inland from the shore and were also found in varying states of production inside an extinct volcano. She also studied Easter Island ethnology. She is reputed to be the first female archaeologist to work in Polynesia.

Of Pitcairn, she wrote, "The whole atmosphere is extraordinary; the visitor feels as if suddenly transported, amid the surroundings of a Pacific Island, to Puritan England, or bygone Scotland. It is a Puritanism which is nevertheless light-hearted and sunny, without hypocrisy or intolerance."[11] She felt that "The standard of life compares very favourably with that of an English village."[12]

Mrs. Routledge agreed to take two brothers, Charles and Edwin Young, as deckhands aboard the *Mana* on her return trip to England. As unofficial emissaries from Britain's minuscule colony, the boys were invited to Buckingham Palace on August 27, 1915, for an audience with King George V and Queen Mary. The *Times* reported, "The King and Queen had a long conversation with the two young men about the conditions on the island and its people."[13] Mrs. Routledge wrote, "The Islanders have been described as the 'Beggars of the Pacific,' and, on the contrary, have also been depicted as saints in a modern Eden. Needless to say they are neither the one nor the other, but inheritors of some of the weaknesses and a surprising amount of the strength of their mixed ancestry."[14]

The First World War

One might have thought that the opening of the Panama Canal on August 15, 1914, would have brought a steady stream of visitors to Bounty Bay. Instead, the First World War limited seriously the number of ships that stopped. Islanders worried about food shortages during times of drought, there being no reliable source of outside supplies. Pitcairners were equally hungry for news. Mrs. Scoursby Routledge indicated that on her visit islanders asked for newspapers with pictures of the war and no other type of reading material. On November 26, 1916, when the steamship *Ruahine* brought soldiers ashore on their way home from Europe to New Zealand, one wrote, "To these innocent folk the news we brought proved very welcome and exciting, especially that from those of us who had been at the Front, and were able to give a short history of the war."

Magistrate Gerald Robert Bromley Christian wrote in January 1917, "We haven't had any mail since 1913 too long altogether — but we have had news quite frequently from those steamers that pass through the Panama Canal, telling us about the progress of the War and its terrible slaughter of human lives." On April 20, 1917, the Australian ship *Australplain* arrived. A crew member wrote, "The Islanders were keenly interested in the war, and were glad that 'Uncle Sam' was entering into it. Two of the Islanders are serving with the Allies now."[15] The *Australplain* brought the first mail in several years, seventy-three letters, as well as $2,500 in presents from America. Women received dresses, men were given suits, and an organ was hauled up the steep slope for everyone's enjoyment.[16]

Benefits of the Panama Canal

After the war ended on November 11, 1918, Pitcairners began to realize the benefit of being on the Panama-Auckland route. The distance from Balboa, Panama, to Pitcairn is 3,520 miles and from Pitcairn Island to Wellington, New Zealand, 3,006, for a total of 6,526 miles. Ships that sailed directly from Panama to Wellington without a stop at Pitcairn saved only four miles, covering a distance of 6,522 miles. Pitcairn was definitely and most conveniently on the route. Passenger ships' captains found it advantageous to allow their guests a brief stop over at Pitcairn. Ships of the Shaw Savill and Albion and the New Zealand shipping companies became familiar sights and its officers familiar visitors. During busy periods ship arrivals averaged one a week.

A virtually unknown civil servant, Gerald de Leo Bliss, postmaster at Cristóbal, Panama, was a major benefactor of the Pitcairn community. From 1920 until his retirement in 1934, Bliss and his wife Marbella Anna assisted Pitcairners by organizing Pitcairn mail coming through Panama and assigning it to ships bound for Adamstown. Bliss was responsible for cutting delivery time from six months to as little as two weeks on some ships. According to the island postal administration's website, "Mrs. Bliss became an indefatigable bargain hunter for the always-cash-short islanders, purchasing, among other large items, Pitcairn's first wood-fired domestic stove."[17]

Eduard Laeffler, Carving Master

A little-known Central European wood carver also benefited the Pitcairners. Souvenirs to be sold to passengers had long been the islanders' major industry. By the 1920s the quality of curios had deteriorated, according to anecdotal evidence from passengers. Collectors were offered coconut shells inscribed "Pitcairn Islands," shell beads and bracelets, plaited pandanus mats and some needlework. Upon receiving cash for these goods, the vendors would rush to the ship's store to purchase manufactured items unobtainable in their remote colony.

Pitcairn patriarch Andrew Young related to the author that in the 1920s, a Bohemian Czech named Eduard Laeffler somehow found his way on to the island and instructed the people in ways to improve their carving. Laeffler brought expertise and taught them to carve miro wood lovingly and painstakingly; they carved sharks, turtles, *Bounty* ship models, walking sticks and other curios. The islanders owe much to this man about whom little is remembered, except that he had died October 10, 1925, at age seventy-five.

Unfortunately, by the time Laeffler arrived, most of the miro wood had been used for fuel. As a result, islanders continue to go to Henderson Island periodically to replenish their supply. Islanders also kill small sharks so they can mount real teeth in their wood carvings of wall-mounted sharks. The great prize that one might bring away from a Pitcairn visit is an exquisitely carved model of the *Bounty*. So important to each family was the sale of curios that, "once the bell — signifying arrival of a ship — sounded whilst a marriage was being celebrated, the crowded church emptied at once, and the bride, bridegroom, and officiator were left alone."[18]

Since the coming of frequent passenger ships, the traditional "shareout" from trading as a community had become infrequent; rather, from the 1920s and 1930s individual curio entrepreneurs sold artifacts and produce to passengers and ships' chefs and kept the profits for their own households. A passenger at the time stated, "They were keen on obtaining light clothing and small articles useful to the womenfolk of the community, such as hooks and eyes, buttons, needles, cottons, soap, scent, paper and envelopes.... Books were not in demand, but they freely accepted daily newspapers and illustrated magazines."[19]

A Report to the Right Honourable Winston Churchill

On June 14, 1921, Shaw Savill and Albion Company's four-masted steamer *Ionic (II)* arrived from Liverpool on the first of seventy-five stops it would make at Pitcairn until 1935. Aboard was Britain's High Commissioner for the Western Pacific, Sir Cecil Rodwell, K.C.N.G.,

This model of the *Bounty* is the "top of the line" of Pitcairn curios. Carved in 2003 out of miro wood by Pitcairner Terry Young, it is typical of fine island craftsmanship. Bohemian visitor Eduard Laeffler taught islanders to make wood carvings in the 1920s. Photo by Barbara Kirk.

and Lady Rodwell. From start to finish this official visit was an unmitigated disaster. A record of the day's events is included in Sir Cecil's report to the Right Honourable Winston S. Churchill, secretary of state for the colonies. It is dated June 25.

Sir Cecil reported to the future prime minister that, when the ship arrived, a boat brought Edward McCoy aboard. McCoy advised Captain A. H. Summers to anchor on the northwest side of the island, a mile from shore. "Soon after we had come to anchor a second boat came off, having sailed round from the other side of the island. The crew brought bad news. A third boat, while being hauled ashore at the main landing, had been lifted by a breaker and had crushed three men against the rocks. One was reported to be dead and the others dying." Rodwell was unable to land until midday due to the emergency, and then because "an eight-foot swell was running, the process of transference from ship to boat was long and hazardous ... and the landing was almost equally difficult." The high commissioner found himself in two feet of water coming ashore, and then he started up the Hill of Difficulty. "The path to the village is no more than a goat-track and lies along a ridge some 500 ft. above the shore, and to reach it we had to scramble up the face of the cliffs from the top of which there is a further laborious ascent through the bush." Commissioner and party "straggled up to the summit, whence a steep descent led to the village."

Rodwell enumerated for Churchill the inhabitants' problems: First, the small chance of finding seven able men out of 170 people who "are by no means illiterate, but ... are slow thinkers," to serve as public officials; second, illegitimate births; and third, a secure way to ship produce to market. "At present," he explained, "it is precarious owing to the uncertainty as to the arrival of steamers. Sometimes the fruit is not ready. At other times a steamer is expected and the fruit is packed and taken to the beach ready for shipment, but the steamer passes without calling." Rodwell listed as a problem the lack of an island postal system, a situation which required letter writers to ask someone on a passing ship to mail their letter for them when they arrived at a port, and to pay the postage at that port. Rodwell recommended establishment of a post office and a postage stamp issue for Pitcairn.

Since the morning's accident, Alphonso Christian and Walter Fisher Young had died. The *Ionic's* physician, Dr. H. W. Mann, and two physicians among the passengers cared for the third victim, who was to recover. Rodwell told Churchill that during his single hour ashore he found no "signs of degeneracy and imbecility" which had been observed by Captain Dyke in his report in 1897. "Possibly," the high commissioner explained, "former observers have been prejudiced by the theory that inter-marriage over a period of years inevitably results in degeneration. This, I believe, is by no means the case where the original stock is sound...." Dr. Mann agreed that had he found "no evidence of degeneracy."

After disembarking only three hours earlier, Rodwell and his party were ready to leave. It was then they found that "The hardest part of the journey" for the "weary and bedraggled" party was getting back aboard. "Each in turn had to stand in the stern of the boat till the swell raised it to the level of the accommodation ladder and then jump for it." Landing had consumed two hours and the return trip to the ship an hour and a half.[20] That had left the High Commissioner for the Western Pacific no more than sixty minutes ashore to gather facts for his official report to the Right Honorable Winston Churchill.

Improvements

Three improvements came to the island in the 1920s: a post office was opened; radio communications were established; and for the first time a longboat was motorized.

One result of High Commissioner Rodwell's report was establishment of a post office. Because authorities assumed that no money was available on the island, mailing privileges had been free for Pitcairners. Mail was marked "No Stamps Available." Eventually, New Zealand authorities alleged that islanders and crews and passengers from passing ships were abusing the free franking privilege; for example, visitors could mail their souvenirs and even soiled laundry home at no cost. Therefore, from June 7, 1926, Pitcairners paid for postage. From that date to October 1940, the Pitcairn postal service was a sub-agency of the New Zealand Postal Department. New Zealand stamps were sold at a post office located in the Pitcairn court house. The postmaster was paid ten pounds a year, a sum that exceeded the total amount of stamps sold.

In the early 1920s Fred Christian and Andrew Young learned Morse code and with the use of a wireless set asked ships to stop to take mail. In 1926, the Marconi International Marine Communication Company gave the islanders a Marconi crystal receiver. It became possible with this more powerful device to send and receive messages from ships up to a hundred and fifty miles; early warning of ships' arrivals allowed curio sellers to complete projects and bring them down to the Landing to maximize their time aboard. Islanders were also able to relay messages to New Zealand and beyond.

By 1937, radio operator Andrew Young was able to listen to ships at a distance of a thousand miles and to transmit messages four hundred miles. In 1938, R.M.S. *Rangitaga* brought two technicians with four and a half tons of components to improve the radio station. The technicians set up an amateur radio station, VR6AY, to be operated by Andrew Young and later by Tom Christian. On April 6, 1938, VR6AY broadcast a show entitled "Salute to Pitcairn island," which was picked up by ham operators in Los Angeles and then went out over the Blue Network stations throughout the United States.

In the 1920s Pitcairn had four wooden longboats. Each had been fabricated on the island. Each was manned by a team of fourteen oarsmen. In 1928, New Zealander Arnold Hare and his family arrived. Hare and his three sons brought a gasoline-powered bus engine and in four weeks they installed the engine in one of the boats. On August 24, 1928, the motorized *Helen Ware*, named after Arnold's wife, carried fifty-eight people on a circle tour around the island. In the next few years, islanders used both motorized launches and sail boats for fishing and to approach ships.

1927: If at First You Don't Succeed ...

Few people have tried harder to land on Pitcairn than Richard Bentley Fairclough. The young man had wanted to live among Pitcairners since July 3, 1921, when he arrived from Ireland aboard *S.S. Paparoa* enroute to Auckland. Fairclough was much impressed by the moral character of islanders who had come aboard. In an attempt to return in order to stay and live among them, he worked, saved his money and booked passage on the steamer *Dorset* and reached Bounty Bay on September 8, 1922. Only then was he to learn that authorities restricted the right to land to those who had prior approval. Without a landing permit, which he had failed to procure from the High Commissioner's office, he was not allowed to disembark.

Fairclough returned to New Zealand and worked five years to save money to try again to reach Pitcairn. Because he claimed descent from a *Bounty* mutineer, he was able to obtain a landing permit. On June 20, 1927, the *Rotorua* brought Dick Fairclough to Pitcairn a third time, and this time he was welcomed as a long-term temporary resident. He became house-mate of bachelor William Christian. Dick Fairclough stayed for over ten years, and was eventually joined by his widowed sister, Jessie Westall.

1929: Another Hasty Report

Eight and a half years after Sir Cecil Rodwell visited Pitcairn, authorities sent another official to report on island conditions. On December 1, 1929, the ship R.M.S. *Corinth* brought Mr. H. G. Pilling, assistant to the High Commissioner for the Western Pacific. Met on arrival by chief magistrate Richard Edgar Christian, Pilling "proceeded to the shore" in a boat to which "a somewhat primitive motor engine had been installed." "Drenched to the skin by spray from waves beating against the sides of the boat," Pilling then climbed the Hill of Difficulty, "carved out of the face of a cliff," as he stated. Here he was welcomed by residents.

Assistant High Commissioner Pilling made a brief visit to the school, but as students had left for the afternoon, he glanced at exercise books left on desks and judged their work to be "of a very elementary standard." After looking into several homes, Pilling climbed three hundred feet to look at agricultural plots. Pilling next had the populace assemble at the courthouse so he could congratulate them "on their sentiment of loyalty to the Throne and on the proud position which they held as members of the British Empire." After spending less than two hours on the island, Pilling was able to file a report for his superior's consideration.

Pilling presented his opinion of those of the two hundred people he saw: "In appearance the islanders resemble the usual type of Polynesian half-caste to be seen throughout Polynesia. They appeared to me to be of good physique, the majority with bright intelligent faces, but here and there were to be noticed some with the dull bucolic type of countenance usually associated with out-of-the-way villages in isolated districts.... I noticed no obvious signs of degeneracy, but the bad condition of their teeth was remarkable. Many appeared to have all their front teeth missing at quite an early age."

Pilling reported that Chief Magistrate Richard Christian had complained "bitterly" that islanders were no longer obedient, that few wanted to assume elected posts, and "that immorality and promiscuous living was becoming more common...." Pilling expressed regret that the "idealistic communism of previous days is disappearing and that individualistic tendencies are on the increase." Assuming that more could be learned in two weeks than he had learned in two hours, Pilling concluded that a "Senior Officer of the High Commission Service ought to live there for two to three weeks for the purpose of studying local conditions thoroughly...."[21]

CHAPTER 22

What Depression?

Earthly Paradise or South Seas Appalachia?

For most of the civilized world, the 1930s were a decade of Depression; for Pitcairners, normally living under depressed conditions and with rich soil to grow ample food, the economy of the 1930s was close to normal. A visitor likened Pitcairn homes and personal appearances to those of America's poverty-stricken Appalachia. Nevertheless, as Electa Johnson noted of the people during her visit in 1936, "They sincerely believe that Pitcairn is an earthly paradise and that those in the outside world, which they only half understand, cannot possibly be as happy and well off as they are on Pitcairn."[1]

While disease, alcohol, tobacco, blackbirding, emigration and armed strife diminished the population of indigenous Oceania communities, Pitcairn was a community that continued to grow. From the 45 people who returned from Norfolk by 1864, due to a healthy birthrate of 2.5 per annum between 1864 and 1937, and a healthy lifestyle, the population reached its apogee in 1937 at 233. It had risen nearly four and a half times in three-quarters of a century. Pitcairn lost few people through emigration because, as an observer wrote, "The people of Pitcairn are very loath to part with any member of their community, and if an adventurous spirit is revealed in a young man which prompts him to leave Pitcairn, the older people will try hard to dissuade him from leaving, pointing to all the unhappiness and wickedness which exists in countries far from the peace of Pitcairn."[2]

They Came, They Saw, They Wrote

A handful of observers enable us to examine Pitcairn life in the 1930s. Irving and Electa Johnson visited for the first time in 1934 aboard the yacht *Yankee*. Electa — or Exy — recalled that as a result of the recent publication of Charles Nordhoff and James Norman Hall's *Mutiny on the Bounty*, her husband Irving decided to sail to Pitcairn from the Galapagos. "I remember well our arrival," Electa wrote. "The Pitcairners came out in their longboats and jumped on board. The were not a prepossessing lot as most of them had no front teeth and their clothes were rather shoddy. We felt they looked like the mutineers themselves and we retreated behind the wheel. Parkin [Christian, the chief magistrate] came toward us and said in his soft voice, 'Don't be afraid; we are your friends,' and with that we did indeed become friends."[3]

Australian film-maker Charles Chauvel visited in the early 1930s and took motion pictures of Pitcairners to show as segments of his film *In the Wake of the Bounty*. Chauvel told about his Pitcairn experience by publishing a book with the same title. James Norman Hall described the island during a brief stopover in 1933. Dr. Harry L. Shapiro was ashore for ten busy days in December 1934 and January 1935. Chairman of the Anthropology Department at the American Museum of Natural History, Shapiro saw Pitcairn as a laboratory where he could study a population whose genealogy had been well documented for nearly a century and a half. When he returned, he wrote *Heritage of the Bounty*.

In 1937, Dr. Rufus Southworth, a physician from Ohio, spent four and a half months treating patients. Southworth had previously visited the island in 1934, aboard the *Yankee*. Dr. Southworth lived with the Roy Clark family, and Shapiro with the Burley Warren family. That more outsiders did not come to stay is explained by the fact that the chief magistrate refused nearly all requests, except requests by *Bounty* descendants and by Seventh-day Adventists such as the school teacher Agnes Ross, and the dentist *Cooze* whose services were desperately needed. Both were New Zealanders. Agnes Ross wrote letters as well, which have been preserved and published. As a result, 1930s Pitcairn Island lives in vivid description.

The Risky Business of Landing

As the *Rangitata* with Dr. Southworth aboard approached Pitcairn Island in total darkness, Southworth saw "Lights bobbing up and down a mile or so distant [which] showed that the Pitcairners were already out.... The powerful searchlights from the port side illuminated the four whaleboats (each 36 feet long) that were jumping up and down. They were rowed by either twelve or fourteen oars. Three of them were loaded with men and women; the fourth had only the oarsmen on board. Two long ladders, rope with wooden steps, were dropped from C deck and in a moment nearly all in the boats climbed up and on the ship."[4]

Islanders carried with them "bananas, watermelons, many colored baskets and Panama like hats, woven in Pitcairn, full rigged models of the *Bounty*, fishes and small vases carved from the dark wood obtained on Henderson Island."[5] In 1937, craftsmen sold an estimated ten to twenty pounds' sterling worth of curios on each ship. Dr. Southworth was brought to shore in one of the boats without any lights to guide the rowers. As Roy Clark commented, "The Pitcairners seem to know the way by instinct."[6]

Descriptions of the Islanders

Of the Pitcairners, Dr. Shapiro wrote, "I had expected to see definite indications of the Tahitian contribution to their mixed Anglo-Polynesian origin. Instead, the men, en masse, were more like a group of Englishmen — dock workers — with ugly, knobby hands and feet, roughened and calloused by labor. They wore nondescript garments, the gifts of passing vessels or bartered from the crew of the New Zealand Shipping Company steamers. ... Their complexion was ruddy and weather-beaten and the hair dark, although with a suggestion of fairer color here and there. The almost universal loss of teeth had produced a curious sucking-in of the cheeks and a collapse of the mouth."[7]

Members of the Seventh-day Adventist community in other countries sent packages of clothing to the women. Shapiro reported, "One woman on the island made a comment that will strike every woman as pathetic. She told me that she had never had a new dress or enjoyed the feminine ecstasy of selecting a dress for herself."[8] However, a woman with money from the sale of souvenirs, and infinite patience, could send to Montgomery Ward or another mail order company for new clothing. Observers noted that the people went barefoot except on Sundays, when they wore shoes made of canvas and rope and pandanus leaves.

Pitcairn's women lived long in the 1930s; those age sixty to eighty-five outnumbered men three to one. The oldest of the women was Mary Ann McCoy — known as "Aunt Ann" and described as blind and fragile. She had been born in 1851. Visitors were taken to meet the sole survivor of the third generation of Pitcairners. Aunt Ann was the only surviving islander who had lived on Norfolk, returning with the party which arrived in 1864. Yet, she was unable to satisfy expectations that she would somehow know intimate details of life and death among the mutineers a hundred and forty years earlier. Shapiro explained visitors' disappointment: "It was natural to expect that [the mutineers and companions] would have frequently retold their exploits to an eager audience of children, and those listeners would transmit the story in turn to a newer crop of ears — and so on unto the present. But ... I was told almost to the very phrases the accounts I had read for myself...."[9]

Pitcairners at Home

The homes that the mutineers constructed had been largely destroyed in 1858 by the shipwrecked crew of the *Wild Wave*. They had been replaced by frame houses whose walls were rough boards, overlaid. Most had corrugated iron roofs, from which rain water fell into large vats, which was the family's water supply. Saving rain water posed a problem, however, as mosquitoes bred in the stagnant containers. "There are few places I have ever been that could boast of so many mosquitoes," Dr. Southworth complained, but "luckily they are not of the malaria or yellow-fever bearing type." Some houses had glass windows but if they had screens they were not mentioned by the observers.

Shapiro described Burley Warren's living room floor as consisting of "wide, roughly-cut, but smooth boards.... The walls and ceiling were hung with wall paper which needed replacing. But so hard is wall paper to come by that no doubt Burley preferred retaining his tattered paper to having none at all...." A couch and table, both produced on the island, "and an old and elaborate bureau shared another wall with a harmonium of the same vintage. Besides crippled kitchen chairs, the only other furniture was a stout chest whose nicked and battered condition lent a nautical air to the room."[10] Shapiro had a bed in his room and, for a closet, nails on which to hang his clothes. Shapiro judged the furniture to look as if it "had been furnished from an unpretentious suburban attic."[11]

Homes were lit by electric and kerosene light. Victrolas produced music from scratchy records. James Norman Hall wrote that "In Adamstown it is easy to imagine that one is in some settlement far back in the mountains of Virginia or Tennessee. The same primitive conditions prevail, and the same clannishness among the people whose faces bear the same stamp placed there by isolation and a crude hard manner of life."[12]

Lifestyles

Like their Tahitian ancestors, Pitcairners enjoyed two substantial meals — breakfast at ten and dinner about four. "The Pitcairners do not use a knife and fork when eating," Dr. Southworth observed, "for them the spoon answers every need.... As far as forks are concerned, everybody knows the precedence held by fingers over forks in the matter of creation."[13]

Pitcairn's community was essentially an extended family. "Young Edward, seeing a light in John's and Mary's house as he passes, just drops in and without a word sits down, may or may not join the conversation and may as unceremoniously depart. Similarly, Henry may decide on the spur of the moment to invite himself to a meal in progress at David's house. A place is made for him at once, without surprise and without question."[14] Southworth commented, "Often I see young people, or even older persons, living in homes as if they were members of the family, only to learn later that their real homes are elsewhere."[15] This casualness may be explained by the fact that families were (and are) interrelated and by the Polynesian propensity to participate whole heartedly and gladly in raising one another's children. Thus if Young Edward barges in on Mary, it is as if a close relative has come home. Dr. Shapiro commented that in such intimate circumstances, "secrets, family or personal, are not easily concealed.... The transgressor is known, and must suffer the judgment of the community."

Shapiro stated, "The days when the virtue and chastity of Pitcairn women were recognized as inviolable by the hard-boiled crews of whaling ships have disappeared." During the fifty years preceding the mid-thirties, morality, according to Shapiro, had deteriorated, resulting in "practically a quarter of all births being illegitimate" and "a considerable number" of births to married couples premature. Even when marriages had been sanctified by ceremony or long-term commitment without ceremony, "a roving taste in sex relationships" existed.[16]

One moral problem that probably did not exist was abuse of alcohol. Island Adventists considered abstinence from drink a pillar of their piety and morality. The islanders drank water. There was no evidence of milk drinking. A few drank coffee or tea. Shapiro commented, "Even to this day the islanders abhor intoxicants. None were to be seen, and no one privately dropped a word that a wee drop might good for the health."[17] In 1937, while attending a national conference of the American Women's Christian Temperance Union in Washington, D.C., Miss Emily McCoy of Pitcairn Island told a reporter that all of her two hundred fellow inhabitants were members of the W.C.T.U.; presumably Miss McCoy was speaking metaphorically. The reporter commented that the fact was "quite phenomenal, considering that the original Pitcairn islanders were as rough and rum-swoggling a bunch of sailors as ever sailed the seven seas," and that two generations previously, "the existence of the island was threatened by a series of rum brawls in which both men and women got roaring drunk and went entirely berserk." Whether Miss McCoy gave that information to the reporter or whether he invented it somehow is not stated in the article.[18]

Adamstown

Dr. Southworth described the village in a letter to his family:

Adams Town begins at the edge where the narrow path up from the landing joins the broad path known as "Public Road." On the right, just before entering the village, is a small wooden house used as a post office and for other purposes. Back of the post office and up perhaps fifty feet is a level on the edge of the cliff overlooking Bounty Bay.... The first few houses on each side are located in the section known as "Big Fence." It then continues in the main due west, following along the side of a hill with houses to the left above and to the right below. Extending less than half a mile, Public Road ends at a great banyan tree which it divides into two nearly equal parts.... Taking the path leading a bit north of west the prison house is passed on the right; across is the public forge where the *Bounty*'s anvil stands.... This path extends to a graveyard a hundred yards father [sic] on leaving on the right the public press for sugar cane.[19]

Dr. Shapiro wrote, "There was no trace of arrangement order of any kind. Branching off from the main road were a succession of small paths, and from these stemmed others, no one of which kept to a straight line. Curving, twisting, crossing back and forth, these lanes, determined by convenience, formed a veritable maze...." Shapiro described the Square as "a community center — a flat open area about one hundred feet square and about six to ten feet directly above the road. Here were a two-storied, many-windowed church, like a New England meeting house without a steeple, the courthouse, and the signal bell suspended on a crossbar."[20]

Church

Pitcairn in the thirties remained very much a church-going community, dedicated to the belief that the second coming of Christ was imminent. As Southworth explained, "From the present upset condition of the world, the Adventists believe that the end of all things is at hand." He referred of course to the Great Depression, Hitler's threat, dictatorial Marxism-Leninism in the Soviet Union, and Japanese expansionism. This apocalyptic conviction, at least according to Pitcairner Roy Clark, had "many of the islanders decidedly improvident for the future."[21]

In addition to multiple Saturday church meetings, the extended family would gather to pray and sing hymns together and to read the Bible. James Norman Hall, a guest in the home of Ben Young, recalled that "Uncle Ben Young brought out the family Bible for evening worship. All gathered around the table, which was lighted by a kitchen lamp, and listened with grave attention while a chapter was read from the Psalms. Then they got down on their knees while Uncle Ben led them in prayer."[22]

The church was at the center of community life. The two-story structure was fronted by a porch that led into a hall with two staircases. Both stories had meeting rooms, but the one on the first floor was where the principal Sabbath service was conducted. Uncomfortable wooden benches, a pulpit and an organ constituted the sanctuary's furniture. Each story had eight windows on each long side. A church bell hung from a crossbar nearby. When it was rung once, Pitcairners assembled for religious services; two bells meant a meeting of all residents. Three strikes summoned men to public service, four meant a share-out of food from a ship, and five meant "Sail ho!"

Friday was known as Preparation Day because work that was done daily had to be completed before sundown, as no work would be done on the Sabbath. Dr. Southworth explained: "All the food for the Sabbath is cooked; the floors of the house are scrubbed and everything put in apple pie order."[23] Moreover, the men shave before sundown, don fresh clothing and shoes, "which constitutes a real act of devotion, almost penance, for these good people accustomed to go barefooted the rest of the week."[24]

When Dr. Harry Shapiro went to church in December 1934, he decided to "sit through

The Square is the hub of Pitcairn life. Here are found the court house, the church, cooperative store, government offices, library, etc. People meet here for public occasions. The buildings are painted white and gray and are neatly kept. Photograph by Robert Kirk.

all of the services." He attended Sabbath School at 7:30 a.m. He was joined there by "practically every able-bodied man, woman and child."[25] Hymns, a prayer, a reading, and an appeal for funds for Melanesian missions were followed by the congregation breaking into five smaller classes and taking their places in opposite corners of both floors of the church. Eleven o'clock service followed in the upper floor. It included hymns, Scripture readings, communion, prayer and a sermon by Roy Clark. Dr. Southworth attended church on Easter and remarked that "no attention was paid" to it as a special day; in fact, he wrote, "they do not observe any day of the Church calendar not even Christmas."[26]

A tenet of Seventh-day Adventism is tithing. Church members gave ten percent of the money earned from selling curios or ten percent of their produce. Islanders were reported in the early 1930s to give two hundred pounds sterling a year to Adventist missions in the Pacific, Asia Minor and South America.[27] Those tithed fruits and vegetables that were not sold in sufficient time to a passing ship were stored in the tithe house. There "these perishable articles of food merely rot away," Shapiro noted.[28]

After the service, Shapiro followed all of the men into the anteroom, not knowing what to expect. "As I stepped into the anteroom ... I saw a pile of white enameled basins and pitchers and a stack of hand towels. The men divided into two equal groups, the members of the one providing themselves with towels, basins, and pitchers of water; those in the other group removing their shoes and rolling up their trouser legs." The men then paired up, one group washing the feet of the other, before reversing positions and having their own feet washed by the men they had serviced. "This was the foot washing ceremony — the symbol of humility."[29] Not until the early tropical sundown on Saturday could secular activities be pursued and games such as dominoes be played in island homes.

Dr. Southworth described a funeral which he attended. All dressed in their "Sunday" [the doctor meant Saturday] clothes. Eight pallbearers wore dark blue suits, which were actually naval uniforms donated by officers of passing ships. Hymns and prayers on the verandah of the dead man's house constituted the ceremony. The pallbearers carried the casket to the public road, followed by family members and then the rest of the people. At the grave site, mourners sat at the edge of the grave, where "demonstrations of grief were marked and rather voluble." More hymns and prayers and a few speeches about the "next world" preceded lowering the coffin into the grave.[30]

Charles Chauvel wrote that "There is a tragedy and loneliness stamped upon the features of the Pitcairn people," which he attributed to their adherence to Adventism. "Their new religion has brought to them a mass of modern 'taboos' as fantastic as any of the tribal inhibitions of the Polynesian savages of yore." Chauvel mentioned prohibitions against dancing, tea, and popular music.[31] Electa Johnson disagreed with Chauvel's viewpoint, stating that "the general advantages of Seventh Day Adventism as practiced on Pitcairn are very great. Their faith and their consequent attitude of kindness, temperance, and peacefulness can only be admired. The people are absolutely sincere and conscientious."[32]

An Accusation of Murder

The Courthouse "was a single large room, one end of which was partitioned off as a post office. The remainder of the room contained about fifteen long benches. Pictures of King George V and Queen Mary hung on the wall. When the chief magistrate held court, Chauvel wrote, the penalty was seldom more severe than catching rats. "When serving a 'rat-penalty,' the sentenced man must kill a specified number of rats and prove the killing by presenting their tails to the Magistrate."[33]

In 1937, when Mr. J. S. Neil was sent to Pitcairn from High Commission headquarters in Fiji to examine and improve the laws, he was asked to try the first murder case in four decades. Most of the island's 233 people crowded into the courthouse to witness the trial of a woman accused of murdering her sick husband by poisoning his tea. When Neil told the constable to bring in the prisoner, he was told the prisoner was already in. Neil found her sitting among the public observers. Neil explained the accusation to her. She replied that her husband had been sick and "he just died...." Neil entered a plea of not guilty and called the first witness. He was informed there were no witnesses. The woman, he soon understood, was a "troublesome character" whose husband had died a day after drinking tea. Neil adjourned the court for lunch and after lunch the room filled again. Neil dismissed the case as having no substance and gave the gathering "a simple address ... on the principles of British law...."[34]

School

Students worked seated at benches and tables in a fifty-foot-long open room while teachers presided behind desks. "Religious texts" dominated the walls. School through much of the 1930s was taught by two Pitcairn men and Miss Agnes Ross from New Zealand. The headmaster until about 1932 was American-born Roy Clark, and from 1937, Fred Ward. Clark told Shapiro that "on the whole ... the children are neither very eager nor apt pupils." Children who saw their life roles as weaving baskets or manning whaleboats when not tilling soil may have questioned the usefulness of memorizing names of England's medieval monarchs.

Attendance was compulsory from ages six to fourteen. Shapiro counted forty-four pupils. Class began at 6:30 a.m. and continued for three hours. Pupils went home for breakfast, which was served at 10 a.m. Younger children studied reading, writing and arithmetic and older students added history, geography and other subjects. When not in school, children swam and surfed. Their kites had tails of banana bark, and their tops were made by sticking a coconut leaf through the center of a dodooee nut.

The islanders, having received a basic education, continued to read what was sent them from abroad—out-of-date newspapers, magazines from England and the United States, and religious tracts. Pupils who saw a limited existence for themselves often found their lessons in history and geography had paid off when they had opportunities to work on ships or to travel with money earned.

Another Shipwreck

On September 11, 1933, the two-masted schooner *Pro Patria* arrived with a cargo of coconuts. Residents were glad to trade produce for coconuts with Captain Winnie Brander. Roy Clark recalled, "Bag after bag was carried off, until not another nut remained. Our own supply on the island is low since a hurricane some years ago, followed by a disease in the plants, so when the opportunity comes to increase our supply it is a delightful time."[36] After two days the ship left, carrying seven Pitcairn men to Mangareva; they were Arthur Young and his three grown sons, a boy surnamed Christian, and two Warrens. James Norman Hall was aboard. After fifty hours the boat was wrecked on Timoe Island, one of the Gambiers.[37] One crew member was killed. The survivors rowed to Mangareva. From Mangareva, Hall found passage home and wrote *The Tale of a Shipwreck* about his experience.

The seven Pitcairners were stranded on Mangareva. During the next several months the island council debated whether to send a boat to Mangareva to rescue the men. As no boat seemed suitable for the long voyage, they failed to do so. It was not until February of the following year that Captain Irving Johnson of the schooner *Yankee* brought the seven home. With them came Ruan, a Mangarevan girl of sixteen, accompanying Pitcairner Sterling Warren. Captain Johnson married Sterling and Ruan aboard ship and Pitcairn acquired a new resident.

Agriculture

Previous fears that agricultural production would be inadequate were obviously unfounded, as the Pitcairners fed over two hundred inhabitants and exported a substantial amount of fruit. The soil is rich, but the flat and arable eight percent of the island is about the size of New York City's Central Park.

In the center of Aute Valley, James Norman Hall found small, scattered gardens containing taro, yams, sweet potatoes, beans, bananas, guava and orange trees. Resident Arthur Young informed Hall that the volcanic soil was so rich that the same crops could be planted in the same field year after year, although islanders used only hoes, shovels and spades to till the soil. Hall, a resident of Tahiti, commented, "I have never seen an island more fertile. Christian might have searched the Pacific over without finding another refuge, so perfectly suited to his purposes whether for concealment or for sustenance."[38]

Some crops were seasonal. In June all residents turned out for the sugar harvest and the grinding of cane. A visitor wrote: "The people make their own grinding machines out of heavy timber and empty nail drums. They make their own salt from sea water. But the most interesting industry of all is the making of [*ti*] molasses. It is like wheat honey."[39] Arrowroot was, and is, a favorite food. In the Pitcairn winter the islanders pull and harvest the root as the first step in baking arrowroot biscuits. It is a laborious process. First the roots are peeled and washed, then crushed into a pulp, washed again and strained. The pulp is then strained through a sieve and dried until it becomes a fine powder suitable for baking.

Successful growth of oranges depends on good weather conditions, including adequate water. A freeze or drought can destroy a crop. By 1937, islanders sold oranges for an estimated £1,800 to £2,000. Dr. Southworth described an additional challenge to the growers, a challenge that southern California and Florida growers did not face: transferring three hundred crates, each containing 144 oranges, from a longboat to a ship. In April 1937, a steamer approached from Panama to pick up a shipment of oranges. A wild storm threatened and the captain radioed that the weather was too bad for his ship to stop. The weather dramatically improved within an hour's time and at nine in the evening the captain indicated that he would, indeed, stop to load the cargo. Undaunted by pitch blackness, the intrepid boatmen ferried orange crates out to the ship, and as the last of the three hundred crates were hustled aboard, "the storm broke again with redoubled fury. Everybody scrambled back into the boats and started for the Landing. Not only the wind blew harder and harder and the seas, that had subsided a little, became bigger and bigger, but the rain came down in what was almost a cloudburst. In the inky blackness five of the boats made the pass successfully. The sixth ... piled up on the rocks, being badly damaged before it was finally brought to the landing. Luckily, none in the boat was harmed."[40] The following month, on May 12, in an attempt to load seven hundred cases, one boat was wrecked but none of its crew was badly injured.

Medicine and Health

Accidents continued to be the leading cause of injury and death. Dr. Shapiro counted nineteen deaths by accident listed in the *Pitcairn Book of Records* from 1864 until his arrival in 1934. Add to these deaths by lockjaw, internal injury, and spinal injury, and about twenty-two percent of deaths on Pitcairn could, during those seventy years, be attributed to accidental causes. Consumption and typhus accounted for eleven percent each; "old age" was attributed as the cause of seven deaths. Seventeen deaths were those of infants under one year.

Without a permanent physician, islanders relied on native herbs and a supply of pharmaceuticals for most contagions. For serious illness or injury, there was no quick evacuation to a hospital. But there was hope for medical attention: If a ship were nearby, if the ship had a physician, if the captain were willing to stop, and if the physician were willing to brave the waves that crashed onto rocks guarding Bounty Bay, then the acute patient might have the benefit of trained care.

Dr. Southworth practiced on Pitcairn from March 2 to July 18, 1937. He counted 558 treatments and examinations that he had performed in four and a half months; these included treating forty-six different injuries and diseases. He saw as many as twenty-three patients in a day. He found an island of slightly hearing-impaired folk and wrote that one lady was "greatly astonished at the improvement in her hearing" when he removed "a plug of wax nearly an inch long from each ear."[41] The temporary physician also dealt with residual coughs from influenza outbreaks which regularly occurred after the islanders had gone aboard a passing steamer. Epidemics were so frequent that to differentiate one from another, each epidemic was named for the ship. "I was surprised," Dr. Southworth told his family, "to find to what an extent the good people of Pitcairn consider this sickness as a matter of course and do not ask for medical help unless they are feeling quite badly."[42]

While Dr. Southworth was in residence, the High Commissioner for the Western Pacific sent a visiting physician to treat islanders and write a report on island health. He was a Dr. Duncan Cook. When Cook assembled the islanders to tell them the purpose of his stay, he cited among his credentials having worked among the Maori, New Zealand's Polynesians. Southworth reported that Cook's statement "did not make the best impression on his listeners, who like to think of themselves as English rather than Polynesians."[43]

Cook summarized his findings: "Relatively speaking, ... this small isolated community has a medical service which meets with practically all their requirements and does not cost them anything." Cook allowed that medical emergencies remained and would remain a problem. "I recommend that a medical officer should be sent every two or three years for the purpose of treating all cases of sickness and examining all the population...."[44] Cook's recommendation did not consider those who would have to wait two or more years in pain or discomfort for a doctor's appointment.

Shapiro wrote that no Pitcairn woman out of sixty who were examined had all of her teeth and that nearly a third of those women had no teeth. The men were somewhat better off, five males having all of their teeth.[45] The well-functioning island sugar mill may have been a contributing factor to tooth decay. During the 1930s, Pitcairn had a full-time dentist, and the dentist had critics. Dr. Cooze, an Adventist from New Zealand, came to Pitcairn in 1928 with his wife, father, and two children. He told islanders he had come to improve his health. Shapiro reported that soon after Dr. Cooze began his practice, most islanders were eating their roasted goat with new false teeth. "Uncle" Ben Young told James Norman Hall in 1933, "We've got a dentist here now, from New Zealand, but my goodness, he don't know much about his trade. We can do better work for ourselves than he does."[46]

When Dr. Duncan Cook wrote a report for the High Commissioner in 1937, he stated of the inhabitants: "The teeth are bad, few reaching the age of twenty without requiring either a complete or partial artificial set, and children suffer from caries [decay of bone or teeth] at a comparatively early age."[47] Dr. Cooze was to remain until 1945, when he returned to New Zealand.

Celebrating the Coronation — Twice

Trade aboard ships was particularly brisk in the months leading to the coronation on May 12, 1937, of King George VI and Queen Elizabeth; New Zealanders stopped at Pitcairn as they made their way to London on the Auckland-to-Panama route. At midnight on May 11, the island bell was rung and guns were fired to mark the beginning of festivities. At six the following morning, "It seems as if everyone who had a gun wished to see if it was in good order," Dr. Southworth wrote.[49] At noon the islanders assembled at the Square, women dressed in white with shoes and stockings, men in donated merchant marine officers' uniforms complete with brass buttons and insignia. Only the children remained barefoot. Benches for the audience were set up in front of the courthouse. Roy Clark led a prayer, Dick Fairclough explained the history of the Stone of Scone, schoolchildren recited, boys sang "Britannia the Pride of the Ocean," and girls sang "Waterloo." Dr. Southworth then spoke in glowing terms about the British Empire, the new king and queen, and Pitcairn and its heritage. "Items by Older Folks" followed, consisting of recitations and song. At the conclusion, all of the islanders rose to their feet and lustily sang "God Save the King."

Six days later the islanders celebrated the coronation again. This command performance came at the request of Mr. Niel from the High Commissioner's office and Dr. Cook; they had arrived too late for the May 12 festivities. The events of May 18 began with a half-mile boat race. After the race, men outfitted themselves once again in merchant marine officers' uniforms and paraded from Shady Nook to the courthouse. Dr. Cook took the opportunity to outline his proposals to inoculate islanders, and Mr. Niel gave gifts to most of the populace, including candy to the children. Parts of the entertainment of May 12 were then repeated.

Pitcairn was probably the only imperial possession which not only celebrated the coronation twice but whose entire — or nearly entire — population participated.

Playing Pitcairn Cricket

When the population was two hundred or more, it was possible to field two eager cricket teams. The losing team had to prepare and serve dinner featuring wild goat meat for the entire community.[50] No cleared land flat enough for a proper cricket playing field existed, but the best available field appeared to be "the Valley," the high plateau where plantations are located. Enough land was cleared of grass and bushes that two wickets could be set up on either side of a field. A slope provided a natural grandstand for spectators.

The reader who has no concept of the rules of this British game is at no disadvantage, because Pitcairners did not play by them, or by any other apparent rules. *The Guide to Pitcairn* explained, "There is no batting order: men and boys push and grab and the victors, flourishing their bats, take up a stance at the crease, surrounded on the leg side by their own team impatiently waiting for the chance to push and grab again.... The prevailing stroke is a hearty and lofted sweep to mid-on, for the grass, scrub and hillside pitch make other strokes almost worthless, and the ball is enthusiastically chased by all fielders within range, and by a good number of excited children as well when it vanishes into grass and lantana scrub."[51]

Dr. Southworth related his initiation into the sport: "I went in last and succeeded in hitting the first ball bowled. In true fashion I tossed the bat away when I ran, only to be called back to retrieve the bat. Fortunately, I hit the ball into a clump of bushes and had time to go back, grab the bat, and reach the opposite wicket, my partner (or whatever he is called) making a run." After taking some motion pictures of the action, and "Judging that my contribution would not materially affect the score, I went down the hill before the second inning commenced."[52]

Admiral Byrd to the Rescue

Isolation was increased when the short-wave radio station VR6AV broke down and had to be sent back to the United States in the spring of 1939 for repairs. Eight months later the repaired equipment languished at Panama, waiting for transportation, while, during the first months of the Second World War, the islanders received no news from the outside world. Radio operator Andrew Young lamented in a letter that a landslide had damaged boats in Bounty Bay, rats had eaten the island's crops, and supplies were low.

Rear Admiral Richard E. Byrd arrived on December 13, 1939, aboard the USS *North Star* on his way to Antarctica. Byrd's name was already synonymous with polar exploration. In 1926, he and pilot Floyd Bennett had flown over the North Pole, and in 1928 he established a scientific station that he named Little America at Bay of Whales, Antarctica. The following year Byrd and three companions flew over the South Pole. He continued to lead expeditions in the 1930s, which brought him to Pitcairn enroute to the southern-most continent.

The description that Admiral Byrd transmitted by wireless to the Navy Department was of a destitute Pitcairn community: "Aided by blinker signals from a cliff and her own search-light, the vessel approached within half a mile off shore before Captain Isak Lystad brought her to anchor. She was boarded immediately by hungry, poorly clothed islanders bearing palm-leaf baskets, wood carvings, cocoanuts, papayas, avocadoes, woven hats and birds' feathers which they offered in exchange for food and clothing."[53] Byrd gave his hosts 4,000 pounds of flour, 3,700 pounds of sugar, 10 crates of potatoes and some drums of gasoline. Byrd's technicians repaired station VR6AY, and his two physicians treated ailing islanders. In addition, islanders viewed the first motion picture most had ever seen; unfortunately Byrd did not tell the Navy Department the name of the movie shown in the ship's main salon. Admiral Byrd returned on February 25, 1956, and presented a gift of a hundred dollars to the island general fund.

End of a Depression Decade

The 1930s were, in a sense, the apogee of Pitcairn civilization and culture, when the island's population reached its all-time high. Although the islanders lived in some degree of poverty as they always had, they endured the thirties because their poverty was not substantially worse than it had ever been. Generally they were able to grow sufficient food for their needs. Much worse was to come in the next six years. Hunger would visit the islanders from time to time while the Second World War isolated the community.

CHAPTER 23

War and a Windfall: 1939–1959

War Again

On September 3, 1939, when the United Kingdom declared war against Adolf Hitler's Germany, Pitcairn, as a British possession, found itself also at war. The Second World War brought hardship and sacrifice to Pitcairners but the island itself was not attacked. Fewer ships stopped and when they did, the islanders sold or bartered fewer curios and less fruit. Several ships that had previously called were sunk by enemy submarines early in the war. *Rangitane*, a passenger liner which had stopped on May 31, 1940, was sunk in November north of New Zealand's Chatham Islands. *Napier Star*, a cargo ship, was at Bounty Bay on July 27, 1940, and was sunk on December 18 south of Ireland; eighty-four of the ship's crew were killed. The passenger liner *Remeura*, which visited Pitcairn on July 28, 1940, was torpedoed and sunk on August 26 off Scotland. On August 13, 1940, the steamer *Huntingdon* was at Pitcairn and six months later was torpedoed and sunk south of Iceland.

On June 15, 1941, Blue Star Line's *Australia Star* stopped, one of the few ships to come during wartime. Third navigation officer James Boyce, who judged it "the most interesting day of my life," was impressed by longboats coming out to the ship: "As they approached, we saw there were many women and children, some very young babies held by their mothers. The oarsmen were stocky and muscular, wearing straw hats such as their ancestors wore in the eighteenth century Royal Navy. Once alongside they swarmed up the side like pirates. Babies were hoisted up in baskets, and it was astonishing how quickly 150 people came aboard."[1]

With fewer men, Pitcairn's women had more work to do, including earning money for church tithes by selling aboard ships. Their situation was made nearly impossible because, for their protection, Pitcairn law forbade women to go aboard visiting ships. One seventy-three-year-old widow complained in a letter that the new law was "very hard on single women and widows who have no men to do for them; for that is the only way that they can get money to pay their tithes or collections in church and Sabbath school...."[2]

Captain Johnson of the *Yankee*

On January 31, 1940, the ninety-foots long *Yankee* under command of skipper Irving Johnson arrived. Two feet longer than the *Bounty*, but with only a third of the *Bounty*'s crew count — and no breadfruit other than in the galley — the sailing schooner, built in 1897, was comfortable. Johnson gave the islanders a new iron vise and took away the hundred-and-fifty-year-old vise from the *Bounty*, which he gave to the Mariner's Museum in Newport News, Virginia; utility, sadly, was seemingly more important to the community than its heritage.

During the *Yankee*'s stay the supply ship *Ruahine* arrived from New Zealand, bringing four islanders home as well as much-needed supplies for which islanders traded fruit. At the shareout which followed, "a representative from each of the 56 family units gathered on the [courthouse] porch with empty pails and basins. One man filled each of the containers evenly with flour, while another counted out biscuits, four to a family."

The Johnsons noted that the islanders had sailed a longboat to Henderson Island once during each of the previous three years because carvers needed to replenish their supply of miro wood. Irving's wife Exy wrote, "They took their lives in their hands for this task. The first voyage was successful. The second time they were becalmed fourteen days and early ran out of food. The third time they could not find the low island and ran into such a storm that the boats nearly foundered." Irving Johnson offered to take a group to Henderson and back. The night they sailed back, "The men, worn and tired, sang hymns all the way."[3]

1940: Stamps Bring a Windfall

Until 1926, Pitcairners sent letters without charge. From 1926 to 1940, they purchased stamps of New Zealand in their own post office to frank mail. Of inhabited British possessions, only Pitcairn and remote Tristan da Cunha in the South Atlantic had no stamps of their own. Over eighty other British countries and colonies had issues that either depicted local scenery and a small picture of the monarch, had only a picture of the monarch, or had been overprinted with the country's name. Collectors bought those stamps, paying at least face value. If a philatelist bought a set with a face value of roughly two pounds, aside from production and distribution costs, these tiny perforated pieces of paper represented pure profit for the country or colony in whose name they were issued. Officials reasoned that if *Bounty*-related events were pictured, given the popularity of British colonial stamps in general and the *Bounty* saga in particular, Pitcairn stamps could — and would — bring in a great deal of income from philatelists.

In May and June 1937, when J. S. Niel, of the High Commissioner's staff, did fact-finding on the island, he recommended: "To provide the additional revenue necessary" for the school, public works, communications and the upkeep of boats, "I can only suggest an issue of Pitcairn stamps. I can see no other source of revenue."[4] On April 14, 1940, Mr. Harry Evans Maude, Native Lands Commissioner, arrived from the High Commissioner's office with his wife. Because of the unavailability of transportation home in wartime, the Maudes spent eight months on Pitcairn. He too recommended that the colony issue its own postage stamps. At that time Britain was locked in a titanic struggle with Hitler's war machine, and issuing special stamps for the use of a couple of hundred isolated subjects in a fly-speck colony might have been assigned the lowest conceivable priority, particularly as their overseas correspondence was minimal and internal correspondence non-existent. However, the Crown Agents responsible for colonial stamp issues immediately set about contracting with artists and printers to work up a set of stamps for Pitcairn.

These artists and printers, under wartime conditions that included intensified German air attacks on south-east England, did a magnificent job. Pitcairn issued a set of eight stamps that captured the imagination and money of philatelists worldwide. The Crown Agents showed admirable restraint by making the highest value a mere two shillings six pence, while other colonies' high values were ten shillings or a pound. The set's affordability added to its popularity among collectors. On October 15, 1940, Roy P. Clark, the postmaster, and his helpers spent hours franking first-day covers in the tiny post office. Besides a vignette of King George VI, these stamps showed scenes of the island, its location on a map of the Pacific, pictures of William Bligh and of Fletcher Christian, John Adams and his house, a breadfruit tree, and of course, the *Bounty*. Interestingly, the postal administration honored two deceased criminals who, after endangering the lives of their captain and crew members, had made off with and destroyed an entire Royal Navy vessel.

Neil and Maude's idea was brilliant. The initial set of definitives turned on the spigot that brought a steady stream of cash to the island government. The income provided sufficient funds to maintain public buildings, pay teachers' salaries, build a new school and schoolmaster's house, as well as make improvement to the Landing. Money from sale of stamps paid for the island's first resident nurse, Evelyn Totenhofer, who arrived in April 1944.

In the first decade, the island government cleared a hundred thousand pounds. Islanders had never dreamed of such a windfall. Philately continued to fund public activities in the following decades. By 1957, when an attractive set of definitives that showed island scenes and Queen Elizabeth II appeared, philatelists bought up a total of 20,000 pounds sterling worth, and by the mid 1960s, over 29,000 pounds reached the public treasury.[5] From 1940 to his

The famous first issue of stamps, 15 October 1940. Note the king's appearance on 4 stamps with mutineers Adams or Christian. Money from stamp sales brought a windfall of profits which became the island's chief financial resource.

retirement in 1958, Roy P. Clark assiduously promoted philatelic interest in Pitcairn's issues and painstakingly corresponded with stamp collectors who wrote to him.

A Revised Law Code

In addition to facilitating the issuing of stamps for Pitcairn, H. E. Maude assisted the islanders in simplifying and clarifying the laws. These are known as the *Pitcairn Island Regulations, 1940*. The laws did not differ considerably from those of earlier days. Probably no English-speaking community in the world had more restrictions and admonitions containing the word "goat." In addition, the laws prescribed fines and/or imprisonment for using abusive or threatening language, profane or obscene language, spreading untrue reports, crying "Sail ho" when no ship was in sight, physical assaults, disorderly conduct, or insulting the court. The law took note of adultery, indecency and even cohabitation outside of marriage. The minimum age for marriage was set at seventeen for males and fifteen for females. Males from sixteen to sixty were liable for public service and to man the island boats when called on. Public service might have been a nuisance to some men, but it was in lieu of paying taxes.[6] Anyone under age twenty-one "who shall smoke tobacco in any form whatever" could be fined one pound.[7]

Island at War

On the same day that Admiral Nagumo's carriers headed out to destroy American forces at Pearl Harbor, two Japanese armed merchantmen, the *Aikoku Maru* and the *Hokoku Maru*, departed from the Marshall Islands to serve as raiders on the Panama-Auckland route. On December 12, 1941, five days after the attack on Pearl Harbor, they sunk the ship *Vincent* near Ducie Island. These two twin-screw high-speed merchant vessels were armed with deck guns and torpedo tubes and were able to carry seaplanes. The two ships took aboard survivors of the Vincent's crew of thirty-eight. These men became POWs.

On January 1, 1942, the two Japanese ships prepared to bomb the Matson Navigation Company's 3,270-ton freighter *Malama* somewhere between Pitcairn and Mangareva. Captain Malcolm R. Peters and his crew "surprised the Japanese pilot by scuttling" the *Malama* rather than allow the Japanese to have the honor.[8] When survivors climbed aboard, they were thrown into holding compartments with survivors of the *Vincent*. No evidence suggests that Pitcairn Islanders knew that dangerous Japanese ships were patrolling the colony's waters.

Germany also posed a danger to Pitcairn; historian R. B. Nicolson wrote that the presence of the radio station "probably saved" Pitcairn from attack by the *Komet*, a German raider. Rear Admiral Eyssen might have raided Pitcairn except for fear that radio reporting of the event would have jeopardized another more important action he intended.[9]

Tiny Pitcairn made a significant contribution of men to Commonwealth forces. According to *The Pitcairn Miscellany*:

"Boyd Christian served in Crete, was wounded and taken prisoner to Germany for the duration of the war.

"Clement Coffin served in Egypt for two years Was wounded at El Alamein and sent back home. Discharged in 1945.

"Chester Young served in Crete, Egypt, New Caledonia, and Norfolk Island. Was wounded and discharged in 1943.

"Ray Young served in four ships carrying supplies and troops in the Atlantic and Pacific. He was wounded in the thigh in Algiers when the *Awatea* was sunk by a torpedo.

"Robert Young served in six ships carrying supplies and troops in the Pacific. He was injured twice, once coming from Fiji, and the other off the coast of New Zealand.

"Walma Warren served in the ground force for two years. Went overseas to Japan and Singapore after the war.

"Wilfred Warren was on final leave, ready to leave for overseas, when he was accidentally killed.

"Percy, Vincent and Burnell Young, Joe Christian, Sterling and Andy Warren served in the Home Guards in New Zealand." On Pitcairn, forty-three men were assigned look-out duties, watching for the approach of enemy craft. In addition the island donated two hundred cases of oranges to the New Zealand Red Cross and five hundred carved canes to the Lord Mayor of London's charity for disabled veterans.[10]

To secure its island dependencies without the expense of garrisoning Henderson, Ducie and Oeno, the Shaw Savill and Albion ship *Corinthic* was asked to place signs on the islands, stating, in the name of King George VI, that they were property of the Crown and to erect a pole on each island and hoist a Union Jack. Some months later the *Corinthic* crew passed Henderson and noticed a swastika flag had replaced the Union Jack. Going ashore they found a notice stating, "With apologies to King George VI, this island is now the property of the Greater German Reich."[11] No Germans were present.

A seven-man radio team from New Zealand arrived in January 1944 aboard the U.S. War Shipping Administration's Liberty ship *J. Sterling Morton*. Unloading equipment for two transmitters and a meteorological station took eleven days. A team of lookouts was stationed on Pitcairn from January 1944 to November 1945, waiting for a Japanese attack that never came. Part of the PAN Expedition, these men operated a medium-frequency broadcasting station. When the team returned to New Zealand, the station was turned over to the High Commissioner for the Western Pacific for use by the people of Pitcairn.

Swiss Family Robinson on Pitcairn Island

In July 1944, resident Jessie Clark wrote to the *Honolulu Advertiser* that on the nineteenth residents spotted a small ship offshore flying the flag of neutral Switzerland. "Could it be the Swiss navy?" Jessie reported islanders asking.[12] Instead it turned out to be Mr. and Mrs. Mark-Walder, their son, and their cat and dog arriving from Tahiti. This war-time Swiss Family Robinson had set out on a world cruise before the war broke out, and when sailing home became dangerous due to enemy naval activity, they stayed in Tahiti for five years. Because of his wife's ill health, Mark-Walder decided to sail to South America in an attempt to return with her to Switzerland.

When they anchored off Pitcairn, a storm caused their twenty-five-ton schooner, *Trondhjem*, to drag anchor. Three island men came aboard to help. Roy Clark described the *Trondhjem* rising "high on a wave in a last anguished attempt at escape then [falling] upon the rocks. Masts and spars, booms and blocks, squeaked and groaned.... Sails flapped uselessly in the wind, ropes swung purposeless, in the air."[13] Soon the schooner settled between two rocks, which tore a hole in its side. The Swiss family became refugees on Pitcairn, waiting for a ship's captain to take them to Panama. The family had no money and the Pitcairn council claimed everything except personal items that could be salvaged from the wreck. On August 19, the

Federal Steam Navigation Company's *Northumberland* took the Mark-Walders to Wellington, New Zealand, as paying passengers after the council paid them for the goods salvaged and church members took up a collection for their expenses. Once in Auckland they were farther away from home than when they had set out, but Roy Clark reported that they eventually arrived home.

Peace and Destruction

Islanders knew the war must be nearly won when, on July 11, 1945, *R.M.S. Ruahine* returned, the first passenger vessel they had seen in five years. Pitcairn's chief material gain from the war was a "flying fox," a crane which New Zealand engineers contributed to offload cargo and lift it to the Edge, three hundred feet above; islanders no longer had to carry heavy objects up hill from the Landing.

While Pitcairn suffered no damage from a war-time enemy, weather brought significant destruction. On New Year's eve 1945, a tidal wave destroyed twelve fishing boats, a longboat and the boathouse at Bounty Bay. Two other longboats were badly damaged by a fallen beam. Part of the jetty was washed away and boulders were pulled on the shore. Then, on April 1, 1946, a tidal wave smashed into the harbor again, carrying off twenty-four fishing canoes and a thirty-eight-foot longboat.

A Controversy over Education

During the immediate post-war period a general feeling seemed to prevail that the quality of education was deteriorating on Pitcairn. A year had passed between the time that one teacher, Pastor Watson, had left and another, Brother F. P. Ward, arrived, and during that year no school was conducted. Both had been sent by Adventist administrators. Shortly after his return in 1947, Brother Ward closed the school, located at an area called Niger, below the Square. The building badly needed repairs. Although materials were available, Adventist leaders on the island were blamed for failing to repair the schoolhouse. The high commissioner's office in Suva, Fiji, was alarmed that school was, and had for some time, been in abeyance; moreover, "They had also been critical, for some time, of the varying abilities of the school teachers over the years and also the standards of instruction."[14] As reported in *Time*, "British inspectors who had seen [teachers] at work found that few of them had ever read a book outside school, knew little about teaching a course, could barely spell themselves." As a result, English speakers on Pitcairn were "slipping into a droning dialect all their own."[15]

In 1948, the High Commissioner for the Western Pacific, Sir Leslie Brian Freeston, summarily took over responsibility for education from the Adventist church. The education officer was now to be appointed by the New Zealand Department of Education for a two-year term. He was also to be the representative of Pitcairn's governor (the High Commissioner), and he would serve as advisor to the island magistrate and the council. Thus, the governor's office would oversee island finances and justice as well as education. Revenue from stamp sales would pay the teacher's transportation and salary.

On July 21, 1948, the first government-appointed teacher arrived from New Zealand with his wife and daughter aboard the steamer *Awahou*. He was Alan Watkins Moverley, an experienced educator, age forty. Moverley's arrival marked the first time the Seventh-day Adventists had lost control of any of their schools in the Pacific islands. Because the old school building was no longer usable, Moverley taught classes in the home of Norris Young, the island magistrate. About twenty pupils attended in the early 1950s. Pupils were ages five to fifteen. Secondary school was conducted through correspondence with a New Zealand institution and under Moverley's supervision.

Herbert Ford stated, "Upon his arrival, Moverley, an atheist, throws all the school's religious books into the sea." When he left in 1949, Moverley vowed to "get all the Adventists off the island." Moverley apparently influenced the High Commissioner's office to the extent that a new pastor, Norman Ferris, was at first denied a government-issued permit to land at Pitcairn. Ford wrote that many other factors aside from Moverley's stance "play a part in what is seen as a growing church-state battle."[16] Adventist historian Malcolm Bull stated that people became polarized and "This time of open and covert criticism proved to be a very difficult one for the church and the island and eventually led to more serious problems on the island over the next few years."[17]

Pastor Norman Ferris, having at last been permitted to land, stated that "the great majority of the Pitcairn family were loyal at heart, and were deeply grieved over these strange and disturbing actions."[18] An anti–Adventist feeling caused fear that "all contact between the church and the islanders might soon be cut by government decree."[19] The government permitted Gordon Branster of the Adventists' Central Pacific Union Mission to visit Pitcairn; Branster arrived in August of 1952, aboard the *Ruahine*, and worked with a measure of success to rebuild unity among members of the island's Adventist community.

When the *Awahou* brought the Moverleys, it also brought building materials for a new school. The new school was to be financed from stamp sales. The materials were unloaded over a period of three weeks and then carried up the Hill of Difficulty or hoisted on the flying fox. A site had been chosen at Pulau, a half mile from Adamstown. Three builders from Fiji and the men of Pitcairn erected the pre-fabricated school and teacher's house over a period of several months. Authorities equipped the school with a library, film projector, piano, phonograph, sewing machines, typewriters and other technical training tools. The building would be used until October 2006, when a new school building was completed.

While teaching on the island, Moverley made a study of Pitkern, the local language, and published a book on the subject with philologist Alan Ross, *The Pitcairnese Language*. In his spare time, Moverley experimented with varieties of trees to improve island fruit culture. Mrs. Moverley taught sewing and organized island women to help sew school uniforms. Moverley died in 1953 in England while working on his doctorate.

In spite of the use of a modern education facility, students — at least according to their instructors — were not academic. Roy Clark recalled that when he was education officer in the 1950s, school was dismissed when ships arrived. Clark introduced the standard American report card that he had grown up with in California schools. Clark wrote, "The children simply looked at the report cards and threw them aside, and I do not believe that one was carried home to parents."[20] In spite of compulsory schooling, adults read magazines, if they read at all. A teacher told Australian journalist Ian Ball in 1971 that island elementary school pupils were two or more years behind students in the same grades in New Zealand. Students of high school age were even further behind, in his estimation. The students did not read, according to the teacher, nor, according to Ball, in spite of a small library at the square, did their elders.

The Return of the *Bounty* Bible

In 1950 Pitcairn issued a stamp picturing the *Bounty* Bible. It is the Bible that mutineer Adams used to instruct the second generation. Today it is the chief historical attraction in the church. It is three inches thick, and measures five by seven inches. It contains an Anglican prayer book and the metrical psalms. The table page and the date of publication had at some time been removed.

The Bible had been gone from Pitcairn Island for 111 years. On July 17, 1839, the whaling ship Cyrus, out of Nantucket, arrived, and departed with what should have been the community's most precious possessions, both the *Bounty*'s Bible and Fletcher Christian's, known as the Pitcairn Bible. John Adams, grandson of the mutineer, gave the ship's Bible to the *Cyrus*'s carpenter Levi Hayden. Mary Christian, daughter of Fletcher, gave Hayden her father's Bible. Hayden had apparently been a most charming guest during his two weeks among the residents to have been entrusted with the two most precious religious objects on the island. Hayden promised to have both volumes rebound and returned to the colony. Instead, Hayden gave the Pitcairn Bible to a mariner's church in Boston, the Fort Hill Seamen's Bethel. It was later acquired by the New York Public Library and displayed in the Rare Book Room. In 1896, the *Bounty* Bible was presented to the Connecticut Historical Society.

When the islanders eventually learned the *Bounty* Bible's whereabouts, education officer A. W. Moverley appealed to the British Colonial Service to press for its return. The Connecticut Historical Society agreed, and asked the British ambassador in Washington, Sir Oliver Franks, to assume responsibility for its delivery. Franks had it sent first to England. In England, it was expertly rebound and delivered to Buckingham Palace to be viewed by King George VI and Queen Elizabeth. A special courier carried the Bible to Fiji aboard the *Rakaia*. When the Rakaia, to the courier's surprise, stopped at Pitcairn, he was unable to hand over the treasure. He had been ordered to bring it to the high commissioner's office in Suva, which he did. On February 19, 1950, Mr. H. A. C. Dobbs, deputy commissioner for Pitcairn, brought the Bible with him from Fiji aboard the *Rakaia*. On February 22, islanders saw Mr. Dobbs present the Bible to Chief Magistrate Warren Christian, and on the Sabbath, February 25, a special service was conducted to commemorate its homecoming.

Government

Mr. H. A. C. Dobbs stayed for several weeks into March, 1950, and reported to his superiors on "the state of affairs" on the island:—

1. the tendency to form factions and feuds which has been commented upon by nearly all outside observers has certainly not diminished; if anything, it is on the increase;
2. the Maude Constitution is not being properly observed, council meetings are haphazard and disorderly, public meetings are rare;
3. the policemen do not investigate cases and court cases are infrequent;
4. rules about women visiting ships are not enforced, and the behaviour of islanders on the ships is often deplorable....

Dobbs recommended that the high commissioner appoint the island police officer and an "Inspector of Police"; that a jail be rebuilt; and that officers from the high commissioner's office make more frequent visits.[21]

In 1952, the government in London enacted an Order in Council that transferred jurisdiction from the High Commissioner for the Western Pacific to the governor of Fiji. Pitcairn gained the status of crown colony. The governor of Fiji was given the title "Governor of the Pitcairn Islands." A governor of Fiji might or might not during his term ever set foot on Pitcairn, but generally someone from his office was sent out from time to time, as Dobbs had been. In October 1953, the governor sent Mr. J. B. Claydon to report. Claydon stayed from October 31 to December 26 and reported that islanders seemed contented.

Pitcairners remained among the Crown's most loyal subjects. When Queen Elizabeth II was crowned in Westminster Abbey on June 2, 1953, the community began celebrating on May 31. The three-day festivities included games, parades, a concert, a church service, and fireworks. Islanders who gathered around a short-wave radio in the courthouse heard the ceremony clearly. Because of the time difference with London, it was three in the morning before the radio announcer described Elizabeths being anointed by the archbishop of Canterbury. On the afternoon of coronation day a public dinner was served in the courthouse. Dessert featured a three-tiered "coronation cake" topped by a replica of a royal crown.

Essentially, Pitcairn remained much on its own, a subject of imperial benign neglect. Pitcairn's village-size population was sufficiently small that each adult could have a say in local governance, making Pitcairn in many ways a direct democracy. To carry out their wishes and to judge legal cases, islanders continued to elect the chief magistrate every three years and two assessors annually. The chief magistrate was also the ceremonial head of the community; in 1953, for example, Chief Magistrate John Christian and his wife represented Pitcairn in Fiji when they were received by Queen Elizabeth II and Prince Philip during their visit aboard the royal yacht *Britannia*.

When necessary, which was not often, the magistrate and assessors met as a court of justice. When island leader Parkin Christian visited the United States in 1956, a television interviewer expressed an interest in law and order Pitcairn-style:

"Do you have a policeman?" the interviewer asked.
"Aah corse we's gotta policeman."
"Well, what does he do?"
"Oor, he meks out gun licences."
"Do you have a jail?"
"Yea shure we's gotta jail."
"Does anyone ever go into it?"
"Oor yeers."
"How many ever go in?"
"Plaanty."
"What do they go in for?"
"Oor ... To sweep it out."[22]

Parkin Christian exaggerated. The jail did actually find some use in the 1950s. The island court had jurisdiction over criminal cases, the penalties of which did not exceed ten pounds' fine or three months' imprisonment, and civil cases that involved amounts under ten pounds. The loser in these cases had the right to appeal to a supreme court in Fiji. When a local law did not cover a matter under dispute, the laws of England applied.

Two Vast Improvements

Though national coffers were depleted from fighting World War II; providing increased services to her citizens; arming herself in the Cold War against the Soviet Union; and putting down colonial insurrections in places such as Kenya and Maylaya, the British government was generous to Pitcairn's minuscule population. The Colonial Development and Welfare Fund paid for one of Pitcairn's motorized launches, a movie projector, and new equipment for the radio station. It funded improvements at the Landing as well. In 1951, the first diesel plant was installed to bring lighting to the school and to private homes. *The Pitcairn Miscellany* commented, "A walk around the village at nights, when all plants were operating, and one would hear a variety of poppings and sputterings as the different types of engines vied with each other to disturb the evening hours. Each had its own particular beat and rhythm, easily distinguishable one from the other; and everyone could tell just by listening what plants were operating on any particular night. Power operated from 6 to 11 pm every night but Friday, when it went off at 10."[23]

In 1952, short-wave radio communications were improved. A wind charger powered batteries for the radio transmitter. Islander Tom Christian listened for ships' calls in the mornings and transmitted in the afternoons. Tom was exempt from other public duties such as road work or boat maintenance, and he received the pay due to a skilled technician. One day when a community member needed medical help that was not readily available, Tom radioed to passing ships; one ship agreed to turn around so its doctor could treat an islander stricken by acute appendicitis. The islander's life that Tom helped save was that of his sister.

Ships and Trade

Roy Clark recalled that in 1950, each boat had fourteen oars, requiring a crew of fourteen. The four boats in use at the time were *Ho Ho, Nuni, Surprise* and *Barge*. Each of the longboats had its own crew. Boys were apprenticed on the boats at fourteen and became crew members at fifteen. Crews were reluctant to change personnel once they had learned to trust one another in their arduous task; thus, the same men would work together as a well trained and synchronized team, from around age fifteen to sixty-five. The consequences of failure in their operation were too great to experiment with other combinations of members or to include inexperienced visitors. Even the expertise and precise team work of the crews were often no match for the elements; Clark described "boats caught on the crest of huge waves and driven with incredible speed directly and uncontrollably onto the rocky shore."[24] Had "Longboat Maneuvering" been an Olympic event, the "Pitcairn Fourteen" would have been quadrennial gold medalists.

Visitors noted that islanders climbed up aboard ships barefoot, with feet calloused and toes wide spread. They clambered up with fruit, and packing sacks full of carved flying fish, wooden tortoises and boxes shaped like open Bibles. When a ship came on the Sabbath and was unable to stay until dark, they offered their wares to passengers as gifts; however, the pious islanders gratefully accepted donations for them. As Adventists, they could not bring themselves to do actual business on a Saturday. Islanders counted fourteen Sabbaths during which they missed opportunities to trade in one year alone. Moreover, according to Roy Clark, when Pitcairners did board a ship on the Sabbath, they handed out Adventist literature.

When the Cunard Line *Caronia* arrived on February 9, 1954, islanders were eager to sell souvenirs to its 1,200 passengers. On that single day, sellers reportedly realized five thousand dollars, many families making several hundred dollars. Roy Clark told a friend that the *Caronia* was the largest passenger liner ever to call. Gathering up artifacts, going out to the ship, conducting business aboard with passengers and crew, returning to the island through the treacherous rocks, carrying the boats from the shore to their sheds, hauling cargo to the village, and then participating in the shareout of any public goods from the ship might take from sunup to after sundown. H.E. Maude noted that in the 1950s Pitcairn received more ships than Noumea, New Caledonia; Apia, Samoa; or Papeete, Tahiti.

In 1956, when photographer Luis Marden arrived aboard the *Rangitoto*, operated by the New Zealand Shipping Company, the longboats came out to the ship to sell curios and to bring Marden ashore. "Welcome to Peet-kern," said Parkin Christian, age seventy-three. Marden described the islanders whom he met that day: "The features of the Pitcairners, both men and women, were more strongly European than I had expected. They were tanned and brown skinned, but most were no darker than sunburned, brown-haired Englishmen. The women looked more Polynesian than the men."[25] Before the *Rangitoto* left in about an hour, the islanders had finished selling their curios and fruit aboard and raced to the ship's store to buy "lollies" and other items not readily available on their island.

The curio trade was serious business. About sixty percent of all curios were sold aboard ship and the rest by mail. Mail orders became important because fewer ships stopped each year. In 1956, sixty-five made calls, but by 1965, only forty-one.

All of the money was not spent in expensive ships' shops. Tom Christian studied in California in the 1950s for his broadcast license, and in Newbury Park he met Eddie Pullen, chief engineer for the Seventh-day Adventist *Voice of Prophecy* radio station. After his return, Tom would collect money from islanders and send it to Eddie. Pullen would order goods, supplies and equipment from Sears, Roebuck and send the goods by whatever ship was available. In addition to manufactured goods and processed foods, Pitcairners saved money to send their children to be educated in New Zealand, or in case they themselves needed passage to Auckland for medical treatment.[26]

Some Famous Visitors

Several well-known personages came to Pitcairn in the postwar period. With the exception of Thor Heyerdahl, who was interested in archaeology, the others came because Pitcairn was on their ship's route.

Pitcairn enjoyed its first visit from a member of Britain's royal family when, on February 19, 1947, *R.M.S. Tangitiki* brought the Duke and Duchess of Gloucester and their sons, Prince William and Prince Richard. Prince Henry, the duke, was the king's younger brother. Their royal highnesses were returning home after the duke served as governor general of Australia, a largely ceremonial office to which he had been appointed in November 1943.

In 1953, a ship stopped offshore carrying six-foot three-inch Salote, queen from 1918 to 1965 of the Polynesian kingdom of Tonga. Tonga was the last remaining kingdom in the South Pacific, and was a semi-autonomous British protectorate. Her Majesty was enroute by royal invitation to Queen Elizabeth's coronation. Adventist Pastor and Mrs. Norman Ferris were rowed out to the ship and the queen emerged from her cabin to walk around the deck with Mrs. Ferris, whom she had met previously. Her Majesty did not come ashore.

In 1956, Norwegian archaeologist and author of *Kon Tiki* Thor Heyerdahl arrived aboard the trawler *Christian Bjellan*. He not only came ashore but did the islanders an inestimable favor. Heyerdahl told of transporting Pitcairners to Henderson Island and back: "On its shores sixty passengers felled twenty-five tons of miro wood in a single day. The palm-fringed beach looked like a scene of a pirate battle as the colorful throng of Pitcairn people of all ages dashed into the surf with crooked branches and maneuvered the logs out to the boats rearing and plunging in the reef."[27] Parkin Christian told Heyerdahl that the supply should satisfy their carving needs for four years.

Sir Anthony Eden, who had served as Britain's Conservative prime minister for a little over a year and a half, arrived aboard *MS Rangitata* on February 12, 1957. A month before he had resigned following the Suez Crisis. His health and political career had been shattered by his abortive attempt to save the canal from a takeover by Egypt's Nasser. Recently created Earl of Avon, Eden sought warm weather and distance from Westminster. At Bounty Bay, the seas were so stormy that, as an islander recalled, "The boats received a heavy thrashing that night, and fruit, curios, and personal gear were awash in them."[28] Only Parkin Christian, Andrew Young and a few other hearty souls rowed out to the ship to wish the Earl and Countess of Avon well.

The easiest way to visit Pitcairn, of course, was to stay aboard ship and admire it from a distance, as did her Royal Highness Princess Alice, countess of Athlone, in March 1962. Chief Magistrate John Christian boarded the *Athenic*, bound for Auckland, presented flowers to the wife of the late Queen Mary's brother, and asked that the islanders' good wishes be conveyed to Queen Elizabeth. *The Pitcairn Miscellany* commented, "Quite a few of the local people also met her Royal Highness, and it was interesting to hear her comments. All were thrilled to be given the chance of meeting a member of our Royal Family."[29]

The *Bounty*'s Anchor! Who Cares?

In February 1957, skipper of the *Yankee* Irving Johnson dove down and found the *Bounty*'s anchor and brought it to the surface. Pastor Lester N. Hawkes described what happened next. "The islanders pounced on it to collect whatever they could. Large lumps of rust scale were taken. Among the most valuable pieces was the hemp rope knot which was still tied to the ring. These items were sold overseas.... After the salable parts were taken away the interest in the anchor diminished." Hawkes reported that he tried to get a team of men to help drag the anchor up to the Square, but "no one was interested."[30] With the help of Floyd McCoy, who read books on Pitcairn history, Hawkes chipped and treated the anchor against rust, painting it with cod liver oil and varnish. Some islanders then tried to tip the anchor back into the sea. When the governor of Fiji and Pitcairn was due to arrive, Hawkes appealed to the men's civic sense and they dragged it up the Hill of Difficulty. It now decorates the public square in Adamstown.

Time Out from Work

Each year started and ended with festivities as islanders took time off from their usual heavy schedule of work. On New Year's a men's team vied with a women's team in a tug-of-war contest, the women often pulling the men over. Amazingly, families managed to get away on vacation on their two-square-mile island. Their vacations took them to rustic camps built on the plateau. One family had "a good-sized, well-made house ... furnished with three comfortable beds and several reclining chairs...." The views were dramatic: "Eastward and far below lie the plantations; then beyond is the peak at the extreme northeast part of the island.... Due north is Bounty Bay beyond which the blue sea extends as far as the eye can reach. A little farther west Adams Town, so completely hidden by the growth on the hillside that little, if any, of it can be seen. But nothing can hide Mount Lookout — the most westerly point of land on Pitcairn where Christian's Cave is located."[31]

Back down the hill, a motion picture projector provided relaxation and entertainment at least once a week. Some movies were favorites and were repeated several times. *Mutiny on the Bounty*, not surprisingly, was the most popular. Islanders reportedly enjoyed seeing Fletcher Christian portrayed as an admirable hero and Bligh as an uncouth brute.

On July 31, 1957, the first Royal Navy aircraft carrier to come to Pitcairn and the first helicopters to land provided a needed diversion for the community. The carrier was HM *Warrior*, a ship that could accommodate forty-eight planes on its spacious deck. The August 1957 edition of *Pilhi* reported, "Soon two helicopters were hovering around; and when the first landed, out stepped Commodore Hicks to greet Council members. A party including Parkin, Andrew, Vernon, Ivan, Pastor, and the Teacher were taken off to breakfast on the carrier. An hour or two later the men of the island went aboard to trade.... In the afternoon the sailors came ashore to roam around and fill shirts with oranges, mandarins, and whatever could be found while the women and children went out to the carrier to enjoy a party lunch of buns, cake and ice cream...."[32] After giving each Pitcairner a signed Bible, the commodore arranged for a pyrotechnic display that lit up the sky.

Extended-family celebrations included elaborate meals with dozens of dishes. Birthdays are major party days on Pitcairn. All close relatives, which could easily amount to a majority of the population, are invited. All are seated at a long table, covered by a cloth which is

The anchor of *HMAV Bounty* was brought up in 1957, but the only interest shown by islanders was to salvage rope and rust in order to sell them as souvenirs. Adventist Pastor Lester N. Hawkes finally persuaded men to drag it to the Square, where it remains. Photograph by Robert Kirk.

hidden by many different dishes, in the celebrant's home. Grace is intoned: "Bless this food kind Father, bless it for our soul's use and make us thankful, Amen." As the official Pitcairn guidebook stated, "Pitcairners are solid trenchermen with a taste for sweet delicacies, which they mix appreciatively with meats and vegetables on the single plate that serves through the meal. Conversation about the food and the capacities of the eaters begins to slow and complimentary belching brings a glow of satisfaction to the hostess, who bustles from the oven ... to the table with more food and steaming cups of cocoa and tea." "So long as you get enough," the host reminds his guests.[33] Birthdays and holidays called for humpus bumpus, which consists of mashed ripe bananas with arrowroot flour, baked as fritters; or eddie, which is bananas cooked in coconut milk. Flora Christian explained, "Eddie — that's Lucy's husband — he like it, so that's why they call it for him."[34] Potta is stewed taro greens in coconut milk.

The Mystery of Bob and Moko

What follows is a shaggy chimpanzee story. In Vancouver, British Columbia, John and Diane Wells, both teachers, built a sea-going yacht, which they dubbed the *Flying Walrus*. Their plan was to see South Sea islands, to work for a while in New Zealand, and then to sail around the world over the period of a couple of years. In Papeete they met a Floridian in his late twenties. He said his name was Robert Tomarchin. Bob Tomarchin introduced his year-old pure-white chimpanzee as Moko. Tomarchin had returned to Tahiti after being deported by French authorities from Papeete to Fiji when he was unable to produce money for a return ticket. This time he was able to show travelers checks as well as valid papers for Moko. Tomarchin never told John and Diane his source of money or his profession.

On July 18, 1957, John and Diane Wells, Bob Tomarchin, and Moko sailed out of Papeete Harbor on the *Flying Walrus*. They told port authorities they were bound for Mangareva, Pitcairn Island, Raivavae, and Tubai before heading for Auckland. On August 10, John and Diane arrived at Pitcairn without Bob and Moko. Diane came ashore for the day and mentioned that they had had to drop an unreliable crewman off on an unnamed island.

On September 7, Shaw Saville Line's ship *Corinthic*, under the command of Arthur Jones, sighted a man and what appeared to be a child on Henderson Island. Reasoning that they were Pitcairners on an excursion to cut miro wood, Jones sailed to Pitcairn, where he was told all Pitcairners were accounted for at home. Tom Christian radioed Governor Sir Ronald Garvey in Fiji to report the sighting; Garvey advised the Pitcairners to go to Henderson to investigate. Two days later the ship *Pioneer Isle* from the United States arrived at Bounty Bay, and its captain readily agreed to transport two longboats and their crews, under command of Floyd McCoy, to Henderson Island. When the longboats made their way to shore after the seven-hour trip, an exultant Bob Tomarchin tearfully hugged Pitcairner Pervis Young in gratitude for having been rescued. "You have saved my life," Tomarchin told Young. "There are thousands of rats and they have eaten all my supplies."

When asked how he had come to be on Henderson Island, Tomarchin explained that when Moko ate Diane Wells's vitamins, she became "excited" and insisted he and Moko leave the boat for a few days. Tomarchin said the Wellses left him with a few supplies and promised to return shortly. Captain Jones of the *Corinthic* offered to transport Tomarchin — but not Moko — to Panama. Tomarchin refused to go without Moko and decided instead to go to Pitcairn with his chimp.

When the rescue crews offered to gather up Tomarchin's possessions, they found that he had a fully-erected nylon tent, forty-four gallons of water, twelve cases of food, a radio and batteries, a gramophone with records, candles, a bed, fishing gear, a rubber raft and rubber canoe, and a rifle with a thousand rounds. Tomarchin packed his books and travelers checks into his suitcase and boarded one of the longboats for Pitcairn. Tomarchin told Tom Christian he had gone to Henderson to dig for buried treasure. The Pitcairners were unable to reconcile Tomarchin's wildly conflicting stories, but they had already agreed to take Bob and Moko home with them and they kept their promise.

The twenty-three-hour journey was over rough seas, but the boats arrived safely. Tomarchin and Moko were invited to stay as guests in the home of Parkin Christian. Governor Garvey radioed that Tomarchin, who had no official approval to stay, was to be removed from the island on the next available ship, and that if the ship's captain refused to take Moko, Moko could be destroyed or dealt with at the islanders' discretion.

Meanwhile in Rarotonga, John and Diane Wells were arrested for abandoning Tomarchin at Henderson Island. The Wellses insisted that Tomarchin had chartered their vessel, paying them to take him to Henderson Island with a boat load of his gear.

On September 13, 1957, the ship *Rangitane* arrived at Pitcairn and when it left, Tomarchin went with it but this time without Moko. Charles and Charlotte Christian allowed Moko to stay with them. Betty Christian recalls Moko, dressed as a child, walking hand in hand with one of his hosts through the village.

In Auckland, Tomarchin was fined ninety-eight pounds after being charged in court with stowing away on the *Rangitane*. He told an Auckland newspaper, "I want to get my chimp back again. I am very attached to Moko." Having acquired sufficient money somehow in Auckland, Tomarchin was able to pay his way to Pitcairn the following year, and this time to take Moko away with him.

Tomarchin and Moko next were spotted in New York City, where Moko appeared on television. When Moko allegedly became too strong, Tomarchin sold him to the Bronx Zoo for two thousand dollars. Regretting his action, he offered the zoo double the amount for Moko's return. When the zoo refused, Tomarchin stole Moko from the zoo and took the chimp to Mexico. Retaken by authorities in Mexico, Moko was returned to the zoo. According to Herbert Ford, extensive searches of web directories have failed to turn up a Robert Tomarchin anywhere in the United States. Thus ends a Pitcairn Island shaggy chimp story.[35]

Miscellany, 1959

The first issue of the monthly newsletter *The Pitcairn Miscellany* was published April 16, 1959, by Education Officer Ernest Schubert. Ernest and his wife Betty explained that they regularly busied themselves answering individual messages and questions about life in the community and decided that a single-sheet newsletter would suffice to reply to many correspondents. Schubert's predecessor had published a news-sheet called *Pitcairn Pilhi*, which had a run of eighteen months and had ceased publication. Therefore, recalled Schubert, "One sleepless night, the idea came to me of recording the events of Pitcairn daily life in a regular newssheet, sponsored by the Island School. Older children help stuff envelopes in which three consecutive issues, constituting a quarterly update, are sent to hundreds of subscribers worldwide. Each envelope is stamped and canceled, making the envelopes themselves objects of philatelic interest."[36] *Miscellany* has continued to publish virtually without interruption and has been an important source of information about island life for nearly a half century.

CHAPTER 24

Population in Freefall: 1960–1979

Increased Isolation

When attorney David Silverman, an American, visited Pitcairn in the 1960s, he wrote, "One can grasp the true isolation of Pitcairn only from the top of the island. There ... one can turn in a complete circle and see nothing but the white-flecked cobalt disk of the Pacific, enclosed by a ring of horizon as hard and unbroken as if drawn with a compass."[1] A feeling of isolation increased for those who stayed, as friends and relatives moved off the island in the 1960s and 1970s.

Pitcairn at Age 170

What was Pitcairn like 170 years after its founding? When Donald McLoughlin visited in 1958, as legal advisor from the governor's office, his "overall impression was that of a reasonably prosperous, hard working law abiding and contented little community. They undoubtedly had their minor differences among themselves but these were not really serious and I considered them as having no significance."[2]

In 1960, retired postmaster Roy Clark described his community in detail: "There are 27 families (comprising husband, wife, and children) six widows, and seven widowers. Those of marriageable age are 14 — eight men and six women. In addition there is one divorcee, one spinster, two bachelors, two grass widows, and two husbands with wives abroad. Children of school age number 37.... There are 10 boys and 11 girls under school age, making a grand total of 147 people on the Island."

Clark counted 57 occupied and 29 vacant homes. Occupied homes contained 37 stoves, 12 refrigerators, 7 washing machines, 42 telephones, 57 sewing machines, and 14 typewriters. Music in homes and church was made possible or augmented by "11 organs, 4 pianos, 1 violin, 1 mandolin, 12 radios, 2 recorders, 3 radiogramophones, 17 phonographs, 18 ukuleles, 6 guitars, 1 piano accordion, and a few mouth organs." In 1960, the colony had its own band, consisting of a trombone, four cornets, an E-flat bass, tenor horn, kettle drum and "one instrument of unknown name."

Clark's inventory of animals included: "25 dogs, cats unnumbered; poultry by the

Boat sheds protect the island's longboats and canoes from the elements. Men carry canoes, but longboats are launched and rehoused on a metal track. Looming above is the peak known as Ship Landing Point. Photograph by Robert Kirk.

hundred, but not a single singing bird. There are a few goats and sea birds, as well as a scattering of sparrows." Six, among "a number of" canoes, used outboard motors; and the islanders owned together a launch and four longboats. "No TV," Clark continued, "no buses, no trams, cars, trains, planes — in fact, nothing that carries except wheelbarrows. No taxes to pay and no bills to foot. No store to buy from and no money in circulation. We have a rock in the Pacific five miles round and two miles through."[3]

The great attraction, the reason some stayed and those who went departed in some reluctance, was probably a feeling of community. Homes appear to have been open to all family and friends to a degree that eliminated a sense of privacy. David Silverman wrote: "The visitor, unworried by lack of invitation, drops in, perhaps joining a conversation in progress, perhaps picking up a magazine to leaf through it silently. He departs when the mood strikes him, having made no claim to being entertained, although both host and guest may find enjoyment in the visit."[4]

Emigration

Ironically, as the islanders began to enjoy improved homes and amenities such as electricity and better communications with the outside world, they left Pitcairn in greater numbers. The decline was dramatic. From a high of 233 in 1937, the population fell to 136 by 1954 and then more or less leveled off. In 1958, twenty-four people left for New Zealand.

From a total of 128 in 1962, the population declined to 86 the following year. In 1974, fifty-six people clung to their island home.[5] "Christians were most numerous at twenty-five, followed by thirteen Youngs, eleven Warrens, four Clarks and three Browns."[6] By then, a third of native-born Pitcairners lived in New Zealand and Australia. About half of these expatriates returned to visit family, but few stayed as permanent residents.

The school was affected when an average of twenty students in the 1950s fell to ten in 1974. When a new term started on January 27, 1975, eight students' names appeared on the roll. One pupil, Marlene Christian, was slated to go to high school in New Zealand; and Kerry Young, visiting her grandfather Andrew, was ready to leave with Marlene on the next ship bound for Auckland. The editor of *The Pitcairn Miscellany*, who served also as school-master, lamented, "That will mean that the roll be at six, and two of the six are mine, so there will be only four Pitcairners at school."[7]

Residents left for various reasons; the story of Langford and Iris "Pony" Warren is illustrative. In 1958, Pony needed to have her appendix removed in New Zealand. Without a compassion grant for transportation, it became necessary for Langford to find work in New Zealand in order to pay for transportation, surgery and living expenses. Langford went to work in the construction industry. Because Langford had lucrative work, the couple did not return to Pitcairn, but instead built a home in Auckland and stayed on, although in 1995, they came back to visit relatives.

In the August 1963 issue of *The Pitcairn Miscellany*, retired postmaster Roy Clark sought to explain the exodus:

> One factor of dissatisfaction is that more than half the island homes receive government pay, while the others have no regular income. Fifteen families draw pay cheques, while 14 do not. Other reasons for leaving the island are:
>
> 1. The lure of money. The high wages paid in New Zealand.
> 2. Labour on the island has become too arduous and increasingly toilsome. This has been brought about by the multiplicity of blights, destroying insects and weeds, not to mention the destructiveness of termites and wood borers that are working havoc in the island dwellings, and the lack of trees for lumber to rebuild or repair.
> 3. The lack of ships to supply the islanders with a substantial income to secure the necessities of life.

Clark continued by enumerating lack of "advancement or improvement in personal achievements," increasing visitations of epidemic diseases, "a break-up of communal life," summed up as "soon-coming disintegration of Pitcairn as a community of people."[8] When the New Zealand Shipping Company stopped making regular calls, trade decreased and, as a result, migration to New Zealand accelerated.

In 1964, the *New York Times* reported the population to be eighty-three, but more alarming, with fourteen men needed to man longboats, the males between ages fifteen and sixty numbered only fifteen. With only four shipping lines still calling with a maximum passenger load of eighty, and the threat of radioactive fallout from French nuclear testing in Mururoa Atoll, the island, according to the Times, "may soon be abandoned."[9]

If Pitcairners had considered abandoning their home, they had an invitation to move to Norfolk. In 1970, Norfolk Islanders urged the government to make land available to their Pitcairn cousins. Nearly half— 589 — of Norfolk's 1,232 people were descended from *Bounty* stock. The *Honolulu Star-Bulletin* explained that Pitcairners liked their island and did not want to move. "Nearly everyone has modern stoves, refrigerators, telephones and other appliances as the island is well supplied with electricity by its power generator." Cars, motorcycles, motion pictures, and a cooperative store had made life sufficiently comfortable that Pitcairners said thanks but no thanks.[10]

On New Year's Eve 1974, Tom Christian wrote with a real sense of alarm: "Young folks are leaving, others still wish to go. What is our future? Today there are 56 Pitcairners and five outsiders here — the lowest population in 100 years.... This year we have had two births and three deaths. Thirteen Pitcairners have left for New Zealand — some for medical treatment, hoping to return; some for other reasons; and some to see the world and perhaps to stay. There seems to be real concern by the few here that perhaps time is running out for Pitcairners and Pitcairn, if our numbers keep falling."[11] In 1975, Tom appealed to Pitcairners who had left to "come and repopulate a dying land." He reminded expatriates that though life might be challenging on the island, Pitcairn did not have vice and crime and drugs. Later in the year six young expats returned.[12]

Ambassador Parkin Christian

In July 1964, former magistrate Parkin Christian gave an interview to a reporter for the *Honolulu Star-Bulletin*. Seated in the Hawaiian Mission of the Seventh-day Adventist Church, at eighty the oldest Pitcairner was enroute to visit a son and granddaughters in Australia. He had already been to Canada and the United States as a roving good-will ambassador. "In Ontario, Canada," he told the reporter, "I meet a Bligh descendant. It was supposed to be Blighs and Christians coming together again. But he afraid I hold a grudge. Ha, I tell him that be like holding a grudge against Adam."

In regard to the island economy, Parkin stated, "Ships not call at Pitcairn anymore like the old days. Only four cargo ships stop now, about three or four time a year. Hardly any passengers. Big ships they now go to Tahiti instead." As a result, he continued, "We can't sell our goods. Fruit — bananas, pineapples oranges, mangoes — go to waste by the ton. So our wood carvings." Nevertheless, he admitted. "We happy. Can't be sulky all the time."[13]

Dilapidated Homes and Creeping Bush

When the *Mataroa* stopped in October 1951 enroute to Wellington, a passenger noted that the island looked as if it were wild bush, with cultivation noticeable only around Adamstown. Roofs of auburn-colored rusted iron could be seen, half hidden by palms, oranges and banyans. Five radio masts pointed toward the sky on the island's peak.

In the 1950s and '60s, while inhabited homes were being improved, uninhabited dwellings became food for termites. In 1963, a resident complained in a letter to *The Pitcairn Miscellany* about the "tumbling-down dilapidated houses, — the vacant residences that have fallen in to disrepair many years back that are an eyesore and a disgrace to our better judgment." The writer recommended using the boards for fire wood and to plant trees and flowers on the sites. "Ever [sic] the growing of weeds would be more attractive to the eye."[14] When Australian Frank Clune spent a week at Pitcairn in 1964, he noted eight percent of the cultivated areas had reverted to wilderness.

The man who broadcast most widely the sorry state of the island's homes was Australian journalist Ian Ball. In 1971, Ball brought his wife, three children and two photographers to Pitcairn for nearly a month. His intention was to write a book about the islanders. Only

A typical Pitcairn home of the late twentieth century. Homes are continually under siege by termites and by the elements. Most have been improved with aluminum windows, corrugated roofs, cement floors and modern materials. Homes abandoned by emigrants are found in varying degrees of deterioration. Photograph by Robert Kirk.

twenty-two households remained. Ball noted that the seven members of his party increased the population by 8.2 percent. Seventy-three-year-old Christy Warren commented that if his thirty grandchildren returned from New Zealand, the population would increase by a third. The Balls and their photographers were taken to shore in a diesel-powered island launch; it was named the *Rosalind* after Rosalind Amelia Young. They were welcomed warmly as guests into island homes.

"Welcome to Peet-carn Island," chief magistrate Pervis Young greeted them. Young hoped none of the visitors was sick, as three-quarters of the islanders were only now recovering from a flu brought by a cargo vessel from New Zealand. Nine men, the minimum number for safety, manned the longboat. Ball likened the trip into the landing as analogous to riding "a surfboard in powerful seas and over dangerous rocks."[15] His nervousness was appropriate; in fact, the following year a boat was smashed on the rocks and the crew members were thrown into the waves, sustaining some serious injuries. Radio operator Tom Christian's leg was broken.

The Balls were to live in the home of Warren and Millie Christian. Warren and Millie gave up their bed to Ian and his wife, while they slept in a smaller bedroom. A Ball daughter had a tiny room which Warren had built especially for her. After a good night's sleep, Ian Ball set about describing his hosts' home and the village in general. He found "rickety, tottering dwellings." Ball described the houses as they were: unpainted dwellings made from whatever useful material was available to the islanders — rough-cut lumber, dunnage from passing ships, etc. He found termites on the verge of "claiming total victory" against walls that sagged atop "casual foundations." Ball stated that inhabited and uninhabited homes looked to him much alike. These disparaging remarks and particularly the supercilious tone in which they were made served to make Ball in particular and journalists in general unwanted on the island.

Ball found rooms containing "the rich disorder of old attics, and on the walls of his hosts' living room a calendar and pictures of the ship *Pitcairn* and a plaque that read 'To Mother,'" a souvenir from the Empire State Building. He noted a picture of Christ and "a small, dingy" picture of the Queen, Prince Philip and the royal children. When his hostess, Millie Christian, cooked early breakfasts for Ball's family, a meal she added from her busy schedule to accommodate her guests, she took food from a refrigerator whose amateur paint job Ball gleefully described as "almost lost beneath the workaday grime of hands that have opened it."[16]

As untidiness is not a Polynesian nor a Melanesian trait, Ball suggested it could have had something to do with the Adventist conviction that the world would end soon, commenting that "they are preoccupied with the concept of an afterlife and heavenly rewards to a degree I have rarely encountered in other societies."[17]

When Glynn Christian, a descendant of Fletcher, visited Pitcairn a few years later, he found that residents "had biting criticism for recent publications about Pitcairn, and writers who had described it as unwelcoming and squalid." In his hosts' defense, Glynn wrote, "Certainly they hoard everything — string, paper, glass and metal. This is simply facing up to the reality of living in isolation and with the unreliability of the rest of the world."[18]

Christmas Festivities

Islanders' attitudes toward Christmas had changed since Dr. Harry Shapiro's visit in 1934; they now celebrated the holiday. Christmas festivities underscored the close family relationships among Pitcairners and their hospitality toward strangers. Islanders made certain at Christmas time that the Balls and their children partook of the communal celebration. Because Christmas fell on a Sabbath, parents waited until Saturday night to go house to house putting gifts in baskets children had hung outside because tropical Adamstown was devoid of chimneys. Ball commented, "By both bloodlines and social necessity, these people are members of a single family, and this was never more apparent to us than on this Christmas night as the islanders made their rounds in the milky moonlight."[19] The next day, the populace assembled in the court house to avoid the rain, and there exchanged an estimated thousand gifts among them.

Governing

The governor holds the power of "revocation and alteration" of any laws the council makes, but "alteration is usually confined to textual amendment to make the meaning and intention of the rules legally exact."

On September 2, 1970, the council enacted the Pensions Ordinance to provide payment to all residents over sixty-five who resided there at least five of the last twenty years. Pensions were also available to those who were physically or mentally handicapped and needed financial assistance. Payment was NZ$9.24 per month. Residents paid no taxes.

On October 10, 1970, when Fiji became a sovereign nation, the British high commissioner in New Zealand was named Pitcairn's governor. He was Sir Arthur Galsworthy; M. E. Daymon became commissioner for Pitcairn.[20]

Goats v. Trees

Rosalind Amelia Young called attention as early as the 1890s to the inescapable fact that, although the island had bountiful forests when the mutineers arrived, a hundred years later, "during which wild goats have roamed in herds over certain portions of the island, many of the trees have disappeared. The soil, thus made bare, has severely suffered by being washed away by heavy rains, and scarcely a trace of the once luxuriant growth of trees remains. Viewed from the sea, the island in two or three places presents a bare and sterile appearance."[21] Goats did not bear sole responsibility for denuding parts of Pitcairn; trees had been felled for houses, boats, heating and cooking, and carvings. Firewood for cooking and heating had been a staple product available for sale or trade aboard ships.

From 1947 onward, Captain Arthur C. Jones of *MS Corinthic*, a frequent Pitcairn visitor, helped the islanders begin reforestation. On each trip to Pitcairn Island, Jones brought — from New Zealand — Norfolk pines, kauri, phoutakawa and wattle trees. Fences were erected around young trees to protect them from destructive goats.

In the 1960s, the government encouraged the planting of miro on Pitcairn for future harvesting. Islander Jacob Warren recalled that his dad, also Jacob Warren, was given the job of planting miro. His work included "chopping the undergrowth, sowing seeds, planting seedlings, and then fighting the goats and fires." With his assistants, Warren planted over 90,000 seedlings on three sides of the island. The first major harvest took place in 1983. Wood was cut in even lengths, debarked and shared evenly among the island's carvers.[22]

By the mid–1950s, an annually elected Goat Master oversaw an estimated four hundred of the shaggy beasts. The Goat Master made certain that goats were branded to indicate their owners, and organized periodic hunts to keep their numbers at a manageable level and to provide meat for periodic feasts.

Islanders were divided on the goat issue. During the Cold War, the Pro-Goaters argued for the animals as an emergency food supply in case hostilities made shipping impossible and cut the island off from supplies. Anti-Goaters, many of whom were probably vegetarians, pointed to erosion and desecration of the land.

In 1973, *The Pitcairn Miscellany* described the latest goat roundup, a description that suggests the goats' domain was vast:

> Anyone passing Big Fence on the morning of the 15th could be excused for thinking that he had tumbled back in time to the mid nineteenth century Cimarron. The "cowboys" were mounted on steeds that wheeled and turned as if in anticipation of the chase. The trail boss issued his final orders as one or two late-comers thundered up; then, with a whoop, the men mounted and charged up the hill in a cloud of dust and spitting Honda exhausts. Eight hours later, a very tired bunch of men returned to the village. They had chased goats three quarters of the way round the island in order to catch kids for marking. From Tauama they went, through Faute Valley, Outer Valley, Ginger Valley, Orlior, Tedside, Goathouse, below Pulau, and finally caught the last of the bunch up at Anderson's Place. The goats thoroughly enjoyed it.[23]

"Downtown" Pitcairn

Ian Ball found the public square tidier than private dwellings. The post office was an important location on the Square. It found little use most of the time but was exceedingly busy immediately before and after ship arrivals. Postmaster Oscar Clark described the room: "On entering through one of two doors, you will see on the wall facing the entrance two framed pictures of Her Majesty, Queen Elizabeth II, and H.R.H. Prince Philip. The hardboard walls are bamboo in colour and the ceiling white. On the serving counter are two metric scales for parcels, and on a working counter is a metric scale for letters. There are 27 individual P.O. boxes.... On the wall to the right of the main entrance you will see on display stamps which have been issued over the year." When a ship brought mail, according to *The Pitcairn Miscellany*'s editor, "the Postal staff begins sorting the mail. As they go about their task, the Square gradually fills up with folks who wait in earnest for their mail." When letters and packages have been sorted, "Pitcairn's unofficial Mayor, Morris Warren, is asked to ring the bell; and then the once patient crowd surges forward to receive their letters." Waiting for mail to arrive from another part of the world tested everyone's patience. A letter sent from Pitcairn on January 17, 1977, for example, arrived in England six months later; while the reply, dated June 29, 1977, arrived November 24.[24]

In addition to the church, court house, and post office was a co-op. The cooperative store was the recommendation of Mr. F. E. M. Warner, assistant commissioner to Pitcairn. The first location was the school art room at Pulau. Open two hours a week beginning July 9, 1967, it was this Pacific outpost's version of a small supermarket. On the first day it was open, the store was nearly sold out in two hours; islanders spent NZ$210. On June 23, 1969, the permanent store, having been constructed, was open for business. Everything is brought in by ship, with the profits going to the island account. Islanders unpack each crate, price each item and place it on the shelves. Customers find shelves nearly bare several weeks after the last supply ship. Ian Ball found canned peas, beans, tomatoes, and peaches in stock; perhaps they remained because many items in the cans could be picked fresh in family gardens. Potato chips, "lollies" (candy), condensed milk and canned spaghetti — which Pitcairners were said to enjoy cold — had long since been bought up.

Vehicles

On the last day of 1964, the Pitcairn agricultural revolution began. Island farmers had used hoes and unique wooden Pitcairn wheelbarrows. The steamer *Corinthic* brought tractors and two experts from the Fiji Department of Agriculture to show Pitcairners how to assemble and use their new machinery. "Bells and whistles" on these vehicles included bulldozer blade, ripper, bucket, winch, trailer, transport box, cordwood circular saw, plow, tandem discs and other tools. These tractors were funded through the Colonial Development Welfare Act, financed by the taxpayers of the United Kingdom.

In the Square and on the roads were Honda motorcycles. Tom Christian had ordered a Honda in 1966 in order to motorize his mile-and-a-half commute up to the radio station at Taro Ground. Soon many other residents had to have one too, sending their orders and awaiting arrival of the supply ship.

Pitcairn's first motor car, a Morris Mini Moke, arrived in 1967. The central Pacific Union Mission of the Seventh-day Adventist Church had donated it to the islanders. Less practical than motorbikes, its range of travel was severely limited by the lack of roads. By 1969, sufficient traffic was kicking up mud and dust that rules were published: If you are entering the main road, give way to traffic; all traffic must keep left — that includes operators of wheel barrows; use hand signals to show you will turn; observe the speed limit of thirty miles per hour; be courteous. A survey at the end of 1976 found three Mini Moke cars, thirty-eight motorcycles and twenty Pitcairn wheelbarrows. In May 1969, the editor of *The Pitcairn Miscellany*

1960's: Traffic jam Pitcairn style. *Left to right:* Marona Young drives a Mini Moke, Elwyn Christian transports a girl on a motorbike, Charles Christian pulls a trailer, and Wallace Warren mans a traditional Pitcairn wheelbarrow. Courtesy of Pitcairn Island Study Center, Pacific Union College, Angwin, California.

observed hopefully, "If we could keep Pitcairn free from traffic fatalities we would be a unique country in this modern world."[25]

French Nuclear Testing

According to the *Bulletin of the Atomic Scientists*, in 1955 the United States had proposed to use Pitcairn Island as a testing area for hydrogen bombs. Scientists and supporting staff would have been headquartered on Henderson Island. Pitcairn seemed to American officials a truly ideal hydrogen bomb target. It was one of the most isolated islands in the world, far away from major inhabited communities. The small population could be relocated elsewhere at minimal expense. Fortunately, British authorities felt that worldwide sentiment would oppose moving the mutineers' descendants out in order to blow apart their historic home.

By the 1960s, France, rather than the United States, would pose the greater threat to the people of Pitcairn. Algeria won independence from France in July 1962, and as a result, the French lost their nuclear test site in the Sahara Desert. Although Britain, the United States and the Soviet Union halted testing in 1963, when they signed the Partial Nuclear Test Ban Treaty, France insisted on more tests. France had no Pacific possession as isolated as Pitcairn and, in 1963, announced plans to detonate nuclear weapons on Mururoa Atoll. In the Tuamotu archipelago, Mururoa is 580 miles from Adamstown.[26]

Author David Stanley wrote, "Obviously, an atoll, with its porous coral caps sitting on narrow basalt base, is the most dangerous place in the world to stage underground nuclear explosions."[27] That Pitcairners were well aware of the danger is evidenced by an editorial in *The Pitcairn Miscellany* in November 1962: "[H]ere on Pitcairn fears for our safety are being expressed because of the small distance which separates us from this proposed testing ground. To the South of Mururoa lies nothing but water until the Antarctic continent is reached. To the north and west there exists a vast extent of ocean over which any nuclear fallout which may be created can be dispersed, but would there be some unexpected change in weather conditions Pitcairn Island could be in an extremely dangerous position."

People in South Pacific communities from Australia to Chile protested French nuclear testing in what they considered their backyard. Pitcairners had real reason to worry about the effects of nuclear fallout; in fact, the detonation on July 2, 1966, shook Adamstown buildings. An islander said he had seen a flying seabird drop suddenly out of the sky. From July to October, 1966, five Royal Air Force technicians were stationed in Adamstown to monitor the atmosphere during French testing. In 1970, *The Pitcairn Miscellany* reported two more bombs were detonated during five weeks. "On both occasions the noise was heard from here. It resembled someone having a good bang at a set of drums, or rather like distant thunder." On May 6, 1973, the sailing vessel *Fri* arrived at Bounty Bay from New Zealand, enroute to Mururoa Atoll, where Captain David Moodie intended to stage a protest. On August 15, French commandos stormed the *Greenpeace* and the *Fri* and placed their crews under arrest.[28]

In 1974, an international outcry forced France to detonate its weapons underground, boring deep into Mururoa. By then France had detonated forty-one nuclear devices above ground. Between 1974 and 1996, France concluded 181 subterranean tests.

On August 6, 1985, the eight members of the South Pacific Forum, an organization of self-governing nations founded in 1971, declared the South Pacific Nuclear Free Zone. China and the Soviet Union signed the treaty. France did not. French president Mitterand halted testing in 1992, and when French president Jacques Chirac ordered resumption in 1995, the organization Greenpeace sent two vessels to the site. The French impounded the ships and deported their crews.

Protests caused France to end its program in January 1996. The Centre d'Experimentations du Pacifique decommissioned the site at Mururoa. Pitcairn islanders' worries, however, are far from over. Radioactive groundwater continues to flow from fractures in the atoll. Rising cancer rates in French Polynesia are in all probability a result. Fish in the entire area have been contaminated.[29]

Health and Medical Treatment

Although Pitcairners have a healthy diet and most get exercise in their work, they are still prone to transmitted disease from visitors. In 1959, for example, 95 percent of the people were struck by influenza. All but five or six of a hundred and twelve residents were downed again by influenza two years later. Most flu sufferers could be treated on the island and almost all recovered. Islanders were understandably defensive about communicable disease when forewarned; when a ship arrived in 1961 with reported measles aboard, for example, all trading was done "over the side" with minimal human contact. In addition, ten percent of the residents were said to suffer from asthma.[30] Some maladies required evacuation, which were never quickly or easily accomplished. Although the wife of the Seventh-day Adventist pastor was always a trained nurse, and resident Royal Warren was trained as a nurse, there was little either could do to help the several people who suffered appendicitis attacks; in such cases, ships in the vicinity would be contacted in hope that the ship's doctor would come ashore to treat the patient. Some were sent to New Zealand for surgery.

When the public bell rang signifying that an accident had occurred, all men reported immediately to the Square for assignments as members of a rescue party. Royal Warren opened the dispensary. The "accident bell," at least according to *Miscellany* accounts, was ringing frequently in the 1960s and '70s. It is uncertain if Pitcairners are more accident prone than people in other communities, but the record continued to be full of horrendous occurrences: In 1961 a child, Terry Young, had a watermelon seed lodged in his windpipe and was evacuated to New Zealand. Terry was the first Pitcairner to receive a Compassion Grant to go to New Zealand for medical treatment. Each grant had to be approved by the governor, but it saved island families from inordinate expense. A physician removed the seed in an Auckland hospital, and the child returned to his parents, Sam and Vula.

The Pitcairn Miscellany published accident reports much as George Hunn Nobbs's *Pitcairn Register* had done in the previous century: "Clifford was unloading timber from a ship in to the longboats below, when his left little finger was almost entirely severed, as the rope slipped." "Little Glenn Clark had a serious fall from a tree and hurt his eye...." "Warren had been standing on a rock, fishing, when it gave way. He fell heavily onto the rocks below and then into the water." "Pastor slipped and fractured his left leg." "Last week Jacob had a very nasty accident to his eye. He was hammering a steel peg to pin down a line, when it sprang up and hit his glasses. His glasses broke and pieces of glass cut his eyeball." "Nancy had been on a fishing trip with Charles, Charlotte, and Les; and in trying to negotiate a crack in the cliff wall, she slipped into it and would have fallen right down into the sea had she not wedged herself tightly into the crack, with her back to one wall and her knee to the other." She was extricated, but with a badly cut knee and lacerated back.

It was normally Tom Christian who stayed up nights at the radio station pleading with passing ships to send a surgeon ashore, but in 1973, "Tom Christian had caught his big toe in the chain of his Honda whilst trying to get home from a day's fishing at Tedside." Not long after, "While crossing the rocks to Glennie, Irma suffered a fall and landed on jagged rocks 12 or 15 feet below the route she had been following." "Steve Christian met with an unfortunate accident whilst playing in the Square ... injuring his thigh and apparently fracturing it at the joint." "Brian's heavy fall from his bicycle left him with a greenstick fracture of the left forearm and considerable pain." When Albert climbed the rope ladder to the ship *Cap Vilano*, "the whole apparatus came away from the ship's side, flew across the five feet of water between the boats and the ship, then across the first boat.... Albert fell 20 feet down the side of the ship, landing on his back across the gunn'el of *Boxhead* [a longboat], from where he bounced into the water between the ship and the boat." In 1967, *The Pitcairn Miscellany*'s editor expressed his wish "that some retired G.P. would spend part of his retirement at Pitcairn."

In 1972, Dr. David Gibson, a physician from Texas, came to practice during a short stay and examined a number of residents. He wrote: "It would be difficult to find a comparable population anywhere in the world as healthy, robust, and physically fit as these people. I am amazed to see 50- and 60-year-olds trotting up and down steep paths of this little island. It is nothing to see Pitcairn men of more than 70 scrambling up rope ladders to the decks of ships like only 20-year-olds elsewhere might do. Apart from minor surgical procedures there really is not much to do." Gibson found life expectancy of Pitcairners to be as good as, if not better than, that of residents of the United States.[31]

The All-Important Curio Trade

Births, deaths, departures of emigrants, cruise ship days, and unloading the regular supply ship, *New Zealand Star*, were among the more important events on Pitcairn Island in the last half of the twentieth century. Manning the longboats had become easier due to installation of outboard motors. In 1967, according to the editor of *The Pitcairn Miscellany*: "The good old sailing days are over, and there is no more 'lashing it' with 14 oars pulling against wind and tide. The launches have made seagoing life all too easy. Maritime life on Pitcairn for the younger generation is one of ease compared to the hardships encountered in the days of the oar and sail."[32] Yet, for the boatsmen as well as for the passengers coming in or going out, waiting for the right wave and the signal from shore to be propelled into the calm of the inner cove required one to endure "this lolloping, jolting, rocking, undulating, swinging, swaying, teetering, sickening vacillatory motion ... while the smell of the fruit, diesel fumes, bilgewater etc., merely adds more tremors" to a sick stomach.[33]

Islanders worked continually to produce salable curios. David Silverman wrote: "Nearly every household is a small factory, with bench, lathe, gouges, chisels, and planes...."[34] Frank Clune explained that "A fifteen-inch length of mirau [miro], six inches thick, is hacked roughly by a sharp whittling knife into a more definite shape. Then comes a slow job with rasp, glass scraper, fine sandpaper, and before your eyes is a sleek albacore with graceful fins and tail, leaping from the water in ecstasy."[35] Clune observed that everyone had a wheelbarrow and that "on Ship Day the path through Adams Town is as busy as Queen Street, Auckland," as islanders brought curios to the Landing.[36]

The number of ships that stopped had diminished from forty-eight in 1972 to twenty-three by 1981. Ball insisted, "most of the men and women find the hawking of curios a humiliating experience, conscious always that they themselves are being examined by the tourists as human curios."[37] On the contrary, other observers feel that the curio sellers of Adamstown see the opportunity as a magnificent social occasion to meet new people and to renew acquaintance with shipboard personnel who stop frequently. They are able to purchase necessities and luxuries from the ship's stores, and to be treated to desserts or entire meals. The visit is a rare chance for non–Adventist islanders to enjoy an alcoholic beverage or two. Pitcairners are outgoing people. They give the appearance of enjoying making friends aboard ships as much as, if not more than, making money. Their memories of ships past and people aboard are prodigious; when visitors return, islanders profess to recall them from previous visits.

A Cruising Ambassador

In 1962, Chief Magistrate John Christian was offered a seventy-day around-the-world voyage aboard the liner *Willem Ruys* as a guest of Royal Rotterdam Lloyd Shipping Co. Ltd. Because descendants of the mutineers, particularly those named Christian, are instant celebrities when they turn up abroad, the company publicized John Christian's presence onboard. The cruising magistrate found media representatives waiting for him at Panama as the ship prepared to transit the canal. Press, broadcasting networks and dignitaries were invited to meet John at Fort Lauderdale, Florida. The *Willem Ruys* went on to Bermuda, Plymouth and Rotterdam. At each stop he was welcomed by the Seventh-day Adventist community and by the media. In Rotterdam and Amsterdam John met the burgomasters and officials of Rotterdam Lloyd. After touring several Dutch tourist sites, John reboarded and headed back to Pitcairn via Southampton, Port Said, Colombo, and Melbourne. In Sydney and Auckland, John met with Pitcairn expatriates. A highlight of his voyage was being able to spend an evening with his sister, Elsa, in Auckland. On reaching Adamstown, John commented, "Holland is a fine place, but for me Pitcairn is still the best."[38]

Going to Church

Australian writer Frank Clune attended the single-story church in 1964. The church had been constructed ten years previously. Pastor Walter Ferris, "a benevolent-looking patriarch with grey hair" led the singing of "To God be the Glory, Great things He hath Done," calling on "sixty lusty-voiced Pitcairners."[39] Ferris and other pastors were appointed for two years by the president of the Central Pacific Union Mission in Auckland.

Ferris was kept busy on the Sabbath. *The Pitcairn Miscellany* stated that "The Services of the Church on Pitcairn comprise four main phases. There is Sabbath School (this is divided up into a children's division and an adult division); there is the Divine Service at 11:15 A.M. In the afternoon of the Sabbath, the Missionary Volunteer programme is held. Then of course, there is the Tuesday prayer meeting at 7 P.M.; a part of this midweek service is the usual *Faith for Today* half-hour 16-mm movie. Seventh-day Adventists around the world are a very missionary-minded people; but on Pitcairn this phase of life can be missing altogether, though some work is done on passing ships." With its precariously low population, Pitcairn can scarcely afford to send many residents abroad to prosyletize.[40]

Clune described a baptism. After several months of attending church classes, candidates for membership in the church were immersed in the waters of *Bounty* Cove. Clune watched five girls and a boy wait their turn. The pastor placed a hand beneath the neck of Kathleen Clark, "then gently bends her backwards until her body is covered in water, at the same time saying, 'I baptize thee in the name of the Father, and of the Son, and of the Holy Ghost. Amen.' Returned to an upright position, she takes a handkerchief from her pocket and hands it to the Pastor, who wipes her face. In this manner all are baptized."[41]

Young people joined the Seventh-day Adventist Pathfinder Club in which "Pastor and his wife, along with five willing counselors, are endeavoring to keep 26 lively boys and girls interested in the aims and ideals" of this organization which was compared to the Boy or Girl Scouts. Wearing bright green uniforms, the Pathfinders in 1967 climbed aboard the cruise liner *Sagafjord*, and "Some 400 spectators ranged around, many looking from the promenade deck above. Then, to the beat of the drum, down the deck they marched singing lustily, 'For We Are the Pathfinders Strong.' Recitations, marching and more singing followed."[42] In the late 1960s the future of the Seventh-day Adventist Church on Pitcairn Island seemed promising.

Miss Jennifer Toombs, Artist

By 1966, philatelic sales were sufficiently important to justify bringing the most prolific designer of Pitcairn's stamps, Miss Jennifer Toombs, from London to Pitcairn. She accompanied a representative of the Crown Agents, the organization which arranged for colonial stamp issues. Her purpose was to accumulate ideas for future designs and events to be commemorated. Described as "a slim, dark-haired young lady in her middle twenties," Miss Toombs had already designed several Pitcairn issues. During ten days Toombs sketched, photographed and tape-recorded. She saw all significant landmarks: the flying fox, the Court House, government offices, the church, the *Bounty* Bible, the *Bounty* anchor, John Adams's grave, library, post office, the bell, Thursday October Christian's house (the oldest on the island), the school, radio station at Taro Ground, outdated island wheel barrows and the Hondas which had replaced them.[43] She photographed and sketched so as to have visual material from which to design future stamp issues.

In 1968, Pitcairn abandoned the cumbersome pound sterling and began to use the New Zealand dollar. This decision called for two more lucrative definitive stamp issues; in 1967, authorities surcharged existing supplies of the 1964 definitives with decimal values, and then came out with a definitive issue in 1969 with entirely new designs illustrating events of the *Bounty* mutiny and its aftermath.

Revenue from the sale of postage stamps to collectors rose dramatically in the 1970s from NZ$100,069 in 1972–73 to nearly five times as much in 1978–80.[44] This windfall subsidized the school, radio communications, the telephone service, the free dispensary, the library, publically owned boats, the community hall, old-age pensions, and road maintenance. In addition, stamp sales paid for two hostels which were built for use by official visitors. These modern two-bedroom houses had running hot and cold water and indoor toilets. Construction provided temporary paid work for some island men. Ball speculated presciently, "if world philatelists ever were to lose their interest in Pitcairn issues, the island 'economy' would crumble...."[45]

A Sovereign Republic of the Pitcairn Islands?

If Pitcairners had wanted to renounce their allegiance to the Queen, the United Nations was eager to offer encouragement. In 1968, the UN General Assembly Special Committee on Colonial Affairs recommended to the General Assembly that seventeen colonies and territories in the Caribbean and Pacific be granted self-determination and independence. Incredibly, Pitcairn was on the UN's de-colonization list. Were Pitcairn to become a sovereign nation, the Pitcairn Islands would be eligible for United Nations membership and a seat in the General Assembly. Had the sovereign Pitcairn government sent off representatives to the UN and ambassadors to New Zealand, Britain and the United States, Adamstown would have been dangerously depopulated.

In a short-wave radio interview with the Voice of Prophecy radio station, Tom Christian recommended playfully that the UN bring all sixty-six Pitcairners to UN headquarters in New York to voice their own opinion on independence. In the UN Building, he suggested, islanders could sell souvenirs, stamps and handicrafts to delegates and staff.

A Very Royal Visitor

On February 21, 1971, Prince Philip, Duke of Edinburgh, Queen Elizabeth's husband, made an official visit aboard the 3,990-ton royal yacht *Britannia*. It is unlikely the Prince was dispatched to Adamstown to head off an independence movement; nobody outside of the UN took Pitcairn sovereignty seriously. Rather, the prince was representing his wife by making royal visits to Commonwealth communities. Coming from Easter Island enroute to Rarotonga in the Cooks, he was accompanied by his uncle, Lord Louis Mountbatten, last viceroy of British India, and Mountbatten's daughter and son-in-law, Lord and Lady Brabourne. *The Pitcairn Miscellany* reported, "all members of the community who were fit and able were invited aboard the Royal yacht to welcome the visitors and attend a party on deck. After boarding the yacht, all members of the community were introduced to Prince Philip and then, having moved onto the upper deck, were served refreshments and had the opportunity to meet and speak with His Royal Highness and other members of the party. During this interval the Royal Marine Band played light band music on a lower deck." The community disembarked at 6 P.M.

The next morning Prince Philip and his party came ashore and were taken up the Hill of Difficulty in Mini Mokes. Standing at the verandah of the courthouse, the prince listened while the villagers sang the national anthem. Philip charmed the people by saying, "I just wonder what would have happened [in 1790 among the mutineers] if somebody had prophesied — they didn't have a Pastor in those days to prophesy — I wonder whether he would have found something in the Bible to prophesy that 181 years later a Royal Yacht would anchor in the same place as the *Bounty* had anchored, and that here we would be all friends and all sunshine and all happiness." The prince was taken into the courthouse for morning tea, to the post office and dispensary, and then transported by Mini-moke to Taro Ground to have a look at the radio station. Later at the school, children sang and were each rewarded with a packet of sweets by His Royal Highness.[46]

The prince expressed a desire to meet every single islander, so he visited those in their homes who were too infirm to have gone in the morning to the public square. While visiting in island homes, the prince was undoubtedly pleased to see his picture hung with that of the Queen. However, in one home a portrait of the sovereign with teeth blackened out decorated the wall, and when he saw it, Philip remarked wryly, "I had no idea my wife had lost that many teeth."[47]

The prince gave the islanders his picture; it remains mounted in the courthouse. Islanders gave him several carvings. As the royal party sailed away at sunset the community sang their famous "Goodbye Song" to their Queen's husband. Prince Philip remains the highest ranking member of the royal family to have visited the island.

A Safer Landing Place

A major harbor improvement was accomplished in 1976 and 1977. All longboats must enter or leave through a narrow channel. If a hard left-hand sweep is not made correctly and immediately after entering, boats can be — and have been — bashed on rocks. On relatively calm days the surf pounds relentlessly.

A team of Royal Engineers worked on improvements with Pitcairners for nine months. Three hundred and fifty tons of stores were brought in during the first ten days. After equipment was assembled, they improved a path leading to a stone-crusher at Tedside; from there, they brought 220 tons of crushed rock to the site. In addition, 60 tons of sand and 25 tons of cement were used. Eighteen island men were employed on the project for an equivalent of 2,353 eight-hour days.

The Landing from the Hill of Difficulty. In the early 2000s the road was paved and the jetty improved, as were the harbor and the Landing. Nevertheless, Pitcairners still risk life and limb when they venture out in their longboats. Photograph by Robert Kirk.

The workers drove 172 steel piles to extend and strengthen the jetty. According to *The Pitcairn Miscellany*, "450 cubic yards of rock-fill was placed inside the piles and the structure completed by placing 145 cubic yards of concrete to form the deck and wave wall, after the necessary timber framework had been built. Finally, 250 tons of rock was placed on the seaward side as protection." The new jetty was first used on November 12, 1977.[48]

The slipway, through which two- and three-ton longboats are hauled in and out of the water, was also improved. Islanders themselves completed that project. As the *Miscellany*'s editor explained, "Basically the new slipway comprises two steel channels laid in concrete running the length of the boathouse and down to the high-water mark.... In essence, the whole concept was to make things easier when putting the boats to sea." The editor described the final product: All the island men pulled and "Away went the boat literally like greased lightning and into the harbor...." That is perhaps because a man with a paintbrush was assigned to grease the skidway.[49]

Why Pitcairn International Airport Does Not Exist

While on the island to complete the jetty, engineers studied the possibility of building an airfield. If planes could be landed, medical evacuations would be easier, mail could be expedited, and travelers could shave days from their journeys. *The Pitcairn Miscellany* reported, "The length of airstrip required by the airline operating out of Tahiti is 985 yards. The maximum length of strip which could be provided in Aute Valley is 660 yards; but even to do this would be a major construction task, requiring more plant than is on the Island and taking many months to complete. Clearly no such work could be considered unless it was known that there were aircraft willing and able to use it."[50] As a result, by the 1980s, Pitcairn's minimal population resigned themselves to living without the hope of air service. Pitcairn Island remained the most isolated inhabited community on Earth.

CHAPTER 25

Dreams of Smiley's Millions ... And a Dream Realized

The 1980s: A Minimal Population

In 1981, the British Nationality Act made Pitcairn a British "Dependent Territory." This act of Parliament had little or no actual impact for Pitcairners, even if the dwindling numbers of inhabitants had been aware of it. That year, the chief magistrate was Ivan Christian, who had served since 1976 at a salary of NZ$1,130 per year. His two councilors were paid NZ$298. The people over whom Ivan presided numbered fifty-four. Two years later, the population was only forty-five. An islander said, "I think Pitcairn is on her last leg. The manpower now is getting down so low — what are they going to do about it? They may come right to the point they can't manage. What they'll do — whether they'll send people here or move the people — I don't know."[1]

What was the quality of life on Pitcairn in the early 1980s? The official guide book states, "A soil and climate that yield food liberally; generous friends overseas; trading aboard ships and by mail; no taxation; and a tolerant New Zealand which allows access and work without impediment are the Pitcairners' inheritance...."[2] These advantages, and reluctance to leave family and beloved surroundings, are among the reasons all of the islanders did not abandon their island home.

The minuscule community may live in a starkly beautiful tropical paradise with fruit ripening on the vine and stars poking through swaying palms, but, as their numbers dwindled, their lives were hardly idyllic. Fewer people were left to do the work. The islanders were always busy. Ed Howard, writing for *National Geographic*, called them "the hardest working people I've ever lived among...."[3]

One task was rebuilding their homes. Termites had been a particular scourge, necessitating replacing beams, flooring and siding from time to time. A subsidized building scheme that commenced in 1984 helped islanders afford to make repairs and improvements. From New Zealand came building materials at half cost, the British government paying the other half and all freight charges. Thus, modern materials slowly replaced hand-hewn planks. Aluminum-framed windows and concrete floors would deter termites. Electricity from generators allowed amenities in the twenty-two occupied homes: electric stoves, refrigerators, freezers,

TVs for showing videos, and even electric coconut graters. Concrete floors had carpeting. Nevertheless, if life were to be truly comfortable, Pitcairn still needed millions of dollars for replacing and improving homes, boats, communications, roads, and public buildings. At the beginning of the 1980s some felt confident that the money would soon be on its way, not from the British authorities, but from an eccentric multimillionaire.

Dreams of Smiley's Millions

In the early 1980s, British author Simon Winchester visited nearly every one of Britain's remaining colonial possessions to gather material for his book *The Sun Never Sets*. Colonies like Grand Cayman and Hong Kong were easy to get to, but Pitcairn frustrated Winchester; like many visitors and would-be visitors, he made logical attempts to get to the island and concluded that his best option, a ten-hour layover ashore — if the seas were sufficiently calm for him to land — was hardly worth the effort and expense. As a result, Winchester did not visit Pitcairn to gather material for his book.[4]

Instead of visiting Britain's last Pacific island possession, the journalist drove to Frog Level, Virginia. In Frog Level lived one A.M. "Smiley" Ratliff, a fifty-seven-year-old divorced multimillionaire. Smiley had made a fortune in coal mining. In addition to mines, Ratliff owned a motel, a shopping center, thousands of head of cattle, and around twenty thousand acres of the best farm land in Grundy, Virginia. He wanted to trade his lucrative empire for isolation. Ratliff wanted to separate himself permanently from the "evils of Communism, Freudian analysis, big government, narcotics and Elvis Presley."[5]

In 1981, Smiley Ratliff sailed 4,500 miles around the South Pacific on a rented sailboat with a hired crew. Smiley sailed in search of his own private paradise. One day he happened upon Henderson Island. After scaling the cliffs and struggling through the dense undergrowth, he envisioned "crops growing, cattle grazing, some decent housing, a jetty down at the beach, solar electricity." Smiley sailed over to Pitcairn, where he found the islanders to be "kind and gentle, almost Christlike; they're what man was meant to be and once was," he said. Because Communism, Freudian analysis, big government, narcotics, and Elvis Presley's music were not present on uninhabited Henderson, Smiley Ratliff offered Britain's Foreign Office a million dollars to lease it; some reports have the figure as high as five million. Smiley now began to dream of transforming Henderson into his private Shangri-la; Pitcairners began to dream of what they would do with Smiley's millions.

But Smiley's millions would never arrive. When the World Wildlife Fund heard about the scheme, they reminded the Foreign Office of its obligation to preserve this incomparable natural habitat of sea birds, coral reefs, and diverse fauna for which Henderson Island is known. The British government informed Ratliff that the island was not for lease. "It's got where you can't do anything anymore without first checking it out with some idiot," Smiley concluded.[6]

Carl Lipscombe — on the Rocks

Smiley Ratliff's millions might have allowed islanders to improve their harbor by further extending and strengthening the jetty. His money would have brought an airfield to Henderson and made emergency evacuation easier. That the money evaporated before it materialized was more lamentable to some because the factor of island life that can never be improved is the fury of the surf that attacks the shore. For two hundred years boats of varying sizes have been dashed against Pitcairn's merciless rocks. In late 1975 it happened again. Skipper Carl Lipscombe lost his yacht *Fairwinds* when a storm during the night caused her to break up near where the *Bounty* was burned. Lipscombe had left the boat unattended.

On October 13, 1989, Lipscombe returned, this time aboard the yacht *Aviva*, bringing a single passenger from Mangareva. That passenger was to be the first of many that Lipscombe intended to ferry between Pitcairn and Mangareva aboard the regular service he proudly inaugurated. By radio, Lipscombe told the Pitcairn longboat crews that he would anchor at Tedside. When the men prepared to go out to the yacht, all they saw was a broken hull and debris bobbing in the surf. Lipscombe's Aviva had been smashed into three pieces. Lipscombe soon left Pitcairn on a Chilean vessel. Islanders wondered if he would ever return. They wondered if there would ever be a ferry service to and from Mangareva.[7]

Stick and Tin and Tub

Crews used each longboat perhaps seven or eight years at most because "Continual wetting then drying of the planking, scraping along the skidway, pounding against the jetty while moored, and gashes from the steel flanks of visiting ships" caused the boats to wear out quickly.[8] In 1982, Pitcairners built their last wooden launch. They began selecting timber to fell on August 29 and completed the boat on November 21. At forty-seven feet with a ten-foot beam, *Stick* was the largest boat ever produced on Pitcairn. Nevertheless, diminishing population with fewer able hands demanded more reliable craft.

Tin, received in 1983, was the community's first aluminum boat. A new aluminum launch, which the islanders named *Tub*, arrived in December 1987 on the container ship *ACT 4*. With the arrival of *Tin* and *Tub*, *Stick* was no longer used. On December 17, an island crew sailed *Tub* to Mangareva to pick up islander Meralda Warren; they returned on the 26th. It was the first time anyone had taken a Pitcairn longboat from Bounty Bay to Mangareva.

Recession

In 1985, Pitcairners had to tighten the public belt. Tightening meant putting off the purchase of a wood-to-gas converter to reduce diesel bills, and deferring maintenance on buildings and roads. Postage stamp sales had fallen by almost forty percent. The editor of *The Pitcairn Miscellany* thought the decrease due to global recession, but the downturn in philatelic income has another explanation. During the period of intense inflation in the late 1970s and early 1980s, investors had rushed to collectibles such as art, coins, antiques and, of course, quality stamps. Prices of investment-quality stamps more than doubled. Stamp dealers were able to convince non-collectors and casual collectors that Pitcairn stamps were a good investment. When inflation subsided, so did the value of some collectibles, including the Pitcairn Island new issues that rested in bank vaults and safety deposit boxes. Sales to collectors continued, but sales to investors plummeted.

The Parachuting Cat

Supplies arriving by ship, particularly frozen foods, had to be taken up to Adamstown as soon as possible. Mud made the task challenging. Rain during one week in 1999 made the steep upward track, in the words of *The Pitcairn Miscellany*'s editor, the "worst I had driven on and I must confess to being terrified on the first trip down and then up again with supplies tied to the bike." He mentioned islanders "losing grip and sliding metres at a time, down the steep sections with no way of stopping — losing traction on the way up and wheels spinning, unable to control going back or forward."[9] Something clearly had to be done.

In 1983, a spectacular air drop took place. An eleven-ton D-4 Caterpillar tractor was eased onto the island. It was to be used for road maintenance, particularly for improvement of the slippery path to the Landing. Radio operator Tom Christian reported that, "As the plane circled Pitcairn at an altitude of 1,000 feet, two crates were dropped. One housed the tractor and was suspended by six 100-foot parachutes. The other, under two similar parachutes, contained the canopy and blade for the 11-ton earthmover." The use of the Royal New Zealand Air Force C-130 plane came at a cost to the island council of $25,000. The airdrop was essential because the tractor was far to large to bring ashore from a ship.[10]

Trying to Fit In: The Bewilderment of Martha Petty

In March 1982, Medical Officer Martha Petty arrived in Adamstown with her husband, the pastor of the Seventh-day Adventist church. During their two-year stay, this American woman expressed mixed feelings about living in the Pitcairn community. When they arrived, she wrote, "We felt confused and isolated." Petty found Pitcairn a closed society in that "much of what they think and mean can go without saying." She attributed Pitcairners' mutual understanding to "extensive information networks among family, friends, colleagues, and clients" to which outsiders were not privy. As a result, all seemed to know "every minute detail" of life which they were unable or reluctant to share with newcomers. For example, when the Pettys heard the church bell ring five times they went immediately to the Landing in anticipation of seeing longboats shooting between the rocks to board a cruise ship. In at least one instance they found they were the only ones at the Landing and that no boat had departed. "On other occasions, however, we went to the landing in about the same amount of time as before, only to miss the boat entirely."

Martha Petty found that, except when a ship arrival was imminent, time had little meaning to the islanders. Contrasted with America, where "deadlines and appointments are a serious business with penalties for being late," on Pitcairn, people do what they feel is important at the moment and will put off until another day the task they had planned to complete. Petty conceded that rain and wind may be a factor, and cited an example of the decision made during a sudden onset of superb weather to suspend all activities in favor of a community picnic.[11]

Petty was as baffled by "a maze of paths and dirt roads, which generally have no names" and which bore no street signs as she was by the islanders' unspoken secrets. In two years, she managed to find her away around the community and explored roads she had never traveled before, but she never managed to walk on all of the roads and paths that existed on the tiny island. Some of these paths to abandoned homes may have been in the process of returning to bush.

Petty learned that the Pitcairners she spoke with found it difficult or impossible to think in abstract terms. "Their purpose in life seems to be survival and the enjoyment of life. They have enough drive to make money in order to buy the conveniences they want to make their lives easier and more interesting. But they regard money as only a medium of exchange and not as an end in itself." Despite being baffled by this closed society, Petty concluded that she came to prefer the Pitcairn view of time and found reorienting herself to life in the United States on her return more difficult than fitting in on Pitcairn.[12]

Nuclear Threats and Warships

Pitcairners were criticized in the mid–1980s for trading with crews that were from countries with poor human rights records. An editorial in the July 1985 issue of *The Pitcairn Miscellany* mentioned concerns about the Chilean military dictatorship, but also about France, and the United States. A reader had written to the editor to criticize the islanders' warm welcome in October 1984 of the Chilean navy ship *Esmeralda*. The reader charged that the ship belonged to a nation whose army was notorious "for its cruelty and torture practices" under the Pinochet regime. The editor readily agreed with the writer's viewpoint, but stated that Pitcairn also welcomed the Soviet ships *Mikhail Lermontov* and *Maxim Gorky* in spite of the Soviets' humanitarian outrages.

The editor went on to state that a French naval ship was expected, although "France perhaps provides the greatest threat to our security of any nation." Six hundred miles away, at Mururoa Atoll, the French had long been testing nuclear weapons, and "It is widely known that during this time radiation levels rose above normal levels acceptable to human beings...." The editor explained that radiation from underground testing has caused fish in and around French Polynesia to become contaminated, but that "The state of the fish around Pitcairn is not known and we continue to eat them." The editor also expressed concern that Trident missiles would splash down seventy-five miles from Adamstown. He argued that in spite of the fact that nuclear risk to Pitcairn "is probably greater than in many other places ... all ships are welcome at Pitcairn, because they are all needed."[13] It was apparent that islanders had no intention of boycotting any visiting ships for political reasons; the sale of curios had become too vital to each family's income and ship visits were too few as it was.

1986: The Adventist Centennial

The church continued to flourish in the 1980s. With headquarters in Auckland, New Zealand, the Central Pacific Union governed the Pitcairn Seventh-day Adventist church. In 1986, members celebrated the centennial of the Pitcairn church. Expressing disappointment that no Adventist or Commonwealth officials had accepted invitations to attend the commemoration, they scheduled appropriate ceremonies on October 18, 1986. Missionary John I. Tay had arrived on that day a century earlier.

At nine in the morning a procession headed down the Hill of Difficulty, females dressed in long dresses and sunbonnets or woven hats. Men wore clothing to approximate that worn in 1886. Seven-year-old Timmie Young crowned himself with a top hat and painted on a mustache. *The Pitcairn Miscellany* reported that "Andrew Young, 87 years old, had walked down wearing a very very old seaman's coat. Bernice Christian, same age, came wearing the dress

in which she had met the Queen in 1958. ... Mavis wore a hat woven by her mother in 1933."
Pastor Oliver Stimpson, playing missionary Tay, wore black pants, a white shirt and vest and
black hat and attached a long fake beard to his chin. Three men carried Tay out of the harbor in a row boat and then brought him back in. The islanders sang "Praise God" and climbed
back up the hill for a special church service. A public dinner concluded the festivities.[14]

Coming Ashore, February 1, 1986

On Saturday, February 1, 1986, when the *Lindblad Discoverer* on which the author served
as history lecturer approached Pitcairn, the bell in the square at Adamstown struck five times
and some islanders hurried to the Landing. From there they made their way out to the *Discoverer* which, due to stormy seas, anchored far away at Tedside. They climbed aboard easily
and sold wooden turtles, T-shirts, carved sharks, fans, canes, baskets, hats and beads to passengers. While they were onboard the expedition cruise ship, other islanders prepared to attend
Sabbath services.

Pitcairners dressed in yellow oilskin slickers helped passengers into the longboat *Tin*
from the ship, which was two miles out. Two men sat at the bow, one was maneuvering the
tiller and another hovering over the engine. Visitors literally bounced through the roiling
waters, only to wait for the right wave. The boatload of people hovered expectantly offshore
for eleven stomach-churning minutes. The buoyant boat jumped up and down and up and
down. At last the right wave came and it darted into the Landing, where the *Discoverer*'s pas-

The author posed in front of the "Welcome to Pitcairn" sign at the Landing on February 1, 1986. He
arrived aboard the *Lindblad Discoverer*, the expedition cruise ship on which he served as history-
enrichment lecturer. Photograph by Barbara Kirk.

sengers were greeted by a large sign above the launch shed: "Welcome to Pitcairn." Smiling islanders stood waiting. Passengers expected the Hill of Difficulty to be a challenge, but they climbed, some more slowly than others, while chatting with new Pitcairn friends.

Passengers met nearly all the islanders. They included six Browns; Norma Clark, who was postmaster Roy Clark's widow; twenty-one Christians, nineteen Youngs, the pastor and his wife and the educational officer and his family. Because it was Saturday and because the timing was perfect, most of the passengers went to church. They filed in and filled some empty pews. Pastor Oliver Stimpson welcomed the visitors, obviously thrilled to have a good-sized congregation for at least this one beautiful summer Saturday morning. Near the pulpit in a wooden case is the Pitcairn *Bible*, and behind it a large painting of an island scene and, in large letters for all to see from the wooden pews: "The Lord is My Rock and My Fortress." The pastor said it had been painted by a visiting artist, Eric Were.

The group that sat after services on the long bench at the Square chatting with the oldest islanders, Bernice Christian and Andrew Young, learned about island history. Young told about the arrival and demise of the mutineers. The story of the settlement and aftermath was expected of the island patriarch, yet he told the story without revealing anything that might not be found in the copious literature. But the man himself was a repository of twentieth-century island lore. For years Andrew had been the timer, standing on the shore telling the longboats when to jump into the swell to be thrust toward the beach. "Picken thems times" is what Andrew had done. He recalled the miscues he had given that imperiled boat crews. Like most islanders, he remembered every ship that had stopped in Bounty Bay during his lifetime. Pitcairners have prodigious memories for such things. Tall, tanned and wiry, Andrew was in amazingly good health and said that he had recently circumnavigated the island by rowing his canoe. Bernice Christian sat quietly; perhaps she had heard Andrew's stories before. A little more than two years later, on March 17, 1988, Andrew Young died, age eighty-eight.

Walking about the island, visitors skirted frangipanis, bougainvilleas, hibiscus and fruit trees in great profusion. Ripe bananas and peaches bordered the path at elbow height, inviting the passerby to eat. Islanders explained that the rain that caused their home to be a lush garden had a profound effect on their lives. It could rain for a few minutes, cooling and refreshing people on a hot day. A few minutes later they will have dried off in the hot sun. Rain could fall all day and all night or for days on end or for a month. Conversely, crops could dry up in a withering drought. Roads could be tracks of deep mud — slippery slopes that challenge the pedestrian. During droughts roads became rutted tracks, exacerbated by the wheels of vehicles used by teenagers and adults. Islanders complained about rust, a natural result of rain. Rust invaded vehicles and bored holes in tubs — in anything fabricated of metal.

Islanders told their guests about the joys of their lives — the constant round of birthday parties and occasional public dinners that brought them together on days other than the Sabbath. None mentioned the incredible quiet and darkness that swept across the community after the last generator went off at ten; those luxuries were taken for granted in this lonely place, something that only visitors noticed.

Tom and Betty Christian showed visitors the foundation, plywood decking and framework of their home under construction; it was to measure 2,500 square feet on the ground floor and half as much again on the upper story. "Chez Christian" was clearly to be the nicest home on the island. Tom was able to finance this spacious dwelling as a result of a lifetime of work as island radio officer. Tom and Betty were also adept curio entrepreneurs. They were to have a magnificent view of the sea. There was no comparison between the house in progress and Tom and Betty's century-and-a-half-old home it was to replace. When a supply ship

Andrew Young and Bernice Christian were in their late eighties in 1986, the oldest people in the community. Andrew had run the radio station, timed the launching of boats from the Landing, and traveled extensively. A park has been named for Bernice "Beenie" Christian. Photograph by Robert Kirk.

arrived from Auckland minus some building materials, Tom was understandably frustrated; he would have to wait another three months or more to proceed in the next step of construction. Building, in spite of frustrations due to distances, was easier, Tom told passengers, than when he was a teenager in the 1950s. Then, islanders who wanted to build or repair a home had to cut logs at Tedside with a pit saw. They swam each log out to a boat. The logs were then ferried around to Bounty Bay and lugged uphill to the building site.

Three years later an article appeared about the abandoned houses that passengers noted throughout Adamstown. The teacher's wife, Lesley Harraway, published a letter in *The Pitcairn Miscellany* addressed to former chief magistrate Pervis Young, who had moved away in 1974. She told Pervis that the people in the late 1980s were as kind and hospitable as ever, "Yet the main road through Adamstown is strangely quiet. Old houses, including your own, are gone or slowly decaying under a gentle mantle of Morning Glory. Andrew's house is sadly silent, Henry's house covered in wild bean; no John, Sammy or Maynard, and Christie and Maimi's door is closed forever — but even here some things are the same — Bob's Walley still bears the haunting perfume of Queen of the Night and is full of lush bananas and towering breadfruit."[15]

Lunch during the *Discoverer*'s visit was catered by the ship's culinary staff for passengers and for islanders in the spacious court house. Chief Magistrate Brian Young welcomed the group warmly. Cruise Director Jim Snyder replied that he was delighted to return to strengthen friendship and good relations between the Lindblad staff and Pitcairners. Passengers were gratified by the islanders' friendliness. Glynn Christian wrote of his own visit a few years earlier, "At first we were embarrassed by the generosity and hospitality of the Pitcairners, hardly believing it could be sincere and sustained; but it was."[16]

Tom Christian, a direct descendant of mutineer Fletcher Christian, posed at the construction site of the new home he was building in 1986 for his wife, Betty, and his daughters. Tom expressed frustration at shipments of building materials that failed to arrive for months. Photograph by Robert Kirk.

Passengers were escorted out the short distance to see John Adams's grave, and to Pulau, the site of the school. They found the most astonishing fact about the school is not the small number of attendees, but the play yard — a tilted slope, guaranteed to send a missed ball into the Pacific. The school yard is a reminder that flat land anywhere on Pitcairn is in very short supply.

When the *Discoverer*'s captain gave cases of beer to members of a boat crew to thank them, some crew members gladly accepted. Prohibition of alcohol had been tested on March 26, 1984, when a secret ballot gave voters a chance to decide if Pitcairners could obtain licenses to import alcoholic beverages. Sixteen voted no, and only six yes. William Buckley, the conservative columnist, famously stated about some of the Pitcairn men after he came to the island as a cruise lecturer aboard the *Sea Cloud* on April 17, 1987, "none of them will take a drink, except the ones to whom you offer a drink."[18] What Buckley may or may not have understood is that every drinker was not a hypocrite, because not every islander is an active member of the Seventh-day Adventist church.

A Soaking-wet Departure

In an article about the *Discoverer*'s visit, *The Pitcairn Miscellany* related that one boat-load, "heading back to the ship, were refreshed by a sheet of water which drenched everyone as it came over the bows."[18] When the boat reached the ship it was evident to all that passengers not only had been soaked to the skin, but in many cases had been knocked off of their benches by the huge wave. Some had been thrown to the floor of the boat. Cameras and purses were filled with water. Concerned, a staff member asked the oldest passenger, a ninety-four-year-old slightly built titan of American industry, if he was all right. "All right? Of course I'm all right," he trumpeted emphatically. "I fell on a fat lady!"

The Pitcairners came out in another boat to bid the visitors goodbye. Bobbing in the pulsating water a few yards from the ship, they sang:

> In the sweet bye and bye,
> In the beautiful land beyond the sky
> We shall part never more,
> When we meet on the beautiful shore.

As they made their perilous way back to the Landing, they must have known that some passengers were crying.[19]

CHAPTER 26

Bicentennial Decade

After Two Hundred Years

The decade of the nineties would be a decade of significant structural and communication improvements on the tiny island, though population decline would remain a real worry. By August of the bicentennial year, the population had sunk to a low of thirty-three and eleven resident outsiders.[1]

Although no British official came to help the residents celebrate, a message arrived from Queen Elizabeth II: "On the occasion of the Two Hundredth Anniversary of the settlement of Pitcairn Island, I have much pleasure in extending my warm congratulations to the Island Magistrate, the island Council and all the people of Pitcairn. Elizabeth R."[2] As in most other years, the descendants burned a replica of the *Bounty*, held a church service, laid a wreath at the grave of John Adams, swam, and enjoyed a public dinner and fireworks. Considering how few of them were present, islanders may well have wondered if tercentennial festivities would take place in 2090.

In the summer of Bicentennial year, island magistrate Brian Young and his Norwegian-born wife Kari traveled to London. They had been invited to represent Pitcairn at Queen Elizabeth's Buckingham Palace garden party. Kari reported that, "if we had imagined an intimate cup of tea alone with the Queen, we would have been very disillusioned by the awful sight of 8,000 tea and lemonade drinkers wandering around on the lawns." When the queen and duke of Edinburgh approached the couple, Kari wrote that "Brian reminded the Duke of their last meeting, when the royal yacht *Britannia* came in 1971, when Brian was still a young boy, ... and the Queen reminded them, 'And Louis (Mountbatten) was with you, wasn't he?'" referring to Prince Philip's late uncle. "We also discussed the decreasing population and the future of Pitcairn," Kari reported, "and by the time close to ten minutes had passed, they said goodbye to us and wandered off to archbishops and lords and ambassadors, leaving us quite dazzled and exhilarated."[3]

Temporary Return Scheme

To encourage population growth, the governor's office and island council announced a program by which former Pitcairners and their descendants who were in good health, between nineteen and twenty-eight years of age, and willing to work, would be assisted to return to Pitcairn for a minimum of twelve months. It was expected that applicants would come from Norfolk Island, Australia, and New Zealand, where the largest communities of *Bounty* mutineer descendants resided.

The island council voted to "provide assistance in finding suitable board with a local family," preferably a family related to the applicant; "provide paid employment in at least one government post"; to provide all medical and dental benefits that were available to residents; and "provide an opportunity for participants to obtain by lease, purchase, or other legal means, a plot of house land suitable for the erection of a permanent dwelling should they wish to settle on Pitcairn...." In addition the scheme offered paid passage from Norfolk or New Zealand and return passage at the end of the stay. If the temporary resident decided to become a permanent resident, the government would give him or her the cash equivalent of a return ticket. The scheme in its first year secured a twenty-year-old electrician and a nineteen-year-old tractor driver trainee, both from Norfolk Island.[4]

The Governor and the Commissioner

Pitcairn had been administered by a governor whose more important title was British High Commissioner to New Zealand. The governor appointed a commissioner to look after Pitcairn affairs; this official was based at the office of the British Consul General in Auckland.

Leon Salt and his family posed in 1986. Salt served as island education officer and his wife aided in editing *The Pitcairn Miscellany*. Salt would later be named commissioner, a title which he explained meant "Island Go-fer." Photograph by Robert Kirk.

The commissioner, until he retired in 1995 after twenty-three years of service, was Garth Harraway. A former Pitcairn education officer, Harraway served as government advisor to the chief magistrate and council. Harraway was succeeded by former Pitcairn Island education officer Leon Salt. In response to a query about his job, Salt wrote: "My job title is Commissioner for the Pitcairn islands. Sometimes I think it means Gopher for the Pitcairn Islands...." "Gophering" included deciding what stamp issues would be designed and printed each year. When Salt determined that basket weaving was a desirable stamp topic, he secured photographs of the process from islander Meralda Warren. Salt commissioned artists to draw up rough drafts of stamps, secured the governor's approval of subject and design, and then sent the designs to Buckingham Palace for approval. He then contracted with a printer and decided on quantities to be sent to Adamstown and to philatelic distribution agents. By the summer of 1992, Pitcairn had issued a total of 370 stamps over 52 years. Subjects included the most obvious ones — Bligh, Christian and the *Bounty*— as well as stamps to honor specific cruise ships that called, turtles, fish, birds, and even the peculiar island wheel barrows designed for navigating precipitous terrain.

Salt purchased medical supplies for the islanders, T-shirts with island imprints to be sold to tourists, school supplies, fuel, hardware, building supplies, machinery and parts. In emergencies, Salt arranged for ships to evacuate islanders for medical treatment. Salt evaluated applications for temporary residence, and then ran background checks and secured permission of the island council and the governor before granting permission for entry. He assisted the governor in selecting education officers for two-year appointments. He traveled frequently to Pitcairn and he represented the island at large stamp shows, and at regional conferences such as that held at Noumea, New Caledonia, by ministers of culture from the Pacific area.[5]

Supplies and the Cooperative Store

The most important task that Harraway and Salt performed was arranging the arrival of periodic supply ships to keep the cooperative store filled, and to make certain goods individuals had purchased abroad were delivered to Pitcairn. Four supply ships a year brought flour, meat, cereals, canned foods, potatoes and other food products. When *Act III* arrived in July 1991, *Miscellany* described what went on: "Then for the next nine hours, whenever the longboats were at the landing every available body was fully occupied carrying bags, boxes, containers, and trays into the Landing Store Shed where the higgledy-piggledy stack of assorted stores and supplies grew higher and higher and more jumbled."[6]

A report in 1991 stated that the store was open twice a week for an hour each time. Residents could purchase groceries, sundries and "carving needs." The store clerks accepted New Zealand or American dollars, or pounds sterling. Because some goods were lost into the sea in the process of transferring them from ship to shore and some spoiled or became rusted before they could be sold, the coop's members agreed to a twenty percent markup on each item stocked.[7]

The Challenge of Generating Income

The commissioner's and magistrate's major challenge was finding sufficient public income to finance services. At the end of 1996, island magistrate Jay Warren lamented the decline of public revenue from the sale of stamps. From a high in 1981-82 of NZ$919,000, income had fallen to NZ$446,000 in 1995-96, or by forty-eight percent. The magistrate warned that "government expenditure exceeds income by close to a hundred percent and the substantial reserves built up during the seventies and early eighties are rapidly eroding. Forecasters have predicted bankruptcy in six years unless the trend can be reversed." Warren suggested the shortfall might be reduced through mineral exploration on the tiny rock, sale of Pitcairn phone cards and additional coins to collectors, and the sale of fishing licenses.[8]

To supplement funds from declining stamp sales, Pitcairn issued its own commemorative bicentennial coins on January 15, 1990. Silver and cupro-nickel dollar coins were produced, as were 2,500 fifty-dollar silver pieces and 500 two-hundred-and-fifty-dollar gold coins. It is unlikely that anyone used the coins on the island for trade or tithing; these attractive disks were sold to collectors.

Throughout the decade the handicraft industry remained the single most important source of islanders' private income. In May 1994, *The Pitcairn Miscellany* reported, islanders cleared US$27,000 by selling curios on two ships, the *Odessa* and the *Royal Viking Sun*; the two cruise ships had arrived only three days apart. "Without this bonus," the editor wrote, "no Pitcairner would be able to buy the VCRs, stereos, freezers, washing machinees [sic], motor bikes or stoves which have made such a difference to the standard of living on Pitcairn."[9]

Wood from Henderson made curio carving possible. Longboats had to be used both ways because freighters had discontinued loading longboats onboard and taking islanders one way. Because of the minimal population, the island Council now needed to approve these trips. Approval was necessary because, with half the population gone, and with the longboat crew off island, those who remained would be unable to leave Pitcairn or even meet a ship; moreover, those left at home would have to maintain all of the gardens.

In 2002, during his two-month stay, Sean Bercaw joined an expedition to Henderson. "It sounded so simple," Bercaw recalled, "overnight by longboat up to Henderson, a day of cutting, day loading, and overnight back to Pitcairn; less than 3 days and the island would have a large supply of raw material for their carvings." After reaching Henderson Island early on a Tuesday morning, the party set up camp and "set forth with axes and chainsaw" to cut miro and tau wood. Because these scrubby trees were "scraggly and branchy," the men and women had to search for wood with adequate diameter and color. Tramping through thick jungle, they cut quickly what they could find. After cutting came the hard part: "In a simple but elegant procedure the logs are laid out on the beach near the water's edge, hitched together with a long line, and then towed over the coral reef and out to sea by a hawser from one of the longboats," Bercaw wrote. "The backbreaking part is the hand over hand hauling of the logs up out of the water into the boats and then unhitching and stowing them in the bilges."

Back in Bounty Bay after the voyage home, the workers unloaded logs onto the Landing and divided them for their owners. Men then brought the logs up the hill by tractor and delivered them to the owners' houses. After that, the bark having been stripped off, the wood was dried for four months before it could be carved.[10]

A further challenge to islanders working to generate private income came during the 1990s, when the New Zealand government reclassified Pitcairn as a "developed" rather than a "developing" entity. This form of flattery was costly to islanders who mailed souvenirs and honey. The letter rate tripled to NZ60¢. An airmail letter, which incidentally went by ship to Tahiti, was NZ$1.20. The book sold by islanders, *The Pitcairn Guide*, cost a purchaser $15 but mailing was an additional $10. Pitcairn honey cost $4 per jar for postage, and the cost for an American receiving a carved *Bounty* model — the top of the line in Pitcairn artifacts — was NZ$42 in postage. High parcel rates resulted in fewer mail orders.[11]

Pitcairn: A Century Club Favorite

Pitcairn is considered a discrete geographical entity — at least by the Century Club, the club for travelers who can prove visits to a hundred or more countries, and by the *Guinness Book of Records.* Mr. Jarl Harienmark of Munka-Ljungby, Sweden, set foot on Pitcairn in 1992 while the supply ship on which he traveled was being unloaded. Getting his feet onto the Landing and having his passport stamped were important to this traveler to 171 countries and 41 non-sovereign territories. With his Pitcairn passport stamp secured, the world-roaming Swede had only seven more territories to visit in order to have been to all of the world's "countries." It is a rare that a cruise ship destined for Pitcairn does not have one or more Century Club members aboard. Some will take a cruise for the sole purpose of getting their passport stamped by immigration officer Meralda Warren.

The Basics: Electricity and Water

By 1991 a power station containing three generators operated from 9 A.M. until 1 P.M. and from 5 P.M. to 10 P.M. Residents were charged only for the power they used, which was supplied from fuel that arrived in drums. The editor of *The Pitcairn Miscellany* added, "Generally we leave power on longer at night if the longboats have to go out to a ship as we have large flood lights at the landing and overlooking the harbour."[12] Some homes had their own generators, which were used at times that public power was not available and to power their refrigerators and freezers. Power was often used in the evening to enjoy video movies.

Pitcairners had lived for a century and a half without electricity, but the island would never have been habitable without water. Natural springs are insufficient for daily needs, so water is collected in cisterns. At the pastor's house, for example, rain water ran down the indentations in the corrugated iron roof and gutter system and was collected. The capacity of the container was about six thousand gallons. As Pastor Thurman C. Petty, Jr., explained, "An inch of rainfall produces .62 gallons per square foot. Since the mission roof has an area of about 1,800 square feet, it should accumulate about 1,100 gallons of water from a one-inch shower."[13] Average rainfall amounts to seventy to eighty inches a year.

An Improved Pitcairn

The 1990s saw several improvements in the lives of residents:

• Air mail drop: In 1992, islanders enjoyed the benefits of the first airmail service in five years. The population headed up to Aute Valley to wait for a New Zealand Air Force Orion Kiwi 041 to drop five parachutes loaded with a half ton of mail. After the drop, four postal workers sorted letters and parcels while islanders reportedly chuckled at covers marked "No Air Service."[14]

• Museum: Since the early 1990s, a small museum has been open in Adamstown. The island council hoped that cruise ship passengers would pay to view the modest collection. The

The Landing has been subject to improvements during nearly every recent decade, but there is no way engineers can tame the elements that make boarding ships hazardous. Note the "flying fox," a gigantic hoist, in the background. Photograph by Robert Kirk.

governor presented two lockable display cases and islanders supplied a few *Bounty* and pre–European artifacts as exhibits. The main problem in assembling a collection was that those community members who had *Bounty* artifacts or other items of interest were reluctant to turn them over. Overseas friends of the islanders sent books, articles and photographs. The natural history displays include examples of Pitcairn Islands' flora and fauna. Old machinery, a layout of stamps, cannonballs, and copies of *National Geographic* magazine that featured the island round out the collection. On the other hand, important *Bounty* artifacts have left the island. McCoy's kettle can be seen in the Norfolk Island Museum; the *Bounty* rudder is in a museum in Fiji; the *Bounty*'s gudgeon and pintle are in the Otago Museum in New Zealand; the *Bounty* vise and anvil — taken by Irving Johnson in 1937 — are in Mariners Museum, Newport News, Virginia. Since 1966, it has been illegal to remove any *Bounty* relic from Pitcairn without the governor's written permission. But there is not much left to remove.

- Landing Area: By 1992 Bounty Bay was made safer for the "Pitcairn navy" and the Landing was improved. Over two tons of rocks were removed from the entrance. The slipway for boats was repaired, and widened to make launching easier. The landing area was enclosed by 71 Akmons, which are one-and-a-half-ton concrete blocks. Back-fill leveled off the tops of the Akmons.

- Telecommunications: In June 1985, worldwide telephone communications had been introduced on Pitcairn, and calls could be made or received twice daily. Calling time was billed at NZ$1.70 per minute. The New Zealand Telecom discontinued that link through Wellington in 1992. To replace it, in early 1992, the International Maritime Organization announced it would provide Inmarsat satellite service. Although islanders could call any time, the cost increased to NZ$15.00 per minute. Five years later an Inmarsat M Planet One system was installed; if islanders used phone/fax cards, their costs were cut to NZ$7.50 per minute, still prohibitive for most users. Instead islanders use amateur radio, and the Pitcairn Island Amateur Radio Club VP6 PAC operates Radio ZBP. About a dozen amateur licenses have been issued.

• Seismic Station: In early 1996, the United States government installed a seismic station near the Landing. As part of a worldwide network of test centers to monitor and predict major quakes, the station contains an instrument pier firmly attached to bedrock inside a two-room vault. Seismometers mounted on the pier by Allied Signal Aerospace of Albuquerque, New Mexico, send signals through a remote satellite data link directly to Albuquerque for analysis. Technicians installing the system trained islanders to maintain it after they had left.

• Rat Eradication: Rats probably had been brought to the island by earlier Polynesian inhabitants and were already present when Fletcher Christian stepped ashore. More might have landed from the *Bounty* to join their fellow rodents. They had become a sufficient nuisance that in 1997, the commissioner arranged for Wildlife Management International Ltd. of New Zealand to send a team of six pest control specialists to Pitcairn and later to Oeno to eradicate them. The team, dubbed the "Ratpile," spent eight weeks cutting 800 tracks all over Pitcairn and laying out poison pellets. All six of Ratpile's crew then checked 7,635 bait stations over a period of three or four days. The project was financed by the Overseas Development Administration and the World Wide Fund for Nature. When crew members were unable to find a live rat, they reported their project a success. Birds, plants and invertebrates could flourish without their most formidable predators.

• Honey Production: In 1998 and again in 2001, the South Pacific Commission in Suva sent James Driscoll, an apiarist, to help start a viable honey industry. By 2000, bee keeping had become a profitable activity, the product of the hives being sold aboard cruise ships and by mail. When competition among fifteen bee keepers with forty-four hives lowered individual profits, families formed Pitcairn Island Producers Co-operative, or Pipco. Honey, judged among the most pure in the world, has become a mainstay of family income.

The Tragic Wreck of the *Wiggy*

Had harbor improvements been completed in May 1991, they would probably not have saved the *Wiggy*, a yacht which arrived from Easter Island. St. Paul's Point is at the southeast corner of the island, between Down Rope and Bounty Bay. On May 12, Eric Bennett and Rosalind Owen sailed their yacht toward the island. At daylight the forty-three-foot boat crashed on rocks adjacent to St. Pauls. *The Pitcairn Miscellany* reported that Rosalind Owen's radio signals were not received when the ship began to sink and that "Rosalind remained at the radio as long as possible sending the distress calls before managing to find her way through the water to where Eric was clinging desperately to a mast. Eric supported her while being battered between the rocks and the mast. Waves continued to crash in and Rosalind was continually ripped from his grasp, only to be washed back to his arms. Rosalind was slammed against the mast severely. One final time the sea ripped Rosalind from his grasp and Eric was forced helplessly to watch her float away face down in the water." Eric made his way somehow to Big Fence. Rosalind's body was later found and she was buried at the island's cemetery.[15]

A New Health Center

In 1990, the British government promised to fund through the Overseas Development Administration a new health center. A carpenter and electrician arrived from the Cook Islands and organized local men into a work force. Construction of the 1,800-square-foot facility, directly opposite the church, began in April 1996 and was completed in June. The cost was NZ$430,000; building materials shipped in from New Zealand accounted for nearly half that amount.

A reception area leads into a dental clinic, treatment room, pharmacy, laboratory, ward, and x-ray room. The center is operated by a visiting nurse, a member of the Seventh-day Adventist church; she is often the spouse of the pastor or teacher.

Visiting physicians were brought from New Zealand or Australia by the administration for two or three months to assess the needs of the community. In 1996, Dr. Anders Kallgard found that "the general health is good," and that most of twenty Pitcairners who had died between 1974 and 1993 were older than eighty-two. Dr. Kallgard identified as problems moderate asthma, and obesity. Obesity had never before been mentioned as a problem until the arrival of four-wheel-drive Hondas that made walking up and down hills optional.

Steve Christian, who had studied dentistry in New Zealand for three months, was able to do extractions, and, as a result, "not one of the adult islanders had any of their own teeth left...."[16]

Because the island had no permanent physician, acute appendicitis continued to be life threatening; in December 1994, eighteen-year-old Shawn Christian, son of Steve and Olive, had an inflamed appendix. The radio operator sent calls to eight shipping lines asking for immediate transportation. Thirteen days later the *Melbourne Star* picked up Shawn, and eight days after that a surgeon in Auckland removed his appendix. According to *The Pitcairn Miscellany*, "Olive recalls, as a hideous nightmare, the time she had to wait two months for the same operation several years ago; Raylene had to wait six weeks. Dobrey's brother, Pervis, was saved by the arrival of a doctor on the island. The doctor said at the time if he had been one hour later, he could not have been saved.... And then we have the sad cases of Nola's mother and Tom's sister who were unable to be helped."[17]

Medical attention and prescription drugs for all residents were provided at no charge. If a patient needed to be evacuated to New Zealand, either a shipping company allowed free passage or the government paid for it through a compassion allowance. In addition, the patient who went to New Zealand and his or her spouse would be given a living allowance while there. In April 1996, a ship called the *Tourcoing* from New Zealand evacuated Thelma Brown, whose leg suffered a serious blood clot. Because *Tourcoing* had to divert from its route, it had to pay another vessel to leave the berth *Tourcoing* needed in Auckland and for a crane to offload the other vessel; as a result, Thelma's evacuation cost *Tourcoing*'s owner, Gilfoyle Shipping Services Limited, an estimated NZ$100,000. Thelma had her clot removed and her life was saved.

As spacious as the new clinic was, according to *The Pitcairn Miscellany*, it could not accommodate accident victim Brenda Christian. On September 26, 2006, the former mayor "was Down Pulley on a fishing trip, about to get out of the boat onto the rocks. A big swell caused her to fall back into the boat, impaling the top of her foot on a fishing spear lying in the bottom." The spear's barbs embedded themselves into Brenda's foot so the spear could not be pulled out directly. In order to move her, Brenda's companions strapped the spear to her leg and brought her to the medical center. Because both the foot and spear would not fit through the doorway at the same time, Dr. Peter Modlmayr performed surgery outside. *Miscellany* reported that Brenda soon recovered.[18]

Unraveling Land Records

Many landowners had left Pitcairn never to return and their crop land was overgrown. Some residents had no title to land or use of insufficient land for their needs. Necessity for islanders to grow their own food compelled a rethinking and adjustment of land ownership. In 1992, the legal issue of land use and ownership was addressed. The governor's legal counselor, Donald McLoughlin, argued that two hundred years earlier, "Whilst the whole island may well have been appropriated to the families of the mutineers, it would appear that this was on the basis of communal ownership with rights on the part of individuals to mere occupancy and not ownership. This concept is common in Pacific island communities and presumably had its origins in Tahitian custom...." Proceeding from his assumption, McLoughlin argued that from "this basic communal system ... existing land customs on Pitcairn have evolved ... gradually converting the right of occupancy into that of ownership."

In the case of one parcel, the owner had died in 1997 and his appointed trustee had also died, leaving no clear owner or user. Some absentees had made verbal promises that "trustee caretakers" could use their land. As McLoughlin explained, "The land records, although required to be kept up to date, were in fact in a hopeless mess and completely unintelligible. No survey has ever been made of the island and, whilst boundaries have by law been required to be regularly maintained and inspected this was not done."[19]

The situation had become so complex and inequitable that the Pitcairn Land Court revised the law. The revision is set out in Part V, 17 (i); it states: "Any person who is registered ... as the owner or lessee of any land ... and who intends to leave Pitcairn island for a period longer than six months shall make application to the Court ... of some fit and proper person ... to be named ... as the caretaker during his absence from the island." The island council was given the power to serve at least a month's notice and then to take unused land "to be held in trust for all inhabitants" or to demolish an unused dwelling.[20] The council is able to tax the land of non-residents or "land held by a resident, in excess of his or her reasonable needs" in order to ensure "sufficient land is available for reallocation...."[21]

In 2006, the Pitcairn Islands Office in Auckland took the process of redistribution a step further when it sent a notice to all known land holders: "As from 1 December 2006 all existing freehold land titles on Pitcairn will be suspended, and Land Allocation Title may be issued instead. In addition, an annual land tax for unutilized land will be introduced, at a rate for the first 12 months of NZ$ 0.50¢ per square metre for nonresident owners." The notice warned that if landowners did not notify the government of their claim, their claim would cease and their lands would be reallocated. Nonresidents could notify the government that they claimed ownership, in which case they would be taxed.[22]

Miss Dea Birkett v. a Closed Society

In the mid-nineties, Dea Birkett, a London-based author, wanted to write a book about a visit to Pitcairn Island. She convinced Royal Mail to sponsor her to go to Pitcairn to do a report on the workings of the island postal system. Having been dealt with harshly by some writers in the past, the island council would not have admitted her had they known her profession and the real purpose of her visit. Her report on life among the dwindling population resulted in a book with an ominous title, *Serpent in Paradise*.

Birkett came away with the impression that Pitcairn is a closed society to which only an occasional outsider, one such as Kari Young from Norway who married a Pitcairner, can gain admittance. As Martha Petty had recognized in the early 1980s, a visitor could never be privy to esoteric vibrations that caused the closed community to exchange signals without seeming to communicate with one another. Birkett described their mental and physical synchronization when she described picking arrowroot: "The Pitcairners worked, not as a set of dedicated individuals, but as part of an organic whole. It was the same when they went out to trade on a ship, unloaded supplies at the Landing or hauled *Tub* into the boat shed. They moved as if choreographed, with the rhythm coming from within the group itself."[23]

Dea Birkett lived as a guest of Irma and Ben Christian. Birkett was impressed by the islanders' relative affluence. She noted that Irma owned "three industrial-size deep freezers, three cookers, two video machines, two TV screens, a heavy-duty microwave, a food processor, an electric frying pan, a deep-fat fryer, and two kettles." Irma considered freezers essential when nobody could be certain when a supply ship would arrive. Fortunately the island generator, off from eleven in the morning until six in the evening, was not off long enough to defrost her freezers' contents if she turned the thermostat to the coldest temperature.

Good Yachties and Bad Yachties

Arriving in June 1997, aboard the yacht *Kialoa II*, Lynn and John Salmon were met on the dock by Meralda Warren, the island police chief. Meralda told the Salmons to come and find her house if they wanted their passports stamped. So much for formalities. The Salmons counted thirty-five people in all; these included the pastor and his wife, the medical officer, an astrologer, and a young man working his way around the world. Islanders explained to Lynn that population was lost as teenagers went to Palmerston North, New Zealand, to study at the Seventh-day Adventist secondary college, and did not return.

After being transported up to Adamstown in all-terrain vehicles, the Salmons were put up at private homes. Chatting with Meralda and looking over the island register, the Salmons noted a large number of yachts and only a few cruise ships recorded as having stopped. Some yachts, they were told, arrived two at a time.

Pitcairners told Lynn they appreciated some yacht captains and wished others would stay away. Some owners offered to take islanders to Mangareva or Henderson. They cheerfully paid for provisions supplied by Pitcairners for them to take away. Others arrived "in sorry shape and with bad attitude." Either they had brought inadequate provisions and money for a trans-Pacific voyage, or they viewed the islanders as yokels easy to swindle. Though unrewarded or inadequately compensated, the islanders continued to show their traditional hospitality by supplying these "freeloaders" with food and water.

Touring the school, Lynn found the class "full of Huckleberry Finns and Becky Thatchers — shoeless, boisterous and more likely to be the subject of a book than reading a book."[24]

Another Constitutional Change

In 1998 the constitution was revised yet again. The foremost island officer was no long the chief magistrate, but now a mayor. He or she was to be elected for a three-year term. The mayor was one of ten members of an island council. Others consisted of four directly elected legislators, a directly elected chair of the council, two members appointed by the governor, one commissioner — also appointed, and an island secretary. Appointed members served at the governor's pleasure, while elected members were chosen yearly during Christmas week.

Internet and the .pn Domain Suffix

A lucrative income source is the Pitcairn pn. internet domain suffix. Every country has a suffix assigned by the IANA (Internet Assigned Names Authority). Britain has been assigned *.uk*. Pitcairn's is *.pn*. The Pitcairn postal authority's website, for example, is <*www.stamps.gov. pn*>. The suffix was assigned before Pitcairners acquired the use of internet. Before the council realized it, islander Tom Christian and Nigel Roberts of Britain's Channel Islands had gained title to what was to prove a lucrative domain name. Companies and individuals willingly pay to register under a domain. When they realized they had lost a valuable income source, all but two Pitcairners signed a petition to have the suffix restored to them, and in April 2000 they were rewarded when the domain name was taken from Tom Christian and his partner and reassigned to the island community. By 2001, over seventeen hundred *.pn* internet domain names had been registered. Registrations bring in hundreds of thousands of dollars to the island government.[25]

Fewer Ships

At the end of the nineties, thirty-five to forty ships a year visited Bounty Bay, but in 2003, Pitcairners were saddened to greet the crew of *America Star* for the final time. *America Star* was one of the Blue Star Line ships which had called since 1981; they were *Melbourne Star*, *America Star*, *Sydney Star* and *Queensland Star*; Pitcairners had formerly known them as *ACT III*, *IV*, *V*, and *VI*. At one time or another several Pitcairners had sailed aboard at least one of these ships, and islanders had formed personal friendships with officers and crews. Pitcairn Commissioner Leon Salt expressed sadness at the loss: "The Blue Star captains would call me by satellite phone from the other side of the Panama Canal and ask if I had any excuse for them to stop at Pitcairn. Sometimes I'd only have the mail. I'd say 'there's only the mail' and they'd say 'that'll do' and they'd stop for two hours. They just could not go past."[26]

With increased containerization aboard giant super cargo carriers, the new destination became Port Chalmers on New Zealand's South Island instead of Auckland. Pitcairn was no longer on the route, nor was it possible to unload giant containers into longboats. Blue Star joined a list of other lines that no longer stopped: Shaw Savill and Albion Shipping, NZ Shipping Company, Ellerman-Buckness Lines, White Star Line, and Port Line.

A Changing Society for a New Millennium

Pitcairn's mayor, Steve Christian, age 48, and his wife Olive, 46, were invited to Chicago at the end of 1999, to help civic authorities ring in the new millennium. The city had invited two representatives from each of 175 countries and territories. Dazzled by the metropolis, Steve exclaimed, "To walk into McCormick Place and see the immensity of the area, the people." Olive disclosed that she looked forward to passing through Los Angeles on her way home to look for her favorite movie actor, Clint Eastwood.[27]

The Seventh-day Adventist Church is the only church on Pitcairn. Pastors are appointed for two-year terms. Since 1950, the *Bounty* Bible has been the church's great treasure. Worship services take place on Saturday. Photograph by Robert Kirk.

The community that Steve and Olive left to travel to Chicago numbered thirty-four, and other residents brought the total to forty. Stamp and coin sales, the generosity of the British and New Zealand governments, income from the internet *.pn* domain designation, donations from friends abroad, and curio sales allowed the islanders to enjoy an enviable standard of living and to improve personal amenities and the island's infrastructure throughout the 1990s. As the New Zealand government recognized, Pitcairn Island had indeed become a "developed" colony. Yet, if more people were to leave, those who planned to stay were perennially haunted by the possibility of having too small a population to continue as a viable community; the fear of having to evacuate as their ancestors had done in 1831 and 1856 was always present.

Solutions to the population drain were not always palatable to the close-knit community. For example, in 2001, Wellesley, a construction consortium from New Zealand, proposed to construct two airports, a four-star hotel and two lodges. They promised the islanders no more than thirty visitors at any one time and ten percent of the profits. Opposition, particularly to an airfield on Henderson Island, came from conservation groups and from the islanders themselves.[28] According to Professor Herbert Ford, the plan died a slow death in the wake of legal problems which beset the islanders in the early 2000s.

Population decline was most noticeable in church attendance. In 2000, Pastor John O'Malley counted only eight attendees at Sabbath services. Ray Coombe, assistant to the Adventist Church president in the South Pacific, stated, "A handful of faithful members remains, and the church is committed to maintaining its presence and influence on this historic island." The fall-off in membership was attributed in part to members' moving away and transferring their membership to Adventist churches in their new communities. "Although an Adventist culture prevails, Pitcairn Island is no longer the pristine example of the past," Coombs stated without explaining what he thought made it less "pristine." On May 19, 2001, the "church" was downgraded; it ceased to exist as an entity designated a church and the Pitcairn congregants were informed they worshipped as part of a "company." Church members were invited to transfer their affiliation to other Adventist churches if they so wished.[29]

But by the dawn of the new millennium a declining population and falling church membership had been eclipsed by a truly monumental problem.

CHAPTER 27

Island on Trial

Rumors of Rape

The first years of the new millennium have been the most painfully challenging for the islanders since the 1830s, when islanders lost relatives during the removal to Tahiti and then fell under control of a tyrant. While community members enjoyed dramatic improvements in their standard of living in the late 1990s and early 2000s, seven Pitcairn men were put on trial in Adamstown for sex crimes. Observers were shocked that multiple charges of rape should be leveled in a community that prided itself on the fact that so few crimes had been identified that the hinges of its jail had rusted, freezing the door open. The trials took place in September and October 2004. When six adult males were convicted, many predicted that Pitcairn would soon have to be evacuated due to lack of workers and boat crew members. Not only were the men on trial, but so was the fate of the community.

In 1996, Pitcairn seized the attention of British law enforcement authorities. A father filed a complaint in England that his eleven-year-old daughter had been violated while visiting the island. Detective Superintendent Dennis McGookin of Kent, England, was dispatched half way around the world to investigate. Superintendent McGookin stated: "There is alcohol-related crime and violent crime and firearms laws are being broken all the time."[1] When they heard the allegation, island men argued that they carried guns to shoot goats or to shoot breadfruit out of trees and were not breaking any laws in doing so. Islanders denied allegations of alcohol-related offences and violent crime. Pitcairn's reputation as a pious community had come under further attack just the week before announcement of McGookin's allegations; Dea Birkett's *Serpent in Paradise* appeared in book stores. Birkett's account of her four-month stay in Adamstown portrayed the islanders rather negatively, though it contained no accusations of sex crimes. Islanders felt betrayed by Birkett.[2]

Investigators determined after some time that the eleven-year-old visitor was in a consensual relationship with a teenage Pitcairn boy. But the matter did not end there. As a result of McGookin's mention of guns, alcohol and violent crime, the British government decided to investigate further by sending a second police officer from England to its smallest colony. In October 1997, Gail Cox, a constable from Maidstone, Kent, arrived on a six-week assignment ostensibly to train island constable Meralda Warren in police procedures. Had there been a direct flight, she would have traveled 9,250 miles, but Cox had to approach

Pitcairn by a circuitous route. After a twenty-four-hour flight to Auckland, Cox had flown to Wellington to confer with the governor, and then back to Auckland. From Auckland she flew to Tahiti and then to Mangareva. From Mangareva she sailed to Pitcairn aboard the ship *Te Manu.*

Cox's assignment was funded by a thirty-thousand-pound British government budget item, labeled The Pitcairn Island Good Government Fund. A Foreign Office spokesperson said, "We haven't discussed whether the officer will be armed yet. We can't rule it out at this stage."[3] Cox set about establishing a seemingly trusting relationship with some of the island women. When she returned and submitted her report, Cox's superiors sent her back to Pitcairn for two months. This time, in 1999, when officer Cox gave a woman a pamphlet about sexual harassment, the woman realized that an incident that she said had occurred when she was eleven or twelve was unacceptable. She confided in her mother and her mother told Gail Cox the details. Cox reported the allegations to her superiors.

British authorities suspected that similar abuses may have been widespread, so Kent police, under assignment from Whitehall, began an extensive investigation. Officers were sent to the South Pacific. They interviewed not only all women living on the island, but female former Pitcairners living in New Zealand, Norfolk Island, and Australia. Kent police were obligated to tell each female they interviewed that under United Kingdom law they were eligible for statutory compensation for victims of crime. Reportedly, compensation was NZ$4,000. "We got disclosure after disclosure, it was staggering," an officer reported.[4] In all, thirty-two women claimed to have been abused while living in Adamstown. As a result, seven men on Pitcairn were charged as were six in Australia and New Zealand. Kent police named "a further seventeen men as abusers during the investigation."

Because charges had been made, British authorities felt it necessary to follow through and see that judicial procedures were completed. The accused would be tried under Britain's Sexual Offenses Act of 1956. On May 21, 2002, all subjects living in British Overseas Territories became British citizens, although they had previously been subject to British law. Although an island court system had long been in place, the British government felt it necessary to create a special court system for the trials. Because Pitcairn's governor was in Wellington, the British government decided that the trials should take place in New Zealand. In December, 2002, the New Zealand legislature passed the Pitcairn Trials Act that would have allowed the proceedings to be held in Auckland. However, the defendants on the island challenged the decision and won the right to be tried in Adamstown.

An Inundation of Outsiders

At last, Pitcairn Island had the full attention of the British government, though not the kind of attention that most islanders had long waited for. In late 2002, Governor Richard Fell spent two weeks on Pitcairn. Fell called the community members together and explained that he had three jobs. He served as British High Commissioner to New Zealand, which is tantamount to being ambassador to a Commonwealth nation. In that capacity, he promoted trade between New Zealand and Britain, and presided over cultural and other events. In addition, Fell was British High Commissioner to the autonomous nation of Samoa. Fell's third job was governor of Pitcairn, and in that capacity, he made all laws, approved appointments, and oversaw finances. He told them he would appoint all personnel for the upcoming trials.[5] Some felt it unfair that one appointee in New Zealand should personally assign prosecutors and defense attorneys as well as judges. They felt the fate of their two-centuries-old community rested on Fell's selections.

In 2003, court personnel from New Zealand visited Pitcairn to hold a preliminary hearing. The ship *Braveheart*, which brought trial personnel to Pitcairn after they had flown to Mangareva, was chartered at NZ$3,500 per day. *The Pitcairn Miscellany* reported, "The legal team consisted of Chief Justice Charles Blackie, Judge Jane Lovell-Smith and Judge Russell Johnson, public prosecutors, public defenders, New Zealand and British Police, a communications technician, a court registrar and court crier." The editor of *The Pitcairn Miscellany* stated in parentheses: "One wonders how British taxpayers would feel paying the thousands of dollars for a court crier when his only function was to declare the court open and closed!" *Miscellany* observed that "The court's formal attire contrasted sharply with the seven defendants' best informal dress." The editor concluded, "However things will never be the same on Pitcairn and some four years after the investigation began, the stress and a split community remain with us."[6]

Extensive construction and improvements were planned so the trials could be held in the rustic courthouse. Ships began to arrive weighed down by building materials and heavy equipment. Ironically, the accused men — who constituted the majority of able adult males — met ships in longboats and transported the equipment and construction personnel to the Landing. The accused were paid five dollars an hour to build their own prison and to erect a fifteen-foot-high fence around it. In 2007, it was estimated that annual operation of the jail would cost US$950,000 per annum; the British taxpayers would pay the New Zealand Department of Corrections for stationing guards in Adamstown. In ordering a prison built to accommodate exactly six prisoners and committing to annual maintenance fees before the trials began, British court authorities seemed to know the trials' outcome before the first gavel was pounded.

Britain's taxpayers contributed about NZ$5.5 million, while the European Union gave NZ$4.3 million for necessary infrastructure improvements. Among the projects were a six-bedroom government-owned guest house, a police station, a large warehouse, and extensions to the hostel. The courthouse was upgraded with carpeting, electronic gear for long-distance communication, and new furniture. In addition, workers improved roads and added several large water tanks. To organize the work, Britain sent the former governor of their Caribbean colony, Montserrat, as well as a retired Foreign Office official, and a civil engineer.

Probably Worth a Try

In November 2003, Mr. Paul Dacre, public defender for the accused, argued in the Pitcairn Supreme Court, sitting at Papakura in New Zealand, that the British could not try island residents because Pitcairn was not then — and had never been — a British colony. Dacre reminded the court that the earliest description of the mutineers in Britain had been as pirates, which in a sense, having stolen a ship and all of the goods aboard, they were. Pirates, Dacre reminded the judges, are by law stateless persons and as such they were no longer British subjects. The mutineers, Dacre asserted, by the very act of mutiny against the sovereign, "cut irrevocably, and severed, their ties to the United Kingdom." They had, in fact, established a separate state. Dacre argued that in regard to the twenty-four members of the second generation, "At law, illegitimate children took the nationality of their mothers at birth, which in this case would have been Tahitian." Dacre pointed out that every January 23, the populace celebrates the mutineers' destruction of the king's property by burning a *Bounty* replica in the cove; this act is "a symbol of the attitude of the Pitcairn community toward the British government and particularly an indication of their independence."

Crown Prosecutor Simon Moore argued vigorously that Pitcairn was indeed a British colony. Among his points was that the islanders had asked Captain Elliott of the *Fly* in 1838 to help them write a constitution and laws. They had begged for protection from the Royal Navy; this voluntary submission, he asserted, confirmed their British nationality. Defender Dacre countered that the British government failed at the time to confirm the relationship, and that the islanders' request was "a sign of civilized self-government by a people able to sustain their independence." Dacre reminded the court that when the islanders left for Norfolk in 1856, Pitcairn ceased to be a British settlement. When it was repopulated, the returnees came to an uninhabited place that was not under British jurisdiction. Moore quoted *Halsbury's Laws of England*: "A settled colony reconquered or ceded back after conquest or cession does not lose its status as a settled colony."[7]

In April, 2004, the Pitcairn Island Supreme Court ruled against Dacre's motion. The three judges stated that the mutineers were British citizens and were unable to withdraw their allegiance to the Crown; their twenty-four children were also British subjects, and so were all of their descendants. The prosecutor stated that Pitcairn fell under the British Settlements Act of 1887, which empowered "Her Majesty the Queen in Council ... to establish all such laws and institutions, and constitute such courts and officers ... as may appear to Her Majesty in Council to be necessary for the peace...." Furthermore, in 1898, colonial secretary Joseph Chamberlain directed that under the provisions of the Order in Council, 1893, for Pacific island settlements, "the said order in Council shall be exercisable in relation to the British Settlement known as Pitcairn Island...." The judges reminded Mr. Dacre that islanders willingly used stamps with the monarch's picture, as well as coins and had accepted an armorial ensign for Pitcairn. They reminded him how islanders in 1971 had restated their loyalty at the time of Prince Philip's visit. The judges emphasized that Pitcairners readily accepted British subsidies.

The court ruled that "Whilst the Public Defender has been able to point out to us instances of disappointment on the part of residents for periods of Imperial neglect, or confusion on the part of some naval officers or civil servants as to the actual political status of Pitcairn from time to time, the inexorable move towards incorporation into the British legal system is firmly evident...."[8]

Mr. Dacre appealed the decision to the Privy Council in London, the highest court of appeal. The Privy Council upheld the ruling of the three judges. According to the ruling, Pitcairn has been and remains a British possession. Chief Judge Lord Hoffman concluded: "Seldom has there been a more unrealistic argument."[9]

All in the Family

Ian Ball wrote following his visit in 1971, "In a conventional family, it would be a perverted member who prattled willingly to a stranger about the secret vices and nastiness of his kin. The tendency is to hush up the wrongdoing of a family member that society at large has not detected. This, too, I believe happens on this island. Squabbles and human imperfections are resolved quietly within the family."[10] Ball's observation is one explanation for the attempt by the editor of *The Pitcairn Miscellany* to bury in the March 2003 edition the most important island news story of the last two hundred years. The other reason for sublimating the announcement of the charges to be made is that the education officer was appointed by the governor and served at the governor's pleasure; he may have been directed to downplay this piece of shattering news. The paragraph is well worth quoting as an example of how to deemphasize an unwelcome fact: "March has been a busy month on Pitcairn. There were public meetings, fishing, parties and public works. Painting of the Co-op store by the girls was particularly impressive. There was a visit by a cruise ship, a freighter and several yachts. We had at various times many visitors on the island." The days, he stated, were hot, hot, HOT with high humidity. And then, buried discreetly within this pile of mundane trivia: "In addition Pitcairners learned that some of the men here were to be charged with sexual offences."[11]

The Great Fear

In more than a few Adamstown homes lived a man accused or a woman abused. Victims and their families would have to deal on a daily basis with the accused, and this in a community where secrets are virtually impossible to keep. It is phenomenal that wronged families did not lash out violently against neighbors.

The great fear of Pitcairners — beyond punishment, beyond being abused, beyond having their pious reputation ruined, beyond having keepers living among them — was the possibility of having to abandon their isolated rock. The great fear was of being forced to move elsewhere. In October 2002, Betty Christian, whose husband Tom had not been accused, stated with some alarm, "Our very existence is at stake. We are like one family, and whatever decision is made we are the ones who will suffer. Regardless of our differences and problems, none of our people wants to see Pitcairn closed down and abandoned."[12]

Because outsiders continued to land prior to the trial, Pitcairners began "feeling dismayed." The editor of *The Pitcairn Miscellany* lamented that the millions being spent on trials might have been more usefully spent on an airfield, sealing of the main road, a breakwater for the jetty, a new school house and a reconstructed public hall.[13]

On the eve of the trial, a correspondent commented: "The Pitcairn family is now bitterly divided. Most locals consider the defendants have been unfairly targeted and resent the imminent intrusion of prying eyes, including those of journalists, long banned from the island. A minority welcome the trial as an opportunity to cleanse Pitcairn's soul, but they are fearful of speaking out by name. The two camps are barely on speaking terms...."[14] Herbert Ford said that islanders resented particularly the governor's inviting six reporters to monitor the trials. The presence of the media was not a legal requirement. Rather than lashing out at the accused, many islanders seemed to become defensive of their tight community's autonomy and privacy. An undercurrent of public anger at outside intrusion prompted Governor Fell to ask that islanders turn in firearms for the duration of the trials; this was the first time all arms had been confiscated since Joshua Hill, the "Mussolini of Pitcairn," had done so for his own protection 170 years previously.

Six months before the trials began, the author lectured about the mutiny and Pitcairn history aboard MV *Discovery*, sailing from Valparaiso to Auckland. The chief complaint heard by *Discovery* passengers was that outsiders had "taken over" their island home and that they felt they were "living in a goldfish bowl." They missed their privacy, as individuals, and as a self-contained community. One lady disclosed that families have always dealt with private family problems and that they were perfectly capable of dealing with them without the interference of outside officials. They resented what one characterized as "airing linen in public."

Pitcairn Island longboat during visit of *Discovery World*, February 9, 2004. Note the mix of islanders, social workers, the governor's representative and others present for the sexual-abuse trials. Smiles mask tensions. Photograph courtesy of Robert Cook.

One woman said she would have preferred a process similar to the "truth and reconciliation" sessions that had proved useful in South Africa in the aftermath of apartheid. Rather than hold trials, several islanders asked the governor for a mediator to conduct restorative justice sessions which might satisfy accusers.

Passengers were told by at least two people that sex with young girls and sex outside of marriage has been going on for two centuries; Pitcairners were, as several reminded visitors, as much Polynesian as English. One island woman volunteered in casual conversation that she had first had sex at twelve and that it was part of their Polynesian heritage. Meralda Warren said she had never been raped and did not think any girls had been raped. She explained that sex among teens was normal in Polynesia and that Pitcairners should not be held accountable to British morals and law. One man explained that the population was so small that each man had few eligible female choices; he gave an example of a twenty-year-old male faced with the choice of waiting for a thirteen-year-old to come of age, or of taking a woman old enough to be his mother as a partner. All other women were already married. This lack of choice, he explained, was a reason for some men's moving to New Zealand.

A forty-six-year-old woman resident explained to a reporter that she had first had sex at twelve. "To us, it was everyday life on the island. I just feel that the boys are being punished for something that I don't consider to be a crime." She argued, "No one told us there was a certain age for it. It was just like — your body feels like it was just the thing to do."[15]

Pastor Neville Tosen, who had returned to Australia after two years on Pitcairn, told a reporter, "It took me three months to realize they were being abused. I tried to raise the subject at a meeting of the island council and one gentleman replied: 'Look, the age of consent has always been 12 and it doesn't hurt them.'" Tosen continued, "I think the young girls were conditioned to accept that it was a man's world and once they turned 12, they were eligible." Tosen related that when he had asked mothers and grandmothers about the issue, "their reply was that nothing had changed. We went through it too; it's all part of life on Pitcairn."[16]

Commissioner Salt Sacked

On September 12, 2003, immediately before the trials, Governor Fell fired Leon Salt, former education officer, and island commissioner since 1995. Salt was replaced by businessman Leslie Jaques. Fell stated that Salt's actions "amounted to either disobedience, neglect of duty and/or willful misconduct in the terms of his employment arrangement." Salt, a descendant of three *Bounty* mutineers, wrote for *The Pitcairn Miscellany*, "I have been devastated by my unjustified dismissal from the post of Commissioner to Pitcairn. To date, I have been given no reason for the dismissal apart from an alleged break down of trust and confidence."[17] A New Zealand Employment Relations adjudicator refused to reinstate Salt because, according to TVNZ, "Salt was secretly trying to undermine British attempts to prosecute Pitcairn Islanders wanted for rape and underage sex offences." Salt was awarded NZ$432,700 in compensation for his dismissal.[18]

A Time of Trial

In September 2004, the Pitcairn Supreme Court, as constituted by the governor, put seven Pitcairn men on trial at the courthouse in Adamstown. They were charged with fourteen counts of rape, two of gross indecency, and thirty-seven of indecent assault. The offenses were said to have dated over a period of three decades, from 1969 to 1999. The judges ruled that they would try the cases without a jury and stated: "All parties will be aware of the practical difficulties around constituting a jury of 12 people independent of the accused on Pitcairn, even if the law so provided."[19] Other than the accused, islanders stayed away from the trials; only four were reported having attended as spectators.

Six women testified by video-link from New Zealand, while two accusers who still lived on Pitcairn testified in person. A fifty-one-year-old woman on video-link said she had not told anyone of being raped at age eleven or twelve "out of guilt, out of shame, out of nobody would believe me." She said, "It was just the normal way of life back on Pitcairn, how the girls are treated as though they are a sex thing."[20] One woman testified that she was raped every time she went to get firewood.[21]

The judges were said to be convinced by the six women who testified by video-link, some of whom spoke of psychological and emotional damage resulting from their experiences at the hands of the accused. The judges sentenced six men and exonerated one.

• Island police officer Brenda Christian sat beside a defendant as he was being sentenced. It was her brother Steve Christian, age fifty-three. Although he served as the island's engineer, dentist, longboat coxswain, and radiographer, and had been mayor, Steve was sentenced to three years in prison.

- Randy Christian, Steve's twenty-eight-year-old son, was sent to prison for six years.
- Len Brown, at seventy-eight the oldest of the defendants, was sentenced to two years in prison, but subsequently was allowed to serve his time in home detention.
- Dave Brown, Len's son, was sentenced to community service for indecent assault.
- Terry Young, age forty-two, was sentenced to five years.
- Dennis Christian, age forty-nine, was the island postmaster. His sentence was community service.
- Jay Warren was not convicted of any crime, and to the delight of his wife Carol, walked out a free man.

When the trials were over, officials were sent to implement the sentences and to help Pitcairners rebuild their society. In addition to the pastor and education officer, to whose presence they had long been accustomed, and a doctor whose presence was most welcome, they were asked to accept the presence of a police officer, the governor's representative, two social workers, and seven correctional officers.

The Women's Appeal

Attorneys for the convicted men filed motion for review by an *ad hoc* Pitcairn Court of Appeal sitting in Auckland. The appeal to review the cases was denied. The convicted men then appealed to the highest court in the Commonwealth, the Privy Council in London. In an undated internet message after the appeal hearing in Auckland, twenty-one women, most of whom lived on Pitcairn and Norfolk, asked for funds to defray attorneys' fees for the appeal to the Privy Council, scheduled for July 2006. The women estimated they would need NZ$100,000. The women complained that the trial had been unfair for the following reasons:

1. No jury trial, the defendants were not judged by their own peers, but by judges.
2. The defendants were accused and convicted according to a British law that had never been promulgated on the island....
3. The allegations from several Pitcairn women about police promising compensation during interviews were not investigated by the courts.
4. There was no legal counsel available to Pitcairners until ... two years after the investigations started ... thus giving lots of time for media speculation and bias to grow.
5. The Pitcairn justice and court system was created after allegations were made and some were made even after the decision to prosecute and lay charges."[22]

On October 30, 2006, the Privy Council ruled against the plaintiffs. All appeals had been exhausted.

Two More

On January 8, 2007, former Pitcairn resident Shawn Christian, living in New Zealand, married his sweetheart Michelle Purvis. The following day, the Pitcairn Island Supreme Court, meeting at Papakura District Court in South Auckland, convicted Shawn of raping a ten-year-old girl on Pitcairn Island in the 1990s. The same court convicted former Pitcairner Bryan Young of raping two girls on Pitcairn, the youngest when she was seven. Five days later the two boarded a ship for Pitcairn Island, where a jail cell had been reserved for them. TVNZ commented, "The verdicts bring to an end an ugly chapter in the island's history."[23]

Rebuilding a Viable Community

Convicted Mayor Steve Christian gave up his office. In November 2004, the seven-member governing council chose the island's first female chief executive — ex-mayor Steve's sister, Brenda. Brenda had grown up on Pitcairn before living in Britain for several years. At eighteen, Brenda had captivated visiting journalist Ian Ball: "If ever the island enters the Miss Universe contest, she is the logical choice for 'Miss Pitcairn,'" he wrote.[24] In annual elections a little more than a month later, Jay Warren defeated acting mayor Brenda. With most of the men convicted, women were elected to the council; they were Meralda Warren, Olive Christian, Carol Warren, and Lea Brown.

By early 2006, Commissioner Leslie Jacques, whose background was banking and finance, was busily putting together a package of projects to make Pitcairn and its people increasingly self-supporting. Island income in fiscal 2004-05 was NZ$746,000, whereas public expenditures were a little over a million dollars. Economic aid from Britain and the EU in fiscal 2004 was NZ$3,465,000 (US$2,310,000). This money went largely to trial costs and improved infrastructure.

Commissioner Jacques stated that his goal was to create a sustainable economy, to provide full employment, improve the standard of living, and improve communications and regular scheduled transportation abroad. Moreover, he hoped to see a gain in population through immigration so that the island would have 120 to 150 people. The British government promised a further NZ$9 million to improve Pitcairn's economy and infrastructure; that amounts to around US$200,000 per Pitcairner who had not been sentenced. Among income sources, Jacques pinpointed:

- Increased philatelic income. Sales of stamps had fallen eighty-five percent in five years. The new commissioner outsourced stamp issues to "experts" in Wellington, obviously hoping for more income from philatelists.
- Leased use of the island-owned *.pn* website domain would earn an estimated hundred thousand dollars a year.
- Leased fishing rights in the thousand-square-mile Pitcairn Islands Economic Zone would bring in more dollars.
- A larger honey output from six thousand to a projected twenty-four thousand 250-gram units per annum would make money for members of the bee keepers' cooperative.
- An extended breakwater at a cost of NZ$13.5 million would help cruise ship captains feel comfortable sending their ships' tenders ashore; currently, Jaques said only about ten captains sent passengers ashore.
- The slipway on which boats are launched — paved with tons of concrete poured over reinforcing steel bars.
- Improved websites by which internet users could buy island-made artifacts on a "shopping trolly."
- Development of tourism and promotion of eco-tourism. A proposed freighter service from Auckland to Pitcairn once every three months would enable ex-Pitcairners living in New Zealand to spend four or five days on the island, or a full three months on vacation. Leslie Jaques projected 200 to 250 tourists a year.
- A new museum of *Bounty* and island artifacts. Erecting this building came only after the frustration of seeing the building materials by-pass Bounty Bay when weather conditions prevented unloading from a freighter. The materials sailed on to Antwerp, Belgium. On the second attempt, rough seas once again prevented unloading, and the cargo continued on to

Auckland. Only on the third approach, in December 2004, were materials landed. Officials hoped that the NZ$80,000 museum would induce passengers to leave their cruise ships and pay an admission fee to have a look at Pitcairn history.

- Completion of a cement-paved road up the Hill of Difficulty. This was essentially done by early 2006 to a width of three meters. A galvanized iron railing was installed to prevent vehicles from going over the side.
- Videoconferencing facilities to assist in medical consultations with New Zealand physicians. They would also facilitate learning at the school.
- Private phones linked to the New Zealand system.
- Increased internet bandwith.
- Television broadcasts via satellite.
- Wind generators to supplement the diesel generators which provide power only ten hours a day.
- The creation of more government jobs on the island.
- Fourteen percent increases of pensions for seniors.
- A scheme by which islanders could upgrade their homes to accommodate tourists.
- A new schoolhouse, and provisions for adult instruction. The school built in 1948 was pulled down in June 2006 and a modern school erected on the same site at Pulau.
- Assisting Pitcairners with particular skills to return.

Mr. Jacques named his scheme "Partnership to Peace and Prosperity."[25] By September 2006, residents could enjoy private phones, fast internet, live television, and videoconferencing. The supply ship *Taporo VIII* had begun making the 1,367-mile voyage (2,200 km) from Tahiti five times a year on what was projected to be a regular schedule. In addition to these ambitious projects, Pitcairn at last had a series of resident physicians on three-month assignments. In fact, on March 3, 2007, resident Nadine Christian delivered a daughter, Adrianna Tracey Christian, with the help of Dr. Alistair McDonald of New Zealand and a nursing assistant. Adrianna was the second baby to be born on Pitcairn Island in twenty-one years.[26]

By early 2008, it was obvious to Pitcairn islanders that their economy was being transformed as rapidly as their traditional culture. Businesses opened in Adamstown for the first time ever. On Wednesdays only, Olive Christian operated a beauty salon cleverly named Hair Today, Gone Tomorrow. Fridays found the entrepreneurial Olive running Christian's Cafe, the community's first restaurant. On opening night, August 24, 2007, Olive served thirty-six diners. Carol Warren opened a take-away food service for those who wanted to avoid cooking other nights of the week; its name is Delectable Bounty. Impressively large new houses were replacing older dwellings. Wooden steps leading to Christian's Cave, St. Paul's Pool and Gannet's Ridge invited tourists to roam about with less danger of slipping. Five wind turbines were being erected by Australian firms to supply electricity twenty-four hours a day. Coffee was being grown for export. The ship *Braveheart* brought and took away islanders, officials, and visitors twice a month.

Future of an Icon

In 2001, British Overseas Development Minister Clare Short was quoted as saying that Britain should help to resettle the entire population "alongside psychological help and counseling for those who need it."[27] Short is only one of a long line of observers in the last half century who have predicted that the island is on its last legs and will soon be abandoned. It

View of Pitcairn Island from aboard ship. So long as the descendants of mutineers remain on "the rock" the world's greatest sea tale will remain alive. Photograph by Robert Kirk.

is tempting to make such a dire prediction, particularly after the loss of manpower due to the outcome of the trials.

In reply to the author's emailed query, "In your opinion, does Pitcairn have a future?," Carol Warren, the mayor's wife, replied, "I'm positive we have a future here on Pitcairn and it will be a much better place when we finally see the last of the outsiders and then we might be able to move forward and rebuild Pitcairn's good name again."[28] Carol Warren's goal and that of Governor Fell were the same — the survival of the community — but their methods of achieving survival appeared in early 2007 to be as far apart as Pitcairn is from the nearest continent.

It is impossible to make a prediction about Pitcairn's destiny because it is impossible to see into the future. While nobody denies the problems of inadequate population and internal dissention, the island's well-wishers around the globe — and they are many — do hope the descendants of the mutineers continue living on their lush rock, certainly through the twenty-first century and at least well into the next. These descendants are the living embodiment of the world's most cherished sea-foam saga. They are the heirs of odyssean voyages, surging passions, of steamy romance. They are the guardians of what was once an earthly uptopia — and may well be again.

Chapter Notes

Introduction

1. "We Like our Privacy Too," *Pitcairn Miscellany,* September 1986, p. 1.
2. Among the most useful websites are: Pitcairn Island Website, maintained by Paul Laureau of Minnesota, <http://lareau.org.pitcairn.html>. The Pitcairn Study Center at Pacific Union College site, maintained by Herbert Ford, <http://library.puc.edu/pitcairn/pitcairn/index.stml>. The government of Pitcairn website, <http://www.government.pn>. The Yahoo Pitcairn Island discussion group, <http://groups.yahoo.com/group/FRIENDSofPITCAIRN/>. The Pitcairn Island Study Group, largely focused on philately, <http://www.pisg.org>.
3. Greg Dening. *Mr. Bligh's Bad Language* (Cambridge: Cambridge University Press, 1992), p. 347.
4. The making of the 1935 mutiny film was marred by tragedy. San Miguel Island off the coast of Santa Barbara in California was used for shooting scenes of events taking place on Pitcairn Island. The *Bounty* was a barge with props necessary for on-board scenes. In late July, as *Time* reported, "a heavy squall struck the *Bounty,* swept away a water tank support, swamped the barge, spilled 25 technicians into the water." All were saved except cameraman Glenn Strong, who drowned. "Death on the *Bounty,*" *Time,* 5 August 1935.
5. "Bligh Relics Yield *Bounty* at Auction," *Chicago Sun-Times,* 22 September 2002.
6. "The Challenge of Pitcairn," *St. Petersburg Times,* 26 June 2005, p. 5.

Chapter 1

1. John Hawkesworth, *An Account of the Voyages Undertaken by Order of His Majesty for Making Discoveries in the Southern Hemisphere,* vol. 1 (Dublin: James Potts, 1775), p. 278.
2. Hawkesworth, pp. 277–78.
3. Dea Birkett, *Serpent in Paradise* (New York: Doubleday, 1997), p. 87. Among the best descriptions of the three island dependencies are those in Stephen Pendle-

ton, *Atlas of the Pitcairn Islands* (Visalia: Stephen Pendleton, 2006).
4. "Pig Study Helps Trace Pacific Islanders' Origin," *Santa Rosa Press Democrat,* 17 March 2007, p. A10.
5. Marshall Weisler, "Archaeology of Water Valley, Pitcairn Island," *Pitcairn Miscellany,* July 1991, pp. 2–3.
6. Jared Diamond, "Paradise Lost — Lost Civilization on Pitcairn," <http://www.looksmart.com/Discover/html>.
7. Jared Diamond, *Collapse* (New York: Viking, 2005), p. 123.
8. Diamond, *Collapse,* p.132.
9. Diamond, *Collapse,* p. 134.

Chapter 2

1. Eric Williams, *From Columbus to Castro* (New York: Random House/Vintage Books, 1984), p. 129.
2. Williams, p. 226.
3. William Bligh, *The Mutiny on Board* H.M.S. *Bounty* (New York: New American Library, 1961), p. 19.
4. Bligh, p. 21.
5. Bligh, p. 24.
6. Patrick O'Brian, *Joseph Banks: A Life* (Boston: D. R. Godine, 1993), p. 62.
7. O'Brian, p. 64.
8. O'Brian, p. 89.
9. O'Brian, p. 91.
10. George Mackaness, *The Life of Vice-Admiral William Bligh* (New York: Farrar & Rhinehart, Inc., 1931), pp. 48–49.
11. O'Brian, p. 233.

Chapter 3

1. William Bligh, *The Mutiny on Board* H.M.S. *Bounty* (New York: New American Library, 1961), p. 13.
2. Richard Hough, *The Bounty* (New York: Penguin Books, 1984), p. 50.
3. Richard Hough, *Captain Bligh and Mr. Christian* (New York: E. P. Dutton & Co., 1973), p. 302.

4. Patrick O'Brian, *Joseph Banks: A Life* (Boston: D. R. Godine, 1993), p. 234.

5. Hough, *Captain Bligh and Mr. Christian*, p. 303.

6. George Mackaness, *The Life of Vice-Admiral William Bligh* (New York: Farrar & Rhinehart, Inc, 1931), pp. 64–65.

7. Sven Wahlroos, *Mutiny and Romance in the South Seas* (Topsfield: Salem House, 1989), p. 245.

8. Hough, *Captain Bligh and Mr. Christian*, p. 277.

9. Bligh, p. 25.

10. James Morrison, Journal, <http://image.sl.nsw.gov.au/Eboind/oy515a1221000.html>; Sir John Barrow, *The Mutiny of the Bounty* (Boston: D. R. Godine, 1980), p. 63.

11. Bligh, p. 39.

12. Morrison.

13. Bligh, p. 40

14. Bligh, pp. 53–54.

15. Morrison.

Chapter 4

1. William Bligh, *The Mutiny on Board* H.M.S. *Bounty* (New York: New American Library, 1961), p. 60.

2. Bligh, p. 71.

3. James Morrison, Journal, <http://image.sl.nsw.au/Ebind/oy515/a1221000.html>.

4. Glynn Christian, *Fragile Paradise* (Boston: Little Brown, 1982), p. 95.

5. Bligh, p. 111.

6. Bligh, p. 132.

7. Morrison.

8. Morrison.

9. Morrison.

10. Bligh, p. 134

11. Morrison.

12. John Fryer, Testimony, <http://www.law.umke.edu/faculty/projects/trials./*Bounty*/fryertranscript.html>.

13. Morrison

14. Bligh, p. 139.

15. Bligh, p. 140.

16. Morrison; Wahlroos, p. 59.

17. Morrison.

18. Wahlroos, p. 61.

19. Robert B. Nicolson, *The Pitcairners* (Sydney: Argus and Robertson: 1965), p.14.

20. N. A. M. Rodger, *The Wooden World* (New York: W. W. Norton, 1996), p. 113.

21. Gavin Kennedy, *Captain Bligh: The Man and His Mutinies* (London: Gerald Ducksworth, 1989), p. 10.

22. Rodger, p. 227.

23. Morrison.

24. Wahlroos, p. 54.

Chapter 5

1. John Fryer, Testimony, <http://www.law.umke.edu/faculty/projects/trials/*Bounty*/fryertranscript.html>.

2. William Bligh, *The Mutiny on Board* H.M.S. *Bounty* (New York: New American Library, 1961), p. 137.

3. Bligh, pp. 139–141.

4. Bengt and Marie-Therese Danielsson, "Bligh's Cave," *Pacific Islands* Monthly, June 1985, p. 25.

5. Bligh, p. 162.

6. Bligh, p. 160.

7. Bligh, p. 154.

8. Bligh, p. 186.

9. Bligh, p. 190.

10. Sir John Barrow, *The Mutiny of the Bounty* (Boston: D. R. Godine, 1980), p. 91.

11. Barrow, pp. 94–95.

12. Greg Dening, *Mr. Bligh's Bad Language* (Cambridge: Cambridge University Press, 1992), p. 288; Sven Wahlroos, *Mutiny and Romance in the South Seas* (Topsfield: Salem House, 1989), pp. 101–02.

13. Barrow, p. 13; Glynn Christian, *Fragile Paradise* (Boston: Little Brown, 1982), pp. 186–87.

Chapter 6

1. H. E. Maude, *Islands and Men* (Melbourne: Oxford University Press, 1968), p. 6.

2. Sir John Barrow, *The Mutiny of the Bounty* (Boston: D. R. Godine, 1980), p. 14.

3. Maude, pp. 5–6.

4. Few details are known of the ordinary seamen's backgrounds, but we may surmise that Isaac Martin, the only American aboard, was born in Philadelphia and that he was the same Isaac Martin who had served aboard the privateer *Jason* during the American Revolution. When a British man-of-war captured the *Jason* four days before General Cornwallis's surrender at Yorktown, Martin probably opted to enter British naval service to obtain a pardon for participating in the rebellion. If that is the case, he probably served aboard Royal Navy and/or merchant vessels during the years 1782–89, when he signed aboard the *Bounty*.

5. *Times*, 16 December 1815, quoted in *Pitcairn News*, 19 January 2005, <http://www.pitcairnnews.co.nz/050119.html#times18151216>

6. Sven Wahlroos, *Mutiny and Romance in the South Seas* (Topsfield: Salem House Publishers, 1989), p. 291.

7. David Howarth, *Tahiti: A Paradise Lost* (New York: Penguin Books, 1985), p. 156.

8. Barrow, pp. 114–18.

9. Wahlroos, p. 172.

10. Barrow, p. 117.

11. When Edwards was there, Palmerston was uninhabited, but today Palmerston Islanders are — like Pitcairn Islanders — a hybrid English-Polynesian people. The village at Palmerston reminded one of Adamstown. Some seventy years after *Pandora's* visit, Palmerston was settled by one William Marsters (originally Masters), a seaman from Gloucestershire, England. Marsters is noted for having married three sisters from Penrhyn Island. Today Marsters families live on Home Island, one of thirty-five drops of land that compose Palmerston. They represent descendants of the twenty-one children sired by William with his three wives before he died in 1899 at age seventy-eight. When the author visited Palmerston in 1987, he found that they all spoke English with a nineteenth-century Gloucestershire accent. Like Pitcairners', their houses were made from ships' planking, in this case from ships that wrecked on their reef. The Palmerston Island church is filled with pews taken from a wrecked ship. The island's young

ladies sang "There is No Girl Like a Marster Girl for Me," following by selections from the *Hit Parade of 1946.* Pitcairners and Palmerston Islanders are the only English-speaking, Protestant, Anglo-Polynesian communities in the South Pacific. Palmerston Island is under the jurisdiction of the Cook Islands.

12. Barrow, p. 110.

13. Wahlroos, p. 156.

14. *Royal Navy Articles of War—1757,* <http://www.hmsrichmond.org/rarticles.htm>

15. Glynn Christian, *Fragile Paradise* (Boston: Little Brown, 1982), p. 184.

16. Wahlroos, p. 100.

17. Wahlroos, p. 225.

18. Barrow, p. 61.

Chapter 7

1. H. E. Maude, "History of Pitcairn Island," in A. S. C. Ross and A. W. Moverley, *The Pitcairnese Language* (New York: Oxford University Press, 1964), p. 48.

2. John Buffett, "A Narrative of Twenty Years Residence," *The Friend* 4 (1846), p. 2.

3. Trevor Lummis, *Pitcairn Island: Life and Death in Eden* (Brookfield, Vermont: Ashgate, 1997), p. 48.

4. Robert B. Nicolson, *The Pitcairners* (Sydney: Angus and Robertson, 1965), p. 4.

5. Rosalind Amelia Young, *Mutiny on the Bounty* (Honolulu: University Press of the Pacific, 2003), p. 39; Walter Hayes, *Captain from Nantucket* (Ann Arbor: William L. Clements Library, 1996), p. 41.

6. Sven Wahlroos, *Mutiny and Romance in the South Seas* (Topsfield: Salem House Publishers, 1989), p. 275.

7. Nicolson, p. 54.

8. Young, p. 40; Nicolson, p. 54.

9. Hayes, pp. 95–98.

10. Mas a Tierra's first long-term inhabitant was Alexander Selkirk, seventh son of a Fifeshire, Scotland, shoemaker. Having become a crew member whose presence aboard can be characterized as insufferable, Selkirk was put ashore in 1704 by Captain Stradling of the ship *Cinque Ports.* He remained on Mas a Tierra alone, with goats and cats his only companions, for four years and nine months until he was rescued by pirate-explorers Woodes Rogers and William Dampier. Selkirk's story was told in 1712 by Rogers in *A Cruising Voyage around the World.* Inspired by reading Selkirk's experience, Daniel Defoe produced *The Life and Strange Surprizing Adventures of Robinson Crusoe of York, Mariner,* his 412th — and most memorable — publication. Mas a Tierra is known today as Robinson Crusoe Island.

11. Hayes, p. 45.

12. Caroline Alexander, *The Bounty* (New York: Viking, 2003), p. 351).

13. Lummis, p. 109.

14. Hayes, p. 85.

Chapter 8

1. Rosalind Amelia Young, *Mutiny on the Bounty* (Honolulu: University Press of the Pacific, 2003), p. 41.

2. Arrel Morgan Gibson, *Yankees in Paradise* (Albu-querque: University of New Mexico Press, 1993), p. 315.

3. Walter Hayes, *The Captain from Nantucket* (Ann Arbor: William L. Clements Library, 1996), p. 64. Porter established a post at Nuku Hiva in the Marquesas, Fort Madison; and a village, Madisonville, both named in honor of America's fourth chief executive. When the Taipi tribe on Nuku Hiva killed one of Porter's marines, he and his men marched up the valley, burning houses and murdering numbers of Polynesians. Porter forced chiefs to write their marks on a treaty that would have made Nuku Hiva the first United States colony in the Pacific, and he forwarded the document to Washington, D.C. Congress failed to annex the archipelago.

4. George Mackaness, *The Life of Vice-Admiral William Bligh* (New York: Farrar & Rhinehart, Inc., 1931), p. 289.

5. *Pitcairn Island Register Book* (London: Society for the Promotion of Christian Knowledge, 1929), p. 32.

6. Mackaness, p. 289; Sir John Barrow, *The Mutiny of the Bounty* (Boston: D. R. Godine, 1980), p. 170.

7. Mackaness, p. 289; Walter Brodie, *Pitcairn Island and the Islanders in 1850* (London: Whitaker & Co., 1851), p. 154.

8. Harry L. Shapiro, *The Heritage of the Bounty* (Garden City: Doubleday Anchor, 1962), p. 68.

9. Robert B. Nicolson, *The Pitcairners* (Sydney: Angus and Robertson, 1965), p. 58.

10. Brodie, p. 154.

11. H. M. S. Richards, Jr., *Mutineers on Pitcairn Island* (Nashville: Southern Publishing Association, 1980), p. 37.

12. The *Times,* 16 December 1815, quoted in *Pitcairn News,* 19 January 2005, <http:www.pitcairnnews.co.nz/050119.html#times18151216>

13. The *Times,* 16 December 1815.

14. Barrow, p. 178.

15. Greg Dening, *Mr. Bligh's Bad Language* (Cambridge: Cambridge University Press), p. 299.

16. Dening, p. 301.

17. Herbert Ford, *Pitcairn: Port of Call* (Angwin: Hawser Titles, 1996), pp. 4–5.

18. Jenny, "Pitcairn's Island," *United Services Journal,* November 1829, pp. 589–93.

19. Nicolson, p. 60.

20. Nicolson, pp. 62–63.

21. Peter Clarke, *Hell and Paradise* (Ringwood: Penguin Books Australia), p. 92.

22. Frederick Debell Bennett, *Narrative of a Whaling Voyage* (New York: Da Capo Press, 1970), p. 35.

23. Nicolson, p. 69; Ford, p. 7.

24. Nicolson, pp. 71–72.

25. Ford, pp. 10–11; Nicolson, pp. 73–74.

Chapter 9

1. Arthur Herman, *To Rule the Waves* (New York: Harper Perennial, 2005), p. 424.

2. Frederick William Beechey, *Narrative of a Voyage to the Pacific* (London: Colburn & Bentley, 1831), p. 66.

3. William Goldhurst, "Martinet or Martyr," *Horizon,* September 1963, p. 48.

4. Beechey, pp. 96–97.

5. George Peard, *To the Pacific and Arctic with Beechey* (Cambridge: Cambridge University Press, 1973), p. 77.

6. Beechey, pp. 96–97.

7. Beechey, p. 67.

8. Peard, p. 80.

9. Peard, p. 72.

10. Beechey, p. 80.

11. Beechey, p. 99.

12. Peard, p. 84.

13. Beechey, p. 84.

14. Peard, p. 87.

15. Beechey, p. 85.

16. Sir John Barrow, *The Mutiny of the Bounty* (Boston: D. R. Godine, 1980), p. 184.

17. H. E. Maude, "History of Pitcairn Island," in A. S. C. Ross and A. W. Moverley, *The Pitcairnese Language* (New York: Oxford University Press, 1964), p. 55.

18. Beechey, p. 87.

19. Peard, p. 90–91.

20. Beechey, p. 89.

21. *Pitcairn Island Register Book* (London: Society for the Promotion of Christian Knowledge, 1929), p. 31.

22. Beechey, pp. 89–90.

23. Beechey, pp. 91–92.

24. Peard p. 92.

25. Beechey, pp. 93–94.

26. Beechey, p. 120.

27. Peard, p. 79.

28. Beechey, p. 107.

29. Peard, p. 93.

30. Rosalind Amelia Young, *Mutiny on the Bounty* (Honolulu: University Press of the Pacific, 2003), p. 149.

31. Herbert Ford, ed., *The Miscellany of Pitcairn's Island* (Mountain View: Pacific Press Publishing Association, 1980), p. 139.

32. John Buffett, "A Narrative of Twenty Years Residence," *The Friend* 4 (1846), pp. 27–28; Robert B. Nicolson, *The Pitcairners* (Sydney: Angus and Robertson., 1965), p. 79.

33. Harry L. Shapiro, *The Heritage of the Bounty* (Garden City: Doubleday Anchor, 1962), p. 75.

34. Frederick Debell Bennett, *Narrative of a Whaling Voyage* (New York: Da Capo Press, 1970), p. 33.

35. Buffett, pp. 27–28.

Chapter 10

1. Herbert Ford, *Pitcairn: Port of Call* (Angwin: Hawser Titles, 1996), p. 14.

2. John Buffett," A Narrative of Twenty Years Residence," *The Friend* 4 (1846), p. 34.

3. David Silverman, *Pitcairn Island* (Cleveland: World Publishing Co., 1967), p. 148.

4. Lt. J. Orlebar, *Midshipman's Journal* (London: Whittaker, Treacer, and Co., 1833), p. 20.

5. Robert B. Nicolson, *The Pitcairners* (Sydney: Angus and Robertson, 1965), p. 93.

6. Orlebar, p. 20.

7. Buffett, p. 34; Frank Clune, *Journey to Pitcairn* (Melbourne: Angus and Robertson, 1967), p. 134.

8. Buffett, p. 34.

9. Sir John Barrow, *Recent Accounts of the Pitcairn Islanders* (London: Royal Geographic Society, 1833), p. 6.

10. Orlebar. p. 21

11. Walter Brodie, *Pitcairn Island and the Islanders in 1850* (London: Whitaker & Co., 1851), p. 158; Barrow, p. 3.

12. Barrow, p. 3.

13. Barrow, p 5.

14. Orlebar, p. 16.

15. Orlebar, p. 24.

16. Orlebar, p. 20.

17. Barrow, p. 5.

18. Frederick Debell Bennett, *Narrative of a Whaling Voyage* (New York: Da Capo Press, 1970), pp. 30–31.

Chapter 11

1. Frederick William Beechey, *Narrative of a Voyage to the Pacific* (London: Colburn and Bentley, 1831), pp. 81–82.

2. It was Barrow who had first suggested to the Admiralty lords that Napoleon spend the rest of his life on St. Helena following the emperor's defeat in 1815 at Waterloo.

3. H. E. Maude, "History of Pitcairn Island," in A. S. C. Ross and A. W. Moverley, *The Pitcairnese Language* (New York: Oxford University Press, 1964), p. 287.

4. Spencer Murray, "The Pitcairners' 1831 Move to Tahiti," Pitcairn Islands Study Group *Pitcairn Log* (April-June 1997), p.6; Robert B. Nicolson, *The Pitcairners* (Sydney: Angus and Robertson, 1965), p. 97.

5. Maude, p. 290.

6. Sir John Barrow, *Recent Accounts of the Pitcairn Islanders* (London: Royal Geographic Society, 1833), p. 6.

7. Sir John Barrow, *The Mutiny of the Bounty* (London: John Murray, 1831), p. 192.

8. Maude, p. 292.

9. Barrow, *Recent Accounts*, p. 7.

10. John Buffett, "A Narrative of Twenty Years Residence," *The Friend* 4 (1846), p. 21.

11. Barrow, *Recent Accounts*, p. 8.

12. Brodie, pp. 72–73; Maude, p. 296.

13. David Howarth, *Tahiti: A Paradise Lost* (New York: Penguin Books, 1985), p. 41.

14. Howarth, p. 172.

15. David Stanley, *South Pacific Handbook*, 7th ed. (Emeryville: Moon Travel Handbooks, 2000), p. 135.

16. Herman Melville, *Typee, Omoo, Mardi* (New York: The Library of Americana, 1982), p. 513.

17. Frank Clune, *Journey to Pitcairn* (Sydney: Angus and Robertson, 1966), p. 136.

18. Clune, p. 137.

19. Maude, p. 68.

20. Buffett, p. 35.

21. Maude, p. 302.

22. *Pitcairn Island Register Book* (London: Society for the Promotion of Christian Knowledge, 1929), p. 36.

23. Herbert Ford, *Pitcairn: Port of Call* (Angwin: Hawser Titles, 1996), p. 16. Driver is credited with labeling the American Stars and Stripes "Old Glory."

24. Frederick Debell Bennett, *Narrative of a Whaling Voyage* (New York: Da Capo Press, 1970), pp. 28–31.

25. Bennett, p. 37.

Chapter 12

1. Harry L. Shapiro, *Heritage of the Bounty* (New York: Doubleday Anchor, 1962), p. 81.

2. Robert B. Nicolson, *The Pitcairners* (Sydney: Angus and Robertson, 1965), p. 118.

3. John Buffett, "A Narrative of Twenty Years Residence," *The Friend* 4 (1846), p. 50.

4. Shapiro, p. 82.

5. Rosalind Amelia Young, *Mutiny on the Bounty* (Honolulu: University Press of the Pacific, 2003), p. 78.

6. James Norman Hall, *The Tale of a Shipwreck* (New York: Houghton Mifflin Company, 1934), p. 89.

7. Shapiro, pp. 91–92.

8. Walter Brodie, *Pitcairn Island and the Islanders* (London: Whitaker and Company, 1851), p. 160.

9. Frank Clune, *Journey to Pitcairn* (Melbourne: Angus and Robertson, 1966), p. 141.

10. Brodie, pp. 160–64.

11. Clune, p. 141; Brodie, p. 161. On May 2, 1829, Charles Howe Fremantle (1800–1869) took possession of all of Western Australia in the name of King George IV. A city in Western Australia bears his name. His rise in rank was continuous, and in 1864 he was created a full admiral of the Royal Navy.

12. Shapiro, p. 85.

13. Clune, p. 139.

14. Shapiro, p. 87.

15. Nicolson, pp. 114–15.

16. Shapiro, p. 83

17. Shapiro, p. 88.

18. Frederick Debell Bennett, *Narrative of a Whaling Voyage* (New York: Da Capo Press, 1970), pp. 54–57.

19. Rev. Thomas Boyles Murray, *Pitcairn Island* (London: Society for Promoting Christian Knowledge, 1860), p. 182.

20. Shapiro, p. 85.

21. Shapiro, p. 88.

22. Shapiro, p. 83.

23. Young, pp. 77–78.

24. Young, p. 82.

25. Nicolson, pp. 125–27. Samuel Clemens (Mark Twain) fictionalized Hill's rule in his story "The Great Revolution on Pitcairn," published in 1903. In this story, the lives of the people who "have lived in deep Sabbath tranquility" and were governed by laws that were "simple to puerility" were interrupted by the arrival of an American adventurer, Butterworth Stavely — Twain's version of Joshua Hill. Like Hill, Stavely became dictator; unlike Hill, Stavely had himself crowned — as Emperor Butterworth I. Twain knew there were no horses on Pitcairn, so instead of an imperial carriage, Butterworth I was trotted about in a "gilded imperial [Pitcairn] wheelbarrow." Like Hill, Stavely would be ignominiously deposed.

26. *Guide to Pitcairn*, 4th ed. (Auckland: British Consulate-General, 1982), p. 13.

27. Arthur Herman, *To Rule the Waves* (New York: Harper Perennial, 2005), p. 449.

28. Brodie, p. 82.

29. Arrel Morgan Gibson, *Yankees in Paradise* (Albuquerque: University of New Mexico Press, 1993), pp. 144–45.

30. Nicolson, p. 137.

31. Young, p. 91.

32. Shapiro, p. 177.

33. Sir John Barrow, *Recent Accounts of the Pitcairn Islanders* (London: Royal Geographic Society, 1833), p. 5.

34. Brodie, p. 81.

35. Nicolson, p. 137.

36. Brodie, pp. 89–91.

37. Nicolson, p. 139.

Chapter 13

1. Arrel Morgan Gibson, *Yankees in Paradise* (Albuquerque: University of New Mexico Press, 1993), p. 148. One scholar calculated the American whaling fleet's aggregate capacity as 233,189 tons with a value of $21,075,000. Non-American whalers in 1846 numbered 230. Alexander Starbuck, *History of the American Whale Fishery* (Secaucus: Castle Books, 1989), p. 98. In peak years such as 1846, American whalers are estimated to have killed 4,253 sperm whales per annum, yielding an average of 25 barrels of oil from each whale. Granville Allen Mawer, *Ahab's Trade* (New York: St. Martin's Press, 1999), p. 344.

2. Starbuck, p. 97.

3. J. C. Furnas, *Anatomy of Paradise* (New York: William Sloan Associates, 1948), p. 214.

4. Rosalind Amelia Young, *Mutiny on the Bounty* (Honolulu: University Press of the Pacific, 2003), p. 94.

5. Thomas Cochrane (1775–1860) was a major figure in movements for Latin American and Greek independence. He served as naval officer of Chile, Brazil and Greece. In 1844, Cochrane rejoined the Royal Navy and rose to the rank of admiral by 1854. A Latin American historian characterized Cochrane as "bad-tempered and grasping," but on occasion capable of "great bravery and occasional self-abnegation." Hubert Herring, *A History of Latin America* (New York: Alfred A. Knopf, 1961), p. 576.

6. Walter Brodie, *Pitcairn's Island and the Islanders* (London: Whitaker & Co., 1851), pp. 164–65.

7. Herbert Ford, *Pitcairn: Port of Call* (Angwin: Hawser Titles, 1996), p. 23.

8. Brodie, p. 167.

9. *Pitcairn Island Register Book* (London: Society for the Promotion of Christian Knowledge, 1929), p. 42.

10. *Pitcairn Island Register Book*, p. 52.

11. John Buffett, "A Narrative of Twenty Years Residence," *The Friend* 4 (1846), p. 27.

12. Buffett, p. 3.

13. Buffett, p. 28.

14. Buffett, pp. 55–57.

15. Rev. Thomas Boyles Murray, *Pitcairn: The Island, the People, and the Pastor* (London: Society for Promoting Christian Knowledge, 1860), p. 193.

16. Frank Clune, *Journey to Pitcairn* (Melbourne: Angus and Robertson, 1966), p. 152.

17. Lady Belcher, *The Mutineers of the Bounty* (New York: Harper & Brothers, 1871), p. 210.

18. Young, pp. 96–97.
19. Belcher, p. 205.
20. Murray, pp. 153–66.
21. Clune, p. 153.
22. Belcher, p. 204–08.
23. Murray, p. 200.
24. David Silverman, *Pitcairn Island* (Cleveland: World Publishing Co., 1967), p. 132.
25. Murray, p. 195.
26. Belcher, p. 213.
27. *Pitcairn Island Register Book*, p. 72.
28. Murray, p. 210.

Chapter 14

1. Granville Allen Mawrer, *Ahab's Trade* (New York: St. Martin's Press, 1999), p. 177.
2. *Pitcairn Island Register Book* (London: Society for the Promotion of Christian Knowledge, 1929), p. 45.
3. *Pitcairn Island Register Book*, pp. 47–48.
4. *Pitcairn Island Register Book*, p. 51.
5. *Pitcairn Island Register Book*, p. 54. The pre-literate islanders of Tikopia, a Polynesian "outlier" in the Solomon Islands, came closer than George Hunn Nobbs to identifying the cause when they convinced themselves that they contracted influenza from the shrill sound of the ship's whistle that signaled the arrival of the annual missionary contingent.
6. *Pitcairn Island Register Book*, pp. 69–71.
7. *Pitcairn Island Register Book*, p. 40.
8. See chapter 19 for an explanation of Pitcairn Island place names.
9. *Pitcairn Island Register Book*, p. 41.
10. *Pitcairn Island Register Book*, p. 47
11. *Pitcairn Island Register Book*, pp. 61–62.
12. *Pitcairn Island Register Book*, p. 65.
13. Rev. Thomas Boyles Murray, *Pitcairn: The Island, the People, and the Pastor* (London: Society for Promoting Christian Knowledge, 1860), p. 295.
14. Rosalind Amelia Young, *Mutiny on the Bounty* (Honolulu: University Press of the Pacific, 2003), p. 112.
15. *Pitcairn Island Register Book*, p. 85.
16. *Pitcairn Island Register Book*, p. 93.

Chapter 15

1. Walter Brodie, *Pitcairn's Island and the Islanders* (London: Whitaker & Co., 1851), p. 2.
2. Brodie, p. 13.
3. Brodie, p. 7.
4. Brodie, pp. 30–32.
5. Brodie, p. 101.
6. Brodie, p. 23.
7. Brodie, pp. 95–96.
8. Brodie, p. 100.
9. Brodie, p. 94.
10. Rosalind Amelia Young, *Mutiny on the Bounty* (Honolulu: University Press of the Pacific, 2003), p. 105.
11. Brodie, p. 21.
12. Brodie, p. 29.
13. Rev. Thomas Boyles Murray, *Pitcairn: The Island, the People, and the Pastor* (London: Society for Promoting Christian Knowledge, 1860), p. 213.
14. Murray, p. 217.
15. Murray, pp. 293–94.
16. "Pitcairn's Island," *Illustrated London News*, 6 November 1852, pp. 373–74.
17. Caroline Adams, Letter to William Dillon, 10 November 1851.
18. *Pitcairn Island Register Book* (London: Society for the Promotion of Christian Knowledge, 1929), p. 75.
19. Named for the admiral are Port Moresby and Fairfax Harbour in Papua New Guinea, and Moresby Island in British Columbia.
20. "Pitcairn's Island," pp. 373–374.
21. Lady Belcher, *The Mutineers of the Bounty* (New York: Harper & Brothers, 1871), pp. 220–23. M. Fortescue Moresby (1827–1919) later settled in Sydney and became a noted painter and photographer.
22. "Pitcairn's Island," pp. 373–74.
23. Murray, p. 209.
24. Belcher, pp. 222–23.
25. Murray, p. 243; Harry L. Shapiro, *The Heritage of the Bounty* (Garden City: Doubleday Anchor, 1962), p. 104.
26. James Morris, *Heaven's Command: An Imperial Progress* (New York and London: Harcourt Brace Jovanovich, 1973), p. 358.
27. Murray, p. 220.
28. Murray, p. 92.
29. Murray, p. 295.

Chapter 16

1. *Pitcairn Island Register Book* (London: Society for the Promotion of Christian Knowledge, 1929), p. 50.
2. Walter Brodie, *Pitcairn Island and the Islanders* (London: Whitaker & Co., 1851), p. 105.
3. Miller's earlier adventures rivaled those of Buffett, Nobbs and Baron de Thierry. Miller had fought with Wellington in the Peninsular War against Napoleon's forces, had been in the company that invaded Washington, D.C., in 1813 and burned the White House, fought against Andrew Jackson at New Orleans in 1815, and helped to liberate Chile and Peru from Spain.
4. A. Grove Day, *Hawaii and its People* (Honolulu: Mutual Publishing, 1993), pp. 60–61.
5. *Pitcairn Island Register Book*, p. 67.
6. Rev. Thomas Boyles Murray, *Pitcairn: The Island, the People, and the Pastor* (London: Society for Promoting Christian Knowledge, 1860), p. 146.
7. Brodie, p. 170.
8. Murray, p. 169.
9. Brodie, p. 105.
10. Brodie, p. 171.
11. Brodie, p. 173.
12. Murray, p. 228.
13. Murray, pp. 240–41.
14. Murray, p. 233.
15. Frank Clune, *Journey to Pitcairn* (Melbourne: Angus and Robertson, 1966), p. 165.
16. Norfolk Island, <http://www.pitcairners.org/bloodlessgenocide2html>.

17. Robert B. Nicolson, *The Pitcairners* (Sydney: Angus and Robertson, 1965), p. 159.

18. Peter Clarke, *Hell and Paradise* (Ringwood: Penguin Books Australia, 1986), p. 69.

19. Clarke, p. 105.

20. Robert Hughes, *The Fatal Shore* (New York: Alfred A. Knopf, 1987), p. 460.

21. Clarke, p. 107.

22. Stephen Fremantle (1810–60), son of Admiral Sir Thomas Fremantle, was the younger brother of Charles Fremantle (1800–69), who, it will be recalled, signified approval of Joshua Hill's rule two decades previously.

23. Murray, p. 319.

24. Murray, p. 321.

25. Clune, p. 167.

26. Norfolk Island.

27. Lady Belcher, *The Mutineers of the Bounty* (New York: Harper & Brothers, 1871), p. 257.

28. Belcher, p. 267.

29. Belcher, pp. 307–08.

30. Murray, p. 399.

31. Norfolk Island

32. Clune, p. 181.

33. In the early 1980s, Doris Buffett, sister of billionaire Warren Buffett, made contact with singer Jimmy Buffett ("Margaritaville") to ascertain if they were related. Unable to establish their relationship because, according to a genealogical researcher in England, the Buffett family was "very obscure," Doris and Jimmy nevertheless traveled to Norfolk Island in 1983. There Doris Buffett found "oodles of Buffets"—actually forty-six—and Jimmy performed a concert to benefit the island's Central School. They failed to establish beyond a reasonable doubt a family connection to the Buffetts living on Norfolk at that time. Ethan Smith, "'Uncle Warren' Buffett and 'Cousin Jimmy,'" *Wall Street Journal*, May 2, 2005, p. 1.

Chapter 17

1. Rosalind Amelia Young, *Mutiny on the Bounty* (Honolulu: University Press of the Pacific, 2003), p. 138.

2. Frank Clune, *Journey to Pitcairn* (Melbourne: Angus and Robertson. 1966), p. 182.

3. Mayhew Young was born in 1827 and named for captain of the *Topaz* Mayhew Folger, who was the first to find John Adams at Pitcairn.

4. Herbert Ford, *Pitcairn: Port of Call* (Angwin: Hawser Titles, 1996), pp. 56–57.

5. Capt. Josiah N. Knowles, *Wreck of the Wild Wave*, <http://www.nobbly.com/archive/stories/wild-wave.html>.

6. "Romance of a Shipwreck," *Harper's Weekly* ,27 November 1858, p. 764.

7. Knowles.

8. Lady Belcher, *The Mutineers of the Bounty* (New York: Harper & Brothers, 1871), pp. 355–58.

9. "News from Pitcairn Island," *New York Times*, 29 August 1863, p. 3

10. Knowles.

11. H. E. Maude, *Slavers in Paradise* (Canberra: Australian National University Press, 1981), pp. 116–19.

12. Maude, p. 182.

13. Young, p. 167.

14. Belcher, pp. 360–63. Charles Wentworth Dilke entered Parliament in 1868 as a Liberal. In 1879 Benjamin Disraeli predicted that Dilke would one day be prime minister. Before and after his first marriage, Dilke had been the lover of Ellen, Mrs. Thomas Eustace Smith. He was then accused in a divorce case of seducing the Smiths' daughter Virginia, wife of member of Parliament Donald Crawford. The highly publicized trial which followed ended Dilke's chance of living at Number 10 Downing Street.

15. Young, p. 159.

16. Young, p. 186.

17. Young, p. 215.

Chapter 18

1. Rosalind Amelia Young, *Mutiny on the Bounty* (Honolulu: University Press of the Pacific, 2003), p. 189.

2. Young, p. 196.

3. "A Pitcairn Island Romance," *New York Times*, 3 December 1872.

4. Young, p. 198.

5. H. E. Maude, "History of Pitcairn Island," in A. S. C. Ross and A. W. Moverley, *The Pitcairnese Language* (New York: Oxford University Press, 1964), p. 91. McCoy apparently stood out as first man in the community: On February 21, 1890, the wooden ship *A. G. Ropes* of New York called, and Captain Rivers recorded that "at 7 o'clock we greeted on board our ship Mr. McCoy, the king, and sixteen others, Adamses, Christians, Youngs, etc...." Herbert Ford, *Pitcairn: Port of Call* (Angwin: Hawser Titles, 1996), p. 104.

6. De Horsey, Rear Admiral, *Pitcairn Island: Report Received* (London: H.M. Stationery Office, 1878); Young, 203–211.

7. Young, pp. 216–18.

8. Timothy F. Jones, M.D., "Mass Psychogenic Illness," *American Family Physician* 62 (12): 2649 (15 December 2000).

9. Young, p. 222.

10. Ford. p. 84.

11. Young, p. 223.

12. Young, p. 219.

13. Condition of the Pitcairn Islanders, Enclosure 2 in No. 1 (London: H.M. Stationery Office, 1884). Such was the reputation of Chief Magistrate James Russell McCoy that Jack London made him the shining hero of his story "Seed of McCoy." In the story, the chief magistrate boards a burning vessel, the *Pyrenees*, just off Pitcairn, and after arranging for someone to govern in his place in the village in case he is away for as long as two years awaiting transportation home, McCoy pilots the ship with a fire in the hold to Fakarava in the Tuamotus. Tension mounts as the fire's intensity increases, while captain and crew become exceedingly—though appropriately—anxious. It is only the demeanor of McCoy—"a mysterious emanation of the spirit, seductive, sweetly humble, and terribly imperious" that saves the ship's company. Writer London contrasts McCoy's "ineffable serenity and peace" with the actions of his ancestor Will, who threw himself into the sea in an alcoholic fit. Jack London, "The Seed of McCoy," in A. Grove Day and Carl Stoven, eds., *Best South Sea Stories* (Honolulu: Mutual Publishing, 1964), 76–106.

14. Maurice Allward, *Pitcairn Island* (Stoud: Tempus Publishing Ltd., 2000), p. 68.

Chapter 19

1. See A. S. C. Ross and A. W. Moverley, *The Pitcairnese Language* (New York: Oxford University Press, 1964); Harry L. Shapiro, *The Heritage of the Bounty* (Garden City: Doubleday Anchor, 1962), pp. 184–90; *Pitkern Phrase Book*, <http://www.lareau.org/pitlang2.html>.

2. Luis Marden, "I Found the Bones of the *Bounty*," *National Geographic*, December 1957, pp. 62–66.

3. *Guide to Pitcairn*, 4th ed. (Auckland: British Consulate-General, 1982), pp. 61–63; Pitcairn Island Place Names, <http://www.lareau.org/pitplace.html>.

4. Rev. Thomas Boyles Murray, *Pitcairn: The Island, the People, and the Pastor* (London: Society for Promoting Christian Knowledge, 1860), p. 307.

5. Dr. Bob Kendrick, "By Yorley Gwen?" *Pitcairn Miscellany*, October 1985, p. 3.

Chapter 20

1. Rosalind Amelia Young, *Mutiny on the Bounty* (Honolulu: University Press of the Pacific, 2003), p. 235.

2. Herbert Ford, *Pitcairn: Port of Call* (Angwin: Hawser Titles, 1996), p. 115.

3. "The Pitcairn Islanders Now-A-Days," *New York Times*, 11 December 1895, p. 5.

4. Healdsburg College was the forerunner of Pacific Union College, a Seventh-day Adventist institution operating today in the hills above the Napa Valley in the town of Angwin, California. P.U.C. contains the Pitcairn Islands Study Center, a major repository of Pitcairn books, articles, pictures, movies, and documents.

5. Harry L. Shapiro, *The Heritage of the Bounty* (Garden City: Doubleday Anchor, 1962), p. 115.

6. Young, p. 253.

7. *Guide to Pitcairn*, 4th ed. (Auckland: British Consulate-General, 1982), p. 17.

8. Shapiro, p. 117.

9. Shapiro, pp. 264–70.

10. Correspondence (London: H.M. Stationery Office, 1884).

11. Ford, p. 137.

12. "Home of the Mutineers," *Brooklyn Daily Eagle*, 15 October 1899, p. 39.

13. Ron Edwards, "Murder Rarely Reported on Pitcairn," Pitcairn Islands Study Group Pitcairn Log (April-June 2001), pp. 5–7.

14. Young, pp. 260–61.

15. "News from Lonely Pitcairn Island," *New York Times*, 6 July 1902, p. 25.

16. Ford, p. 170.

17. Ford, p. 181.

18. Frank Clune, *Journey to Pitcairn* (Melbourne: Angus and Robertson, 1966), p. 210.

Chapter 21

1. Herbert Ford, *Pitcairn: Port of Call* (Angwin: Hawser Titles, 1996), p. 134.

2. "Dearth of Women's Apparel," *New York Times*, 11 July 1900, p. A1.

3. "Here's a Chance to Get Rich," *Brooklyn Daily Eagle*, 20 July 1900, p. 2.

4. Knowling, George F. S., Further Correspondence (London: H.M. Stationery Office, 1901).

5. Donald McLoughlin, Laws of Pitcairn, Part 8, <http://library.puc.edu/Pitcairn/pitcairn/govt-history 08.shtml>.

6. Harry L. Shapiro, *The Heritage of the Bounty* (Garden City: Doubleday Anchor, 1962), pp. 271–78.

7. David Silverman, *Pitcairn Island* (Cleveland: World Publishing Co., 1967), p. 164; H. E. Maude, "History of Pitcairn Island," in A. S. C. Ross and A. W. Moverley, *The Pitcairnese Language* (New York, Oxford University Press, 1964), p. 96.

8. McLoughlin, Part 8.

9. Shapiro, pp. 286–90.

10. McLoughlin, Part 10.

11. Katherine Routledge, *The Mystery of Easter Island* (New York: AMS Press, 1978), p. 309.

12. Routledge, p. 399.

13. Ford, p. 171.

14. Routledge, p. 313. After she returned to her London home, Katherine Routledge published *The Mystery of Easter Island* in 1919; it was sufficiently popular to warrant a second edition. By the late 1920s Katherine was reported to be seriously ill. Symptoms of her illness were manifested in 1928, when she ejected William from her home by the front door and his clothes into the street from an upper window. Soon after, William had her abducted and forced into an ambulance. William had his wife admitted to a mental asylum, where she died in 1935.

15. Ford, p. 172–74.

16. "Joy on Pitcairn Island," *New York Times*, 8 July 1917, p. 70.

17. Notable Figures of Pitcairn, <http://pitcairn.pn/NotableFigures.html>. Herbert Ford, director of the Pitcairn Study Center, nominated Gerald de Leo Bliss to be honored on a 2002 Pitcairn postal issue. It would be astonishing if Dr. Ford, Pitcairn's unofficial "ambassador-at-large," were not one day commemorated by a Pitcairn Islands stamp.

18. Routledge, p. 311.

19. *Pacific Islands Year Book, 1942* (Sydney: Sydney and Melbourne Publishing Co., 1942), p. 357.

20. Sir Cecil Rodwell, *Report on a Visit to Pitcairn Island* (London: H.M. Stationery Office, 1921).

21. H. G. Pilling, *Report on a Visit to Pitcairn Island* (London: H.M. Stationery Office, 1930).

Chapter 22

1. Irving and Electa Johnson, "Westward Bound in the *Yankee*," *National Geographic*, January 1942, p. 90.

2. Charles Chauvel, *In the Wake of the Bounty* (Sydney: The Endeavour Press, 1933), pp. 134–35.

3. Electa Johnson, "Foreword," in Dr. Rufus Southworth, *A Doctor's Letters from Pitcairn* (n.p., n.d.).

4. Southworth, pp. 27–28.

5. Southworth, p. 37.

6. Southworth, pp. 27–28.

7. Harry L. Shapiro, *Heritage of the Bounty* (New York: Doubleday Anchor, 1962), pp. 6–7.

8. Shapiro, p. 159.
9. Shapiro, p. 15.
10. Shapiro, p. 13.
11. Shapiro, p. 161.
12. James Norman Hall, *The Tale of a Shipwreck* (New York: Houghton Mifflin Company, 1934), p. 63.
13. Southworth, p. 115.
14. Shapiro, p. 169.
15. Southworth, p. 75.
16. Shapiro, pp. 169–70.
17. Shapiro, p. 163.
18. Claude Allen, "Pitcairn Island's Population of 200," *Daily Gazette*, 16 June 1937.
19. Southworth, p. 51.
20. Shapiro, p. 12–14.
21. Southworth, pp. 33–34.
22. Hall, pp. 65–66.
23. Southworth, p. 32.
24. Southworth, p. 44.
25. Shapiro, pp. 242–43.
26. Southworth, p. 49.
27. Chauvel, p. 130.
28. Shapiro, p. 176.
29. Shapiro, pp. 244–45.
30. Southworth, pp. 53–54.
31. Chauvel, pp. 130–31.
32. Irving and Electa Johnson, pp. 86–87.
33. Chauvel, pp. 129–30.
34. Maurice Allward, "Murder on Pitcairn?" The Pitcairn Islands Study Group *UK Log* (July 2004), p. 23.
35. Shapiro, p. 172–73.
36. Herbert Ford, *Pitcairn: Port of Call* (Angwin: Hawser Titles, 1996), p. 228.
37. Uninhabited Temoe Island is the easternmost island in French Polynesia, and is 290 miles west-north-west of Pitcairn. Timoe is the island closest to the Pitcairn Islands.
38. Hall, p. 56.
39. Julius Grigore, Jr., "Inside the Pitcairn Island Family" (Balboa, Panama: typescript, 2003), p. 11.
40. Southworth, p. 63.
41. Southworth, p. 39.
42. Southworth, p. 141.
43. Southworth, p. 102. Twenty-first-century islanders are uncertain if family outhouses, euphemistically called 'the duncan,' were named in honor of Dr. Cook's visit.
44. Duncan Cook, M.D., *Medical Report* (Suva: Office of the High Commissioner, 1937), p. 76.
45. Shapiro, p. 206.
46. Hall, p. 61.
47. Cook, p. 69.
48. The United Kingdom had three reigning monarchs in 1936. King George V (1910–36) died in January, to be succeeded by his son David, who styled himself Edward VIII. On December 11, Edward VIII abdicated for "the woman I love," Wallis Warfield Simpson, an American divorcee with two living former husbands. The throne devolved to the man biographer Sarah Bradford called "the reluctant king," Bertie, who became King George VI (1936–52). He was the father of Queen Elizabeth II.
49. Southworth, p. 84.
50. Islanders obviously enjoyed goat banquets. Charles Chauvel wrote, "If a Pitcairner wrongly or accidentally shoots another man's goat, the offended man is authorized to proceed immediately to the mountain crags to bag one of his offender's goats in return. Sometimes in his chase he shoots the goat of another family, and before long half the people of Pitcairn become entangled in a goat slaughter which characteristically terminates in a great feast in which many wronged goats are offered in a spirit of laughing sacrifice." Chauvel, pp. 128–29.
51. *Guide to Pitcairn*, 4th ed. (Auckland: British Consulate-General, 1982), p. 35.
52. Southworth, p. 121.
53. "Byrd Wires Story," *New York Times,* 20 December 1939, p. 15.

Chapter 23

1. Herbert Ford, *Pitcairn: Port of Call* (Angwin: Hawser Titles, 1996), p. 260.
2. "War Brings Increasing Privation," *Honolulu Advertiser*, 12 December 1940, p. 1.
3. Captain Irving and Mrs. Johnson, *Westward Bound in the Schooner Yankee* (New York: W. W. Norton & Company, 1936), pp. 41–44.
4. J. S. Niell, *Pitcairn Island General Administrative Report* (Suva: Office of the High Commissioner, 1937), p. 24.
5. David Silverman, *Pitcairn Island* (Cleveland: World Publishing Co., 1967), p. 106.
6. "Instructions for the Guidance of the Local Government," *Western Pacific High Commission Gazette*, 29 December 1941.
7. "Pitcairn Island: Won, a Constitution," *Time,* 17 August 1942, p. 32.
8. Herbert Ford, "World War II Came Early," Pitcairn Islands Study Group *Pitcairn Log* (September-November 1988), pp. 5–7. The *Hokoku Maru* was sunk in November 1942 by the Indian Navy in the Indian Ocean, and the *Aikoku Maru* was destroyed at anchor at Truk on February 17, 1944.
9. Robert B. Nicholson, *The Pitcairners* (Sydney: Angus and Robertson, 1965), p. 172; "Another Piece of History," *Pitcairn Miscellany*, November 2003, p. 4;
10. Herbert Ford, *The Miscellany of Pitcairn's Island* (Mountain View: Pacific Press Publishing Association, 1980), p. 67; *Guide to Pitcairn*, 7th ed. (Auckland: British Consulate-General, 1999), p. 16.
11. Ford, *Pitcairn: Port of Call*, pp. 259–60.
12. "Swiss Family Adds New Pages," *Honolulu Advertiser* (28 October 1944), p. 2.
13. *Guide to Pitcairn*, 4th ed. (Auckland: British Consulate-General, 1982), pp. 58–61.
14. Malcolm J. Bull, "Halfway to Heaven" (typescript, n.p., 1986), p. 123.
15. "Pitcairn's Progress," *Time*, 23 August 1948, <http://www.time.com/time/magazine/article/0,9171. 799046.00.html>.
16. Ford, pp. 281–82.
17. Bull, p. 126.
18. Norman Ferris, *The Story of Pitcairn Island* (Washington, D.C.: Review and Herald Publishing Association, 1958), p. 118.
19. Herbert Ford, *Pitcairn* (La Verne: El Camino Press, 1972), p. 88.
20. Silverman, p. 192.

21. Donald McLoughlin, "Laws of Pitcairn, Henderson, Ducie and Oeno," Part 8, <http://library/puc.edu/Pitcairn/pitcairn/govt-history08.shtml>.

22. Neville Tosen, "News and Views from our Local Padre," *Pitcairn Miscellany*, February 2000, p. 3.

23. Ford, *The Miscellany of Pitcairn's Island*, pp. 140–41.

24. *Guide to Pitcairn*, 4th ed., pp. 50–51.

25. Luis Marden, "I Found the Bones of the *Bounty*," *National Geographic*, December 1957, p. 730.

26. Irving & Electa Johnson, *Yankee's People and Places* (New York: W. W. Norton & Company, Inc., 1955), p. 88.

27. Thor Heyerdahl, *Aku Aku* (Chicago: Rand McNally, 1958), p. 333.

28. Ford, *Pitcairn: Port of Call*, p. 317.

29. Ford, *The Miscellany of Pitcairn's Island*, p. 143.

30. Ford, *Pitcairn: Port of Call*, pp. 316–17.

31. Dr. Rufus Southworth, *A Doctor's Letters from Pitcairn* (n.p., n.d.), p. 106.

32. Ford, *The Miscellany of Pitcairn's Island*, p. 12.

33. *Guide to Pitcairn*, 4th ed., p. 36.

34. Marden, p. 754.

35. Henderson Island Monkey Story, <www.winthrop.dk/chimp.html>; Ford, *Pitcairn: Port of Call*, pp. 321–22.

36. Schubert, Ernest, "This Is How It All Began," *Pitcairn Miscellany*, February 1999, pp. 3–4.

Chapter 24

1. David Silverman, *Pitcairn Island* (Cleveland: World Publishing Co., 1967), p. xi.

2. Donald McLoughlin, Laws of Pitcairn, Henderson, Ducie and Oeno, Part 10, <http://library.puc.edu/Pitcairn/pitcairn/govt-history-10.shtml>.

3. Herbert Ford, *The Miscellany of Pitcairn's Island* (Mountain View: Pacific Press Publishing Association, 1980), pp. 134–35.

4. Silverman, p. 203.

5. Pitcairn's Population, <http://library.puc.edu/pitcairn/pitcairn/population.shtml>. Stephen Pendleton, *Atlas of the Pitcairn Islands* (Visalia: Stephen Pendleton, 2006), pp. 15–16; *Guide to Pitcairn*, 4th ed. (Auckland: British Consulate-General, 1982), p. 66.

6. Ford, p. 138.

7. Ford, p. 152.

8. Ford, p. 107.

9. "*Bounty* Progeny Leaving Pitcairn," *New York Times*, 9 February 1964.

10. Glen Wright, "Pitcairn Shuns Bid to Move," *Honolulu Star-Bulletin*, 12 January 1970, p. C-4.

11. Ford, pp. 69–70.

12. *Pacific Islands Yearbook*, 14th ed. (Sydney: Pacific Publications, 1981), pp. 373–74.

13. "Parkin Christian's Tale of Pitcairn," *Honolulu Star-Bulletin*, 2 July 1964, p. 2. Another Bligh and another Christian were to meet on November 7, 1971, at Bounty Bay. When the Port Lines vessel *Port Nelson* arrived with twenty-three-year-old Maurice Bligh from England, a descendant of Captain William Bligh of the *Bounty*, he was introduced to Pitcairn's radio operator Tom Christian, descendant of the captain's nemesis. Bligh assured islanders that he came to Pitcairn "in a spirit of good will and reconciliation." Maurice Bligh,

"What Is the True Story?" Pitcairn Islands Study Group *Pitcairn Log* (April-June 1999), pp. 16–19.

14. "The Sixties Recalled," *Pitcairn Miscellany*, May 1990, pp. 1–3.

15. Ian M. Ball, *Pitcairn: Children of Mutiny* (Boston: Little, Brown & Co., 1973), p. 157.

16. Ball, pp. 172–173.

17. Ball, p. 214.

18. Glynn Christian, *Fragile Paradise* (Boston: Little Brown and Co., 1982), p. 225.

19. Ball, p. 261.

20. *Guide to Pitcairn*, 7th ed. (Auckland: British Consulate-General, 1999), p. 45.

21. Rosalind Amelia Young, *Mutiny on the Bounty* (Honolulu: University Press of the Pacific, 2003), p. 44.

22. "Gold of Pitcairn," *Pitcairn Miscellany*, March 1986, p. 1.

23. Ford, pp. 74–75.

24. Ford, pp. 110–112.

25. "The Sixties Recalled," pp. 1–3.

26. Mururoa was discovered by Lieutenant Philip Carteret in 1767, just days after he had discovered and named Pitcairn Island. Carteret named Mururoa "Bishop of Osnaburgh Island."

27. David Stanley, *South Pacific Handbook*, 7th ed. (Emeryville: Moon Travel Handbooks, 2000), p. 261.

28. Ford, p. 40–41.

29. Stanley, pp. 48–49.

30. A. S. C. Ross and A. W. Moverley, *The Pitcairnese Language* (New York: Oxford University Press, 1964), p. 29.

31. Ford, pp. 114–26.

32. Ford, p. 30.

33. Ford, p. 32.

34. Silverman, p. 104.

35. Frank Clune, *Journey to Pitcairn* (Melbourne: Angus and Robertson, 1966), p. 235.

36. Clune, p. 207.

37. Ball, p. 229.

38. Ford, pp. 47–48.

39. Clune, p. 211.

40. Ford, pp. 50–51.

41. Clune, p. 237.

42. Ford, pp. 53–54.

43. "Pitcairn Adventure," *Gibbons Stamp Monthly*, September 1968, p. 1.

44. *Guide to Pitcairn*, 4th ed., p. 31.

45. Ball, p. 305.

46. Ford, *Pitcairn: Port of Call* (Angwin: Hawser Titles, 1996), p. 382.

47. Ball, p. 214.

48. Ford, *The Miscellany of Pitcairn's Island*, pp. 76–77.

49. Ford, *The Miscellany of Pitcairn's Island*, p. 177.

50. Ford, *The Miscellany of Pitcairn's Island*, pp. 77–78.

Chapter 25

1. Ed Howard, "Pitcairn and Norfolk," *National Geographic*, October 1983, p. 520.

2. *Guide to Pitcairn*, 4th ed. (Auckland: British Consulate-General, 1982), p. 26.

3. Howard, p. 521.

4. Simon Winchester actually did succeed in making the trip to Pitcairn after *The Sun Never Sets* had been published.

5. Simon Winchester, *The Sun Never Sets* (New York: Prentice Hall, 1985), p. 280.

6. Jim Warren, "Sick of Civilization's Rot," *Chicago Tribune*, 15 May 1983, pp. 8–9.

7. "History Repeats Itself," *Pitcairn Miscellany*, October 1989, p. 1.

8. Spencer Murray, *Pitcairn Island* (La Canada: Bounty Sagas, 1992), p. 93.

9. "Diary for October," *Pitcairn Miscellany*, October 1999, p. 1.

10. "Airdrop Delivers Tractor on Pitcairn," *Pacific Union Recorder*, 31 October 1983, pp. 1, 8.

11. Martha Petty had identified the exercise of free will that may result in pleasure for Polynesians, though it may cause inconvenience and frustration for visitors. For example, at about the time of Petty's Pitcairn stay, director Dino de Laurentiis was shooting a $25 million epic in Tahiti, a remake of *Mutiny on the Bounty*. At a cost of four million dollars, he had ordered a replica of HMAV *Bounty* in New Zealand and hired a huge auxiliary cast to work with Mel Gibson and Anthony Hopkins. De Laurentiis was disconcerted when Tahitian women hired to decorate the set with their physical presence simply wandered off without permission — to meet their boyfriends, sleep, swim, or lie in the sun. Worse, a van driver, hired to transport equipment, took his minibus home for lunch and a nap. He took with him cameras and film, so that the highly paid actors and two hundred extras were forced to wait for him to return. Bob Dixon, "The *Bounty*," *Pacific Islands Monthly*, September/October 1983, p. 28.

12. Martha Petty, "An American Experiences Life on Pitcairn Island," <http://pettypress.com/PIT%20RE SOURCE/STORIES16.htm>

13. "Super Powers = Super Threats," *Pitcairn Miscellany*, July 1985, p. 1.

14. Irma Christian, "Centennial Celebration," *Pitcairn Miscellany*, October 1986, pp. 2–3.

15. Lesley Harraway, "A Letter to Pervis Young," *Pitcairn Miscellany*, June 1989, pp. 2–3.

16. Glynn Christian, *Fragile Paradise* (Boston: Little Brown and Company, 1982), p. 245.

17. William F. Buckley, Jr., "On the Right," *San Francisco Chronicle*, 14 November 1987, p. B-11.

18. "*World Discoverer*," *Pitcairn Miscellany*, February 1986, p. 1. The *World Discoverer* was lost in a shipwreck in 2001 in the Solomon Islands.

19. A month after sailing from Pitcairn, the *World Discoverer* anchored at Rendova Harbour in the Solomon Islands, some 4,700 miles from Bounty Bay. I hurried through the tiny museum of World War II clippings and spent shells, and walked to the placid lagoon on this most pristine of mornings. A Melanesian in shirt and cutoffs smiled at me. I sensed he wanted a conversation.

"Do you speak English?" I asked.

"Oh, ye-es. I speak English. I am a Seventh-day Adventist minister."

"That is a coincidence," I replied. " Four weeks ago I met Mr. Stimpson, the Adventist minister, when we attended church on Pitcairn Island."

"Oh, yes," the man said, "that is my best friend. We were at college together." Though covering more than 64 million square miles, the Pacific is indeed still a small place.

Chapter 26

1. Pitcairn's Population, <http://library.puc.edu/ pitcairn/pitcairn/population.shml>

2. "Queen's Message," *Pitcairn Miscellany*, January 1990, p. 1.

3. Kari Young, "Island Magistrate's Visit to Royalty," *Pitcairn Miscellany*, January 1991, pp. 2–3. Lord Louis Mountbatten (b. 1900), to whom the queen referred, was Prince Philip's uncle. Mountbatten, along with two family members and a deck hand, were blown up aboard his 30-foot boat on August 27, 1979. The bomb attack at Mullaghmore, County Sligo, Ireland, was attributed to the Provisional Irish Republican Army.

4. "Pitcairn Island Temporary Return Scheme," *Pitcairn Miscellany*, November 1990, pp. 3–4.

5. Leon Salt, "Commissioner's Job," *Pitcairn Miscellany*, October 2002, pp. 1–2.

6. "Another Wait is Over," *Pitcairn Miscellany*, July 1991, p. 1.

7. Oliver Stimpson, "Pitcairn Co-operative Society," *Pitcairn Miscellany*, February 1991, pp. 3–4.

8. Warren, Jay, untitled article, *Pitcairn Miscellany*, December 1996, p. 1.

9. "A Busy Week for Pitcairners," *Pitcairn Miscellany*, May 1994, pp. 2–3.

10. "Henderson: Saga of the Wood," *Pitcairn Miscellany*, February 2002, pp. 1–2.

11. Steve Pendleton, "Postal Rates Punish Pitcairn Islanders," *Linn's Stamp News*, 4 December 2006, p. 42.

12. "Readers Questions," *Pitcairn Miscellany*, October 2000, p. 3.

13. Thurman C. Petty, "Water for Life on Pitcairn," Pitcairn Islands Study Group Pitcairn Log (April-June 2001), p. 8.

14. "Airmail Delivery Comes Again," *Pitcairn Miscellany*, August 1992, p. 1.

15. "Disaster at Bounty Bay," *Pitcairn Miscellany*, May 1991, p. 1.

16. Dea Birkett, *Serpent in Paradise* (New York: Doubleday, 1997), p. 127.

17. "A Close Call," *Pitcairn Miscellany*, February 1995, p. 2.

18. "Brenda's Latest Body Piercing," *Pitcairn Miscellany*, September 2006, p. 2.

19. Donald McLoughlin, "Laws of Pitcairn, Henderson, Ducie and Oeno," Part 13, <http://library/puc. edu/Pitcairn/pitcairn/govt-history13.shtml>.

20. "Land Issues," *Pitcairn Miscellany*, September 1993), p. 5.

21. *Guide to Pitcairn*, 7th ed. (Auckland: British Consulate-General, 1999), p. 24.

22. "Notice to All Owners of Land on Pitcairn," <http://pitcairn.pn/Noticelandowners.html>.

23. Birkett, p. 274.

24. Lynn and John Salmon, "Visit to Pitcairn," <http://thesalmons.org/lynn/pitcairn>

25. IANA Report, <http://www.icann.org.general/ pn-report-feb00.html>.

26. Pam Graham, "Blue Star's Final Appearance," *New Zealand Weekly Herald*, 19 June 2003, p. A-7.

27. Maureen O'Donnell, "Mutiny Relatives Journey to Chicago," *Chicago Sun-Times*, 3 January 2000.

28. Oliver Bennett, "Travel: *Bounty* Islands Fear Tourists," *Independent*, 6 May 2001.

29. "Turning Point for Historic Adventist Community on Pitcairn Island," Adventist News Network (29 May 2001), <http://news.adventist.org/data/2001/04/0991166375/index.html.en>

Chapter 27

1. Jan Corbett and Tony Stickley, "End of a Legend," *Weekend Herald*, 30 June–1 July 2001, p. E-1.

2. Dea Birkett may be the most unpopular person to come to the island in the last quarter century. Reporter Kathy Marks, covering the rape trials, wrote that islander Meralda Warren "marched up" to her and a fellow journalist and "spat out the worst insult she could think of, likening us to Dea Birkett...." Kathy Marks, "Pitcairn Row," *New Zealand Herald*, 26 October 2004, p. A-6.

3. "A Lawless Pitcairn?" Pitcairn Islands Study Group Pitcairn Log (October-December 1997), p. 15.

4. Kathy Marks, "Judgment Day," *New Zealand Herald*, 25 October 2004, p. A-22.

5. Richard Fell, "Letter to Ariel and Josh," *Pitcairn Miscellany*, November 2002, p. 1.

6. "Supreme Court Hearing," *Pitcairn Miscellany*, August 2003, p. 2.

7. Kelly McParland, "Pitcairners' Defense Relies on Mutiny," *National Post*, 25 November 2003, p. A-3.

8. Pitcairn Island Supreme Court, Trials 1–55/2003 Between the Queen and 7 Named Accused (Auckland: British Consulate-General, 2003).

9. Key Pitcairn Argument Lost, <http://tvnz.co.nz/View/page/411365/781885>

10. Ian M. Ball, *Pitcairn: Children of Mutiny* (Boston: Little, Brown & Co., 1973), p. 326.

11. "March Has Been Another Busy Month," *Pitcairn Miscellany*, March 2003, p. 1.

12. Nick Squires, "Rape Trial Could Seal Pitcairn Fate," <http://www.theage.com.au/articles/2002/10/13/1034222679515.html>.

13. "Many Outsiders on Pitcairn," *Pitcairn Miscellany*, March 2003, p. 1.

14. Kathy Marks, "Law Descends on *Bounty* Island," *New Zealand Herald*, September 2004, p. B-2.

15. Anthony Hubbard, "To the Island," *Sunday Star Times*, 26 September 2004, p. A-7.

16. Kathy Marks, Age of Sexual Consent, <http://www.ageofconsent.com/pitcairn/html>.

17. "Ex-Commissioner's Last Message," *Pitcairn Miscellany*, October 2003, p. 2.

18. Pitcairn Islander Fails to Get Job Back, TVNZ, 24 November 2004, <http://tvnz.co.nz/view/news_worldd_storry_skin/460798>

19. Pitcairn Island Supreme Court. The judges were correct; it would be impossible to find twelve Pitcairn Islanders who were not related to one of the accused. Mark Twain had great fun in his fictional account of Joshua Hill's tyranny, "The Great Revolution in Pitcairn," with family relationships: "A stranger says to an islander: 'You speak of that young woman as your cousin; a while ago you called her your aunt.'" The man replied, "'Well, she IS my aunt, and my cousin too. And also my step-sister, my niece, my fourth cousin, my thirty-third cousin, my forty-second cousin, my great-aunt, my grandmother, my widowed sister-in-law—and next week she will be my wife.'" <http://www.laughtergenealogy.com/bin/histprof/misc/bounty3.html>.

20. Kathy Marks, "Pitcairn's Mayor Led the Pack," *New Zealand Herald*, 1 October 2004, p. A-5.

21. "World Will Keep an Eye on Pitcairn" (editorial), *New Zealand Herald*, 27 October 2004, p. A-14.

22. Letter of Appeal from Pitcairn Women, The Justice for Pitcairn Group, <www.newfoundations.com/Pitcairn/Pitcairn/Appeal.html>.

23. Two Pitcairn Islanders Convicted, TVNZ (10 January 2007), <http://tvnz.co.nz/view/news_budgerstory_skin/955368>

24. Ball, p. 290.

25. Angela Gregory, "Pitcairn Looks to Break Out of its Isolation," *New Zealand Herald*, 30 March 2006, p. A-12.

26. "Rare Birth on Pitcairn Island," *Dominion Post*, 2 April 2007, <http://www.stuff.co.nz.4012891a12.html>. The baby's father, Randy Christian, was able to be present during the birth in spite of serving time in jail for sexual offenses.

27. "Pitcairn Sex Offenders Stay Free," *New Zealand Herald*, 30 March 2005.

28. Carol Warren, E-mail to the author, 21 February 2007.

Works Cited

Adams, Caroline. Letter to William Dillon, 10 November 1851.

"Airdrop Delivers Tractor on Pitcairn." *Pacific Union Recorder*, 31 October 1983: 1, 8.

"Airmail Delivery Comes Again." *Pitcairn Miscellany* 34:8 (August 1992): 1.

Alexander, Caroline. *The Bounty: The True Story of the Mutiny on the Bounty*. New York: Viking, 2003.

Allen, Claude. "Pitcairn Island's Population of 200 Inhabitants All Belong to W.C.T.U." *Berkeley* [California] *Daily Gazette*, 16 June 1937.

Allward, Maurice. "Murder on Pitcairn?" Pitcairn Islands Study Group *UK Log*, July 2004: 23.

_____. *Pitcairn Island: Refuge of the Bounty Mutineers*. Stroud, Gloucestershire, U.K.: Tempus Publishing Ltd., 2000.

"Another Piece of History." *Pitcairn Miscellany* 46:11 (November 2003): 4.

"Another Wait Is Over." *Pitcairn Miscellany* 33:7 (July 1991): 1.

Ball, Ian M. *Pitcairn: Children of Mutiny*. Boston: Little, Brown & Co.,1973.

Barrow, Sir John. *The Mutiny of the Bounty*. Edited by Gavin Kennedy. Boston: D. R. Godine, 1980.

_____. *Recent Accounts of the Pitcairn Islanders*. London: Royal Geographic Society, 1833.

Beechey, Frederick William. *Narrative of a Voyage to the Pacific and Beering's Strait*. London: Colburn & Bentley, 1831. <www.digital.library.upenn. edu>.

Belcher, Lady [Diana]. *The Mutineers of the Bounty and their Descendants in Pitcairn and Norfolk Islands*. New York: Harper & Brothers 1871.

Bennett, Frederick Debell. *Narrative of a Whaling Voyage Round the Globe from the Year 1833 to 1836*. London, 1840. Reprint, Amsterdam and New York: Da Capo Press, 1970.

Bennett, Oliver. "Travel: Bounty Islands Fear Tourists will Result in Paradise Lost." *The Independent*, 6 May 2001. <http://www.findarticles. com/p/articles/mi_qn4158/is_20010506/ai_n143 94241>.

Bercaw, Sean S. "Henderson: The Saga of the Wood." *Pitcairn Miscellany* 45:2 (February 2002): 1–2.

Birkett, Dea. *Serpent in Paradise*. New York: Doubleday, 1997.

Bligh, Maurice. "What is the True Story about Capt. Bligh?" Pitcairn Islands Study Group *Pitcairn Log* 26:2 (April-June 1999): 16–19.

"Bligh Relics Yield Bounty at Auction." *Chicago Sun-Times*, 22 September 2002. <http://www. findarticles.com/p/articles/mi_20020927/ai_1245 73345>.

Bligh, William. *The Mutiny On Board H.M.S. Bounty*. New York: New American Library, 1961.

"*Bounty* Progeny Leaving Pitcairn." *New York Times*, 9 February 1964.

"Brenda's Latest Body Piercing." *Pitcairn Miscellany* 48:8 (September 2006): 2.

Brodie, Walter. *Pitcairn's Island and the Islanders in 1850*. London: Whitaker & Co., 1851.

Brumwell, Stephen, and W. A. Speck. *Cassell's Companion to Eighteenth Century Britain*. London: Cassell & Co., 2001.

Buckley, William F., Jr. "On the Right: 'A Visit to Pitcairn Island.'" *San Francisco Chronicle*, 14 November 1987: B-11.

Buffett, John. "A Narrative of Twenty Years Residence on Pitcairn's Island." *The Friend* 4 (1846): 2–3, 20–21, 27–28, 34–35, 50–51, 66–68.

Bull, Malcolm J. "Halfway to Heaven: A Century of Adventism on Pitcairn Island." N.p., 1986. [Typescript; copy in Pitcairn Island Study Center, Pacific Union College, Angwin, California.]

Burt, Alfred LeRoy. *The Evolution of the British Empire and Commonwealth from the American*

Revolution. Boston: D. C. Heath and Company, 1956.

"Busy Week for Pitcairners." *Pitcairn Miscellany* 7:5 (May 1994): 2–3.

"Byrd Wires Story of Pitcairn Plight." *New York Times,* 20 December 1939: 15.

Caesar, Ed. "Pitcairn: The Island of Fear." *The Independent on Sunday,* 19 November 2006. <http://www.findarticles.com/p/articles/mi_qn4159/is_2 0061119ai_n16859034>.

"Challenge of Pitcairn." *St. Petersburg Times,* 26 June 2005: 5.

Chauvel, Charles. *In the Wake of the Bounty.* Sydney: The Endeavour Press, 1933.

Christian, Glynn. *Fragile Paradise: The Discovery of Fletcher Christian, Bounty Mutineer.* Boston: Little Brown and Company, 1982.

Christian, Irma. "Centennial Celebrations on Pitcairn Island." *Pitcairn Miscellany* 28:10 (October 1986): 2–3.

C.I.A. World Factbook — Pitcairn Islands. <http://cia.gov/publications/factbook/geos/pc.>.

Clarke, Peter. *Hell and Paradise: The Norfolk-Bounty-Pitcairn Saga.* Ringwood, Victoria: Penguin Books Australia, 1986.

Claypole, William, and John Robottom. *Caribbean Story.* Book One: *Foundations.* Trinidad and Jamaica: Longman Caribbean, 1980.

Clemens, Samuel (Mark Twain). "The Great Revolution on Pitcairn." In *The Writings of Mark Twain,* Volume XX, 1903. <http://www.laughter-genealogy.com/bin/histprof/misc/bounty3.html>.

"Close Call." *Pitcairn Miscellany* 38:2 (February 1995): 2.

Clune, Frank. *Journey to Pitcairn.* Melbourne: Angus and Robertson,1966.

Condition of the Pitcairn Islanders, Correspondence Relating to, No. 1, Admiralty to Colonial Office. London: H.M. Stationery Office, 1884.

Cook, Duncan, M.D. *Medical Report.* Suva, Fiji: Office of the High Commissioner of the Western Pacific, 1937.

Corbett, Jan, and Tony Stickley. "End of a Legend." *Weekend Herald,* 30 June–1 July 2001: E1.

Correspondence Relating to the Condition of the Pitcairn Islanders, No. 1, Admiralty to Colonial Office. London: H.M. Stationery Office, 1899.

"Couple Prepare for Service on Pitcairn." *Adventist Review* 156 (June 1979): 7.

Danielsson, Marie-Therese and Bengt. "Bligh's Cave: 196 Years On." *Pacific Islands Monthly,* June 1985: 25.

Daws, Gavan. *Shoal of Time: A History of the Hawaiian Islands.* Honolulu: University of Hawaii Press, 1968.

Day, A. Grove. *Hawaii and Its People.* Honolulu: Mutual Publishing, 1993.

"Dearth of Women's Apparel." *New York Times,* 11 July 1900: A1.

"Death on the Bounty." *Time,* 5 August 1935. <http://www.time.com/time/magazomee/article.0,9171,711695,00.html>.

De Horsey, Rear-Admiral Algernon Frederick Rous. *Report to the Lords of the Admiralty,* 17 September 1878. London: H.M. Stationery Office, 1878.

Dening, Greg. *Mr. Bligh's Bad Language: Passion, Power and Theatre on the Bounty.* Cambridge: Cambridge University Press, 1992.

Diamond, Jared. *Collapse: How Societies Choose to Fail or Succeed.* New York: Viking, 2005.

_____. "Paradise Lost — Lost Civilization on Pitcairn Island." <http//www.looksmart.com/Discover/html>.

"Diary for October." *Pitcairn Miscellany* 42:10 (October 1999): 1.

"Disaster at Bounty Bay." *Pitcairn Miscellany* 33:4 (May 1991): 1.

Dixon, Bob. "The Bounty: Once More with Feeling." *Pacific Islands Monthly,* September/October 1983: 28.

Dodge, Ernest S. *New England and the South Seas.* Cambridge, MA: Harvard University Press, 1965.

Edwards, Ron. "Murder Rarely Reported on Pitcairn." Pitcairn Islands Study Group *Pitcairn Log* 28:2 (April-June 2001): 5–7.

Elliott, Molly G. "Pity Pitcairn." *Eastern Horizons* 19:9 (1980): 36–41.

Estensen, Miriam. *Discovery: The Quest for the Great South Land.* New York: St. Martin's Press, 1998.

"Ex-Commissioner's Last Message." *Pitcairn Miscellany* 46:10 (October 2003): 2.

Fell, Richard. "Letter to Ariel and Josh." *Pitcairn Miscellany* 45:11 (November 2002): 1.

Ferris, Norman. *The Story of Pitcairn Island.* Washington, D.C.: Review and Herald Publishing Association, 1958.

"Few Men Left on Pitcairn." *Brooklyn Daily Eagle,* 27 November 1899: 3.

Ford, Herbert. *The Miscellany of Pitcairn's Island.* Mountain View, California: Pacific Press Publishing Association, 1980.

_____. *Pitcairn.* La Verne, California: El Camino Press, 1972.

_____. *Pitcairn: Port of Call.* Angwin, California: Hawser Titles, 1996.

_____. "World War II Came Early to Pitcairn Island." Pitcairn Islands Study Group *Pitcairn Log* 16:1 (September-November 1988): 5–7.

Fryer, John. Testimony of John Fryer. 12 September 1792. <http://www.law.umke.edu/faculty/projects/trials/Bounty/fryertranscript.html>.

Furnas, J. C. *Anatomy of Paradise: Hawaii and the Islands of the South Seas.* New York: William Sloane Associates, Inc., 1948.

Further Correspondence Relating to the Condition of the Pitcairn Islanders, 1899. London: H.M. Stationery Office, 1901.

Gibson, Arrel Morgan [completed with the assistance of John S. Whitehead]. *Yankees in Paradise: The Pacific Basin Frontier.* Albuquerque: University of New Mexico Press, 1993.

"Gold of Pitcairn." *Pitcairn Miscellany* 28:3 (March 1986): 1.

Goldhurst, William. "Martinet or Martyr?" *Horizon*, vol. 7 (September 1963): 42–48.

Graham, Pam. "Blue Star's Final Appearance." *New Zealand Weekly Herald*, 18–19 June 2003: A-7.

Gregory, Angela. "Pitcairn Looks to Break Out of Its Isolation." *New Zealand Herald*, 30 March 2006: A12.

Grigore, Julius, Jr., ed. "Inside the Pitcairn Island Family." Balboa, Panama: 2003. [Typescript; copy in Pitcairn Islands Study Center, Pacific Union College, Angwin, CA.]

Guide to Pitcairn. 4th ed. Auckland: British Consulate-General, 1982.

Guide to Pitcairn. 7th ed. Auckland: British Consulate-General, 1999.

Hall, James Norman. *The Tale of a Shipwreck.* New York: Houghton Mifflin Company, 1934.

Harraway, Lesley. "A Letter to Pervis Young." *Pitcairn Miscellany* 31:6 (June 1989): 2–3.

Hawkesworth, John. *An Account of the Voyages Undertaken by Order of His Present Majesty for Making Discoveries in the Southern Hemisphere.* Vol.1. Dublin: James Potts, 1775.

Hayes, Walter. *The Captain from Nantucket and the Mutiny on the Bounty: A Recollection of Mayhew Folger, Mariner, Who Discovered the Last Mutineer & His Family on Pitcairn's Island.* Ann Arbor: William L. Clements Library, 1996.

Haydon, Simon. "Space Age Hits Pitcairn Island." *San Francisco Chronicle*, 3 January 1992: B-1.

Henderson Island Monkey Story. <www.winthrop.dk/chimp.html>.

"Here's a Chance to Get Rich." *Brooklyn Daily Eagle*, 20 July 1900: 2.

Herman, Arthur. *To Rule the Waves: How the British Navy Shaped the Modern World.* New York: Harper Perennial, 2005.

Herring, Hubert. *A History of Latin America from the Beginnings to the Present.* New York: Alfred A. Knopf, 1961.

Heyerdahl, Thor. *Aku Aku: The Secret of Easter Island.* Chicago: Rand McNally, 1958.

"History Repeats Itself." *Pitcairn Miscellany* 31:10 (October 1989): 1–2.

"Home of the Mutineers." *Brooklyn Daily Eagle*, 15 October 1899: 39.

Hough, Richard. *The Bounty.* New York, Penguin Books, 1984.

_____. *Captain Bligh and Mr. Christian: The Men and the Mutiny.* New York: E. P. Dutton & Co., 1973.

Howard, Ed. "Pitcairn and Norfolk: The Saga of the Bounty's Children." *National Geographic*, October 1983: 508–540.

Howarth, David. *Tahiti: A Paradise Lost.* New York: Penguin Books, 1985.

Hubbard, Anthony. "To the Island." *Sunday Star Times*, 26 September 2004: A7.

Hughes, Robert. *The Fatal Shore: The Epic of Australia's Founding.* New York: Alfred A. Knopf, 1987.

IANA (The Internet Corporation for Assigned Names and Numbers). Report on Request for Redelegation of Top-Level Domain. <http://www.icann.org.general/pn-report-feb00.htm>.

"Instructions for the Guidance of the Local Government of Pitcairn Island." *Western Pacific High Commission Gazette* 54 (December 1941): 29.

Jenny (a.k.a. Teehuteatuaonoa). "Pitcairn's Island — The *Bounty*'s Crew." *United Service Journal*, November 1829: 589–93.

Johnson, Captain Irving and Mrs. *Westward Bound in the Schooner Yankee.* New York: W. W. Norton & Company, 1936.

Johnson, Irving and Electa. "Westward Bound in the Yankee." *National Geographic* 81:1 (January 1942): 1–44.

Johnson, Irving & Electa, and Lydia Edes. *Yankee's People and Places.* New York: W. W. Norton & Company, Inc., 1955.

Jones, Timothy F., M.D. "Mass Psychogenic Illness: Role of the Individual Physician." *American Family Physician* 62:12 (15 December 2000): 2649. <http://www.aafp.org/afp/200011215/2649html>.

"Joy on Pitcairn Island." *New York Times*, 8 July 1917: 70.

Kendrick, Dr. Bob. "By Yorley Gwen?" *Pitcairn Miscellany* 27:10 (October 1985): 3.

Kennedy, Gavin. *Captain Bligh: The Man and His Mutinies.* London: Gerald Ducksworth, 1989.

"Key Pitcairn Argument Lost." <http://tvnz.co.nz/View/page/411365/781885>.

Knowles, Capt. Josiah N., diary of. Wreck of the *Wild Wave* Fourteen Years After: Ship *Glory of the Seas*, at Sea, May 7, 1873. <www.nobbly.com/archive/stories/wildwave.hmtl>.

Knowling, Commander George F. S. Further Correspondence Relating to the Condition of the Pitcairn Islanders. Enclosure in No. 3, 31 March 1901. London: H.M. Stationery Office, 1901.

"Landing Project Completed." *Pitcairn Miscellany* 34:7 (July 1992): 2.

"Land Issues — Law or Custom? Beware!" *Pitcairn Miscellany* 34:9 (September 1993): 5.

"Lawless Pitcairn Island?" Pitcairn Islands Study Group *Pitcairn Log* 25:1 (October-December 1997): 9, 15.

Letter of Appeal from Pitcairn Women. The Justice for Pitcairn Group. <www.newfoundations.com/Pitcairn/PitcairnAppeal.html>.

"Lightening Never Strikes Twice." *Pitcairn Miscellany* 34:3 (March 1992): 2–3.

London, Jack. "The Seed of McCoy." In A. Grove

Day and Carl Stoven, eds. *Best South Sea Stories.* Honolulu: Mutual Publishing Paperback Series, 1962.

Lummis, Trevor. *Pitcairn Island: Life and Death in Eden.* Brookfield, Vermont: Ashgate, 1997.

Mackaness, George. *The Life of Vice-Admiral William Bligh.* New York: Farrar & Rhinehart, Inc., 1931.

"Many 'Outsiders' on Pitcairn." *Pitcairn Miscellany* 46:3 (March 2003): 3.

"March Has Been Another Busy Month on Pitcairn." *Pitcairn Miscellany* 46:3 (March 2003): 1.

Marden, Luis. "I Found the Bones of the *Bounty.*" *National Geographic,* 62:6 (December 1957): 725–789.

Marks, Kathy. "Age of Sexual Consent." <http://www.ageofconsent.com/pitcairn.html>.

_____. "Judgment Day." *New Zealand Herald,* 25 October 2004: A22.

_____. "Law Descends on Bounty Island." *New Zealand Herald,* 27 September 2004: B2.

_____. "Pitcairn Row Gives Glimpse of Mutinous Past." *New Zealand Herald,* 26 October 2004: A-6.

_____. "Pitcairn's Mayor Led the Pack." *New Zealand Herald,* 1 October 2004: A5.

Maude, H. E. "In Search of a Home." In *Islands and Men.* Melbourne: Oxford University Press, 1968.

_____. *Slavers in Paradise: The Peruvian Labor Trade in Polynesia, 1862–64.* Canberra: Australian National University Press, 1981.

Mawrer, Granville Allen. *Ahab's Trade: The Saga of South Seas Whaling.* New York: St. Martin's Press, 1989.

McLoughlin, Donald. *Laws of Pitcairn, Henderson, Ducie and Oeno Islands.* Rev. ed., 1971. <http://library.puc.edu/Pitcairn/pitcairn/govt-history08.shtml>.

McManus, Jenni. "Pitcairn Commissioner Tried to Undermine Sex Trials." *The Independent,* 24 November 2004: 1.

McParland, Kelly. "Pitcairners' Defence Relies on Mutiny." *National Post,* 25 November 2003: A3.

Melville, Herman. *Melville: Typee, Omoo, Mardi.* New York: The Library of Americana, 1982.

Morris, James. *Heaven's Command: An Imperial Progress.* New York and London: Harcourt Brace Jovanovich, 1973.

Morrison, James. Journal of James Morrison on the *Bounty* and at Tahiti, 1787–1792. <http://image.sl.nsw.gov.au/Ebind/oy515/a1221000.html>.

Murray, Spencer. "The Pitcairners' 1831 Move to Tahiti." Pitcairn Islands Study Group *Pitcairn Log* 24:4 (April-June 1997): 6–8.

_____. *Pitcairn Island: The First 200 Years.* La Canada, California: Bounty Sagas, 1992.

Murray, Rev. Thomas Boyles. *Pitcairn: The Island, the People, and the Pastor.* London: Society for Promoting Christian Knowledge, 1860.

Neill, J. S. *Pitcairn Island General Administrative Report.* Suva, Fiji: Office of the High Commissioner for the Western Pacific, 1937.

"News from Lonely Pitcairn Island." *New York Times,* 6 July 1902: 25.

"News from Pitcairn Island." *New York Times,* 29 August 1863: 3.

Nicolson, Robert B. *The Pitcairners.* Sydney: Angus and Robertson, 1965.

Norfolk Island — Bloodless Genocide. <http://www.pitcairners.org/bloodless genocide2html>.

Notable Figures of Pitcairn. <http://www.stamps.gov.pn/NotableFigures.html>.

Notice to All Owners of Land on Pitcairn. <http://pitcairn.pn/Noticelandowners.html>.

O'Brian, Patrick. *Joseph Banks: A Life.* Boston: D. R. Godine, 1993.

O'Donnell, Maureen. "'Mutiny' Relatives Journey to Chicago." *Chicago Sun-Times,* 3 January 2000. <http://www.findarticles.com/p/articles/mi_qn4155/is_20000103/ai_n9599308>.

Orlebar, Lt. J. *Midshipman's Journal on Board H.M.S. Seringapatam During the Year 1830.* London: Whittaker, Treacer, and Co., 1833.

Pacific Islands Year Book, 1942. 4th (war-time) ed. R.W. Robson, ed. Sydney: Sydney and Melbourne Publishing Co., 1942.

Pacific Islands Year Book. 14th ed. John Carter, ed. Sydney: Pacific Publications, 1981.

"Parkin Christian's Tale of Pitcairn." *Honolulu Star-Bulletin,* 2 July 1964: 2.

Peard, Lt. George. *To the Pacific and Arctic with Beechey: The Journal of Lieutenant George Peard of H.M.S. Blossom, 1825–1828.* Barry M. Gough, ed. Cambridge: Cambridge University Press, 1973.

Pendleton, Stephen. *Atlas of the Pitcairn Islands and the Voyage of HMAV Bounty.* Visalia, California: Stephen Pendleton, 2006.

_____. "Postal Rates Punish Pitcairn Islanders in Dealings with Outside World." *Linn's Stamp News,* 4 December 2006: 42.

Petty, Martha. An American Experiences Life on Pitcairn Island. http://pettypress.com/PIT%20RESOURCE/STORIES16.htm

Petty, Thurman C. "Water for Life on Pitcairn." Pitcairn Islands Study Group *Pitcairn Log* 28:2 (April-June 2001): 8.

"Pig Study Helps Trace Pacific Islanders' Origins." *Santa Rosa Press Democrat,* 17 March 2007: A10.

Pilling, H. G. *Report on a Visit to Pitcairn Island.* London: H.M. Stationery Office, 1930.

"Pitcairn Adventure." *Gibbons Stamp Monthly,* September 1968: 1.

"Pitcairn Islander Fails to Get Job Back." TVNZ, 24 November 2004. <http://tvnz/view/news_world_story_skin/460798>.

"Pitcairn Islanders Now-a-Days." *New York Times,* 11 November 1895: 5.

Pitcairn Island Place Names. <http://www.lareau.org/pitplace.html>.

Pitcairn Island Register Book, 1790–1854. Sir Charles Lucas, ed. London: Society for the Promotion of Christian Knowledge, 1929.

"Pitcairn Island Romance." *New York Times*, 3 December 1872.

Pitcairn Island Supreme Court. Trials 1–55/2003 between the Queen and 7 Named Accused. Auckland: British Consulate-General. 2003.

"Pitcairn Island Temporary Return Scheme." *Pitcairn Miscellany* 32:11 November 1990: 3–4.

"Pitcairn Island: Won, a Constitution." *Time*, 17 August 1942: 32.

Pitcairn News, 19 January 2005. <http://www.pitcairnnews.co.nz/050119.html#times18151216>.

"Pitcairn Sex Offenders Stay Free while Lawyers Argue." *New Zealand Herald*, 30 March, 2005.

"Pitcairn's Island from a Correspondent." *Illustrated London News*, 6 November 1852: 373–74.

Pitcairn's Population. <http://library.puc.edu/pitcairn/pitcairn/population.shml>.

"Pitcairn's Progress." *Time*, 23 August 1948. <http://www.toime.com/time/magazione/article/0,9171,799046.00.html>.

"Pitcairn Trivia." *Pitcairn Miscellany* 33:12 (December 1991): 3.

Pitkern Phrase Book. <http://www.lareau.org/pitlang2.html>.

"Queen's Message." *Pitcairn Miscellany* 32:1 (January 1990):1.

"Rare Birth on Pitcairn Island." *Dominion Post*, 2 April 2007. <http://www.stuff.co.nz.4012891a12.html>.

"Readers' Questions." *Pitcairn Miscellany* 43:10 (October 2000): 3.

Richards, H. M. S., Jr. *Mutineers on Pitcairn Island.* Nashville, Tennessee: Southern Publishing Association, 1980.

Rodger, N. A. M. *The Wooden World: An Anatomy of the Georgian Navy.* New York: W. W. Norton, 1996.

Rodwell, Sir Cecil, High Commissioner for the Western Pacific. *Report on a Visit to Pitcairn Island.* Colonial Reports No. 93, June 25, 1921. London: H.M. Stationery Office, 1921.

"Romance of a Shipwreck." *Harper's Weekly*, 27 November 1858: 764.

Ross, Alan S. C., and A. W. Moverley. *The Pitcairnese Language.* New York: Oxford University Press, 1964.

Routledge, Katherine. *The Mystery of Easter Island.* New York: AMS Press, 1978.

Salmon, Lynn and John. Visit to Pitcairn. <http://www.thesalmons.org/lynn/pitcairn>.

Salt, Leon. "Commissioner's Job." *Pitcairn Miscellany* 45:10 (October 2002): 1- 2.

Schubert, Ernest. "This is How it All Began." *Pitcairn Miscellany* 42:2 (February 1999): 3–4.

Shapiro, Harry L. *The Heritage of the Bounty.* Garden City, New York: Doubleday Anchor, 1962.

Silverman, David. *Pitcairn Island.* Cleveland: World Publishing Co., 1967.

"Sixties Recalled." *Pitcairn Miscellany* 32:5 (May 1990): 1–3.

Smith, Ethan. "'Uncle' Warren Buffett and 'Cousin' Jimmy Make Beautiful Music." *Wall Street Journal*, 2 May 2005: 1.

Southworth, Dr. Rufus. *A Doctor's Letters from Pitcairn, 1937.* Foreword by Exy [Electa] Johnson. N.p., n.d. [Privately printed (500 copies); copy at Pitcairn Islands Study Center, Pacific Union College, Angwin, California.]

Squires, Nick. Rape Trial Could Seal Pitcairn's Fate. <http://www.theage.com.au/articles/2002/10/13/1034222679515.html>.

Stanley, David. *South Pacific Handbook.* 7th ed. Emeryville, California: Moon Travel Handbooks, 2000.

Starbuck, Alexander. *History of the American Whale Fishery.* Secaucus, NJ: Castle Books, 1989.

Stimpson, Oliver, "Pitcairn Co-operative Society." *Pitcairn Miscellany* 33:2 (February 1991): 3–4.

"Super Powers = Super Threats." *Pitcairn Miscellany* 27:7 (July 1985): 1.

"Supply Ship ACT VI." *Pitcairn Miscellany* 28:8 (August 1986): 1–2.

"Supreme Court Hearing." *Pitcairn Miscellany* 46:8 (August 2003): 2.

"Swiss Family Adds New Pages to Bloody Pitcairn's History." *Honolulu Advertiser*, 28 October 1944: 2.

Thierry, Charles Philip Hippolytus, Baron de. <http://www.tcara.govt.nz/1966/T/ThierryCharlesPhilipHippolytusBaronDe/ThierryDc/cn>.

Tosen, Neville. "News and Views from Our Local Padre." *Pitcairn Miscellany* 43:2 (February 2000): 3.

Toulmin, Lew. "The Cruising World: Paradise Lost." *International Travel News*, February 2005: 92–95.

Tree, Ronald. *A History of Barbados.* London: Rupert Hart-Davis, 1973.

"Turning Point for Historic Adventist Community on Pitcairn Island." Adventist News Network, 29 May 2001. <http://news.adventist.og/data/2001/04/0991166375/index.html.en>.

"Two Pitcairn Islanders Convicted." TVNZ, 10 January 2007. <http://tvnz.co.nz/view/news_budget_story_skin/955368>.

Van Tilbug, Jo Anne. *Among Stone Giants: The Life of Katherine Routledge and Her Remarkable Expedition to Easter Island.* New York: Scribners, 2003.

Wahlroos, Sven. *Mutiny and Romance in the South Seas: A Companion to the Bounty Adventure.* Topsfield, Massachusetts: Salem House Publishers, 1989.

"War Brings Increasing Privation to Dwellers on Lonely Pitcairn." *Honolulu Advertiser*, 12 December 1940: 1.

Ward, David. "Pitcairn Population Sees Serious

Decrease." Pitcairn Islands Study Group *Pitcairn Log* 24:3 (April-June 1997): 16.

Warren, Carol (Pitcairn resident). E-mail to the author, 21 February 2007.

Warren, Jay. [Untitled]. *Pitcairn Miscellany* 39:12 (December 1996): 1.

Warren, Jim. "Sick of Civilization's Rot, Millionaire Eyes Pacific Island for His Last Hurrah." *Chicago Tribune*, 15 May 1983: 12: 8–9.

Weisler, Marshall, "Archaeology of Water Valley, Pitcairn Island." *Pitcairn Miscellany* 33:7 July 1991: 2–3.

"We Like our Privacy Too." *Pitcairn Miscellany* 28:9 (September 1986):1.

"What's in a Name?" *Pitcairn Miscellany* 31:7 (July 1989): 1.

Williams, Eric. *From Columbus to Castro: The History of the Caribbean*. New York: Random House, Vintage Books, 1984.

Winchester, Simon. *The Sun Never Sets: Travels to the Remaining Outposts of the British Empire*. New York: Prentice Hall, 1985.

"World Discoverer." *Pitcairn Miscellany* 28:2 (February 1986): 1.

"World Will Keep an Eye on Pitcairn" (Editorial). *New Zealand Herald*, 27 October 2004: A-14.

Wright, Glen. "Pitcairn Shuns Bid to Move." *Honolulu Star-Bulletin*, 12 January 1970: C-4.

Young, Kari. "Island Magistrate's Visit to Royalty." *Pitcairn Miscellany* 33:1 (January 1991): 2–3.

Young, Rosalind Amelia. *Mutiny on the Bounty and the Story of Pitcairn Island, 1790–1894*. 1904. Reprint, Honolulu: University Press of the Pacific, 2003.

Index